Latinx Theater in the Times of Neoliberalism

performance works

SERIES EDITORS
Patrick Anderson and Nicholas Ridout

This series publishes books in theater and performance studies, focused in particular on the material conditions in which performance acts are staged, and to which performance itself might contribute. We define "performance" in the broadest sense, including traditional theatrical productions and performance art, but also cultural ritual, political demonstration, social practice, and other forms of interpersonal, social, and political interaction which may fruitfully be understood in terms of performance.

Latinx Theater in the Times of Neoliberalism

✦

Patricia A. Ybarra

NORTHWESTERN UNIVERSITY PRESS
EVANSTON, ILLINOIS

Northwestern University Press
www.nupress.northwestern.edu

Copyright © 2018 by Northwestern University Press.
Published 2018. All rights reserved.

10 9 8 7 6 5 4 3 2 1

Library of Congress Cataloging-in-Publication Data

Names: Ybarra, Patricia A., 1972– author.
Title: Latinx theater in the times of neoliberalism / Patricia A. Ybarra.
Description: Evanston, Illinois : Northwestern University Press, 2018. | Series: Performance works
Identifiers: LCCN 2017027186 | ISBN 9780810136465 (cloth : alk. paper) | ISBN 9780810136458 (pbk. : alk. paper) | ISBN 9780810136472 (e-book)
Subjects: LCSH: Hispanic American theater—History—20th century. | Hispanic American theater—History—21st century. | Theater and society—United States. | Neoliberalism.
Classification: LCC PN2270.H57 Y37 2018 | DDC 792.08968073—dc23
LC record available at https://lccn.loc.gov/2017027186

For Berta Cáceres y los 43 de Ayotzinapa

CONTENTS

Preface	*ix*
Acknowledgments	*xv*
Critical Introduction	*3*

Chapter 1
"Never Any Other Time but This Time No World but This World,"
   or Staging Indigeneity in Neoliberal Times   *25*

Chapter 2
Havana Is (Not) Waiting: Staging the Impasse in Cuban American
   Drama about Cuba's Special Period   *73*

Chapter 3
Neoliberalism Is a Serial Killer   *105*

Chapter 4
Swallowing the '80s (W)Hole: Millennial Drama of the Narcoguerra   *147*

Conclusion
So Go the Ghosts of . . .   *195*

Notes	*201*
Bibliography	*229*
Index	*243*

PREFACE

Latinx Theater in the Times of Neoliberalism emerges from a combination of frustration in the rehearsal room and the throes of political rage. Its first inkling came when I was directing a production of Cherríe Moraga's *The Hungry Woman* in 2006 in the midst of a national debate on immigration policy which resulted in marches and activism throughout the country.[1] The play tells the story of a queer Medea in the midst of a transnational custody dispute on the Mexican border in a post-NAFTA apocalyptic world. Riffing on the classic Medea myth, *The Hungry Woman* is a meditation on geopolitical violence on the border. A dramatic iteration of her famous 1992 "Queer Aztlán" essay, the play confronts the economic violence of the 1980s and 1990s in North America as its characters come to terms with the failures of cultural nationalism.[2] Moraga's critique of the neoliberal project in hemispheric iteration was at the center of my concerns, although I am (at least) a generation removed from the historic Chicano cultural nationalism that frames the play. Staging *The Hungry Woman* made me confront the near impossibility of representing the lived material experience of the neoliberal condition onstage. How exactly does one stage the destruction and denigration caused by savage capitalism in the wake of the demise of the U.S. social welfare state and the move to free-market economies throughout the hemisphere? How can one adequately represent the structural inequality created therein or the spaces it most frequently inhabits? To literally represent the U.S.-Mexico border on stage is to risk reifying its violence in a too localized manner. Alternately, to be allusive (or elusive) is to stage a metaphor devoid of material reality. Four years later, I faced the problem again when I directed *En Las Manos de la Muerte*, a play written by a student about narcotraffic and the enigmatic Mexican popular saint Santa Muerte (Saint Death).[3] Representing the insatiable violence of transnational business risked the play being made into something like a stock blockbuster action movie: a parade of young men making bad choices down there rather than being soldiers of commerce for us up here. I asked myself: How does one render economic violence as viscerally as the physical violence that propels the action of narco-realistic representations? How does one make the connection between these forms of violence palpable? How does one represent transnational consumerism on stage? How and when does one step out of realism so as to avoid reifying violence as spectacle, allowing it to do the political work Tiffany Ana López claims of the violence in Migdalia Cruz's plays?[4] Or, alternately, when does one employ theatrical realism to avoid metaphor? The problem of how to render economic violence and its "real" embodied iterations theatrically without resorting to simplistic metaphors, cheap equivalency, universalism, or over-literalism haunts me years later. Although I have no fail-safe theatrical or dramaturgical solution to these conundrums, the plays and performances I write about in this book sketch out contours of possibility. I adamantly believe that the very problem of representing geopolitical economic violence onstage has consequences for thinking about these problems offstage. It is for this reason that I am dedicated to close reading theatrical performance as a mode of political thinking under neoliberal capitalism.

I define *neoliberalism* as a political and economic philosophy whose proponents espouse free markets and privatization of state enterprises as the mode by which prosperity and democracy are best reached. These policies, which include IMF interventions, NAFTA, shifts in immigration policy, the escalation of border industrialization initiatives, and varied austerity programs have also created the conditions for many of the most tumultuous events in the Americas in the last forty years. These phenomena include the support of dictatorships in the Southern Cone, the 1994 Cuban Rafter Crisis, contemporary femicide in Juárez, Mexico, the Zapatista uprising in Chiapas, Mexico, and the rise of narcotrafficking as a violent and vigorous global business throughout the Americas. In *Latinx Theater in the Times of Neoliberalism*, I explore how Latinx artists' concerns with these conditions in the Americas have encouraged them to develop innovative theatrical modes of representation to address this violence. I use the term *Latinx* to signal a gender neutral cultural signifier, so as to be truly inclusive of all genders of persons of Latin American cultural identity without resorting to a gender binary.[5] This book differs from critical works in Latinx studies that only rarely address theater and performance as a key mode of cultural production; it also stands apart from theater and performance studies texts that primarily consider Latinx theater as a mode of articulating ethnic identity as/or difference. Instead this book concentrates on how Latinx playwrights critique contemporary geopolitics by making theater that reveals neoliberal violence as a systemic condition that is visibly, audibly, and tangibly comprehensible in its variations. There are two questions that I anticipate here: Why U.S. Latinx writers, and why theater? The first question gestures toward the fact that Latin American artists and intellectuals should be privileged as cultural workers and witnesses describing the situation in which they live, especially since U.S. citizens so rarely read and consider their voices. Yet, I would argue that the point of view of U.S. Latinx persons who have affective and familial ties to Latin American sites, histories, and politics are sometimes the most agile at underscoring the particular transnational intricacies of neoliberal politics. On a formal level, the U.S. Latinx writers I consider in this book purposefully and consciously navigate many of the U.S.-based tropes and narratives that are so corrosive in dismissing neoliberal violence:

blaming its victims, naturalizing its effects as inevitable, or suggesting individualistic achievement as the only way out of impoverishment. For many minoritarian subjects, neoliberal discourses rhyme with longer-standing racist U.S. discourses used to explain away inequality as a result of laziness, lack of ambition, or failure to assimilate to mainstream U.S. (capitalist) culture. This makes them particularly sensitive to these mobilizations on a transnational scale. These playwrights are modeling a mode of concern that breaks with earlier models of solidarity, attempting instead to self-consciously use their roles as "halfies"—whose "national or cultural identity is mixed by virtue of migration, overseas education or parentage"—to think rigorously about transnational conditions.[6] Within anthropology, halfie researchers are acknowledged to have some privileged insight into and access to the cultures that they write about, while not being fully immersed members of that culture. Like reflexive anthropologists the Latinx artists I consider use their roles as insiders/outsiders strategically. In fact, many of the artists actually stage their distance from the experience of those they write about, performing a new mode of solidarity based on the differences in experience and identity between author, character, and persona.[7] And even when they are ambivalent about this difference, as in the case of Cherríe Moraga, their use of formal theatrical devices within their works warn against simplistic ideas of authenticity that have derailed many theoretical discussions about identity in neoliberal times.

My answer as to why theater also begins with a qualification. I recognize that many other forms of media may in fact be more influential because larger portions of the population have access to them. Theater targets a smaller and often exclusive audience, making its critique less widely available than other forms. Yet there is some potential in this lesser scope. While there is often pressure in commercial theater to make bankable work, there are independent and university theaters that can afford to flout the desire for capitalist, individualistic heroic narratives. Mass-produced media have a harder time doing this, especially considering the emphasis on test marketing to create the largest possible audience to render greater potential profit. In addition, in the theater, relations between the United States and Mexico in particular, and between the United States and Latin America more generally, are not primarily embedded in a film industry dominated by crime dramas and espionage tropes, meaning that theater does not have to participate in a filmic industrial complex aimed at allaying or escalating U.S. fears about security and criminality in relationship to the permeability of national borders. Certainly, the theater often likes its heroes as much as film does, as the marketing of Matthew Paul Olmos, *so go the ghosts of méxico, part 1*, which I discuss in chapter 3, will make clear. Yet the entrepreneurial ideal is less naturalized because of how we make theater—often in communities of cooperation rather than as primarily solo pursuits. Quite simply, I believe that theater's smallness and its lack of mainstream relevance allow us to tell different stories. (Lin-Manuel

Miranda's hit musical *Hamilton*, about the eponymous figure imagined as a man of color, is an exception, of course, it notably being a tale of entrepreneurship.) In a similar vein, the locality of theater at the site of production can privilege ideas, concepts, narratives, and subject matters that do meet national and international standards of popular interest, expanding the possibilities for representing local, global, and glocal concerns for divergent communities.

Attention to what theater can't do is equally important. The very limitations of the stage—of what can be represented and not—illuminates the (im)mobilities, violence, erasures, temporalities, and cramped sites of neoliberal life in the Americas. For example, theater is largely incapable of depicting the large-scale violence found in feature films and documentaries on narcotraffic or the epic scope of mainstream narco-narratives; theater's alignment of bodies in bounded space points to the limitations of movement across borders and through territory; theater's simultaneous materiality and abstraction—namely, its inability to seamlessly represent reality with real things—articulates how objects transform under transnational capitalism; and, in some cases, the retention of the theatrical frame, rather than its erasure, serves as a reminder of our position as spectators of neoliberal capital as a (dis)organized performance. My claims about theater, here, if universalized, are not new. Herbert Blau, Spencer Golub, Bert States, and Alice Rayner, among others, have made persuasive arguments for the power of theatricality in the theater.[8] What is new about this book is my emphasis on how theatrical strategies reveal the way economic structures displace, discipline, and disintegrate bodies and souls under neoliberal global capitalism in the Americas.

The book's introduction is followed by four chapters, each of which explores a different political, social, and historical phenomenon created by neoliberal economic practices in the Americas. The introduction provides a brief history of neoliberalism, then moves on to explain why Latinx theater is a crucial nexus of political critique. The first chapter considers how Latinx playwrights in the United States engaged with NAFTA, privatization, and economic liberalization by mobilizing indigenous culture, cosmology, and identity within their plays. The works I examine include Cherríe Moraga's *Giving Up the Ghost* (1986/1994), *The Hungry Woman* (2001/2005), *Heart of the Earth: A Popul Vuh Story* (1994), and *New Fire: To Make Things Right Again* (2012); Michael John Garcés's *points of departure* (2005); and Luis Valdez's *Mummified Deer* (2000) and *Earthquake Sun* (2004). This chapter explores the fate of pan-indigenous movements as a ground of social change in the Americas, revisiting the possibilities and failures of cultural nationalism along the way. Rather than dismissing these plays as co-opting indigenous practice, I argue that they reveal long-standing and complicated engagements with theatricality as well as the history of indigenous practice in the Americas over the last forty years. The historical focus of this chapter illuminates the shifting representational practices from the 1970s to present. It is also here that I think critically about post-revolutionary eschatology as a mode of undoing the exoticization of indigenous practices in U.S. Latino theater. The second half of the chapter, which features Michael John Garcés's *points of departure*, reveals how his rethinking of classical dramaturgy in the Americas ultimately leads to the end of the tragic liberal subject as hero. Chapter 2 explores plays about the 1994 Balseros Crisis, during which thousands of rafters left Cuba because of the horrendous economic conditions there. Plays I examine include Eduardo Machado's *Kissing Fidel* (2005) and *Havana Is Waiting* (2001), Jorge Cortiñas's *Sleepwalkers* (1999), Caridad Svich's *Prodigal Kiss* (1999), Nilo Cruz's *A Bicycle Country* (1999), and María Irene Fornés's *Manual for a Desperate Crossing* (1996) and *Balseros (Rafters)*, an opera based on that script (1997). In particular, this chapter considers how theatrical renderings of temporality and motion make shifts in the definition of exile and migrant visible. They also articulate how national narratives of progress—Marxian and capitalist—are upended by the realities of Special Period Cuba. Nested within queer affect, these critiques of "straight" time and history reveal how queer time functions in everyday neoliberal life.

Chapter 3 considers representations of femicide in the Americas, with special emphasis on the killings in Juárez, Mexico, from 1993 to the present. Plays I consider in this chapter include Victor Cazares's *The Dead Women of Juárez-Town & Smiley* (2008), Coco Fusco's *The Incredible Disappearing Woman* (2003), Caridad Svich's *Iphigenia Crash Lands Falls on the Neon Shell That Was Once Her Heart (A Rave Fable)* (2004), and Marisela Orta's *Braided Sorrow* (2008). I also consider two plays by Mexican playwrights, translated and presented in the United States by Latinx artists Christina Marín and Jimmy Noriega, respectively: *Mujeres de Arena* by Humberto López (2004) and Cristina Michaus's *Women of Ciudad Juárez* (2011). My analysis explores the limits of dramaturgical and narrative modes that attempt to display, investigate, or authenticate these acts of violence as crimes that can be solved. At the same time, I consider how the frequent production of documentary plays may be a form of seriality in itself that underscores that in the times of neoliberalism, necropolitical violence is a constant. I move on to consider how many playwrights embrace nonrealistic modes of representing violence as an ethical mode that illuminates the seriality and theatricality of the crimes themselves. While some playwrights redefine the tragic and the obscene (*obscaena*, the literal offstage), others concentrate on the impossibility of becoming other.

Chapter 4 examines plays about narcotraffic that instantiate the relationship between physical and economic violence in the United States and Mexico. I explore how many Latinx playwrights' choices to stray from filmic narco-realism make their plays more effective at revealing the connections between economic opportunity, performances of masculinity, and excruciating violence. I also consider how the emergence of the narcoentrepreneur in the Americas links Foucault's concept of homo economicus to the long history of drug trafficking. Because most of the works I consider were written during and depict the period of Mexico's narcoguerra under former president Felipe Calderón (2006–2012), they also examine how the Mexican state staged violence to its own ends. Plays considered include Victor Cazares's *Religiones Gringas* (2011) and *Ramses contra los monstruos* (2013), Tanya Saracho's *El Nogalar* (2011), Octavio Solis's *Santos y Santos* (1993) and *Dreamlandia* (2000), and Matthew Paul Olmos's *so go the ghosts of méxico, part 1* (2013). My conclusion will illuminate the stakes of thinking theatrically about hemispheric neoliberalism at the cultural moment in which this book was written.

ACKNOWLEDGMENTS

First and foremost, I wish to thank my family for all the sunny (and snowy) days I was allowed to sit in my office and write this book. Thank you for your patience. *Latinx Theater in the Times of Neoliberalism* would not have been possible without the amazing support of so many colleagues at Brown University in the Department of Theatre Arts and Performance Studies, the Center for the Study of Race and Ethnicity in America, the Center for Latin American Studies, and the Office of the Dean of the Faculty.

Series editors Patrick Anderson and Nicholas Ridout were both early and fervent supporters of the project and have been wonderful editors and friends throughout. The entire staff of Northwestern University Press has been fabulous to work with, especially Michael Levine, who believed in it from the start. The anonymous readers were also superb. Thank you for your attention to my work in the midst of doing yours.

My friends in the Latinx Theatre Commons, ATHE, and ASTR, who have been interlocutors throughout the process, have made the book better (and shorter!). Special kudos go to Jon D. Rossini, Marci McMahon, Patricia Herrera, Ramón Rivera-Servera, Harvey Young, Michal Kobialka, and Rosemarie Bank, who have seen many drafts of parts of this book throughout the last decade. The staff of La Artisan Café kept me fed throughout my sabbatical, and they deserve great credit for the productivity of my afternoon writing sessions. Lou Moreno at INTAR was generous and kind in sharing his time and many archives as I did preliminary research.

My greatest debt, of course, goes to the playwrights and directors whose plays and productions I discuss throughout the book. Many of them gave of their time freely in the form of interviews and email conversations about their work. In particular, I wish to thank Victor Cazares, whose play *Ramses contra los monstruos* changed the structure and the subject of *Latinx Theater in the Times of Neoliberalism*, and whose friendship is one of the cornerstones of my life.

Portions of chapter 2 appeared in "Havana Isn't Waiting: Staging Travel during Cuba's Special Period," in *Performance in the Borderlands*, edited by Ramón H. Rivera-Servera and Harvey Young (Houndsmills, U.K.: Palgrave Macmillan, 2010).

A very different version of a portion of chapter 4 was published as "Latino/a Dramaturgy as Historiography," in *Theatre/Performance Historiography:*

Time, Space, Matter, edited by Rosemarie K. Bank and Michal Kobialka (Houndsmills, U.K.: Palgrave Macmillan, 2015).

Latinx Theater in the Times of Neoliberalism

CRITICAL INTRODUCTION

If one accepts that some of the first incursions of neoliberal capital in the Americas occurred in the mid-1960s with the Border Industrialization Act, which allowed the first maquiladoras to arrive on the U.S.–Mexico border, one must also acknowledge that U.S. Latinx theater emerges in the neoliberal period.[1] And, that it continues to dwell there. Although the movement of many Latin American countries to center-left democracies (again) at the turn of the millennium caused scholars to opine that we are moving into a post-neoliberal age, this post-neoliberal era has not occurred.[2] Thus, I suggest that it is important to think of the last forty years as a single neoliberal era, albeit one that has oscillated in terms of its tactics. Which means, as Jon D. Rossini and I have written elsewhere, that Latinx theater has *always* been responding within, if not to, neoliberal conditions understood as such.[3]

This book, however, primarily concentrates on Latinx plays written from 1992 to the present. The playwrights featured in this book, then, are responding to neoliberalism in process rather than in emergence, after the rise and fall of cultural nationalist and Third World solidarity movements of the 1960s and 1970s. The situations they face include forced migration, femicide, state-sponsored terror, and the escalation of transnational business practices that employ violence in various ways; while some of these forms of violence are hypervisible, such as the display of corpses by narcotraffickers, others are silent and invisible, such as the slow death by near starvation caused by the economic pressures of neoliberal life in post-Soviet Cuba. These conditions ask for political critique that privileges making economic violence perceivable and comprehensible.

In order to respond to these conditions, playwrights employ new tactics that both play upon and depart from earlier Latinx theatrical strategies. In the '60s and '70s, Latinx artists who thought transnationally in the wake of decolonization used Third World revolutionary paradigms to resist assimilation into the U.S. mainstream, to protest their marginalization by allying themselves with non-European and non-U.S. liberation movements throughout the world, and to imagine a revolutionary present or near future. These modes of cultural production were also, of course, often explicitly or implicitly anticapitalist but did not interrogate now instantiated modes of neoliberal global capitalism as a mode of violence. In the '90s and 2000s, in contrast, theater artists speak about transnational capitalism from a vantage point that is postrevolutionary and less optimistic.[4] For some of the playwrights in this book, the transition between paradigms is directly related to their embodied or textual return to Latin America, where they encountered the damage wrought by the early decades of neoliberalism. Their trips were journeys, imagined and real, to the roots of their identities, a trope common to Latinx American literature from the 1960s to the present. But in the last twenty years or so, more often than not, these Latinx playwrights' travels have led them elsewhere—to thinking about the politics of migration, capitalism, pan-indigenous solidarity, and state terror throughout the hemisphere. In coming to terms with these histories of oppression in their home countries or those of their parents and grandparents, these playwrights have newly imagined affective, political, and economic ties in the Americas.

These artists' experiences have inevitably revealed the limitations of certain U.S.-based conceptions of identification and dramaturgies of belonging that depend on mainstream conceptions of the frameworks of Latinx identity: unidirectional migration, an emphasis on cultural authenticity, and the assumption of the stability of national sovereignties and national identities. Nonetheless, these plays and the world in which they were born also show that Latinx subjects are certainly not post-identity, post-ethnic, or post-racial in any sense of the words. Racism and neocolonialism clearly persist. I do not, then, disavow ethnicity-based political movements or solidarity movements, or the artwork of people of color as people of color from the 1960s to the present as being out of time or place under neoliberalism. Instead, I ask that we consider Latinx theater in the times of neoliberalism as a transnational, post-nationalist, and (mostly) post-cultural nationalist perspective aware of its own historicity. This paradigm shift sets the parameters for this study. Historically, this book engages a period of neoliberalism in the Americas in which travel/migration (or its stultification), is a primary mode of governmentality; it is also a period in which the idea of progressive time as historical narrative—common to liberal capitalism and communism—has been upended. Lastly, it is a time in which modes of subject formation have radically changed to privilege articulation by U.S.-based capitalism. It is for this reason that I primarily engage with Latinx theater about Cuba and Mexico, whose histories, migration policies, and historiographies are both antagonistic and deeply interdependent with those of the United States. While not dismissing the interdependency or breadth of other hemispheric histories, my concentration on the relationships between the United States, Cuba, and Mexico focuses this book's exploration of the theatrical critique of a particularly necropolitical contemporary neoliberalism as it has developed over the last twenty years. A brief history of neoliberalism in the Americas offers the context for this exploration.

A Brief History of Neoliberalism in Latinx America

I use the term *neoliberal* to point to the historical specificity of the form of capitalism that much of the world suffers under today. This escalation of late capitalism can also be considered under the rubric of transnationalism or globalization, both of which rightfully underscore the intensification of commerce under multinational companies rather than in a network of more orthodox international trade alliances. The problem with using terms other than *neoliberal* or *neoliberalism* to describe this regime is that without specifying this economic regime as an agentive strategy of capital accumulation emergent in the mid to late twentieth century, we risk espousing contemporary capitalism as a natural outgrowth of an inevitable process unhinged from or existing beyond state power. As the regulation of autonomous enterprise zones suggests, the opposite is the case. The escalation of the power of the state is crucial, rather than counter, to the rise of the neoliberal capitalism. By specifying the contemporary era as neoliberal, we avoid homogenizing all modes of capital accumulation from the sixteenth century to the present. After all, capitalism has always been transnational and global.[5] What marks a difference in contemporary times is the combination of the escalation of the horrific working conditions in much of the Third World and Global South, the dismantling of the welfare state in the First World, and the consequential increased prosperity for an ever smaller elite group of speculative professionals as beneficiaries of the system. This complex of inequalities marks the global fruition of neoliberal policies.

Neoliberalism, however, is most insidious as an economical regime that is also disciplinary of subject formation.[6] The neoliberal regime occurs at the level of ideology, policy, and subjectification, meaning that we are evinced to act as neoliberal subjects not only in our actions in response to employment conditions and shifts in social welfare policy, but in all aspects of our lives, including through our quotidian utterances and practices. In short, we are often asked to imagine ourselves within the frame of economic rationality in everyday interactions. This is because the necessary tension so key to the liberal state between imagining ourselves as citizens of a nation state or society and making ourselves instrumental as economic agents of capitalist accumulation has dissipated, if not vanished. This injunction is what distinguishes neoliberalism from classical liberalism, although these political formations share many principles.

As Foucault (and others) remind us, neoliberalism emerges from post–World War Two Germany, where political philosophers theorized about "ordoliberal" economics distinguished from both socialism and pure free-market capitalism. The American version of neoliberalism, in Foucault's view, more widely disciplines all aspects of everyday life than the German version did. Foucault argues this is due to the United States' particular relationship to liberalism: as a way of thinking and being, rather than merely a form of government. The conversion from homo economicus being a man of exchange under liberalism to being an entrepreneur of the self who "produces his own satisfaction" under neoliberalism was especially successful because of this culturally specific formation.[7] The economic theories that made this transformation possible came from neoclassical economic thinkers at the University of Chicago, including Gary Becker, Milton Friedman, and Friedrich Hayek (who came to the United States in 1950). Hayek, in his book *The Road to Serfdom*, went so far as to equate state-controlled economies with the foreclosure of freedom and the emergence of totalitarianism.[8]

While these scholars' foundational principles were incubated in the U.S. academy, they were soon exported to Chile via academic exchange programs in 1950s between the University of Chicago and the Pontifical Catholic University of Chile in Santiago, meaning neoliberalism was a hemispheric project from a very early stage. This decades-long thought experiment resulted in the 1973 coup and subsequent military rule of Augusto Pinochet.[9] Under his dictatorship, Chile was subjected to a form of economic "shock therapy" to kick-start the country's economy.[10] The experiments in Chile (which offered temporary economic gains but an escalation of the poverty rate and eventually the collapse of the economy) were offered as possible solutions to other parts of the hemisphere where socialist governments and protectionist policies were the norm and could be said to be inhibiting capitalist profit making. Although the growth miracle that the economists imagined did not occur, Mexico, Argentina, Brazil, and Uruguay were convinced to try them, much to their disadvantage.[11] In Chile (and in much of the rest of the Southern Cone) the link between economic violence and physical violence is clear.[12] To counter opposition to these policies, the Chilean regime murdered leftist activists regularly, while simultaneously depriving its citizens of many of their basic needs. Despite his prescience, Foucault's emphasis on Europe and the United States stops him from discussing Chile, although it would have allowed him to pursue the true ends of his disciplinary critique. More plainly, the Chilean example reveals the deeply intimate relationship between U.S. military action, state violence, and global disciplinary interventions in Latin American economies. While mindful of this history in the South and Central America, this book largely concentrates on Mexico and Cuba, considering the effects of these policies in later decades. These effects are suffered as femicides, narcotrafficking, economic deprivation, and forced migration. To be clear, the effects listed above are not evidence of collapsed states, as is often understood in popular discourse, but the opposite. As I suggest briefly above, recent shifts in labor regulation and migration that support neoliberal capitalist accumulation depend on strong state power rather than its weakening, despite the so-called demise of the nationally protected economies.[13] This irony is most easily seen in Latin America.

It is no accident, then, that while most theorizations of the neoliberal condition as a disciplinary apparatus emerge from the U.S. academy, some of the earliest and most trenchant critiques of neoliberalism as an imperialist practice come from those most injured by the extension of neoliberal economics into modes of everyday governance—Mexico and the Southern Cone. In this book, I turn to Latin American theorizations of neoliberalism because they more clearly delineate the panoply of effects of moving away from social(ist) democracy rather than simply chronicling the "demise of the welfare state" in the United States in the '80s and '90s. I am also interested in the historical reach an Americas-centered examination affords. In the United States, some scholars of neoliberalism date its emergence either to the end of the Bretton Woods agreement in 1971, which effectively made the U.S. dollar a reserve economy, or to U.S. reactions to the rise of stagflation in 1973. Most, however, wait until the rise of Reagan and Thatcher in the 1980s to historically pinpoint when the basic principles of neoliberalism became espoused as political doctrine on a wide scale.[14] In contrast, like Foucault, I see the roots of neoliberalism in earlier modes of liberal thought; yet unlike him, I prefer to privilege events in the Americas, such as the emergence of the Mexican maquiladora program in 1965, to underscore that the transition to neoliberal formations in Latin America is *simultaneous with* rather than *subsequent to* the '60s in the United States.[15] This is important because accepting this earlier date revises the notion that the global process of neoliberalization, in the Americas at least, was born out of an affective sense of dissatisfaction with radicalism of the '60s in the United States and France. For the purposes of this study, which considers art made a generation after these incursions, centering the process in Latin America reveals how great an effect these events had on Latinx persons, even if they were born within or have resided for much of their life in the United States.

In Mexico, for example, the elimination of protective tariffs for national industries and the intensification of the maquiladora system in the 1980s led to mass migration to the north of the country or to the United States. After NAFTA, this trend became more pronounced as small-scale farming and other forms of sustenance were eliminated. The deprivation which resulted from the collapse of portions of the agricultural sector has raised the appeal of land-based narcotics trafficking and trade as a way to make a living in contemporary Mexico.[16] Narcoentrepreneurship, or the dream of being able to attain riches through narcotraffic, is one of the most vibrant myths of self-making in the Americas. The popularity of narcocorridos is but one example of this mode of imagining.[17] In reality, this happens for very few. Instead, migrants from Mexico and Central America are regularly kidnapped and ransomed on their way north by traffickers who are diversifying their businesses to make a profit. Tens of thousands are killed within the crosshairs of the drug trade whether they are involved in it or not. Drugs make their way north and guns make their way south, while the traversals of those in search of survival are made harder by trade relations that advocate for the movement of products and criminalize the movement of people.[18] In reality, narcotrafficking is the logical extreme of neoliberal capital in the Americas. As Sayak Valencia eloquently suggests, this never places other forms of exploitative "legitimate business" in the neoliberal Americas, such as maquiladoras, under threat; instead, they form a larger narcomachine.[19] The rise of femicide is directly related to this machine.[20] Both narcotrafficking and maquila factory jobs place women's lives in danger by making them targets, whether they are walking down a dark street to catch the last bus to their homes on the outskirts of shantytowns after their shifts at the factory or become collateral damage of the narco-economy at any other time of the day or night.

The effects of economic liberalization, of course, manifest differently on different sites. In the early '90s, Cuban citizens suffered from severe economic violence as a result of the double deprivation caused by the fall of the U.S.S.R., a great supporter of the Cuban agricultural products market, and the continuation of the U.S. embargo. Although socialist Cuba still stands rhetorically as a bulwark against capitalism, Cuba's reaction to this deprivation included the incorporation of limited modes of capitalist entrepreneurship aimed at collecting revenues from tourism in foreign currency to keep the nation afloat. The dire conditions in the Special Period in Time of Peace led to the Balseros (Rafter) Crisis I describe in chapter 2, when hundreds left Cuba on rafts in order to survive, becoming economic migrants rather than exiles. While this exodus is not related to a complete implementation of U.S.-style neoliberal policy in Cuba, the global move toward economic liberalization and Clinton's neoliberal Third Way politics in the early '90s exacerbated the situation.[21] As I write this, we have again possibly changed our travel policy with Cuba, but upcoming actions will let us know the future of this pursuit.

These Cuban and Mexican examples suggest that the movement of goods and bodies in the Americas has shifted under neoliberal rule, as have the modes of violence enacted through and around state power. On one hand, the intense militarization of the U.S.-Mexico border and of the U.S. and Mexican police forces has led to violence against poor citizens, particularly women and indigenous people. At the same time the vagaries and promises of the informal economy—particularly the trafficking of narcotics—is responsible for a culture of impunity wherein the collaboration of the state and the police to procure their own profits leads directly to their failure to protect everyday citizens from harm or death. Or more grimly, as is the case in Guerrero, members of drug gangs are hired as assassins by the state to kill leftists. Given the reality of these hemispheric networks of capital accumulation, it is accurate to say that neoliberal violence is implicitly supported by the U.S. and Mexican governments via trade policies and modes of policing.[22]

Other parts of Latin America, of course, have reacted to and instantiated neoliberalism differently. As Arlene Dávila has so powerfully and succinctly argued in her essay "Locating Neoliberalism in Time, Space and Culture," we need to attend to the specificities of neoliberal projects in relation to different forms of governance, discipline, and economic regimes.[23] What is important in the context of *Latinx Theater in the Times of Neoliberalism* is that the relationship between particular neoliberal policies, disciplinary apparatuses, and physical, emotional, and epistemic violence be made visible, audible, and perceivable; that we understand the complex trafficking of bodies, goods, and ideas as embodied and performative practices that interrogate modes of nationalism *emergent in* rather than *counter to* neoliberal ideology and practice; and that particular mobilizations of neoliberal subjectification, such as the rise of homo economicus–style entrepreneurship, be recognized within a hemispheric context. Equally important is the recognition that in Latin America, inequalities brought about by free-market economic policies have exacerbated inequalities lingering from colonialism, which often based its modes of dominance on racial/ethnic differentiation. I pay special attention to these historical legacies of racism and ethnocide throughout this book.

Aníbal Quijano, Walter Mignolo, and Ileana Rodríguez provide guidance by tracing the complex relationship between Western epistemology, colonialism, liberalism, and their reimagination under neoliberal regimes, revealing how neoliberal practices exacerbate earlier modes of inequality for indigenous and laboring people throughout the hemisphere.[24] Achille Mbembe's conception of necropolitics complements the work of these thinkers.[25] Revising notions of biopolitics that rely solely on the example of the holocaust, Mbembe reveals the deep relationship between colonialism, slavery, and biopower in the late modern world. His most important contribution, however, is linking financial insecurities from the '70s to the present in portions of Africa to forms of resource extraction, war, militia economies, and the management of multitudes. These multitudes become classes of people who are categorized as "rebels, child soldiers, victims, refugees or civilians incapacitated by mutilation, or simply massacred on the model of ancient sacrifices, while the survivors after a horrific exodus are confined in camps or zones of exception."[26] Although Mbembe's examples might best describe conditions in eastern and central Africa, they are useful for thinking through the conditions in border zones in the Americas as they react to this extraction, as Rosa-Linda Fregoso, Sayak Valencia, and Ileana Rodríguez have argued.[27] Particularly useful is Mbembe's linkage between modes of colonialism, finance, and currency instability with the rhetoric of war and biopolitics in the Global South. Working outside of a paradigm which assumes that egalitarian liberal democracy is a default mode of governance in much of the contemporary world and that the countries in the Global South are merely failing to meet this ideal, Mbembe, like Rodríguez, Mignolo, and Quijano, reveals how the legacy of slavery and colonialism make the fulfillment of liberal democracy impossible, fracturing the very idea that liberal democracy can exist without an "other." These conditions haunt the plays I consider in oblique and overt ways as they critique the neoliberal condition.

Latinx Playwriting as Political Critique

Latinx theater thinks about neoliberalism theatrically rather than directly resisting it as a mode of direct social change. At the risk of a disagreement with Marx for a moment, the point of *Latinx Theater in the Times of Neoliberalism* is to consider how a remarkable group of playwrights theorize the world rather than change it. I do this not to underplay these artists' political work. After all, many of the artists I consider here are activists in their own right. But I also want to advocate that Latinx theater artists are theorists, undoing hierarchies of knowledge production that position people of color, particularly artists of color, as authenticity and content providers in an outdated ethnographic frame. The contemporary Latinx playwrights I consider in this book employ Latin American cultural formations, cosmologies, and epistemologies to theorize time, temporality, periodicity, and duration, as well as space and subjecthood under neoliberalism in the Americas.

While their insights are new and historically particular, the political concerns and theatrical tactics of the artists I consider here are not entirely new to Latinx theater. Neither is their commitment to cultural critique. Many Chicano/a, Puerto Rican, and Cuban American playwrights and performers have exposed inequality, unfair labor practices, and the trials of migration, militarization, urban and rural poverty, sexism, racism, and the violence of assimilation from the beginning of their careers. Dramaturgically, many of these playwrights have used and/or critiqued national narratives from host countries or the United States as part of their work. While some playwrights did so through fairly straightforward orthodox family dramas, others pushed at the boundaries of realism by engaging popular Latin American or European forms such as commedia dell'arte or the Mexican *carpa* (tent shows), by using agitprop performance tactics and performing in the streets, by employing nonrealistic representations of spiritual worlds or cosmologies, by creating and embodying fictional personae that played with but undid racist stereotypes, by staging national borders within the frame of theatrical boundaries so as to critique these modes of territoriality, by staging transformations of U.S. American and Latinx identity as theatricalized practices, and by staging history in theatrically innovative forms.

Many Latinx playwrights also attempted to think transnationally before the '90s—through the frame of Third World solidarity and pan-indigenism, often with less than fulsome results. Plays created in the wake of U.S. Chicano cultural nationalism often inadvertently resuscitated tropes of Mexican nationalism aimed at mythologizing the indigenous past rather than advocating for present-day indigenous people, despite their intent, as I discuss in chapter 1.[28] In the 1980s and early '90s, performance art mobilized against the simultaneous militarization of the U.S.–Mexico border and the emergence of free trade. They did this by making art at the border or by exhibiting symbolic and actual violence on brown transnational bodies in galleries, museums, and public spaces. Relationships between the United States and Cuba were also symbolically rendered in body art, exposing the contradictions in U.S. policy. Unfortunately, mainstream cultural exotification, eroticization, and tropicalization often blunted the critique of pieces like Coco Fusco and Guillermo Gómez-Peña's 1992 *Couple in a Cage*, aimed at this purpose.[29] Despite their popularity as subjects of academic discourse, these performances often failed with everyday audiences. Plays about Latin American dirty wars were even less successful. *The Conduct of Life*, *Thin Air: Tales from a Revolution*, and *Death and the Maiden*, three plays from the 1980s and early '90s, took on the military dictatorships in the Southern Cone, but in modes that could be read as allegorical. In the end, these plays often implicitly positioned Latin America as a site of barbarism in relation to the democratic United States, because they did not specify the country or time where the events were happening.[30] These plays' lack of historicity—a tactic often used in Latin America to enable political speech—blunted their critique and led to accusations of naïveté, if not cultural chauvinism.[31] On a formal level, the coded gestures used to speak under dictatorship that were popular in Latin America in times of censorship, such as Chilean and Argentine dramatists' insertion of certain music to gesture obliquely toward violence or torture, were not efficacious in a U.S. context where the norms of political speech were quite different. At other times, productions of said plays attempted to make them speak universally to a commercial audience, effectively displacing the very particular stakes the United States, Chile, and Argentina had in instrumentalizing such violence.[32] Ultimately, setting a play in a generic Latin American setting was simply read as a mode of allegorizing Latin America rather than asking audiences to pay attention to Latin American formal tactics as a mode of understanding hemispheric political violence. Whatever their faults, these plays reveal the beginning of a transnational consciousness, buttressed by the dissemination of information about U.S. involvement in Southern Cone and Central American dictatorships in the mainstream press.[33] Although these plays were largely unsuccessful as political critique, there is something to be learned from their failures. They articulate why contemporary playwrights often move away from allegorical and universalizing modes of discussing violence when talking about Latin America, even when they hope to make larger claims about the mechanics of political violence. The legacy of these earlier plays, however, haunts Caridad Svich's *Iphigenia Crash Land Falls on the Neon Shell That Was Her Heart*, which I consider in chapter 3. *Iphigenia* moves throughout the hemisphere from a Southern Cone dictatorship to the maquilas of the northern frontier of Mexico, refusing to mark national boundaries and histories, while traversing their particular circumstances.[34] Svich's text points to the limits of thinking hemispherically in the contemporary United States, as she reveals the complicated racial and class dynamics within various Latin American communities.

Some of the most visible changes in contemporary Latinx theater in the last thirty years, however, relate to the shifting realities of migration, which has been the traditional subject of Latinx theater writ large. Rather than writing about migration as a linear process or as a singular painful event that marks a transformation of identity, in the 1990s playwrights began to write about migration as a cyclical or recurring process with less determined impacts on identity. Concomitant with this shift was many playwrights' conscious rejection of viewing the host country as the past and the country of arrival as the present. This tension is evident over the career of Chicano playwright Octavio Solis, whose plays increasingly depict multiple border crossings and dwelling in the flux of the Rio Grande.[35] In his plays and those of others, we are less likely to see the border as a secure threshold space. In fact, in some plays, such as Victor Cazares's *Ramses contra los monstruos*, the border is not represented at all; we are either in Mexico or the United States or somewhere else.[36] Meanwhile, in Nilo Cruz's *A Bicycle Country*, a border emerges as a paradigm that describes an ironically bifurcated sea in the midst of the Balseros Crisis, the representation of Cuban exodus from the island being changed from an exilic paradigm to a more ambivalent staging of migration.

Established playwrights have also begun to look differently at history, consciously engaging the 1970s in the United States and the Caribbean as a watershed time that articulated present reality. As Jon D. Rossini and I argue, both Migdalia Cruz and Octavio Solis have framed the '70s as the beginning of a new regime of thinking about transnational labor and the escalation of inequality in U.S. urban areas.[37] And Nuyorican playwrights José Rivera and Migdalia Cruz have explored how poverty in the United States was wrought by the 1980s mobilization of neoliberal policy.[38] Other established playwrights have taken a transnational turn in the middle of their careers. Eduardo Machado's early plays, for example, mostly concern Cuban Americans. When they are about Cuba, they are about pre-Revolutionary and Revolutionary Cuba, as in the case of *Fabiola* (1989), *In the Eye of the Hurricane* (1985), and *The Modern Ladies of Guanacaboa* (1984).[39] Once he traveled to Cuba after the Balseros Crisis, however, he abandoned a purely exilic subject position and began to write plays about contemporary Cuba. In *The Cook* (2004), for example, he navigated the complex contemporary relationship between the United States and Cuba by telling the story of a *paladar* (home restaurant) managed by an Afro-Cuban woman who used to be a cook for an elite family and who had fled to the United States. This play forced him to explore the legacy of racism in Cuba head-on, while lending a critical eye toward entrepreneurship. By departing from (and critiquing) the nostalgic mode that countenanced his earlier plays, he offers a more transnational view of the Special Period.[40] Cherríe Moraga's work, which represents a long-term queer feminist negotiation with cultural nationalism in the United States, moved south differently, shifting from a Third World solidarity paradigm to one based in hemispheric indigenous cosmology.[41] Her fraught journeys are fully explored in chapter 1. Moraga's struggles are productive of transnationally oriented thought. Yet one must be conscious of one's blind spots. As Saldaña-Portillo's incisive critique of how Chicano/a writers often misrecognize the ways in which *mestizaje* upholds the Mexican state's damaging modes of erasing indigeneity suggests, transnational thinking can be fraught with problems even when Latinx writers are articulating new modes of hemispheric identity and solidarity in the face of NAFTA.[42] Her critique does not ask that we dismiss these transnational gestures, however, because they can and do open up spaces for rethinking neoliberalism, as her most recent work, *Indian Given: Racial Geographies across the U.S. and Mexico* makes clear.[43] There she reintroduces the specter of the *indio bárbaro*, a racist term often used to refer to nomadic indigenous northern Mexican peoples, to understand how the narcotraffickers and other cultural commentators in Mexico under neoliberalism have engaged horrific imaginings of colonialist writers to further their needs. Following her lead, I read texts closely, while gesturing broadly to cultural tropes so as to incorporate a form of transnational thinking that allows me to frame Latinx theater's most incisive political interventions in a hemispheric frame.

Dramaturgical Interventions: Interrogating Liberalism

Latinx writers' most recent foray into intellectual transnationalism has sometimes come with what for some critics and readers is a more difficult intervention into U.S. dramaturgy: the choice to interrogate, deemphasize, and/or dispense with U.S. liberal subject formation as the primary mode with which to narrate Latinx experience and identity. Jon D. Rossini has marked this difficulty in José Rivera's *School of the Americas*. Much to the dismay of many critics, Rivera's depiction of Che Guevara privileges dialectical debate rather than heroism based in liberal subjecthood.[44] In the plays I consider, this dramaturgical transformation is not fully replicated; certainly there are characters in them who come into themselves through individualistic choices, which allow them to overcome their circumstances, be successful, become whole selves, or at least avoid death. Saracho's lower class characters in *El Nogalar*, her modern-day adaptation of *The Cherry Orchard* set in a crumbling upper-class Mexican estate, for example, foray into the new world order by becoming examples par excellence of homo economicus for an instant.[45] Dunia, the female servant, wants to unleash herself on the Internet as a mode of changing her situation rather than working in a maquiladora. She abandons selling her labor power and chooses instead to expose her potential personhood to an online market; her erstwhile companion López (Lopahkin) works for the narcotraffickers largely performing the affective labor of stopping his superiors from freaking out so that they don't kill each other or him.

Together, they inherit their employers' property but no guaranteed future. Thus, although they have escaped the peonage of their past, they embody an ideal form of neoliberal individualism and affective laboring suffused with ambivalence. At the end of the play we do not think they are going to be okay, despite their enthusiasm.

As in *El Nogalar*, this form of self-making is interrogated throughout Latinx theater because the neoliberal situations characters find themselves in do not allow complete belief in individual action as efficacious for self-preservation or the care of others. Perhaps this is why many of the plays I consider experiment with nonindividuated protagonists. Michael John Garcés's *points of departure*, for example, stages its indigenous characters as a modern Aristotelian chorus. He writes: "In this case—as with much modern drama—the play is about the chorus. I wanted to keep a ritual formality about it, make the characters both representative of a polis and at the same time individual, and I think that is why the characters are, as you say, blurry."[46] The play's five characters elude individual subjectivity but also do not become an undifferentiated mass, offering a new mode of subjecthood under contemporary capitalism.

Matthew Paul Olmos's *so go the ghosts of méxico, part 1*, in contrast, creates a mass protagonist made up of the ghosts who are the dead victims of narcotrafficking. This mass protagonist is as compelling as the play's hero: a female police chief who tries to stop the violence in her hometown in Mexico. Olmos's narco-dead rise up, revealing that the true heroes of the recent history of northern Mexico are not easily individuated; their actions offer a different sort of mobilization than the soldiers of the war on drugs do. I return to this point in the conclusion.

My analysis of subject formations within plays in *Latinx Theater in the Times of Neoliberalism* reveals how Latinx playwrights' dramaturgical formations (characters, plot structures, mise-en-scènes) model modes of self-making independent of U.S. liberalism, its forms of heroism, and a belief in unidirectional progress. These plays make it plain that the possibility of thinking a way out of or around neoliberal conditions onstage calls upon us to use nonliberal paradigms offstage. As Wendy Brown claims, neoliberal conditions ask that we refuse the U.S. left's attachment to liberal democracy, which as she suggests, was never fully satisfying anyway given its "institutional and rhetorical embedding of bourgeois, white, masculinist and heterosexual superordination."[47] She posits an alternative for "the Euro-Atlantic states":

> A left vision of justice would focus on practices and institutions of shared popular power; a modestly egalitarian distribution of wealth and access to institutions; an incessant reckoning with all forms of power—social, economic, political, and even psychic; a long view of the fragility and finitude of non-human nature; and the importance of both meaningful activity and hospitable dwellings to human flourishing.[48]

One can hardly argue with these suggestions, but they fall (and feel) differently in Latin America and Latinx America, both of which have been so adversely affected by Euro-American liberal democracies. Latinx writers looking south in the last twenty years more openly and strenuously reject *secular* liberalism as the ideal form of government in formerly colonial states because of the secularism as much as the liberalism.

Cherríe Moraga and Victor Cazares explore different forms of eschatology, which aim to erase difference between self and other, past, present and future, so as to unthink the neoliberal. Moraga imagines a world in which the difference between indigenous cosmology and Western progressive time is dissolved, suggesting an end as a beginning; identity follows a similar collapse, offering Latinx subjects a provisional route to join indigenous revolution and cyclical regeneration on the model of the ceremony of the New Fire. In *New Fire: To Put Things Right Again*, Moraga transforms theater space into a ceremonial space, letting theater and performance coexist. In the process, she engages theorizations of activism against neoliberal violence from Latin America, such as those advocated by the Zapatistas and other indigenous solidarity groups outside of the academy.[49] By basing their claim for national citizenship on their participation in cultural practices rather than on a biological notion of identity or a rubric of citizenship based in property ownership, these groups interrogate modes of identity construction key to liberalism, contemporary liberal democracy, and neoliberalism. They also question the universality of secularism and secular progressive time. The Zapatistas perform thinking otherwise, a mobilization not lost on the other playwrights I consider in this book, many of whom were inspired by the 1994 Chiapas uprising. Subaltern studies paradigms support these playwrights' theorizations of these political strategies (as opposed to the implementation of these tactics in activist practice). Displacing the idea of the elites speaking for disenfranchised people as political necessity, subaltern studies scholars argue that subaltern people can speak for themselves, if we learn how to listen. For Latin American subaltern studies, indigenous practice and historiography is a key modality of this form of writing.[50] Moraga's *New Fire* re-performs this listening onstage when she incorporates video footage of meetings with various indigenous groups and has her characters and audiences listen. These excerpts proffer anticapitalist solutions as political possibility within an indigenous frame. By placing the video onstage, Moraga simultaneously demonstrates the very dexterity of theatricality to complicate modes of subject making that have been co-opted by neoliberalism. Many other playwrights follow suit in different and divergent ways, upending modes of truth making first theorized as liberating, such as the *testimonio*.

Interrogating *Testimonio*, Interrogating Realism

Coco Fusco's *The Incredible Disappearing Woman* is a play about a theatrical trick. In it, three Latinx museum workers—Chela, Magaly, and

Dolores—decide who would be best at playing a corpse in a grisly reenactment of necrophilia. In effect they have to decide who is going to play dead when a famous U.S. male artist restages an art project where he had intercourse with a Mexican female corpse he bought south of the border. Their rehearsals of playing dead allow them to tell each other about the atrocities they suffered in Chile, Mexico, and the United States. Their experiences gesture to the Juárez femicide victims to whom Fusco dedicates the play. Fusco's play is effective in part because of how she engages, without reproducing, the testimonial form.[51]

Testimonio is a type of first person narrative that acts as a witness to atrocities caused by state- and non-state-sponsored violence. From its inception, it has been understood as an important form of indigenous and subaltern representation writ large. Although these texts are often authored in the first person, they stand in for the experiences of many others under extraordinary oppression. Often begun as interviews or oral accounts by those directly affected by this violence, *testimonio* emerged in the 1960s and remained strong until the 1990s.[52] John Beverley valorized these works as a mode of truth telling that offered intellectuals throughout the world opportunity for solidarity with subaltern subjects in the wake of revolutionary possibility.[53] For him, this is not a form of "liberal guilt" or "charity," but "an ethical and political response," which supported international human rights movements in the '80s and '90s in response to state-sponsored atrocities throughout Central America.[54] Although his understanding of these texts changed after they were canonized as literature in the United States, he maintains that they can model a radical multiculturalism outside of a U.S. frame of reference.[55] Scholar Alberto Moreiras raises two potential problems with *testimonios*, however: they can reify an abject position for subalterns, particularly subaltern women, and their politics of truth telling may in fact have traps of its own by oversimplifying the very idea of veracity in its claims to formal transparency.[56] Here, one must ask: Is the so-called audience (Beverley's term) for *testimonio* different in the theater, where spectators are hailed as a self-conscious entity, positioned in a bicameral relationship to the stage? How do we deal with the structures of empathy as an emotional apparatus inherent to many forms of theatrical representation? And how are the formal qualities of the *testimonio* incorporated into theater and to what end? The praxis of *testimonio*, after all, rubs strangely against the theatricality of theater, or what Josette Féral would claim is "the result of a series of cleavages (inscribed by the artist and recognized by the spectator) aimed at making a disjunction in systems of signification, in order to substitute other, more fluid ones."[57] Yet, in their attempt to stand in for the non-present beings one can't hear in the First World, these *testimonios* share a set of tactics of representation that bring the two forms (testimony and theater) into a productive tension.

Chapter 3 explores the use of verbatim utterances and documentary materials in relation to remembering the victims of femicide by U.S. audiences. Many of the plays about these events were constructed using tactics from ethnotheater, verbatim theater, and docudrama, mixing U.S., U.K., and Latin American methodologies to divergent ends. While these tactics are sometimes productive in their incorporation of multiple subjectivities, it cannot be ignored that the rise of docudrama and verbatim theater in the U.K. has also been linked to neoliberalism, namely, the Thatcherite dismantling of the welfare state, the disenfranchisement of workers, and the oppression and terrorization of migrant laborers in relation to labor precariousness and paranoia. Yet, unlike *testimonio*, in the face of the fall of socialism and secure notions of social class, these forms of theatrical truth telling often revert to a liberal subject rather than a collective "I" that challenges the sovereignty of the liberal subject, which runs counter to many of the desires of Latinx theater under neoliberalism.[58] Both Lib Taylor and Jon Rossini underscore the ways that verbatim theater ends up considering systemic problems through an individuated, if not entirely liberal, subject.[59] It is for this reason that I underscore how a different set of Latinx artists modify many of these forms of truth telling by employing overt theatricality. Latinx plays' exposure of structural violence also cautions us about how and when one can speak for, with, or in the place of (an)other. These concerns are most crucial when dealing with plays that try to restore or give voice to deceased Mexican female victims of violence. In a different vein, Michael John Garcés's *points of departure* refuses testimonial tactics, precluding easy identification with citizens in Mayan Mexico and Central America, or what Patricia Stuelke would call the "affective commonality" constructed between U.S. and Central American citizens as part of the Central American solidarity movement.[60] Garcés does this by using formal tactics that make it hard to discern what happened and when, critiquing narrative documentary transparency. He also uses fragmented language that chips away at the presence of recognizably bounded characters onstage that allow us to "other" indigenous people even as we harbor sympathy for them. The chapter also takes up plays that consciously spoof or interrogate testimonial forms more cruelly, such as Cazares's *The Dead Women of J-Town and Smiley*, which leads us to laugh at our own complicities in exploitations of sympathy for the other.

Almost all of the plays I consider refuse to privilege realism as an aesthetic strategy. As Chilean scholar Nelly Richard claims, in contemporary neoliberal formations in the Americas, art that underscores the transparency of language can authorize the truth-making apparatus of the state as easily as it can authorize subaltern voices, often serving the ends of radical capital.[61] It is no accident that many of the U.S. Latinx plays I consider choose modes of representation that are not identical to the conditions they are describing nor entirely faithful to the memory of "real" violence. U.S. Latinx theater artists, some more consciously than others, then, have decided that they are best served by not telling the truth exactly as it happened because these tactics risk reproducing the hypervisibility of violence against Latino/as and Latin Americans as a natural, inevitable, eroticized, and fetishized phenomenon that serves the aims of the U.S. state. It is for this reason that debates within literary scholarship of Latin America are so relevant to my scholarship on U.S. Latino/a theater, even though these literary scholars rarely consider theater and performance in their theorizations.

The move against realism makes visible a more general and fierce concern among artists and scholars about representing physical destruction onstage in a violent era. Artists who write about narco-violence and femicide in Juárez, for example, often refuse to represent images of murdered women. They choose other modes of gesturing to violence without reproducing it.[62] In Cazares's *The Dead Women of J-Town*, for example, the most violent acts are displaced to the consumption of a MacDonald's happy meal in the desert, rather than the execution of a woman there. This is because, as Rosa-Linda Fregoso, Ileana Rodríguez, and Rossana Reguillo have demonstrated, violence against female bodies in neoliberal Mexico is a form of expressive language rather than evidence of the failure of language, meaning it can be endlessly reproduced through repetition.[63] Reguillo's nuanced distinction between expressive and utilitarian violence is crucial here:

> Expressive violence is without a doubt preceded by a complex system of pursuit of "profit," but this remains concealed, encrypted, hidden as residual elements in the "message" that is delivered by way of the thousands and thousands of mutilated bodies accumulated in the so-called "war on the narco." In a radical way, and citing Sontag, these messages encrypted in the space of a finite and forever-broken body, may be read as memento mori ("remember you will die"); you will die three times—when you are tortured (the torture that precedes death is almost always unimaginable), when you die, and when your death is converted into data reported in the media (for example, "five heads were found in front of the Attorney General's office"). The signifying chain of expressive *violencias* could not be more eloquent. In its passage through these three arenas, total death becomes pure expression—objectives no longer matter here and the pursuit of profit becomes secondary. What is relevant is the exhibition of the narcomachine as an infinite and inevitable repertoire.[64]

The non-reproduction of realistic violence is a bulwark against being complicit in the system. Appearing as the obscene in the literal sense, as that which should remain offstage but does not, theatrical renderings with all their failures are an important site to think about the nature of economic violence in the last decade—because of their limitations as well as their possibilities.

Exposing Violence through Theatrical Means

So how does one render economic violence visible? One possibility is offered by Victor Cazares's *Ramses contra los monstruos*, which ties together the history of narcotraffic, the AIDS/HIV crisis, and the rise of Juárez as a megacity as the violent products of transnational neoliberalism. His theatrical exploration of this large-scale violence manifests the obdurate refusal of corpses to disappear or be forgotten. Embodied by very real actors who traverse the stage bloodied, these corpses emerge from zipped body bags or jump out of the vats of acid designed to destroy them. Cazares's characters exemplify the unassailable legacy of violence in the Americas through a theatrical refusal to stay dead. Their traversal of life and death gestures toward the falseness of many of other borders that attempt to cleave nations and naturalize the violence of the state. In the theater, *Ramses* allows Mexico past and present and the United States past and present to coexist on one stage. The play materializes theorizations of the relationship between state violence and licit and illicit transnational economies that developed over the *longue durée* but intensified under neoliberalism. Hermann Herlinghaus, Sergio González Rodríguez, and Sayak Valencia have all compellingly theorized cross-border commerce in the neoliberal period in relationship to longer historical trajectories of commerce relevant to this book. Herlinghaus analyzes the pharmacological history of the Americas from the end of the nineteenth century, articulating ties between U.S. affective histories and transnational commerce.[65] His theorization of the U.S.-led drug war argues that this war is part of a longer-term project to control the narcotics economy under modernity. In this sense, the acceleration of this commerce is a pillar of neoliberal discipline and profit rather than being a symptom of its consumptive excesses. Cazares's picture of a burgeoning Juárez accords with Sergio González Rodríguez's history of the area in *The Femicide Machine*. González Rodríguez argues that the rise of Juárez as a megacity from the '70s onward is a major cause of the intensification of femicidal violence. In contrast to many theorizations of neoliberalism, he concentrates on neo-Fordist rather than post-Fordist labor. As he explains:

> The femicide machine is inscribed within a particular structure of the neo-Fordist economy. In other words, it's a parasite of this structure, just as the structure itself was encrusted on the Mexican border. The structure is defined by mass economic regulation on an international macroeconomic scale, and by an assembly line production that differentiates products via flexible automated methods, information technology and specially categorized labor. This economic set-up presents a new, complex, interconnected spectrum of procedures for exploiting labor and resources, while at the same time maintaining more traditional mechanisms of exploitation. These procedures are both tangible and intangible, and their ramifications are global.[66]

The observation that the labor procedures at the border are "tangible and intangible" allows us to think not only about the reality of labor at the border, but about the simultaneous materiality and immateriality of the stage as a realm in which these labor complexities can be staged and thought about. This understanding is especially relevant to Coco Fusco's *The Incredible Disappearing Woman*. The theatricality of women's labor as unauthorized performers, amidst their very real manual labor (they are actually employed as guards and janitors who are asked to stand or perform repetitive movement for long periods of time—not "performers") gestures to the different forms of labor these women are asked or not asked to perform.[67] The materiality of their labor, both material and immaterial, is made abundantly clear.

Cazares's, Solis's, and Fusco's plays all engage Sayak Valencia's conception of *capitalismo gore* and its toxic modes of enacting masculinity.[68] Speaking particularly of the Tijuana-San Diego border (and later the maquila complex in Juárez) Valencia articulates the relationship between capitalist gore and the "femicide machine." She writes: "In the Mexican context, Capitalismo Gore, the phase in capitalism which implies the creation of surplus value through extreme violence—where in effect, dead bodies are the merchandise following a necropolitical logic, the concrete and symbolic practice of governing over death—allows us to think of the femicide machine as an apparatus of the extreme verification of masculinity within a context where macho violence and labour precarity are structural."[69] Valencia's understanding of the performance of masculinity as a mode of capitalist subjectivity that operates alongside the abjection of the necropolitical female body influences my analysis of plays about narcotraffic, especially Octavio Solis's and Tanya Saracho's explorations of this phenomenon in the contemporary United States and Northern Mexico.[70] In Solis's *Dreamlandia*, Lazaro learns to be violent from his father by practicing shooting migrants. That this action is couched within a theatrically rendered pedagogical lesson reveals the performativity of masculinity endemic to the narcotics trade in which his father is trying to inculcate him. In Saracho's *El Nogalar* López's struggles with enacting this masculinity are highlighted, including his constant fatigue at negotiating this form of violence and his anxiety in the face of constant crisis.

Cortiñas, meanwhile, exposes the more quotidian violence of exchange under scarcity with Brechtian visits to a meat market in Special Period Cuba, attenuated descriptions of sex commerce, and complicated exchanges for sleeping pills used to ward off anxiety.[71] Cortiñas's work highlights how neoliberalism emerges as a practice that incorporates low-level (and slow) violence rather than how it operates as a disembodied and abstract ideology. His staging articulates the contradictory effects and affects of advanced capital showcased by sociologists and ethnographers—especially in places like Cuba and Mexico, where the ideology of the state often opposes U.S.-style capitalism and imperialism, even as their policies instantiate its practices.[72]

Of course, one must also crucially think about the implications of staging narco-commerce at all. Mary Pat Brady, one of the first scholars to link close readings of Chicano/a texts to post-Fordist conditions of labor in the U.S.-Mexico borderlands, coins the term *narcospatiality* to define the shifting terrain created by U.S. drug wars and the routes of drug commerce.[73] Her analysis of urban southwestern U.S. and northern Mexican geographies in relation to drug trafficking and consumption complicates theorizations of the borderlands popularized during the 1990s. Brady recognizes the urgency of analyzing stories that articulate the quotidian practices of narco-commerce within national borders rather than concentrating on policing and drug dealing across borders, as many mass-market representations do. Many of the plays I analyze are similarly oriented toward depicting everyday life around transnational commerce rather than staging the actual selling of drugs or police actions. Only one of the plays I consider, *so go the ghosts of méxico, part 1*, introduces a police officer: Mari, a female cop in greater Juárez who refuses to police in a traditional sense. Notably, there are no actual scenes in which drugs are being actively dealt in this play, nor in any other play I write about in this book (although *Santos y Santos* comes close). The avoidance of these scenes, so popular in film, take Curtis Marez's admonition that "the war on drugs is inseparable from mass mediation" seriously.[74] Marez was writing before the most recent era of the narcoguerra, but his comment lays out the importance of refusing to participate in the tropes of mainstream film to avoid becoming an unwitting participant in the drug war and its propaganda. Deemphasizing the rhetoric of borders and boundaries also allows us to "attend to those artistic, cultural and political influences that do not respect national (or cultural nationalist) borders," as José David Saldívar asks us to do as Latino/a scholars.[75] Cazares's and Saracho's work achieves this goal, while not ignoring the very real difference in conditions on the different sides of the border.

Interrogating Progressive Time

As my analysis of the fatigue of *El Nogalar*'s constant middleman López makes clear, Latinx plays consistently reveal the extent to which neoliberal conditions are dependent on an exhaustive (and exhausting) economy of affective and immaterial labor. And this exhaustion almost always complicates or perforates the ideal of progressive time. Unfortunately, some of the most popular academic forms of critique that link labor and temporality only theorize within First World contexts.[76] For example, Lauren Berlant's *Cruel Optimism* primarily considers film in the United States and Europe; pioneering work by performance scholars Shannon Jackson, Rebecca Schneider, Tavia Nyong'o, and Nicholas Ridout also remain within English language performance in the United States and Europe.[77] In this book, I hope to engage and extend their thinking about affect, labor, and temporality to the particularities of Latino/a American cultural production, with its particular rhythms, times, and spaces. In a sense, I try to transnationalize these theorists by dragging them through various postrevolutionary Latin American states. For example, I argue that Moraga's *indigenismo* actively engages what Ridout calls romantic anticapitalism. Perhaps because of my proximity to him and Schneider (they are both close colleagues), this book began to think about time more fully as it was written. I moved beyond rethinking neoliberal time to thinking about neoliberal temporality. Not surprisingly, J. Jack Halberstam, Elizabeth Freeman, and José Muñoz's work on queer temporality tempers how I think about time, movement, and post-national, post-teleological movements in Latina/o America in the neoliberal period.[78] Muñoz's critique of neoliberal straight time, in which he engages Freeman and Halberstam, productively articulates post-nationalist imaginings in Mexico and Cuba. My analysis of queer artists like Jorge Cortiñas, Eduardo Machado, and Victor Cazares, who are all invested in undoing teleological national narratives, indicates they implicitly engage queer temporality as they refine it. Unlike many of the theorists above, some of the playwrights I write about abandon secularism alongside straight time by moving to Christian, Mayan, and Mexican eschatology. The *Merriam-Webster* dictionary defines *eschatology* "as a branch of theology concerned with the final events in the history of the world or of humankind; a belief concerning death, the end of the world, or the ultimate destiny of humankind." Cazares and Moraga engage these end-times as a way to think one's way out of neoliberalism—in ways akin to but not entirely framed by Zapatista discourse; they add a queer touch. By exploring a combination of Latin American influences, they move away from future-oriented queer secular utopias toward an eschatological vision of end-times as now, marking a difference from, but sympathy with, the idea of "cruising utopia."

From the book's beginning, I showcase playwrights who have ambivalence about, if not a resistance to, heteronormative reproductive futurity and orthodox nationalism, committed as they are to reimagining revolution and its temporal and spatial dynamics. My focus on temporality and revolution in relation to indigenous identity in the first chapter complements Alicia Arrizón's and Rafael Pérez-Torres's incisive scholarship on *mestizaje* as a counter-hegemonic form of racialization in the United States, while moving elsewhere.[79] Other chapters take on other temporal interventions. The second chapter reveals changes in the idea of exilic space, time, and revolution in contemporary Cuba as the playwrights engage affective understandings of contemporary neoliberalism. Chapter 3 includes an examination of seriality as a mode of understanding necropolitical violence. Chapter 4 returns to questions of eschatology, revolution, and recursivity, closing the circle on the book's meditation on time. Together, they form a meditation on temporality in the times of neoliberalism.

A Final Note on Transnationalism and Theater

While I aim for a truly transnational scope in this book, many of the scholars and almost all of the playwrights whose work I discuss are based in the United States and have U.S. privileges. I acknowledge this, as do they, but this caveat is not meant to disavow their validity as transnational critics. Rather I aim to work through a different transnational transit by reversing the usual trend—using Latin American scholarship to analyze U.S. cultural production rather than using U.S. scholarship to analyze Latin American texts. In doing so, I hope to counter what Román de la Campa calls Latin Americanism. Latin Americanism presents the idea of Latin America for U.S. consumption in an orientalizing manner, despite claims to the contrary. Although de la Campa concentrates on scholarship on '60s and '70s boom literature, his insights can be applied to recent analyses of Latin American novelists and films about narcotrafficking, whose readers and critics are enamored with the edgy representation of political and physical violence throughout the Americas.[80]

I also wish to reiterate that some of my important theoretical insights about neoliberalism have come from the artists themselves—either through their work or the things that they have said about it. I concentrate on playwrights in *Latinx Theater in the Times of Neoliberalism* because they are making some of the greatest contributions of thought about contemporary conditions in the Americas. As they are quick to acknowledge, their collaborations with dramaturgs and directors have brought their works to fruition. These collaborators have also been important to the evolution of these playwrights' thought and artistry. Yet, I wish to give the stage over to these writers, because it is through their plays that many "long thoughts" about the processes of neoliberal practice have germinated.[81] The playwrights I consider are diverse in their origins and aesthetics, although not in any way representative of Latinx theater as a whole. But most of them work and live in a community of cultural workers who think together as they make art together as Latinx artists. As these writers sat across the table from each other in María Irene Fornés's workshops at INTAR (International Arts Relations, Inc.), directed each other's work, saw each other's work and promoted it, or met at the Latino Theatre Commons or other festivals, they also thought together trenchantly about politics in the Americas.[82] They disseminated images, allegories, and kinesthetic embodiments that accumulate over time and through theater spaces. My chapter on the Balseros Crisis will trace just one of these legacies: that of Michael John Garcés's work as a director of plays about Cuba's Special Period. Recognizing this interdependency and dialogue as productive rather than derivative, namely, as evidence of collaboration rather than co-option, is crucial. By de-atomizing Latinx theater artists' contributions to the public sphere I acknowledge theatrical collaboration as productive of cultural critique in order to open up the possibility of working differently in the times of neoliberalism.

Chapter 1

"Never Any Other Time but This Time No World but This World," or Staging Indigeneity in Neoliberal Times

Unlike the chapters that follow, this one does not center on a single event or phenomena, such as the rise of femicides, the Balseros Crisis, or the recent Mexican narcoguerra. Rather, it traces creative responses to a hemispheric (and global) shift in political possibilities: the fall of socialism, the end of a series of leftist radical revolutionary movements in Central America, and the emergence of widespread neoliberal economic practices, including but not limited to the ratification of NAFTA. I suggest that it is through the exploration of indigenous subjectivities, practices, and cosmologies, many inspired by the Chiapas uprising in 1994, that these playwrights rethink the possibilities of social change in the midst of the demise of global socialism.

I position Latinx engagements with indigenous practices, *indigenismo*, and nonliberal modes of political action from the 1990s to the present as different from these earlier periods in significant ways, although they struggle with many of the same conundrums. I begin this journey by confronting the formal and political difficulties Cherríe Moraga has representing indigenous people onstage in the United States as she develops her political critiques; I then examine how Moraga theorizes indigenous practices, cosmologies, epistemologies, and solidarities as a mode of combatting neoliberalism within a theatrical register, undoing linear time and secular temporality, ultimately by engaging a mode of decolonial thinking that interrogates the frame of theater even as she uses it. A major aspect of her theatrical challenge is a dramaturgical one: the challenge to the dominance of the liberal subject of tragedy. While this chapter is largely dedicated to Moraga's intellectual and aesthetic development, I also engage El Teatro Campesino's recent works and Michael John Garcés's sorely underrated *points of departure* (2005).[1] Garcés and El Teatro Campesino's works also move away from individuation and individual rights within their political dramas. All of these authors move away from traditional progressive time and its dramaturgical equivalent—Freytag's model of plot structure and dramatic action which depends on

25

a concept of exposition, rising action, climax, and conclusion—deploying alternative structures that engage recursive nonlinear modes of dramaturgical movement. In short, they ask their audiences to *move* differently. I consider their revision of dramaturgical structures as a mode of rethinking neoliberal subjectivity through exposing injury and, simultaneously, offering a way to the future. This exploration necessitates a brief historical précis of Mexican *indigenismo*, Chicano/a cultural nationalism (including the theater that was a part of those movements), and indigenous activism in the Americas over the last twenty years, the latter of which has engaged decolonial thinking from both inside and outside of indigenous communities.

Indigenismo and Indigenous Activism in the Americas

Twentieth-century Mexican *indigenismo* was a movement that valorized Mexico's Indian past as part of the national postrevolutionary project to create a distinctly Mexican identity that drew on its distinctive mestizo culture composed of indigenous and European roots. In the '30s and '40s cultural producers were inducted by the state to create art with indigenous iconography to foment cultural pride and identity based on the distinctiveness of indigenous roots. These artworks were often created hand in hand with state-sponsored development projects designed to acculturate various indigenous groups by asking them to learn Spanish and participate in various forms of assimilation to mestizo culture at odds with their cultural and spiritual practices. In the 1960s, Mexican citizens launched a fierce critique of this form of valorization of the indigenous (primarily Aztec and Mayan) past because romanticization of indigenous roots and cultural programs had changed nothing economically for living indigenous people. Despite modernization, many indigenous and poor mestizo citizens did not have access to potable water or other fundamental necessities.[2] Concerns about these inequalities also fueled the Zapatista uprising in 1994, whose adherents pointed to these ongoing disparities as part of their critique of NAFTA. The Zapatistas, while largely comprised of indigenous citizens, strategically used some of the very nationalistic discourses their presence brought into question, reformulating the relationship of indigeneity to nationhood. They called the state on its hypocrisy and exposed the bad faith of Mexican nationalism, which undervalued contemporary indigenous cultures and ignored indigenous reality in its quest to make itself "modern."[3]

In the United States, Chicano/a cultural nationalism emerged in the 1960s as a movement against U.S. assimilationist paradigms of belonging that favored integration into U.S. mainstream culture. This assimilation implicitly, if not explicitly, privileged the European aspects of Chicano/a mixed-race identity. In contrast, Chicano/a cultural nationalists embraced the indigenous aspects of Chicano culture and history by framing the U.S. Southwest as Aztlán, the ancestral homeland of Mexicans who later traveled to central Mexico (a history contained in various codices) and by incorporating indigenous iconography within cultural production. This historiographic intervention was liberating for many Chicano/as, who felt oppressed by Euro-American cultural hegemony. Unlike the movement in Mexico, the Chicano nationalist movement was decidedly not a state project; on the contrary, it was arguably antistatist and hostile to the United States as a nation.[4] The 1971 Spiritual Plan de Aztlán, for example, largely written by *movimiento* poet Alurista, called for retaking U.S. land to (re-)create Aztlán in the American Southwest.[5] Unfortunately, despite their desire for liberation, many Chicano/a cultural workers' representational practices reified Mexican nationalist discourses and visual iconography of *indigenismo* and *mestizaje* without being fully aware of their collusion with the Mexican state.[6] Within the theater, Chicano/a proponents of cultural nationalism not only valorized indigenous cultures, but also rejected the individual as the prime mover of social change. Many theater artists used collective creation practices and forms that abjured individual human characters for allegorical protagonists (such as El Teatro Campesino's *actos*) or protagonists played by many actors or actresses (such as many forms of what Yvonne Yarbro-Bejarano calls "*teatropoesía*").[7] The plays militated for collective political action rather than personal change, buttressed by recourse to Chicano/a common ethnic heritage as mixed-race indigenous people whose history could help them to fight oppression and evolve spiritually.

Given the coexistence of Mexican *indigenismo*, this form of cultural production was fraught on both sides of the border. This problem came to a head in 1974 when El Teatro Campesino (ETC) toured the *Baile de los Gigantes* to Mexico, performing at Teotihuacán. While for ETC this performance, based on aspects of the Mayan *Popol Vuh*, was a good faith effort to embrace indigenous heritage and conceptions of identity and belonging based on communitarian principles, its iconography and theatrical tactics replicated the large-scale spectacles at archaeological sites staged by the Mexican government from the 1940s forward.[8] Their presentation of *La Gran Carpa de las Rasquachis* was also poorly received and roundly criticized. Many Latin American groups decried it for having abandoned its program of social change for the mystification of religion.[9] *La Gran Carpa* involves a man who struggles through life as a laborer and, as a result of refusing to join a union, ends up living in poverty. In the version performed at the Mexico City event, the play was preceded by an indigenous dance to the four directions and ended with a spiritual intercession by La Virgen, who convinced the protagonist to join the union. Valdez, in his defense of the work at the forum that followed, argued that *indigenismo* and faith are compatible within narrations of class struggle. Valdez's commitment to nonviolence, in combination with Catholic imagery, was rightfully viewed as naïve by Southern Cone participants suffering under repressive regimes that formed the bedrock of early neoliberal violence.¹⁰ For the other Chicano companies, the problem was that the play tried to reconcile indigenous thought/*indigenismo* with materialist/Marxist-Leninist politics rather than advocating one paradigm or the other.¹¹ These critiques aside, a careful analysis of the method behind these performances, namely, the practice of the Theater of the Sphere, indicates a more complex critique of capitalist practice than the performances did themselves, anticipating Moraga's and others' work.

Broyles-González's careful analysis of the ensemble's development of the Theater of the Sphere argues that the company's commitment to *indigenismo* was an anticapitalist (and anti-imperialist) project for many of the ensemble's members, who used the training to counter the alienation and devaluation of the human being through capitalist society.¹² This method was inspired by a set of teachers from Mexico City, including *conchero* dancer Andrés Segura and Domingo Martinez Paredes, a linguist of Mayan languages.¹³ Both men espoused the idea of a pan-indigenous identity throughout the Americas, using Aztec and Mayan teachings as the base of their cosmologies. Dedicated to collective practice, the modes of performance inspired by these sources rejected individual liberal subjectivity as a basis for social action even as they made creative use of their sources. Because Theater of the Sphere was an embodied everyday practice not aimed at formal theatrical production, there are few archival traces of the work and thus little information about how the practitioners' participation accorded with anticapitalist practice or was articulated as such in everyday discourse. And, to be fair, the artwork can be ambivalent on this point, as its representational practices are not (and never were) dogmatically Marxist. In this sense, Barclay Goldsmith is right in saying that ETC's and other Chicano/a companies' plays shared a "lack of emphasis on economic metaphors."¹⁴ A more generous reading would frame Valdez as a materialist rather than an orthodox Marxist, who got caught in the difficult bind of trying to create hybrid cosmologies within a theatrical rubric with inherent limitations.

I have belabored this historical moment to counter the dismissal of Chicano/a theatrical work invested in *indigenismo* as necessarily antimaterialist or at odds with economic analysis. Unlike their predecessors, today's artists who engage with *indigenismo* are well versed in economic theory, transnational politics, and the conundrums that come with working one's way through the vagaries of U.S. imperialism. In Moraga's case, her thinking is as beholden to hemispheric anticapitalism as it is to Chicano/a engagement of shared cultural heritage as an emancipatory practice, a claim I will detail below.

Thus, I see the development of Moraga's theatrical *indigensimo* as a productive form of "romantic anticapitalism," to use Lukács's term, or and perhaps even "romantic anti-neoliberalism."¹⁵ Theater, as Nicholas Ridout claims, in a different context, can be a detour, allowing us to think of an outside of capitalism, instead of providing an escape from it. This operation is temporal and historiographical because theater enacts the type of "genuinely revolutionary move" indicated by Walter Benjamin in his "Theses on the Concept of History": "an interruption or substitution of the present with something of the past, something consciously and deliberately repeated." For Ridout, this maneuver replaces the time of the present with that embodied by the "time of theatrical 'presence.'"[16] While Ridout's critique comes from within a European tradition of secular Marxist and Judeo-Christian imaginings, my analysis of Moraga's romantic anti-neoliberalism engages Latin American Marxist, millenarian, and indigenous cosmologies, including that of the Zapatistas. The Zapatistas' desire for making utopia now plays havoc with the progressive teleological and revolutionary timelines of Mexican cultural nationalism. If viewed within recent hemispheric history, Moraga's desire to imagine a time before colonialism not only extends El Teatro Campesino's Theater of the Sphere project, as Ricardo Vivancos Pérez suggests, but also engages the Zapatistas' methods.[17] Her conscious return to indigenous identity and practice is, in Ridout's terms, a detour rather than an escape. And it is a maneuver that is as influenced by the transnational present as it is by the cultural nationalist past.

Indigenous anti-neoliberal movements are, of course, not limited to the work of the Zapatistas. The larger set of actions and visions to which Moraga and Garcés owe their thinking is a hemispheric, and often global, reaction to the individualizing pressures of neoliberal governance and its relegation of difference to categorizations created by market economies and capital accumulation. Indigenous justice movements have repeatedly reimagined the relationship between spirituality, land, and subjectivity, as well as interrogating national sovereignty and the very idea of individual rights that accrues to liberalism. In much of the Americas this activism has been fueled by a renewed interest in mobilizing indigenous identity in the service of social change combined with the need to halt the mass destruction of indigenous lands by multinational companies and states that have sold water and land rights to accumulate profit and/or support precarious economies.[18] While a large-scale review of these movements and their history is outside of the scope of this chapter, it is important to note that the very basis for these movements is a radical challenge to both liberal and neoliberal subjectivities.

Within U.S. minoritarian cultural production, this challenge to liberal subjectivity rubs strangely against an ideology that valorizes the creation of relatable, complex individual characters within novels, plays, and films so as to advocate for the worth of said minoritarian subjects outside of representation. This maneuver is a defense against the use of insidious stereotypes that have been present in U.S. American literature from its inception. Nonetheless, within a historical context of neoliberalism, this mode may not be effective. Instead this dependency performs as unabashed support of what Jodi Melamed calls racial liberalism, a mode of postwar liberalism that separated antiracism from a critique of capital, especially within literature, mobilized "as a privileged apparatus for knowing difference."[19] Melamed's reading of U.S. literary production seeks alternatives to this practice from what she calls the "*race-radical* tradition," turning to indigenous literature to imagine resistance to neoliberalism.[20] Melamed, working primarily within a U.S. indigenous context, argues for how indigenous peoples' reimagination of the relationship of land to human life offers a critique of multicultural neoliberalism's desire to sever culture from a relationship to land within both policy and literature in the Americas. Her literary example, Allison Hedge Coke's *Blood Run*, a free verse play, refuses human subjects as characters, giving voice to other living things so as to resist neoliberal individuation and the severance of culture from land. Although neither Moraga nor Garcés use this strategy, both authors work against liberal forms of subjectivity by decentering liberal tragic heroes and avoiding easily individualized subjects by making their characters blurry, multiple, or emblematic.

The larger legacy of decolonial theory throughout the Americas is also important for understanding Moraga's and Garcés's dramaturgical choices. United States–based scholars such as Chela Sandoval, Latin American cultural studies scholars such as Aníbal Quijano and Walter Mignolo, and global indigenous scholars such as Linda Tuhiwai Smith have all asked their readers to undo and unthink the colonial and imperial governmentalities and theoretical paradigms that have created racialized, gendered, and sexed identities that separate peoples—and allow them to be differentially treated—according to Western epistemologies.[21] In particular, Cherríe Moraga uses Tuhiwai Smith's practice of "knowledge sharing," as a mode of knowledge production. The theatrical demonstration of this tactic is imbedded in *New Fire*.

Both authors inhabit a form of transnational thinking. Garcés, through his artistic work in Chiapas, sees migration in a truly transnational lens, as evidenced by his work with Cornerstone Theater Company, including his production of *Los Illegals* and his direction of a number of plays about Special Period Cuba. Moraga also has a transnational lens. As Sonia Saldívar-Hull argues, Moraga and her collaborators on *This Bridge Called My Back* and *Cuentos* began to theorize women of color feminism in relation to the emergent genre of Latin American female-authored *testimonio* from the early 1980s.[22] Moraga's commitment was heightened by her awareness of U.S. intervention in Central American wars and, presciently, the fact that indigenous people were those most gravely affected by this violence. This awareness persists throughout her oeuvre. Moraga's intellectual transnationalism, then, began before her engagement with cultural nationalism and remained after the height of cultural nationalist influence in her work, which peaked in the early 1990s. In terms of her theatrical and autobiographical writing, the mid-1980s was also the time when she decided to seek out Mexico, by moving to California and beginning regular trips to Mexico. The intersection of these two political commitments results in contradictory representations. To understand the full range of Moraga's theatrical thought and the many challenges theatrical production posed to her ideological project, however, we must begin with her trips to Mexico, where she inadvertently exposes the vagaries of neoliberalism for the first time.

Giving Up the Ghost, or a Theatrical Foray into Neoliberalism, *Indigenismo*, and Queer Time

In the 1986 version of her first play, *Giving Up the Ghost*, Cherríe Moraga stages a return to Mexico for Amalia, a Mexican-born bisexual femme feeling ambivalent about her relation with her Chicana butch lover, Marisa. In a long monologue about her reunion with a former (male) lover in Mexico City, Amalia describes a walk through the Zona Rosa, an area of the city with skyscrapers, nightclubs, and high-end shops, which has seen its luxurious heyday pass. She recounts:

> He was my first latino lover and it is true
> this makes a difference . . . older now,
> both of us, gris y maduro
> like this ground that weeps
> beneath these buildings
> campo frágil
> con memoria tan violento que
> podría destruir los edificios.
> U.S. Embassy. Banco Serfín [*sic*]. Cocktail Lounge. Curio Shop.
> "Regresaré." La Tierra nos recuerda.
> "Regresaré." Nos promete.
> When they discovered the El Templo Mayor
> Beneath the walls of the city,
> They had not realized that it was she who discovered them.
> Nothing remains buried forever.
> Not even memory.
> Especially not even memory.[23]

That Amalia walks through the area with a male partner metonymically links an area associated with tourism (curio shops), U.S. presence (U.S. Embassy), and commerce (Banca Serfín) to her nostalgic heterosexual union with Carlos. Amalia's ambivalence toward queerness is tied to her attachment to Mexico, marking one of the key problematics in Moraga's oeuvre: Mexican national culture's deep connection to heterosexuality and childbearing, which comes with the prohibition of lesbian and/or butch identity. This section of *Giving Up the Ghost* also presages one of her later obsessions—the role of indigenous memory in exposing wounds in contemporary Chicano/a culture. At the end of the passage above, she mentions the Templo Mayor, an indigenous worship site in Mexico City's Zócalo, which is partially covered by the National Cathedral, which was built on top of the Templo to discourage indigenous people from worshiping Mexica gods. Because the cathedral is also a National Heritage site, it is impossible to completely excavate El Templo Mayor, leaving it partially covered. The resulting ruin displays the history of violence underneath Mexican *mestizaje*. For Moraga, this unearthing uncovers the memory of trauma. While Moraga does not mention the Spanish conquest openly, she stages the memory of trauma as sutured to indigeneity.

Her mention of the destruction of the "campo frágil" by a "memoria tan violente" [*sic*] is less allegorical than real: it references the 1985 Mexico City earthquake, which hit the older buildings in the Zona Rosa and the nearby Colonia Roma especially hard. In Amalia's monologue, the earthquake as *memoria* threatens buildings on or near the Paseo de la Reforma, which houses the city's major commercial center and exemplifies the centrality of Mexico's transnational commercial and cultural relationships with the United States and Europe. They include Banca Serfín, which began as the Bank of London in 1864 and was Mexico's first bank; the U.S. Embassy, built in the 1960s under President Kennedy; and the Cocktail Lounge—an English language–named bar which probably dates from the same period. An example par excellence of aspirational liberalism, the Paseo was conceived in the late nineteenth century as the main artery of the city, replete with monuments that would narrate the nation's history from beginning to end. Flanked by homes for the rich, the area served the city's elite early in its existence. By the 1960s, however, it had become a commercial district more accessible to middle-class consumerism, if not middle-class ownership; by the 1980s, the area had lost its luster, becoming a more popular site for street vendors and sex commerce, which are, it should be noted, viable commercial pursuits for the city's poor. The land underneath these buildings was unsteady given that Mexico City was built on a lake, making some portions especially vulnerable. The magnitude 8.0 earthquake in 1985 exposed the faulty foundations of this commercial complex, exacerbating the difficulties faced by a national government under austerity measures.[24] I recount this history at length because for many a historian, this watershed moment signaled the beginning of a post-national neoliberal Mexico that incorporated austerity measures while serving the needs of the rich elite, thus echoing the excesses of the Porfiriato rather than the glory of the Revolution. The mention of Banca Serfín is crucial because it gestures to the transnational history of Mexican banking—a keystone in the Mexican financial crisis—which led to nationalization of banks in 1982. (Ironically, President Salinas privatized these banks in 1991 and 1992.) Indigenous presence in the Zona was strategically erased by elite desires to keep poor mestizo and indigenous vendors out of the area. In this sense, the Zona Rosa is the farthest thing from the Mexico Moraga wants to imagine when she becomes invested in Mexican *indigenismo*; yet

Moraga's nearly real-time snapshot of the '80s Mexican crisis is an important inconvenient memory because it reveals the scars of hemispheric neoliberalism and the tension between nationalist and post-nationalist Mexico at an important historical moment.

The productive tension this memory creates disappears in the 1994 version of the play. There, Amalia's lover Carlos, the Zona Rosa, and the 1985 earthquake are gone. In their place is a scene where Amalia, safe in her hotel room, hears "hombres" who "are already at work, tearing up the Mexican earth with their steel claws. (*Indigenous music.*)"[25] This version not only erases Carlos, but also the inauthentic, transnational or European-inspired aspects of Mexico City. The more generic form of mechanical construction/destruction, gendered as male, is staged as violating the earth, gendered female, without historical referent (although it is linked intimately to Corky's rape.) Theatrically, the earth is linked to indigenous culture through "indigenous music," making the violence therein an allegory rather than a historical critique. What is also missing, or at least transformed in the later version, is the material reality of Moraga's first trip to Mexico City. Moraga first came to Mexico City in 1985, shortly before the earthquake. Her poetic essay "The Ecology of Woman" is set in Mexico City in 1985, where her alter ego, Cecilia, details her hotel room in the D.F., and the seeming pity with which she is viewed by a female hotel worker, who feels bad for a "pobrecita niña viajando sola."[26] It is here (Mexico City, 1985) that Moraga's estrangement from and compulsion to belong to Mexico is born. That Cecilia suffers a miscarriage from a heterosexual liaison in this poem is not insignificant, because it co-articulates a critique of nation with a critique of compulsory heterosexuality, which is so important to her later work. Moraga's feminist allegorical re-visioning of Mexican history has been used productively, if sometimes reductively, to counter everyday sexism and homophobia within Chicano/a culture, as has her use of indigenous memory as a decolonial method. Less attention has been paid to how these methods were created out of her experience of transnational travel and thought. Moraga's earliest Mexican travelogues expose her complicated engagement of indigenous histories and cosmologies, which later became crucial to her critique of neoliberalism—both inside and outside of the theater.

As Jorge Huerta and Yvonne Yarbro-Bejarano remind us, Moraga often develops her ideas by moving between genres: plays, scholarly/critical essays, and poems.[27] As a result, Moraga's texts are palimpsestic, richly layered and multiple. They peel away at sedimented, often contradictory narratives, ideologies, and dramaturgies of gender, sexuality, and ethnicity within Chicano/a, Anglo-American, and Mexican imaginaries. Moraga's very public process of revision adds another layer of possibility. Because she often publishes multiple iterations of each of her plays and essays, she implicitly asks readers to consider each text as thought-in-process. This seeming obstacle to definitive analysis is a blessing. It allows critics to detect subtle shifts in Moraga's thinking, including her changing dramaturgical and theatrical conceptions over time.

This chapter largely focuses, then, on revisions of two of these plays, *Giving Up the Ghost* (1986 and 1994) and *The Hungry Woman* (1994–2001; 2005), in relation to Moraga's development of neoliberal critique within her prose works.[28] This is not to say that there is an easy progress narrative—there is not. Moraga's intellectual journey refuses clean teleology. As Sandra K. Soto has so eloquently explained of examining Moraga's work, "one must pause over and learn from the tensions, slippages, and gaps that are quite disruptive to what otherwise may appear as a smooth teleological narrative of homecoming and enactment of racialized sexuality."[29] My critique of Moraga's hemispheric political and economic violence works takes Soto's injunction seriously. I pay close attention to these "tensions, slippages, and gaps" so as to nuance my understanding of her political theater. I argue that many of these tensions are in fact her wrestling with the challenge of the theatrical conundrums representing *indigenismo* poses.

Theatrical thinking in this period inhibited her ability to be transnationally minded in her *indigenismo*. The edits made in the 1994 version of the 1986 text may be as much the result of the early transformation of her theoretical ideas into theatrical representation as her deepening commitment to cultural nationalism, suggesting the importance of theatricality as a mode of transforming her thought. As Moraga herself suggests, the 1986 version of the play was published without extensive stage directions because it had not yet received a production. I offer that the changes added to the 1994 version go beyond adding stage directions. Instead, she restaged, rewrote, and reimagined the play through production.[30] This staging revealed a tension inherent in many of her other plays I consider: that the imagining of indigeniety as a self-reflexive act of undoing self, time, and the other was often stymied by the desire to make indigenous Mexican culture legible in the theater.[31]

On stage, *Giving Up the Ghost*'s representation of indigeneity must rest on aural, visual, and sartorial cues. Indigenous music is often heard at moments of transformation. The wearing of a rebozo signals a choice to become Indian, and the "suggestion of a Mexican desert landscape is illuminated upstage during scenes evoking indigenous Mexico."[32] For those familiar with Guillermo Bonfil Batalla's *Mexico Profundo*, the idea of "evoking indigenous Mexico" rather than recognizing its present presence denies not only the contemporary existence of indigenous Mexicans throughout Mexico but also their contemporary coexistence with nonindigenous people in urban and rural spaces. Aurally, the world of Moraga's play mixes indigenous *flauta y tambor* music with a Chicana urban soundtrack in the play's present. Visually, however, the indigenous Mexican scenes use desert images on scrims that contrast with the "simple suggestion of an urban setting" in the present, suggesting two separate worlds that do not exist together in the same way that her music does. Despite her prescription for the mix of music in the stage directions that open the play, the choice to use only *tambor y flauta* music to evoke indigenous Mexico in the very love scene Yarbro-Bejerano critiques in an earlier version of the play underscores the point that indigeneity is eroticized as other, and theatrically so. By 1994, Corky, Marisa's younger self, enters with an Indian *bruja* mask when Amalia voices her ex-lover's accusations against her as a "bruja, puta." By concretizing these epithets, Moraga literalizes Mexican woman as indigenous, underscoring these essentializing associations even as she tries to critique the misogyny that created them within a self-consciously performative gesture.[33]

The changes Moraga made in a crucial dream sequence also speak to this problem. In the 1986 version of *Giving Up the Ghost*, Amalia begins her description of a dream with: "I had a dream once. You and I, Chata, were indias, baking something, maybe bread, maybe clay pots, on a wide expanse of beach. We were very happy."[34] In this version, she is clearly imbuing indigenous subjectivity with an almost prelapsarian joy that is taken away once the taboo—lesbianism—is exposed. While Moraga's hailing of Mexican Indianness here and elsewhere certainly functions as what Yarbro-Bejarano calls an "affective category, rather than as a historically, materially situated social location," the incongruity of baking bread or pottery on a beach jumbles many of the signifiers of Mexicanness and domesticity, creating a productive cleavage between the affective nostalgic resonance of the scene and its impossibility.[35] Making "sense" of the scene has its consequences. In the 1994 version, the narration of the dream is separated from the theatrical staging of the dream. At the beginning of the scene, stage directions describe Amalia, Marisa, and Corky sitting together making tortillas instead, in concert with the indigenous *tambores*. This clichéd mise-en-scène, often used to signify women's work and solidarity within Chicano/a theater, is staged here as an indigenous Mexico whose gendered solidarity is broken by an admission of lesbianism.[36] That the narration of the dream, which explains the relationship of the dream to the present, happens later in the scene in the 1994 version of the play suggests an inability to hold the representation of indigenous Mexico and the present together, placing indigeneity in the lost past rather than in the fractured present in a disjunctive mise-en-scène, as it was in the 1986 version of the play. The 1994 version of the play, however, glosses over the productive tensions between affective *indigenismo* and its representation on stage. These tensions will reappear in her revision of *The Hungry Woman*.

The temporal disjuncture in the 1986 version of the play, later erased, also bears note because it may be the seed of Elizabeth Freeman's theorization of queer temporality writ large. In an evocative, but enigmatic moment in the preface to *Time Binds*, Elizabeth Freeman suggests that *Giving Up the Ghost* confronts "on an affective register irreducible to traditional historical inquiry what has been forgotten, abandoned, discredited or otherwise effaced."[37] She claims that in the play "time and history appear as borders, too, alongside the borders between Anglo and Chicana, Spanish and English, the United

States and Mexico, all of which the play complicates and violates."[38] Freeman never returns to the play or explains what she means—although I assume she is talking about Corky/Marisa's playing out of butch identity qua *cholo* aesthetics/Chicano nationalist masculinity.

A careful analysis will bear out Freeman's claim and aspects of this relationship that exceed her analysis. *Ghost*'s temporal disjuncture is both embedded in Amalia and Marisa's cross-generational relationship and embodied by Marisa's split subjecthood as Corky (her younger self) and Marisa (her present self). As in many Latinx plays, in *Giving Up the Ghost*, queer intergenerational relationships are a mode of negotiating with the past. In the 1986 version, the play is set in 1980; Marisa's younger self, Corky, dresses "in the *cholo* style of her period (the '60s)."[39] The dialectical relationship within Marisa's own consciousness is between the 1960s Chicana/o movement of Corky's childhood and her present position "at sea" in the 1980s, where she is trying to sculpt a Chicana butch identity in the age of the Hispanic. Moraga does not register the emergence of a post-nationalism in Mexico or the mainstreaming of Latinx identity in the United States as forces in the play. Nonetheless, part of Marisa's pain comes from her estrangement from the nationalisms in which Moraga invests. Marisa's identity is unhinged both from the Chicana/o *cholo* period of the 1960s and from the Mexican identity of her lover, whose childhood would have come at the height of Mexican socialist nationalism. The disappearances of both of these seeming utopias (which were nonetheless often oppressive to Chicana-Indigena women in particular) are the result of hemispheric neoliberalism. In the United States, the disembowelment of radical identity came with the emergence of a supposedly diverse multicultural subject of capitalism; in Mexico, the 1982 peso crash necessitated the undoing of the rhetoric and practice of the golden age of Mexican cultural nationalism which abjured U.S. culture and capitalism as forms of imperialism. This nationalism's iconicity is replicated in Amalia's costume, which replicates Mexican *traje tipico* (rebozo, long skirt, hair tied back) as much as it marks her as an older femme. By the time Moraga wrote *Giving Up the Ghost*, however, she and her characters were clearly post-Revolutionary, suggesting that both characters perform a form of temporal drag, the productive form of embodying a past iteration in the present that carries the past as a possibility into the now.[40] Thus, Marisa's stone butch *chola* (mestiza) is a disruptive image, in a Benjaminian sense, which points out the paucity of the now without imposing rigid teleology.[41] Although *Giving Up the Ghost* is framed by Marisa's experience and suggests that Amalia is the one who is unable to commit to the relationship, the play argues for the productivity of the search for identity through the vagaries of Mexican and Chicano/a history, whatever the outcome of the particular relationship.

Although Amalia and Marisa's generational gap is maintained in the 1994 revision of *Giving Up the Ghost*, Moraga does not mark the time period of the play or clearly root the characters' sartorial choices in their temporal specificity in this version. The theatrical presence of past ideals as an intervention into the characters' present—a temporal drag—is blunted, undoing the distance between the play's characters and their ideals. The result is a less critical and nuanced engagement with the recent Chicano/a and Mexican past than in the earlier play. This decision may have been one of theatrical exigency, a making accessible and making concrete of abstract or culturally specific concepts from the 1986 version of the text. Nonetheless, the contrast between the 1986 and 1994 versions inadvertently points to the temporal disjuncture at the center of many of Moraga's plays, a form of engaging the past that can serve as a model of romantic anti-neoliberalism and a tool for today's readers against what Sara Warner calls homoliberalism, the mainstreaming of LBGQT identity under neoliberal rule that abandons commitment to radical politics, revolutionary action, and liberation as its center.[42] My exploration of *Giving Up the Ghost* points to how the tensions in Moraga's work are instructive as theatrical and dramaturgical strategies. These tensions become more apparent in her development of *The Hungry Woman*.

The Hungry Woman, or Running on Apocalyptic Time

The Hungry Woman, written between the 1990s and 2005, arguably restages Marisa and Amalia's relationship in a different time and place, with more open engagement with the idea of revolution and neoliberalism.[43] And, I would argue, with the very idea of time itself. Coming a few years and a few plays after *Giving Up the Ghost*, *The Hungry Woman* works through Moraga's ideas in *The Last Generation*, an anthology of essays and poems that represent her foray into revisionary cultural nationalism while gesturing at something left uncontained by that label: the articulation of indigenous eschatology and postrevolutionary discourse in relation to contemporary capitalism. An examination of the essays, which were written later than the poems, is crucial to understanding *The Hungry Woman*.

"The last generation" refers to Moraga's moniker for a dying breed of Chicano/as who are being deracinated through intermarriage and depoliticized through mainstreaming. A literal—and very U.S.-centric—reading of Moraga's title has overly determined interpretation of the collection, largely limiting commentary on the work to dissection of and/or celebration of her desire to go brown, thus disavowing her biracial identity to counter white dominance in U.S. culture.[44] The inspiration for the book, however, comes as much from "a Mexican moment in an indifferent literary world history" as her racialized U.S. reality.[45] In this sense, the last generation gestures to the last generation of secular revolutionaries. Her invocation of the book as prayer and prophecy underscores its spiritual tone. It could also be said that the last generation is the last generation of believers in history as teleology, as progress—a key term Moraga notably puts in scare quotes in the introduction to the volume. As Moraga tells us early in the collection, the end of the Nicaraguan Revolution in 1990 and the five-hundred-year anniversary of Columbus's discovery of the Americas in 1992 temporally bracket the essays.[46] This period also spawned the development of NAFTA, which solidified free-trade capitalism as a primary mode of governmentality in North America. Her essay "Art in América Con Acento" begins soon after the defeat of the leftist Sandinista government. Moraga writes from the rage and sadness inspired by seeing U.S. Latinx persons celebrating this defeat. It is here that she first realizes the conditions that we will soon understand as neoliberal: the mass migration caused by U.S. interventions throughout the Americas. She writes: "When U.S. capital invades a country, its military machinery is quick to follow to protect its interests. This in Panamá, Puerto Rico, Grenada, Guatamala . . . Ironically, the United States' gradual consumption of Latin America and the Caribbean is bringing the people of the Americas together."[47] She goes on to chronicle the huge shifts in migration from many of the countries in the America as well as Southeast Asia. She also uses the term *economic refugees* to describe immigration not directly linked to political persecution, revolution and the loss of wealth, and war, anticipating many of the crises of citizenship categories I explore in subsequent chapters on the Balseros Crisis and passage of free-trade agreements.[48] These conditions inspire her to ask Chicano/a artists to turn their writer souls away from Washington, the U.S. capital, and toward "México Antiguo."[49] As she claims, "that is not to say that contemporary Chicano literature does not wrestle with current concerns, but without the memory of our once-freedom, how do we imagine a future?" Later in the essay she claims she holds a vision of a "radical transformation of consciousness" that will allow people of color to "redefine what 'American' is."[50]

This once freedom in Moraga's work often imagines itself as the time before the conquest, or before the rise of the major civilizations, or at times before the domination of the female by the male in Aztec cosmology. While her imaginings of indigenous cultures can and should be interrogated for their generalizations, her desire clearly links the idea of a preimperialistic time to liberation from the economic conditions of the present. I register this as a form of romantic anti-neoliberalism rather than naïveté. The past that she imagines is not a prelapsarian ideal, but a thought experiment that offers an alternative to the now. Her vision of the Americas is historically specific. The future solidarity of "la raza" she describes no longer accords with José Martí's nineteenth-century idea of America as a united continent unleashed from U.S. imperial domination so important to thinkers in the 1960s and '70s. For Moraga, the events of 1990 destroy this possibility because of the emergence of "a fractured and disintegrating America, where the Northern half functions as the absentee landlord of the Southern half and the economic disparity between the first and third world drives a wedge between people."[51] That she sees this relationship as economic rather than merely imperial marks her difference from many of her peers, gesturing to her future conceptions of the neoliberal.

Moraga's commitment to indigenous thought, history, and cosmology (México Antiguo) is as sutured to neoliberal *economic* conditions as it is to "the breakdown" of her "bicultural mind."[52] If *The Last Generation* stands as her decision to recommit to Aztlán, it also stands as a commitment to social change based neither on the promise of Latin American socialist governments nor a strictly secular idea of revolution; both of these, of course, were hampered by U.S. military interventions and Latin American elites during the late '80s and early '90s. Moraga uses her "Queer Aztlán" essay to conceptualize revolution and nation under these conditions. The essay does begin with Moraga's critique of the largely white radical queer communities on the East Coast and the homophobia and misogyny of the Chicano movement, but it spends nearly as much time laying out her commitment to Ward Churchill's conception of *indigenismo*, which he defines as the concern with the fate of indigenous people being the most urgent political action there is.[53]

Moraga, while sometimes utilizing Mexican statist iconography, is politically astute about indigenous movements in her present. In a telling section of the essay, where she finds herself eating sushi in Vancouver, she links the oppression of the Inuit in Quebec to the impoverishment of Chicano/as in the United States to deforestation and poverty in Brazil. Yet, while she stands on the edge of her balcony contemplating a protest jump at the beginning of this section of the essay, by its end, inspired by the Earth Summit in Rio De Janeiro in June 1992, where indigenous people came together to ask for economic conditions necessary to create ecologically sound communities, she is advocating for a transnational solidarity of indigenous people/people of color to band together against this destruction.[54] She calls on Chicano/as to experience this urgency for change *as indigenous people*. To be sure, there is slippage between Moraga's critique of Chicano/a imaginings of the Indian as "past"—which she places in quotation marks—and her own suggestion that the "road to the future is through the past," meaning the traditional practices of our ancestors. Unlike many other *indigenismo* advocates, however, she is well aware of present day indigenous movements and scholarship by Native academics. The movements she talks about in 1992 were not obscure but were less known by U.S. Americans than they would be after the passage of NAFTA and the 1994 Zapatista uprising. She is also clearly making an anticapitalist statement. As she explains in "Queer Aztlán," "here the Marxist meets the ecologist. We need look no further than The North American Free Trade Agreement (NAFTA) to understand the connection between global ecological devastation and the United States' relentless drive to expand its markets."[55] For her, the revolution she calls for is the end of the United States. It is a revolution based in retaking land: a revision of Alurista's famous Spiritual Plan de Aztlán in the face of neoliberal encroachment. In her newer version, Moraga refuses to dispense with forms of conservation and sustainability that predate modernism, marking an environmentalist bent absent in the original drafts of Alurista's plan.[56]

It is worth noting that Moraga's double legacy of Chicano/a nationalism and transnational indigenous movements permeate many of her plays, articulating her political position. The earliest full length published version of *The Hungry Woman* is bound together with *Heart of the Earth: A Popul Vuh Story*, a play that restages a source text key to Chicano nationalism and to Luis Valdez and ETC. At first glance, *Heart of the Earth* appears to reproduce a certain enchantment with past Mayan culture at the expense of the present. A close reading of the production process and the play, however, belies this simplicity. While the script is single-authored, the production, produced by INTAR, was a collaborative project with Anglo director and puppeteer Ralph Lee. Lee, although not Latino, has a strong connection to Mayan Mexico: he travels to and collaborates with the Mayan theater company Sna Jzt'ibajom regularly. This production was imagined within a transnational frame from the start. As a grant proposal to fund the play claims:

> The Popol Vuh Project will bring to light the rich indigenous history and culture of the Americas, reflecting a new view of the Americas, where North and South are joined by common desire for peace and cultural integrity. Woven throughout The Popol Vuh Project (the early title of the play) are the Mayans' reverence for nature, their comprehensive understanding of the integrated relationship between life and death, and other fundamental spiritually-oriented perspectives that we believe can resonate for both the Latinos that share the same land as the Mayan [sic], as well as for North Americans who may come to know about the Mayan [sic] and Popol Vuh through reading or travel."[57]

The project was imagined in conversations with scholars of Latin America and a diverse range of artists; at one point it even included the possibility of publishing supplemental materials for the play in Spanish, English, and Quiché Maya. Awareness that many Mexicans and Central Americans in New York City are indigenous was clear in promotional materials. The link between peoples in the Americas is theorized not in racial or ethnic terms but as a commitment to peace and cultural integrity. The language in the proposal is striking in that it introduced new modes of solidarity before the Chiapas uprising; given that one of the collaborators regularly visited Chiapas, however, I see the emphasis on nonexclusivity as evidence of knowledge of how the Mayan movement in Mexico and Central America had begun to articulate a transnational vision before the uprising. Moraga, through this collaboration, incorporated this thinking into her theater work.

A more sustained engagement with conceptions of revolution and nationhood, in relation to neoliberalism, gets worked out and over in the course of writing (and rewriting) *The Hungry Woman*. Her dramatic version of the revolution in *The Hungry Woman* is dystopic rather than utopic. Based loosely on Euripides's *Medea*, Cherríe Moraga's tragic protagonist is a queer mestiza who helped lead a revolution in which various groups of people of color founded "independent nations" that "seceded from the U.S. in order to put a halt to its relentless political and economic expansion, as well as its Euro-American cultural domination in all societal matters including language, religion, family and tribal structures, art-making and more."[58] Ultimately, despite the fact that the revolution was dedicated to a fairly expansive goal of "defending aboriginal rights around the globe," and its members' willingness to ally themselves with "any man or woman of any race or sexuality that would lift arms in their defense," the revolution ends with a reactionary swell where hierarchies of gender are (re-) inscribed and queers are exiled.[59] Medea's exile is in Tamoachan, another name for Phoenix, Arizona, where Medea, her lover Luna, her son Chac Mool, and a larger set of family and friends reside.

Moraga's fictional revolution imagines a "future based on a history at the turn of the century that never happened."[60] Set in the "second decade of the early part of the twenty-first century," the play chronicles the failure of her dream in *The Last Generation*. The events that inspired the revolution are political and economic. On one hand, her characters are alternately disenchanted and heartened by events from the '80s and '90s, beginning with the demise of Central American communist and socialist governments and the rise of the Zapatistas. On the other hand, they were clearly reacting to the misery brought on by neoliberal economic conditions. In a line that appears in the 2001 version of *The Hungry Woman* in a slightly different form from her 2002 essay, "From Inside the First World: On 9/11 and Woman of Color Feminism," Mama Sal, the matriarch of Medea's family refers to "[los] transnational corporate patrones" who "had turned the whole global economy" into "a poisoned alphabet soup."[61] Savannah, an African American neighbor, follows by naming "NAFTA, the WTO, GATT, and the FTAA."[62] Although GATT dates to 1947, the other organizations, which gained prominence during the 1990s, the middle period of hemispheric neoliberalism (the WTO is the newer incarnation of GATT), are a crucial part of Moraga's historical narration. Sweeping in scope, her history of the immediate pre-revolutionary period includes the fall of unionized jobs and environmental protection, the militarization of the border, the widespread use of pesticides, the rise of the maquiladora, and, in the 2005 version, the Juárez femicides and the fall of the Twin Towers. They are marked as racialized, gendered, and neocolonial forms of damage done by transnational capital (and imperialism).

Comparing the 2001 and 2005 versions of *The Hungry Woman* elucidates how Moraga formulates a transnational indigenous response to neoliberalism as she exorcises some of her dependence on representational *indigenismo*.

In the introduction to the 2001 version of the play (first written in 1994, revised throughout 2000, and published in 2001) Moraga argues for her link to indigenous history through her experience of monumental archaeological ruins, namely, the experience of "the Templos de México: Monte Albán, Palenque, Tulum and Teotihuacán."[63] Her concentration on central and southern Mexican monumental architecture is at odds with her biographical exploration of her northern indigenous roots in the same essay, a lineage she can't trace with specificity due to this history's erasure in her own family history. In the 2005 version of the play, Moraga more forcefully addresses the cultural specificity of her characters. Its stage directions describe a set with resonances of a kiva located in the northern state of Chihuahua.[64]

More broadly, however, Moraga shifts from representing indigeneity on stage to seeing through the lens of indigeniety onstage—moving from symbolism to cosmology. As she claims in the beginning of the 2005 version: "The world of the play takes place within the indigenous American imagination. That is to say, that a Pre-Columbian and Southwest/Northern Mexico indigeneity is the vantage point through which all action, past present and ancient occurs."[65] This is not to suggest that we move to a form of time that does not recognize temporal distinctions or historical specificity. The addition of a historical prologue that preempts Cihuatateo East's lines—"this is how all stories begin and end"—which opened the 2001 version of the play, suggests she has moved to a more clearly historicized position in relation to indigenous practice.

Moraga's revision of revolutionary temporality and reproductive futurism also shifts between 2000 and 2005. In the 2005 version of the play, Moraga adds a prologue that historically positions Medea in relation to the fall of socialism. She states:

> It was when the Soviet Union collapsed. 1989. I didn't applaud it, for fear of a rampant free market enslaving the globe. But it made revolution . . . possible. If the Union of Soviet Socialist Republics could go, why not the United States of America. Why not? I had been a student of Marx, Engels, Malcolm X, Geronimo, Che and Fidel. A daughter of El Movimiento, the first one and the last.[66]

The prologue concludes, "I had seen it, the revolution I feared and also hungered for, in my lifetime. I could never have imagined I would also witness its demise." Her lines about the fall of the U.S.S.R. are pulled from her "Queer Aztlán" essay, where this fall is linked to being able to think about how a set of sovereign nations could "leave" a nation and recover the land. Simply put, the fall of the U.S.S.R. lets her imagine the end of the United States as nation. By 2002, in "From Inside the First World: On 9/11 and Woman of Color Feminism," Moraga imagines revolution because of the fall of the Twin Towers. She claims:

> For the first time, it occurs to me that as residents of the United States we are finally subject to the global violence we have perpetuated against the non-Western world. What has also shifted is my sense of time. Maybe the revolution I hoped for and feared for *will* be realized in my lifetime. Or maybe I will live only long enough to witness the dreaded violence that anticipates revolution and the erosion of the real quality of our lives.[67]

In the 2005 version of *The Hungry Woman*, she conflates these "negative" imaginings to imagine a time after the revolution, not before it. In the essay, the revolution has not happened yet. Over the course of these years, Moraga goes back and forth on where we are in relation to the revolution, ultimately moving away from secular revolution entirely. This is why I read her comment, "What has also shifted is my sense of time," against the grain. Read straightforwardly, it simply means that the coming of violence against the United States as an imperial state will arrive sooner than she thinks. In a different light, however, Moraga's admission reveals that she is struggling with the problem of secular teleology itself. Thus, her imagination of Aztlán in the negative is not simply a reminder of the persistence of homophobia in communities of people of color, but an admission that the coming of a secular utopia is no longer thinkable within neoliberal conditions. And with that confession, Moraga has to give up the power of the Mexican Revolution and all other cultural nationalist modes of teleology as a dead end.

This dead end includes the Chicano and Mexican nationalist dependency on reproductive futurism. In Mexican nationalist symbolism, the mestizo child (usually a boy), born of one indigenous and one Spanish parent, represented the future of the nation as a culturally cohesive unity. These representations were especially popular in the late '30s and '40s when cultural workers attempted to smooth over the tumult of the Mexican Revolution (1910–20), wherein the revolutionaries attempted to overthrow Porfirio Díaz to create a more equitable society by giving land back to the people who worked it, rather than letting it stay in the hands of landowners. Reacting to the new state's secularity, this vision depended on a Marxian-inspired teleological nature of progress after the revolution, which provided the radical break. The solution was a weakly spiritual but not quite secular inflected discourse centered on the creation of, care for, and forward motion of the mestizo child, who sutured the wounds of the revolution. Fast-forward thirty years across the border to Chicano/a culture and one finds the valorization of female contributions to the movement relegated to the raising of Chicano/a children and sustenance of the nuclear family. Reproduction was, in all regards, a virile metaphor and a powerful one, even for queer Xicana activists. Moraga herself attempts to contribute by having a brown son so as to repopulate the world with indigenous children.[68] Yet in her dramatic fiction, she kills her own son to avoid his oppression and her own.

In struggling with these contradictory discourses, Moraga moves to a different form of thinking about societal transformation first broached in final essays of *The Last Generation*. In that collection, she shifts subtly from a reimagination of a land-based revolution to a millenarian view of the world. Framing the Los Angeles revolts as the end of the Quinto Sol (the fifth sun), "Codex Xerí" suggests the awakening of a new consciousness, a form of thinking she explores more fully in her subsequent essay collection—*A Xicana Codex of Changing Consciousness*. In Aztec cosmology, the fifth sun represents the stage of creation that we are living in now, which began with the rise of the Aztecs. This form of creation is prophesied to end under a giant earthquake. Until then, the sun needs to be nourished by offerings every fifty-two years, after which the sun could decide to rise again or not. In Moraga's conception, the end of the fifth sun is not an ending but a beginning that will involve violence. This beginning asks for a "new breed of revolucionario," who will "burn down the Alamo, Macy's San Francisco, the savings and loan, and every liquor store in South Central Los Angeles!"[69] Although steeped in indigenist symbolism, the call is for the destruction of predatory capitalism. The fact that she believes that this something else will come is revealed in two places. One is at the end of this essay where she claims that "*our Olmeca third eye/ begins to glisten/ in the slowly/ rising/ light.*"[70] The other is at the end of the "Queer Aztlán" essay where she writes:

> As these 500 years come to a close, I look forward to a new América, where the only "discovery" to be made is the rediscovery of ourselves as members of a global community. Nature will be our teacher, for she alone knows no prejudice. Possibly as we ask men to give up being "men" we must ask humans to give up being "human," or at least give up the human capacity for greed.[71]

Her language betrays an eschatological form of thinking and temporality. In "Codex Xeri" she suggests, that "[a]fter these Roman hieroglyphs have been pressed into the printed page, history will have advanced well beyond the time of this writing, but as the Maya understood, a date is not the beginning, but the culmination of history in its totality. What we are witnessing took 500 years of conquest to create."[72] She cites Mayan prophecy, but her description accords with Christian conceptions of eschatology in which all that has happened coexists on the same plane and our individuated selves dissolve. This is, it should be said, a potentially queer move as progressive theologians have suggested.[73] In Mayan, Aztec, and Christian sources, this transformation is preceded by a culminating violence, which for Moraga, like for Victor Cazares, takes place in the neoliberal period. The "end" as she sees it, is happening now.

Moraga's employment of eschatological symbolism from Aztec and Mayan empires harbors Mexican millenarian thinking coincident with the end of the twentieth century and the rise of neoliberal dominance. This belief system parallels the beliefs of contemporary indigenous activists such as the Zapatistas, who, as Paul Vanderwood suggests, "want their utopia right now."[74] Thus, it is through theoretical writings by the Zapatistas and about them, rather than through a purely Chicana/o studies paradigm, that Moraga's later work is best understood. This type of exploration lets us think of the Zapatistas' understanding of their role in history as José Rabasa describes it: as both "eschatological" and "tragic" without being "teleological."[75] Meaning, as Rabasa suggests, that the Zapatistas' role in history is tragic, not because they mark the end of history in an ironic nod to Francis Fukuyama, but because "they mark a continuation in struggle."[76] For Rabasa, the Zapatistas confront "mythical violence" in a mode consonant with Benjamin's understanding of history—which abandons progressive teleology for messianic time.[77] (This, of course, echoes Ridout's own reading of Benjamin in his formulation of romantic anticapitalism.) For Moraga, as for the Zapatistas, this operation breaks down the idea of the "I" without romancing the idea of a fragmented self in a way consonant with orthodox post-structuralism. It also allows her to imagine a mode of nonsocialist and nonnationalist solidarity (linking her to multiple indigenous insurgencies and temporalities that don't respect orthodox timelines). Moraga's move parallels the scholarly turn to historical explanations informed by the Latin American subaltern studies group that emerged from under the ashes of the Sandinista Revolution. Like those scholars, she moves away from a strictly Marxian historical narrative for liberation without abandoning a radical framework for social change or romancing the failure of Marxism.

The Zapatistas' paradigm in particular lets us consider millenarianism as a reasonable, rather than reactionary, strategy for indigenous people in the Americas who suffer the brunt of neoliberal economics. As Carlos Monsiváis suggests, the Zapatistas' discourse acknowledges that their self-conception was as influenced by the Bible, the Popol Vuh, and the Chilam Balam as it was socialist rhetoric. In his eyes, their engagement turned the label millenarian from an "accusation" to "description."[78] The actions of the Zapatista National Liberation Army (EZLN), namely, the demand for the "resignation of the President of the Republic and overthrow of the political system" became in a way to "be realistic" by "demand[ing] the impossible."[79] In the twenty years that have followed the 1994 Chiapas uprising, the Zapatistas have moved from this revolutionary mode to a new form of democracy with a global purview. In this sense, "todos somos indios" becomes a form of governance predicted on strategic allegiance. Moraga, I argue, works toward this type of solidarity, which is not the same as '60s and '70s forms of solidarity that aim for secular revolution, in her theatrical representations. She is, like the Zapatistas, chasing the impossible in real time.

Moraga first refers to the Zapatistas in *The Hungry Woman*, where Mayas are the leaders of the revolution Medea joins. Her statement that the revolution was already spearheaded by the Zapatistas suggests to me both that a) the example of the Zapatistas allowed Medea (and Moraga) to conceive of a revolution wherein the undoing of gender hierarchies within indigenous communities was a touchstone, and b) the Zapatistas exist for her "already" in the eschatological sense, meaning that they, the Zapatistas, were in some sense foretold by the larger history of indigenous insurrection and communitarian practice.[80] The history of the Zapatistas bears this out. Although they failed at getting their demands met by the Mexican state, they succeeded in changing the possibilities of governance. A large part of their program has been to undo the gendered prejudice in Mayan communities and the world; and they existed long before the world became aware of them. Also, more plainly, indigenous women ran huge portions of the EZLN, a fact that is often lost in commentaries of the movement that concentrate on Marcos. It is for this reason that they play such a crucial role in Moraga's thinking. She comes to reconsider the Zapatistas' relevance differently as she moves on in her career.

After *The Hungry Woman*, Moraga stages the Zapatistas not as agents of a particular revolution against the Mexican state that failed in secular time, but instead as an embodied attitude toward imperialism and oppression which asks us to conduct ourselves differently under contemporary neoliberalism. To this end, she includes Zapatistas as characters in a children's play that she mounts at her son's school in order to tell the history of "the people of the corn." This play created a dyadic struggle between greed and the people of the corn's (i.e., Americans') livelihood. Here, the Zapatistas—who are gendered as female and played by girls—bring down greed, "who is forced to succumb to the righteous power of revolutionary resistance."[81] In true teatro style, they replace Greed's placard with one saying "Compartir" (share).[82] Their injunction to share, though simple, effectively gestures to different modes of thinking about land, earth, and resources compatible with transnational indigenous movements, including the Zapatistas own injunctions to the Mexican government asking for rights to collective land use rather than right to property. This mode of thinking is the basis for a critique of Mexico's and many other nations' neoliberal drive to extract land from indigenous collectivities and convert them into property or to extract resources from them to (literally) fuel multinational capital.

While the Zapatistas come at the end of her history, they bring not only revolutionary resistance but a "righteous" power: an attitude designed to continue, fully embodying its moral and religious overtones. Ultimately, then, Moraga's end goal is asking us "to remember" that "second class status in the United States is not a natural born fact."[83] That she imparts this lesson through performing Zapatismo makes the revolt present as a *moda de ser* in the neoliberal age. One might compare this staging to that of *La Gran Carpa de las Rasquachis* to see the subtle differences in their creators' mixture of cosmology and materialist critique. Moraga makes indigenous insurgency the very present instead of a mythic past.

Her 2011 collection *A Xicana Codex of Changing Consciousness* further clarifies her eschatological vision. Critiquing the commercialized version of apocalypse imagined through the perversion of Mayan cosmology, she claims that "Mesoamerican calenderic predictions are being realized daily in the ongoing violence resultant of more than five hundred years of continued colonization and its legacy of slavery, misogyny, and environmental indifference," and that "the apocalypse has already occurred for those of us standing in the line of cruelty's fire."[84] Her resistance to seeing the end as a singular event is also important. This antiteleological stance is underscored in her claims that "life is not a progressive plot line," referencing with the term *plot line* both the norms of dramatic structure and the practices of imaging quantitative data.[85] Given the emphasis on quantitative analysis of experience within the contemporary moment, Moraga's wry commentary has a barbed edge.

It should be noted that it is in *A Xicana Codex* that Moraga first names neoliberalism, mobilizing her critique of both Latin American *mestizaje* projects and U.S. governmentality. It is also there that she most openly frames her political project as being in opposition to liberal multiculturalism. This framing makes Moraga's move to indigenous identified modes of being a conscious rejection of liberal subjecthood and liberal political ideology. In the companion play, *New Fire*, Moraga decolonizes her own dramaturgy to this end. She nonetheless retains an allegiance to theatricality, thus creating a work that defies easy categorization.

New Fire: To Put Things Right Again

New Fire: To Put Things Right Again, while sharing many formal qualities with *The Hungry Woman*, is less a play than a staged ritual of renewal that abandons liberal dramaturgy. The "plot" follows a fifty-two-year-old Chicana named Vero who is trying to heal herself from a childhood rape and a life of internalized homophobia. She does this by going through a series of purifying exercises, including the lighting of a fire that is needed to put things right again. Vero's life cycle parallels the fifty-two-year cycle of the new sun, and the lighting of the fire parallels the period in which one gives offerings so as to forestall the end of the world. While the story follows the history of a single protagonist, *New Fire* works as a rite to remember indigenous people in the present. The substitution of *rite* for *right* not only gestures to the play's ritualistic aspects but to the displacement of a liberal human rights paradigm with performative practice in the face of capital. Vero's name, it should be noted, is a variation of the Spanish (and Latin) word for truth, gesturing to the fact that her journey to self is also a journey toward a larger truth.

Ensemble for *The Hungry Woman*. Codirected by Cherríe Moraga and Adelina Anthony. Set by Celia Herrera. Stanford University. Photo courtesy of Stanford University.

New Fire's set echoes *The Hungry Woman*'s, which was also designed by her collaborator and life partner, Celia Herrera Rodríguez. Images of the codex bleed through a light floor, just as they did in the Stanford production of *The Hungry Woman*.[86] Yet unlike the earlier set, there are more clearly marked areas of the stage for indigenous ritual practice. There is an area of the stage where Celia, as the fire keeper, sits and where tobacco is passed. As she does in *The Hungry Woman*, Moraga attempts to include women of color from many ethnic backgrounds in supporting roles, although the non-Latino characters are perhaps less crucial to the plot than their corollaries in *The Hungry Woman*. These women, who remain on stage throughout, move between the play's parallel worlds—which she calls the "mundane" and the "mythic."[87] The mythic world is comprised of *tzitzimime*—star women who were active during the solar eclipse, which often symbolized a moment of instability in the cosmos.[88] These figures function much like the Cihuatateo did in *The Hungry Woman*. Yet, unlike that play, which used an orthodox tragic form, *New Fire* is structured as a ceremony distilled from research conducted through participation in nontheatrical ceremonies. Over the course of *New Fire*, significant portions of these "real" gatherings, which Moraga and Herrera Rodríguez attended, are projected onto a screen behind them. The

New Fire. Directed by Cherríe Moraga. Set by Celia Herrera. Dena Martinez as Vero with Itzpapalotl (Alleluia Panis). Photo Gregory Villyard.

groups that they sat with include the South Central Farmers of Buttonwillow, Calif.; women of the White Mountain Apache Reservation; Kularts, a Bay Area Pilipino arts organization; the Mexicano/a Danzante community, who served as support for Flor Crisostomo of Humboldt Park, Chicago; and the *familia* of Albertina Vallejo (Purépecha). These sittings were to be exchanges of technology and knowledge among different tribes. The use of the word *tribe* here designates not governmentally recognized groups, but groups allied in a project of community building, allied with her reimagining of the word from *The Last Generation*.[89]

Moraga's idea of knowledge sharing engages that of Maori scholar Linda Tuhiwai Smith, who writes: "Sharing contains views about knowledge being a collective benefit and knowledge being a form of resistance. Like networking, sharing is a process which is responsive to the marginalized contexts in which indigenous communities exist."[90] The incorporation of the video footage of these acts of knowledge sharing creates the co-presence of indigenous identified people in the contemporary United States with the actors on the stage, while also dislodging an exclusive focus on the play's main characters. The oppressions that make indigenous people marginal are revealed but indigenous people are not doubly marginalized through the play's dramaturgy. As Moraga claims,

> *New Fire* was not to be a docudrama, we knew; but, instead we hoped to find our inspiration and grounding for the play through these community exchanges. The end result is that the staged play occurs in conversation with these communities, which are represented through video projections of our encounters appearing at key moments within the body of the play. As the audience experiences the play as ceremony, they do so in *correspondence* with these living practitioners."[91]

In *New Fire*, contemporary indigenous people are presented as coeval with the audience—they are in the same time, if not in the same place. The film makes the indigenous present "present" for audience members who may be unfamiliar with their everyday practices and struggles. Yet there is some distance. Moraga is clear that the play is not a ceremony but that the audience experiences it as such, successfully retaining her sense of theatricality while offering the production as authentic, temporally "real" experience related to earlier ceremonial experiences in the videos.

At the level of content, *New Fire* stages violence in the neoliberal Americas as largely rooted in violence against indigenous people, specifically women. This is clearest in the video of Flor Crisostomo, a Zapotec Mexican woman without documents who took asylum in Adalberto Methodist Church in Humboldt Park in Chicago. The interview explains her act of asylum as a protest against both the U.S. and Mexican governments because neither government supports immigrants in the United States, particularly indigenous immigrants.

"Never Any Other Time but This Time No World but This World" 51

In the video, Crisostomo sees her own oppression as part of a five-hundred-year history and obliquely relays the effect of NAFTA on her ability to support her children, a condition she more clearly laid out in the statement she made when she took asylum in the church.[92] Her testimony, which is the longest of *New Fire*'s video excerpts and is placed at the fulcrum of the play, combines a ceremony by the Mexican Danzante community (with common roots to the *conchero* dancers mentioned earlier in the chapter), with *testimonio*, in effect linking ceremonial healing with political coalition building. Crisostomo makes it clear that the oppression of Mexican people in the United States today is particularly virulent to indigenous people, because indigenous people were disproportionally disadvantaged as workers on small farms replaced by corporate farms fomented by NAFTA and thus came to the United States to work under less than ideal conditions, as Moraga points out in her own writing.[93]

The juxtaposition between Flor's real story and Vero's fictional narrative sets up a parallel between Vero's healing from rape and assault and the conditions that contemporary Mexican women face. And it destabilizes Vero as the subject of the play, although *New Fire* does follow her life journey. The positioning of the Mexican woman as a corporate subject is most visible in scene 8, called "Basura." Here, Vero decries the Juárez killings I discuss in chapter 2:

> VERO: Trash. Basura.
> They said as much
> To middle age abuelas.
>
> (*Vero covers Lola's shoulders with the cloth. She removes it and gathers the mutilated body into it.*)
>
> Come and collect your daughter
> In 30 gallon trash sacks scavenged
> From a Juárez desert . . .
> 878 girls and counting . . .
> I see my familia's "dark side,"
> mirrored in the ponds
> of dissolving black stone
> that are my mother's eyes.
>
> LOLA: Es mi hija
>
> VERO: I know and I forget . . .
>
> (*Lola exits with blanket of body parts. Vero returns center stage. Spiderwoman slowly begins to encroach upon the scene. The fierce beating of the water drum fills the air.*)

VERO: This is the source of our sadness.
(*Raging*).
Women
are so
much
trash!
Pura Basura!⁹⁴

This scene is a transitional moment between Vero's illness and the purging that lets her heal. It is also a crucial piece of text because it shows that Vero is not meant to be an individualized consciousness. She is healed when she admits the social and transnational source of her pain. The mention of the 878 bodies of women killed in Juárez extends the play's list of the dead read aloud before this scene. The inclusion of the women of Juárez also effectively reimagines Vero's consciousness as transnational. When she claims that "this is the source of our sadness" she frames her illness as having as much or more to do with the desecration of women within the Americas than the rape and violence she experienced personally. The healing offered in the play is not a personal one, but a social one. Interestingly, the laying on of a cloth, much like the putting on of a rebozo, occurs in this play as well.⁹⁵ This time, however, rather than making a character "an india" by linking her to the past (as in *Giving Up the Ghost*), the laying on of the cloth links Vero and Lola as indigena sufferers in the present, who work together to heal from a current event. That Lola later wraps this cloth around her "daughter," who is represented by a large garbage bag in which the real remains of the victims are often contained, marks the very impossibility of a complete transformation of the deceased into lived presence. This is the trauma that must be recognized so Vero can heal. This moment of congruence between the too real and the impossible, framed within an openly nonrealistic mise-en-scène with a prop on the verge of real object, successfully exposes the cleavage of real and unreal so crucial to theatricality. This cleavage also gestures to the impossibility of becoming other, an issue that I explore in chapter 3 in relation to theatrical modes of representing femicide. On another level, however, the obsolescence of the garbage bags points to the impossibility of erasing neoliberal violence against indigenous and mestiza women, despite the impetus to do so by various pressures; *New Fire* performs a theatrical refusal of said erasure.

The play also refuses the larger dramaturgy of neoliberalism, although economic conditions are mentioned only obliquely and Marxist materialism is largely rejected as a solution throughout the play. Vero jokes about being a former "stone Marxist" much like one might joke about being a former stone butch who learns to be "touched." And yet, the play's form resists the allure of the individualized subject of liberal humanism so crucial to neoliberalism's success. *New Fire* also resists the temporality of forward-moving progress by instilling a recursive healing process of cyclical renewal, which functions differently from the recursive crisis management I discuss in chapter 4. Mostly, however, *New Fire* resists the speed (and diffusive attention) of representation often inducted into contemporary performance. As one reviewer remarked when he critiqued the show—it is slow.[96] It takes an hour and twenty minutes to move through forty pages of text; ritual performances are allowed their own duration, and the character arc is often interrupted. This asks for a certain attentiveness and patience with the play. It is a kind of "sitting with" all too often glossed over in everyday life. This form of temporal endurance is at odds with both advanced capitalism and orthodox forms of revolution which move fast to a clear goal—whether that be conflict or the accumulation of wealth or data.

New Fire's production and construction parallels Moraga's calls for indigenous consciousness through creative pedagogy for the last ten years through her Rite to Remember and Indigena as Scribe workshops, which offer different ways of being in contemporary neoliberal conditions. In a 2005 interview, she offers that "convincing young people that they are Indian" is key to her political commitments because of how it opens them up so that they "disidentify with the goals of the nation state they are supposed to have allegiance to. And they begin to look at alternate ways of making home, making family, making economic structures, based on models that indigenous people are still trying to practice that have to do with collectivity, that have to do with a reciprocal relationship with the earth."[97] Of course, this thinking risks folkloric oversimplification, but in Moraga's case I see this as a productive detour rather than an escape. It is a consciously performed act, not a return to the authentic. In this she moves away from Chicano/a nationalism and closer to the decolonizing methodologies of Linda Tuhiwai Smith.[98] Moraga utilizes these methods in a transnational mode that does not simply counter neoliberalism through the effects and/or changes made possible by these methods, but by offering a modality of living that imagines otherwise. In this she joins a large number of thinkers who see an allegiance to indigenous practice as a global countermovement to neoliberal ascendency in theory and practice. Moraga's shifting modes of thinking about indigeneity and political change move from transnational-to-nationalist to a transnational/global lens, transforming from a critique of Euro-American dramatic structures to a new mode of dramaturgy. Interestingly, Teatro Campesino, the primary architect of theatrical cultural nationalism follows suit.

The Return of El Teatro Campesino as Transnational Thinker

Moraga's form of recent indigenista anti-neoliberal critique sits cheek by jowl with Luis Valdez's recent work. Valdez, after a long hiatus, returned to representing indigeneity onstage with *Mummified Deer*, a play that combines two "true stories": one about an eighty-four-year-old woman who was found with a sixty-year-old fetus still residing in her and the story of his own Yaqui grandmother.[99] As suggested by a 1999 interview with Victor Payan, writing this play marked Valdez's turn away from linking his indigenous heritage to the Mayans and Aztecs and instead linking it to his northern roots. As he claims:

> Now, I'm claiming my Yaqui origins, and I know that one of the things I have to do in order to claim that is I sort of have to let go of the pyramids. I'm not going to let them go completely, obviously, because I've been studying the Maya for too long and the Aztecs. I'm connected to that, too. But then in order to cross the Rio Petatlan by Sinaloa and to get into Yaqui lands, you know into the Mazas River and the Yaqui River, I have to get out of Aztlán. Aztlán is an Aztec concept. And I have to enter el terreno del Yaqui, you know El Rio Yaquimi. I have to come into the northern deserts. I have to come into Sonora, and I have to rethink and say, okay, what is the value of the Yaqui.[100]

It is important to note that Valdez's conversation on this point is made in the context of President Ernesto Zedillo's visit to California. Although Valdez admits he could not make the protests to show opposition to Zedillo's lack of support for immigrants and his handling of the Chiapas uprising, he clearly understands violence against indigenous people as a form of "ethnic cleansing." Later in the interview he makes a connection between the extermination of the Yaqui and appropriation of their lands in the early twentieth century, revealing a subtle knowledge of transnational (and one might argue by using the term *ethnic cleansing*, an international) frame for understanding the oppression of contemporary indigenous people. He, too, is inspired by Chiapas.

This inspiration perhaps shows up less legibly in his plays than in his interview, as does his critique of neoliberal practices, although the latter lurks in his 2005 play *Earthquake Sun*. *Earthquake Sun*, created over a period of forty years, attempts to rethink the present in relationship to the fifth sun, or the earthquake sun, that Moraga also references.[101] It takes place in the eighth century, the twenty-first century, and the thirty-fourth century and follows the time travel of a young warrior who ends up in the nightmare dystopia of cloned reproduction and hologrammatic experience of the thirty-fourth century. The play is inflected with Mayan cosmology, although it makes only passing reference to contemporary Mayan people. It does, however, reference neoliberal reality in the twenty-first century section. There, one of the brothers comes into being as a coyote who is taking a Guatemalan Mayan family over the U.S.-Mexico border. The play gestures to the sexual violence suffered by the poor mestizo and indigenous women who cross the border for work (Blanca Luna, the "little mother," pretends to be pregnant so as not to be raped), and the reality of drug violence in Central America in the current era. The beheading of Blanca's boyfriend, Jaguar Kan, is referenced as the result of drug trafficking and political/religious persecution simultaneously. The scene where she explains his death attempts mixes Central American and Chiapan reality while tapping into Mayan and Mexican cosmology:

> BLANCA: There was a war. The soldiers came to our mountains, and started taking prisoners. They said we were followers of the Holy Cross.
> EL COYOTE: What's that, holy rollers, aleluyas?
> DOMINGO: Revolutionaries. Defenders of the four corners, the four directions. Our Mayan people are fighting for what little remains of our way of life. They said we were comunistas!
> BLANCA: It's all lies. The drug dealers only want our lands to cut down the trees and plant ambola to grow poppies for their heroin!
> RAQUEL: Worse and worse.
> BLANCA: It's true! They want us all dead! We might as well be dead. We live like ghosts in the mountain jungles.
> EL COYOTE: What do the ghosts hope to find in los estados unidos?
> BLANCA: The birth of the new sun.[102]

Mostly, however, Valdez is interested in writing about the Popol Vuh in a highly mediatized world.[103] For Valdez, the *eschata* (Greek for "last things") works to show what Huerta calls Valdez's belief of death as a beginning rather than an end, which while it has political valences is not political in Moraga's sense, despite their similar inspirations.[104]

Valdez and the Teatro Campesino come closer to rethinking political philosophy in current era through their practice of the spherical actor. Kinan Valdez, Luis's son, is the foremost teacher of this practice today. Concomitantly, the company is staging new theatrical versions of the Popol Vuh and plays about Víctor Jara, one of the most high-profile artists killed under Pinochet's dictatorship. The range of work suggests a movement away from strict cultural nationalism into a more political transnationalism that incorporates the history of neoliberalism. The framing of the contemporary work retains Luis Valdez's commitment to *In Lak'ech*, the belief that you are my other me, which emerged in the 1970s. The practice of acting in relation to this principle breaks down the individual I, as everything I do to you I do to myself. In acting exercises, this opens up the possibility of creating theatrical action not contained by individual human subjects, although the practice is meant to open up the possibilities of human creativity. A recent solo work written and performed by Rubén González, *La Esquinita, U.S.A.* demonstrates a combination of political content and acting training that stands apart from liberal subjecthood.[105] González's play is a solo tour de force where he portrays more than ten characters who are trying to survive in a racially mixed neighborhood after the demise of the Thompson Tire Factory. His virtuosity aside, what is striking is how this acting training transformed a solo show about postindustrial Los Angeles into an exposition of the need to think outside of individual needs in relation to community, and how the very erasure of difference between self and other at a physical level is key to this transformation. Although *La Esquinita, U.S.A.*'s inclusion of a South Asian guru risks veering into abstract spiritualism and orientalism, the confrontation at the end of the play demonstrates the moment of recognizing the enemy as one's other self. Because this conflict largely explodes out of the racial tensions brought about by economic scarcity (as does his main character Daniel's drug habit), the physical precision with which the two characters meld and depart from one another demonstrates the acquittal of the liberal subject as an act of solidarity necessary in this environment.

Kinan Valdez and González acknowledge their use of theater of the sphere techniques in production, suggesting that these were a shorthand which they used to collaborate as actor and director. More pointedly, Kinan Valdez linked his commitment to *In Lak'ech* to its use by the EZLN, suggesting that even though the term predates him and has a different genealogy within the history of ETC, his use is influenced by its recent transnational history.[106] This contemporary gloss on his father Luis's understanding of Mayan philosophy reframes it as a political and consciously transnational mode of thinking under neoliberalism.

This reimagination intersects with new modes of Latinx political thought countering the liberal underpinnings of neoliberalism. Rosa-Linda Fregoso, who wrote early criticism of El Teatro Campesino, including analysis of the principle of *In Lak'ech*, has recently reanimated the term in her call for pluriversal human rights—a form of thinking about rights based in indigenous thoughts.[107] Although she draws her version of the term from Chicana feminist Laura Pérez, not El Teatro Campesino, her vision of *In Lak'ech* resonates both with the more recent work of ETC and Moraga.[108] Fregoso is careful not to reify indigenous thought as homogenous but does ask us to consider indigenous forms of intersubjectivity to decolonize human rights from the frame of liberal subjecthood.[109] Her theorization asks that we think about collective rights, and the interdependency of the collective and the individual, thus combining forms of subject making by Chicano/a artists and the Zapatistas. This form of thinking is one of many modes of undoing neoliberalism that finds its place in Latinx theater.

points of departure: Obliqueness as Neoliberal Condition

My last exploration—that of the work of Cuban-Anglo playwright and director Michael John Garcés—unlike the others, works largely outside any framework of Chicano and Mexican cultural nationalism. Instead, Garcés combines his transnational political consciousness with a commitment to formal innovation that resists symbolism, iconography, or any other form of representational standing in for another. While he shares Moraga's aversion to linear time, reproductive futurism, and singular liberal subjects, he is unconcerned with theatrical legibility, avoiding the representational conundrums that haunt Moraga. Instead, Garcés employs a certain obliqueness of language and referentiality to portray how neoliberalism feels for indigenous populations affected by state violence under these conditions. This obliqueness avoids what Jodi Melamed calls the methods of "represent and destroy" that undergird representations of minoritarian subjects under liberalism and neoliberalism. This method, usually found in U.S. literature, creates stories about fully realized subjects of color in which they prove their worth as subjects (or the lack thereof) through their confrontation with, use of, or submission to violence. This violence often destroys them, as Melamed's phrase "represent and destroy," suggests. In *points of departure*, the characters survive but refuse to be consumed. Garcés's characters' obliqueness works to describe their living conditions within the play *and* acts as a mode of resistance to the audience's consumption of them as characters standing in for "real" people.

Garcés's understanding of these representational practices stems from his own transnational history. He has a Cuban-born father and an Anglo mother, but he was born in the United States and raised in Colombia, where he lived in the 1980s. He returned to Miami to do his undergraduate work before embarking on his professional career, which took him to Chiapas, Mexico. In 2001, Garcés helped create two shows with Sna Jtz'ibajom, a Mayan writers collective there, whose theater wing is named Lo'il Maxil. (This group also collaborated with Ralph Lee, who worked with Moraga on *Heart of the Earth*.) One of the plays he worked on was *Mexico with Us Forever*, which was created by the ensemble (they work as a collective). *Mexico with Us Forever* is a pointed drama about political corruption and *caciquismo* (boss rule) in Chiapas. A gloss on the Zapatista phrase, "Never again Mexico without us," the play follows the story of a mayoral candidate, Jmanel, who pays would-be supporters and later pockets the money that he is supposed to use to pay for town improvements. Because of local tensions, the play has never been staged outside of the headquarters of Fortaleza de la Mujer Maya (FOMMA), Teatro Daniel Zebadúa, and the Casa del Lago.[110] In addition to referencing local political problems, this play also documents the more widespread difficulty getting work in post-NAFTA Mexico. As one character, Jpalas, puts it after he realizes that he is not going to get the job in the coffin factory promised him by the mayor when he was still a candidate—"And now he says that they are going to give me a coffin for myself. So it is better that I go as a wetback to the United States than they kill me."[111] He repeats this desire a couple of lines later. The members of Sna know whereof they speak—many of them have witnessed friends and family leave for the north despite its danger.[112]

Michael John Garcés's introduction to theater in Chiapas came through exploring issues of migration at a time in which the effects of NAFTA—under which I include the militarization of both of the borders of Mexico (north and south) and paramilitary incursion into Chiapas and other places in rural Mexico—are fully realized. When speaking of the experience in an interview with Eisa Davis in spring 2006, Garcés admits that his experience with Sna was informative and important for a number of reasons: one, because of the social power of the drama, and two, because it was especially challenging to work in a collective. In his own words, it "slowed him down." More importantly, he seems to have learned how to be outsider to the community and still work with a collective. As he explains:

> It was an extremely lonely experience. Living in a small room by myself. I'm not and don't pretend to be Mayan or Mexican. The company speaks Spanish and two different Mayan languages with each other, and you're very much welcome, but at the same time you're not, you're emphatically not. The Mexicans in town were not thrilled to have me there; interacting with Mayans I was definitely suspect. And I wasn't really down with hanging out with European tourists. I got a lot of writing done; it was fruitful in that way . . . The more you are accepted by the group, the more you realize you're not part of the group. I'd love to go back, and I'd do it again, but it was a harrowing and wonderful experience at the same time.[113]

I quote Garcés's observations at length because I think the distance that he feels from his collaborators and the difficulty of his collaboration allow him to see indigenous issues in a different light than Moraga and Valdez. Garcés's contact with indigenous people is only through their present—a difficult present in which he is implicated as a U.S. citizen and a Latino without indigenous heritage. While he does not talk about the particular politics of Chiapas in this interview, these politics come out clearly in his play, which I suspect he started to write while there.

Garcés's experience of travel is strangely refracted in the title—*points of departure*. Produced at INTAR in 2006, the play's stage directions do not reference a specific country—only designating the play place as "san bartolomé, a small town in the highlands, at some point in the present."[114] Yet it is clear that San Bartolomé alludes to San Cristóbal de las Casas, Chiapas—the city named after Bartolomé de las Casas, the sixteenth-century Spanish priest who defended indigenous rights. The story is simple. In the first half, a traveler named Márquez, who has been living in the United States, attempts to go back to his home village, Chenahló. In the second half, Petrona, the maid who cleans his hotel room, who is also from Chenahló, migrates to the United States after time spent in a refugee camp. Garcés's decision to write about a handful of characters with no discernable role within the state apparatus actualizes the everyday material reality of his characters and of the contemporary experience of migration. This reality is not lived as a monolithic conflict between indigenous people and the state writ large, but as a more riven set of conflicts within militarized social and economic networks. Those networks might include members of one's own family. An exchange between Márquez and Petrona exemplifies this situation (and its relation to transnational commerce):

> P- if he . . .
>
> M- these dollars. in this book. I. .won't need them. don't give them to your uncle.
> P- they have requested him.
> M your uncle?
>
> if the roads open you should leave. alone. call these numbers. when you get to the capital. it may be enough money.[115]

However obliquely, the play references real conditions. The capital, seemingly, is San Cristóbal. Chenahló, in contrast, is a Tzotzil-speaking town whose Zapatista citizens have been continually terrorized by paramilitary groups. The 1997 massacre in Acteal, where paramilitary soldiers killed forty-five people praying in a church, happened within its municipal limits, as have multiple state-authorized displacements and land seizures throughout the late 1990s and early 2000s. The subject matter of the play, then, comes straight out of Garcés's experience of Chiapas. The maid in the hotel is named Petrona, a reference to an actress from FOMMA who also worked with Sna; the complications of local bureaucracy under *caciquismo* and terror the actors faced is also very real. Yet, by not specifying the site of the play as Chiapas, and referring to UN refugee centers for stateless refugees, Garcés allows his audience to recognize the similarities between conflicts in the late '80s and '90s in El Salvador and Guatemala and late '90s conditions in southern Mexico. For Garcés, these conditions echo some of those he saw in Colombia, which was at the height of conflicts between the military and the Revolutionary Armed Forces of Colombia (FARC) when he lived there in the 1980s.[116] His constellation of experiences shows the extension of networks of violence under neoliberal capital throughout the hemisphere: the FARC conflicts escalated with the rise of transnational drug trafficking; the conflicts in Chiapas and Central America were also part of a larger genocide of leftists.

Garcés also gestures to the longer history of indigenous genocide in a lyrical, but bittersweet exchange between Petrona and Mazapa (indicated as m and p below), which I quote at length.

M- miami . . . tallahassee . . chatanooga . . and . . wichita . . .
P- cha . . ta . . .
M- . . . nooga . . .
P- chatanooga.
M- yes.
P- I hear voices in those names, different voices. wichita.
M- perhaps you will go someday and hear them.
P- no. I will never leave.
M- no.
P- your life, all of those places—
M- no. no. my life, it is here. nowhere else. where have you been?
P- nowhere.
M tell me.
P- nowhere. nachig, yoshib, san bartolomé.
M- I hear voices in those names.
P- you do?
M- when you say them.[117]

All of these names are transliterated from U.S. indigenous languages and refer to sites inhabited first by indigenous tribes. The replacement of one indigenous language of the Americas, which Garcés's characters can't speak publically for fear of reprisal, by a series of other languages registered as place names, traces the history of displacement indigenous people have suffered throughout the hemisphere. Rather than leave these place names as ghosts of a forgotten history, Garcés imbues them with life. Márquez's rediscovery of voices in his personal geography temporarily alleviates his distance from his home as it provides a Brechtian estrangement for a U.S. audience that, in its familiarity with these cities, forgets that these place names are indigenous. More generally, the connections between (im)mobility, memory, and language articulate how his characters' struggles form part of a longer history of violence under colonialism and imperialism. It is no accident that once she comes to the United States, the city Petrona ends up in is Columbus, Ohio, a city whose very name re-members discovery, conquest, and colonization.

Although Garcés acknowledges these long hemispheric histories, *points of departure* dwells stubbornly in a present. Garcés also avoids any temporal sequence that would situate indigenous culture as past. His deft theatrical minimalism paired with the oblique referentiality of his language is the exact opposite of Moraga's dramaturgical *indigenismo*, which works through highly symbolic palimpsestic modes of staging cosmology and historiography. Garcés's play has no symbolism. Its objects do not stand for anything else. No one becomes indigenous because everyone is indigenous. (The cast was composed of Latinx actors, none of which identify solely as indigenous, however.) Garcés's characters identify (or hide) themselves through language and place rather than mentioning their ethnicity because of the conditions mentioned above. On a practical "given circumstances" level, his Latinx actors do not employ costumes to indicate their indigeneity because their characters are hiding their geographical origins, which particular forms of dress would make legible.

Rather than show estrangement between indigenous and nonindigenous characters as many plays about the neoliberal Americas do, Garcés concentrates on how displacement *feels* within and between indigenous communities. *Points of departure* offers not romantic anti-neoliberalism with gestures to an indigenous past, but a rendering of the neoliberal present that asks us to experience the difficulties of recognition that his own characters face when they try to surmise their own identities and pasts. This quest for recognition is largely registered only in language. It begins when Márquez returns from the United States, referred to in the script only as "there," to find out what happened to his family in Chenahló. He stays in a hotel that employs a maid named Petrona, whose memory is as strong as his, as he tries to get permission to go home. Márquez's dealings with a government official and a shopkeeper who sells local crafts (Chenalhó is also renowned for its textiles) end up with all of the characters being tied up and brought into a room, presumably to be questioned, and likely to be hurt or disappeared. Over the course of the first act we find out that Márquez's indigenous name is Mazapa. But even here Garcés does not designate the characters' ethnicity, although the names used are Tzotzil Mayan. Because all of the characters face persecution according to political allegiances in their particular villages, the "tongue" (*lengua*) they speak can make which village they live or lived in apparent. Thus, the obliqueness of their language is their protection. This is as true when they are among themselves as it is when they are interacting with bureaucrats—who, in this play, are also indigenous people with long memories. Perhaps because of his familiarity with Chiapas, Garcés thinks at the level of the pueblo and the language group. *Points of departure* reveals that indigenous people are not always in solidarity. At the level of ideology, this neoliberal reality contrasts with the dreams of cultural nationalism as an emancipatory project. Aesthetically, the result is that Garcés's play avoids recognizable symbolism that could be subsumed by the Mexican state or its ethnic categories.

Garcés's characters' language not only deflects stable designation of ethnic identity but also registers a more general psychic fragmentation in the face of contemporary economic and political oppression. An example is Petrona's conversation with her husband as they are about to leave a refugee camp for the United States. I include a rather lengthy passage to demonstrate how Garcés's oblique language materializes the character's struggles:

    M- there are those there that speak spanish. many.
    P- never again.
    M- there are.

P- never spanish again ever.

M- no one speaks your tongue.
P- our tongue.
M- no longer.
P- here.
M- no one speaks it.
P- there.
M- there, here. no one.
P- anymore.
M- no one.
P- english, then. only. we'll learn.

M- good, yes.
P- yes. good.[118]

Petrona is in a situation where her tongue—her way of communicating with other indigenous people—will eventually be wrested from her. And here, that is exactly what happens. Her hatred of the Spanish language reveals her anger at what it represents: the necessity of hiding her identity, hiding from violence, and the longer history of colonialism. It is also a reminder that English is a third language for many Latin Americans in the United States. Garcés, however, is not simply referencing the linguistic difficulty indigenous people experience when communicating in Spanish and English in a documentary way, as one critic of the play claimed. Nor is he employing this language as a merely formal device, even though it is, in Garcés's own words, "formal."[119] Instead it is a mode of conveying the feeling of fragmentation to an audience rather than explaining it.

As audience members, our encounters with the opacity of the language ask us to read through the lines, experiencing the same difficulty that the characters do when they try to navigate their everyday lives. Garcés's language asks that we give the play absolute attention to understand where we are, as all clues to what is happening when and where are contextual rather than indexical. In the second half of *points of departure*, we move forward and backward between Petrona's experiences in different camps, the United States, and in transport between these places, in nonsequential fashion. Garcés's modes of storytelling challenge not only temporal logic but also any adherence to migration north as a progress narrative. While being in the United States saves Petrona from physical violence, she is not happy there. Her journey has come at the cost of her peace of mind. She "goes back" in her head regularly. And getting "there" has no clear trajectory either. Instead we see a set of decisions to leave but do not witness any arrival, suggesting a journey that is not only not complete but cannot be complete, impeding teleological structures. It is for this reason that I counter critics who suggest that the play does not go anywhere; it actually goes a lot of places, just not in the way in which the reviewers are accustomed. (I wrestle with a similar claim about Jorge Cortiñas's work in chapter 2.) This lack of unidirectional movement is often particular to neoliberal life. In particular, circular migrations, particularly among Central American and Mexican migrant populations, are the norm rather than the exception, as many people, willingly or under coercion, move back and forth as financial pressures and legal injunctions dictate. This reality, as will be evidenced in chapter 4, undoes the very dramaturgy of migration as well as the ideology of a unidirectional ascent to the riches of the American dream undergirding U.S. nationalism.

Garcés's temporal and sequential manipulations are also a revision of nationalist reproductive futurity, and ultimately a critique of the nuclear family so important to dictatorship and post-dictatorship regimes in the Americas. Over the course of the play, Petrona becomes a mother, seemingly both to a son who is disappeared and to two daughters who are born in the United States. Yet because of the temporal disjunction of the play, we are very unclear about her status as a mother. Consider a conversation between Petrona and Xun/Juan before they leave:

> P- nothing for your boy, for my brother nothing.
> M- what happened to domingo wasn't your fault.
> P- his name was tumín.
> M- petrona—
> P- our boy, no name, nothing—
> M- petrona. petrona.
>
> ———
>
> you can do something. for the child inside you, petrona.
> P- not mine.
> M- you can do something for that child.
> P- not your.
> M- petrona. please, I..that is something you can do.
>
> ———
>
> P- not yours. not my—
> M- they will let us go while you are pregnant, petrona. but not after.
> P- and when we are there?
> M- after you give birth? they won't.
> P- and after I give birth? there? to this child, xun?
> M- my name, petrona, is juan.
> P- what then? you and I and this child?
>
> ———
>
> this child inside me is not ours.[120]

This dialogue indexes Petrona's pregnancy clearly, but does not let us know what happened to her son. Interestingly, she refers to him both as "our" son and "yours," creating ambivalence about her own maternity, even though we hear later, through her conversation with Leti, that a male child seems to have been taken from her in the process of leaving San Bartolomé. A more puzzling set of questions arises when she claims "this child is not ours" after the earlier "not yours" and "not my." This dialogue most plainly suggests that the child is a product of rape.[121] More allusively, however, Petrona's comment that the child is "not my" alludes to a different form of abstraction from biologically defined family. Perhaps, the truth of it is that she sees the child as the product of a larger collectivity, as the potentiality of something that is not yet understood. That Petrona temporarily adopts Leti, a young woman in the camps, so they can leave together indicates that her notion of family is not confined to the biological. Kinship here is expansively rather than narrowly defined in crisis. Garces's obliqueness about the biological family gestures to the possibility of abandoning it as a mode of kinship under crisis or, perhaps, better said, the neoliberal condition.

Departing from the Liberal Subject

On a theatrical level, Garcés's innovation revises Aristotelian and U.S. twentieth-century realist dramaturgical norms, to the confusion of some audience members. Petrona, Márquez, Cruz, and the rest are vivid characters; however, their contours, as reviews suggested, "are quite blurry around the edges."[122] Rather than seeing this as a defect, however, I read Garcés's characterization as a distinct departure from forms of individuation that naturalize the liberal subject of tragedy. As I have written elsewhere, the liberal subject of tragedy is obsolete under neoliberal capitalism, in part because the tragedy of aspiration upon which such a liberal hero defines himself is dependent on a distinction between the self within political society and the self defined by capitalist worth.[123] As opposed to the demise of this subject within U.S. American dramas about Anglo male characters, here the erasure of the distinction between these two selves is rendered biopolitically through the legacies of colonialism, imperialism, and grinding, but constant, neoliberal conflict. Rather than restore this form of subjecthood to indigenous male and female characters as a political act, Garcés moves in the other direction, suggesting that one might see more clearly if one undoes spectators' dependence on this type of hero—especially a male hero. (It is not lost on me that the substitution of a male protagonist in the first half with a female protagonist in second half may have exacerbated many viewers' irritation at the play.) This choice is underscored in his intentional triple casting of the male roles in the second half, which blurs the lines between Petrona's husband, brother, and father. They are all indicated with the lower case "m:" which perhaps means male. Referring to the characters by letters obfuscates their individuality as it registers their existence in Leti's head as male voices, rather than differentiated beings. Privileging the female indigenous subject as the preferred conduit for neoliberal experience of migrants in the Americas undoes a dependence on male subjectivity; it also accords with Moraga's dramaturgy that centers on female indigenous experience as the lens with which to view neoliberalism.

Garcés's critique of liberal dramaturgy is in conversation with rather than in direct opposition to Aristotle and the conventions of classical drama. When I asked Garcés about how he chose to engage Aristotle, he provided this response:

> In fact, I would say that my feeling at the time was that it was impossible for a play made in the classical vein to convey a modern, (Central) American reality as I conceived it. So [I was] pushing against those rules, but not disregarding them. [I was t]rying to find the essence of tragedy while deploying them differently.

This deployment also called upon a reimagination of the chorus. He continued:

> The Greek plays focus on royalty, and the chorus is witness. In this case—as with much modern drama—the play is about the chorus. I wanted to keep a ritual formality about it, make the characters both representative of a polis and at the same time individual, and I think that is why the characters are, as you say, blurry. I intended them not to be completely defined, to be types as well as specific characters.[124]

This means that for Garcés, there were "most certainly, no singular heroes."[125]

While it is true that many modern plays are about the chorus in the sense that they are about nonroyal and nonelite persons, I think that Garcés underestimates the uniqueness of his decision to include indigenous citizens as part of an imagined polis. His decision to create such a polis—however much it may artificially extend the myth of Athenian democracy—offers up the idea of a mass protagonist of indigenous people that is not an undifferentiated mass outside of politics, but a group fundamental to politics that is nonetheless not subsumed by existing categories. This innovation is both theatrically and politically utopian, a thinking otherwise, that engages the Zapatistas' most radical suggestions while revising Jacques Rancière's understanding of those who have no part.[126] Rancière's theorization, which is predicated on not being able to categorize the demos as having a certain cultural affiliation, needs to be rethought in Mexican and Central American political contexts.[127] Gareth Williams has posited that the EZLN's Other Campaign, which appeared as part of the highly fraught 2006 Mexican election cycle, constitutes the part of those who have no part because of the very open invitation sent to possible members to join that campaign.[128] Here, I offer that, within representation,

Garces's indigenous migrant characters also constitute a "part of those that have no part," despite their so called cultural affiliation, because of their longstanding disenfranchisement within the very constitution of the political within the Mexican imaginary, where indigenous people are often highly visible, but nonetheless, do not count as citizens in real ways.[129] Characters like Petrona create their place through what Rancière calls dissensus—a "demonstration (*manifestation*) of a gap in the sensible itself."[130] The difficulty of these characters' language, its so-called refusal to be reduced to functionality, make it an example par excellence of said dissensus. That their disruption occurs *within* language, however, is important because it does not recast indigenous people as a mute body who cannot speak, reinscribing colonialist tropes of indigenous silence. Garcés's play renders Rancière's political idea, ironically enough, through an engagement with Greek drama and Aristotle, the very site of the constitution of the demos that Rancière wants to disrupt.

Garcés openly addresses Aristotle's *Poetics* in *points of departure* in relation to the concept of recognition and reversal, ultimately transculturating these terms. In the epigraph, Garcés uses the following fragment of the *Poetics* to situate these key terms: "indeed two parts in the myth, namely reverse and recognition, concern these things."[131] "These things" is the plot.[132] In *points of departure*, the first act, "recognitions," literally charts the characters' recognition of each other and of their shared past. The second act, "reversals," reverses the motion of the play from Mazepa's visit to Mexico to Petrona and Xun's travel to the United States. Of course, this reversal is also a reversal of fate. In an Aristotelian sense, the play does carry out a true reversal—we think that Márquez is eventually going to get back to his village to find the truth, but he ends up passing off the money to Petrona who goes in the opposite direction. The recognition, namely, the "change from ignorance to knowledge of a bond of love or hate," that occurs is Petrona and Márquez's realization of their common history in Chenahló.[133] That this recognition happens simultaneously with a reversal demonstrates Garcés's deep engagement with Aristotle and his accomplishment of Aristotle's ideal form of tragedy.

Because this reversal demonstrates a brief moment of solidarity in the face of neoliberal violence, however, Garcés essentially transculturates Aristotle's terms, redefining recognition for indigenous people in the contemporary Americas. Fate, often seen as abstract in modernity because we are deeply invested in the belief of an individual's control of his or her own destiny, is resuscitated here in a time in which we can no longer (or should no longer) believe in individual human agency as triumphant.

Garcés also transculturates the concept of reversal within the context of transnational migration. On a simple level Márquez's fate goes from good to bad (he, perhaps, has the tragic flaw of hubris, despite Garcés's departure from straight Aristotelianism); Petrona's fate meanwhile goes from bad to good, because she gets to "escape" to the United States. But Petrona's experiences en route to and arrival in the United States are also somehow tragic. She is haunted by memories and alienated from her own daughters, who plan to place her in a retirement community in Braderton, Florida. In a more traditional play, perhaps, we would be asked simply to follow Márquez, feeling for him when he fails to return home, aware of his foolhardiness in trying to get there by any means necessary. In Garcés's double plot, however, we end up following Petrona, not Márquez, and in doing so we are asked to abandon the idea of a clear reversal or a sequential sense of suspense. Petrona's experiences are conveyed out of sequence, which disallows suspense or any sense of moving in a clear vector from ignorance toward recognition. This temporal disjuncture is the reality of migration under neoliberalism.

The role of pity, fear, and suffering endemic to Greek tragedy also has a different resonance because of the role of empathy in relation to spectacles of suffering in the neoliberal Americas—particularly representations of Central American migrants—who have often been staged as always already suffering. It is no accident, then, that Garcés breaks off his epigraphic quote from Aristotle just before suffering is mentioned. This third aspect of tragedy is the silent presence he is trying to transform as he considers the neoliberal Americas, by removing the idea of suffering, or, at least, spectacular suffering, from view and by unlinking this suffering, or the pity or fear we feel for the characters, from the audience's experience of catharsis. He does this with his frankly antidramatic rendering of his characters' everyday lives, which feature everyday acts of survival rather than grand victories or losses against the state. Petrona's everyday life is a remaking of self, just as Márquez's was. It is for this reason that I depart from critic Joy Goodwin, who claimed in her review that

> when Márquez recedes, we are left with a cast of victims who do little to inspire our sympathy. Mr. Garcés leaves a handful of refugees onstage and seems to think it sufficient to point out that they are suffering unjustly. Politically, that may be enough—indeed, the play stirs up concern for victims of distant dictatorships. But artistically it will only take him so far. As his play shows, an audience cares about characters not because they are suffering, but because of what they are trying to do about it.[134]

Garcés's play, in my opinion, shows these refugees doing quite a lot: choosing to be quiet, choosing to leave, and trying to remake family. Unlike dramas that might privilege Márquez's actions against the state as "actions," Garcés makes the case for enduring as a form of action (and in the play, this enduring is a profoundly gendered experience). Factually, Goodwin seems to miss that Petrona, Juan, and Leti suffer not under "distant dictatorships" but very near democracies. Thus, Garcés asks: How exactly are migration and displacement under neoliberalism tragic? And how do we have to rethink our assumptions to understand the quotidian lives of indigenous people in the Americas? In *points of departure*, Garcés argues not only that we have to abandon the grandeur of the tragic hero—an intervention made long before—but that we have to revise our idea of suffering. He asks that we quit using the suffering of the other to inspire sympathy. He is not looking for it, and this is where Goodwin is right: we are not meant to have sympathy in straightforward way for Petrona; we are asked to experience Petrona's fragmentation so as to understand how conditions under neoliberal conditions *feel*. Garcés does not allow Goodwin to valorize or sympathize with Petrona as a hero or an exemplary sufferer despite what she claims. He flouts emancipatory modes of representing the other based in liberal humanism: the creation of recognizable three-dimensional nonwhite characters to which the viewer can offer liberal subjecthood as an act of benevolence. He also does not give any of his characters a heroic struggle that they clearly win or lose so as to activate particular feelings in the audience. Instead he stages durational experiences through voices that are part of collective and a collection of experiences in language that cannot be reduced to empathic relatability or sympathetic pity.

Rather than making characters legible through a melodramatic narrative, Garcés refuses his spectators' customary methods for consuming depictions of transnational violence. His repositioning of the audience avoids what Ana Puga has referred to as "migrant melodrama" in "Migrant Melodramas, Human Rights, and Elvira Arellano."[135] Puga's essay considers social performances that make suffering the price of migrants' admission into the nation state and the deployment of melodramatic forms the way to gain access to rights that they already have under the law.[136] As Puga suggests, the stakes of migrant melodrama interrogate how and when one can make human rights claims without imputing these stereotypes and plot structures. And, as she recognizes, it is usually the people in power of granting or advocating for or against said rights that are the ones who get to frame these social performances.[137] Puga's essay concentrates on the way Elvira Arellano, an undocumented woman who took up residence in the same church as Flor Crisostomo, is portrayed as a typical suffering mother in melodramatic form—a performance that Petrona both engages and refuses in *points of departure*. Scholar Patricia Stuelke takes on this phenomenon in a other era—focusing on the audience mechanism in relation to these spectacles of suffering in the '80s era Central American solidarity movement.[138] She singles out how "indigenous subjects" in particular "have been called upon to perform intractable difference and dramatize their own victimhood in exchange for affective and cultural recognition (as distinct from previous attempts by Cold War developmentalist states, militaries and leftist movements to erase indigenous forms of identity and social organization)."[139] Stuelke is especially critical of how these mechanisms created "audiences" for said performances who wanted to perform the reparative act of solidarity. This paradoxical mode of audience construction erased the difference between us and them through a form of sentimentality that obfuscated and colluded with discourses and practices of privatization advocated by the United States, while also creating a spectatorial position to consume suffering. This operation, in her view, was carried out by the dissemination of representations of violence and pain that enlisted our feeling for the victims as we feel for ourselves and those close to us. In short, the identification with the other *as sympathy* purged rather than reminded viewers of their complicity with the U.S. machine. Although she does not engage it, Stuelke recalls Augusto Boal's critique of Aristotle.[140] As she frames them, offerings of sympathy by U.S. audiences were part of the problem rather than a solution because these viewers and their modes of sympathy were within the affective complex of neoliberal multiculturalism, not outside of it. Stuelke's analysis hinges primarily on documentary films, novels, and *testimonios*, leaving theater virtually untouched as a medium. In fact, her only engagement with theater is her antitheatricalist descriptor for a section of the essay that describes the sympathy complex: "Solidarity's Compassionate Theater."[141]

In contrast, I offer that Garcés's play needs theatrical thinking to undo the very neoliberal affect Stuelke decries. On a literary level, *points of departure* operates as an anti-*testimonio*, a conscious choice given that Garcés cites a *testimonio* as one of the inspirations for the play.[142] Petrona's speech is a clear example:

> P- that bodies leave us that bodies leave that we cast them aside
> as they leave us as there are no bodies as there have never been
> bodies never been flesh never been hands never eyes never hair
> never bellies never veins never sweat never navels never throats
> never the voices of throats the voices of lungs the voices of tongues
> of mouths of teeth voices of lips and the biting of lips the sound
> of voices never at night at play at table at washing at courting at
> prayer never any single being of human sound any flesh to slap
> against flesh to press into flesh slice flesh caress flesh rub against
> flesh hold against flesh club against flesh no flesh for iron to
> strike for fire to sear for smoke to drown for showers to scour
> for wind to gouge for sand to cut for earth to bury no flesh never
> been bodies never any other time but this time no world but this
> world.[143]

The brown woman who speaks here does not make violence plain—she literally talks around the bodies of the dead. She does not use a singular or even a corporate "I" to stand in for the experiences of others. She is not a sovereign subject. In terms of theatrical thinking, the play does not stage any direct violence or narrate it in a straightforward way. It is doubly obscene—literally offstage in a classical Greek dramatic sense as well as being repugnant on a moral level. In direct opposition to the rehearsal of violence at the center of *testimonio* or melodrama, this play makes its audiences imagine these events

points of departure. Directed by Ron Daniels. Sandra Delgado as Pertona. Photo courtesy of Carol Rosegg.

offstage, and this does not give one the perverse pleasure of seeing the end of such pain in the act of witnessing or consuming it.

The emotional tenor of the characters rallies against emotional consumption of pain. Although the play was infused with florid music that displayed intense emotion, the actors played the scenes obliquely, rarely emoting their pain openly within the text. This estrangement and deferral was crucial. The monologue above is a case in point, as it came after an emotional song sung by the actress playing Petrona. In juxtaposition, the actress's refusal to relive the violence in an emotionally orthodox way when she narrates the deaths she has seen and experienced forced audiences to listen to the fragmented formality of her language as language, not emotion. This exercise, for Goodwin is "self-indulgent." In perhaps the best backhanded compliment in recent memory she states that Petrona "delivers long, manic monologues that sound like Shakespeare crossed with Gertrude Stein. Her blurry story frustrates; not only is it vague and confusing, but she takes so long to tell it."[144] The idea that Petrona's pain is not finite nor her delivery of it efficient, makes her speeches a continual indictment of neoliberalism; her monologues reject the idea that one can "get past" such an event, perhaps even questioning whether such an event can be said to be in the past.

Going to the theater to see *points of departure*, then, is not a reparative act. Although Garcés's strategies bear the risk of distancing audience members not experienced with nonrealistic dramaturgy, his experimentation is productive. *Points of departure* conveys how memory, identity, and selfhood are experienced affectively in the midst of crisis and "after" it. The lack of a clear end to suffering inhibits our sympathy—not because the characters in the second act are mere victims, but because sympathy is no longer the point. We are asked instead to immerse ourselves so as to understand the affects of everyday neoliberal violence and, at the same time, to comprehend that this affective reality is an unending neoliberal condition. This type of spectatorship is hard work; it is exhausting (as Joy Goodwin would certainly agree!). But it is also a lesson in learning to listen—differently.

It is telling that after working with Sna and drafting this play, Garcés was hired to be the artistic director of Cornerstone Theater in Los Angeles, a theater long known for creating works with and through listening to communities. It is also no surprise that not long into his tenure he staged *Los Illegals*, a collaboratively created work with documented and undocumented people, about the subject of immigration and labor politics. This work was quite different in form from *points of departure*. Yet, one can see how Garces's experience of Chiapas and his affective staging of the experience of migration make their way into *Los Illegals*. As is often the case with Cornerstone's work, Garcés used a classical text as an inspiration. In this instance, the play is *Fuenteovejuna*, Lope de Vega's play about a community protecting a person accused of a crime by refusing to let him take sole responsibility for it. In *Los Illegals*, the plot is similar: a group of day laborers prevent one member of their community from being accused of a trumped-up charge of assault against a right-wing protester. Alongside this very linear plot, however, are the travel narratives of two migrants—one, Rosenda, who is inside a truck (*adentro*), and the other, Javier, who is crossing outside (*afuera*). These monologues serve as a counterpoint for the struggles of those who have already arrived. Their speeches, like Petrona's, are often fragmented and allusive, walking around rather than spelling out the experience and trauma of the liminal state of transport. They are both delusional and not. Both characters' ability to move is also stymied—Rosenda is stuffed into a truck with others and has nowhere to go; the brutality of the heat makes Javier's forward movement nearly impossible. Both characters, however, embody a kind of agitated stasis. Rosenda embodies a "tremulousness" that "builds into a shudder."[145] As described by Garcés, Rosenda, at some point, "begins to cough spasmodically . . . set[ting] off an explosive wave of coughing around her. It rises, then slowly ebbs."[146] Her embodied trauma is affective rather than emotional for her and the audience. The audience, then, is forced to reckon with the economic violence she faces not through her explanation of it, but through being co-present with her experience of it. This suffering is not individuated but spread upon a mass of other migrants, who become a chorus of coughing. At the end of his journey, Javier also embodies said violence as he struggles in the hot sun. He "stands, vibrating in the air, just able to keep his balance," exemplifying the disorientation of the grueling experience of migration.[147] This disorientation is also present at the end of the play, when Rosenda enters the work center with the other characters, disoriented, but alive.[148] We do not know what happens to Javier, however.[149] He does not arrive to the world the rest of the characters inhabit, although the actor who plays him is lit onstage in subsequent scenes so that the audience remembers Javier. This indeterminacy suggests an elongated experience of migration, beyond the actual crossing as well as the possibility that one may never arrive.

Pointedly, Garcés staged Eduardo Machado's *Kissing Fidel* about Special Period Cuba in the same INTAR season as *points of departure*, which was not long after he took over Cornerstone. The overlaps in theatrical tactics suggested a shared rather than divergent experience of migration by Mexicans, Central Americans, and Cubans. Garcés's divergence from action-oriented dramaturgy made his audiences feel the particular stuckness of migrants throughout the Americas. As I elaborate in the next chapter, this structure of feeling bleeds into his direction of *Kissing Fidel* and *Havana Is Waiting*, two plays about Special Period Cuba. In my analysis, I engage the idea of the impasse in modes that Lauren Berlant has perhaps not anticipated, asking us to think about what a truly transnational critique of cruel optimism would look like in the neoliberal Americas.

Chapter 2

Havana Is (Not) Waiting: Staging the Impasse in Cuban American Drama about Cuba's Special Period

At a talk back after a matinee performance of Eduardo Machado's *Kissing Fidel*, I asked Michael John Garcés about his experience of directing the play, which had an unsettling feel. In contrast to the set, which depicted the lobby of a funeral home with well-appointed seats, an elegant coffee machine, and a wall of red roses, the experience of *Kissing Fidel* was neither restful nor calming. Garcés revealed that the way he created the frenetic feel of the play was to never let the actors sit down for more than a few seconds whenever they were onstage.[1] The effect was a jittery but caged movement where everyone moved, but no one went anywhere. *Kissing Fidel*'s tremulous movement was different in pace than *points of departure*, but the feeling of getting nowhere in confined space despite constant attempts to escape resonated deeply. Both plays, quite simply, made me feel quite tense, while stopping short of making me feel any particular emotions for the characters: an affective mélange. Playwright and director Michael John Garcés has the distinction of having directed all of Cuban American playwright Eduardo Machado's three full-length plays about Special Period Cuba: *Havana Is Waiting* (2001), *The Cook* (2003), and *Kissing Fidel* (2005) in the lead up to finalizing *points of departure* in spring 2006. Thus, despite the fact that as writers Machado and Garcés could not be more different—Garcés's plot-resistant sparse poeticism is as far from Machado's baroque and sentimental Ibsenism as it could be—because Garcés directed them, Machado's and Garcés's plays feel similar. Garcés's experience directing a production of Nilo Cruz's *A Bicycle Country* in 2000 only deepened his connection to the depiction of movement of the Special Period. Going backward from *departure* into Garcés's choreography of the Special Period reveals how U.S.-authored theater about this era in Cuba attenuates affect in the present as a neoliberal condition. This turn of phrase, of course, comes from Lauren Berlant's *Cruel Optimism*, as does my theorization of the impasse.

73

Cruel Optimism is a tour de force in affect studies and an important work of neoliberal critique that engages U.S. and European cultural production articulating the failed promises of late liberal capitalism. Berlant's assertion that the (neoliberal) historical is felt affectively before it is understood in any other way is an especially fruitful observation for thinking about Latinx theater under neoliberalism, particularly Cuban America drama. Cuban American drama seems to be an odd place to introduce Berlant's theorization given the very different historical circumstances within which Cuba has developed as a socialist exception to neoliberal capital. Yet, Cuba has not entirely exiled itself from capital in the last twenty years, making Berlant's observations all the more relevant. None of the plays in this chapter mention neoliberalism by name, but all of them render neoliberal experience, particularly postrevolutionary neoliberal experience, vividly in how they move and feel. Instead of our pain coming from cyclical reactions to a singular traumatic event in the past, today's affective reality is an attenuated low-level reaction to a continued anxiety-provoking set of conditions in the Americas. This is what Berlant calls a "crisis ordinariness" that features constant battles to survive, increased militarization of borders, and attempts to move on to somewhere where conditions might change (but might not).[2] Berlant's departure from trauma theory, with its dependence on wounding events, is instructive because it suggests that our reaction to changed economic and political opportunities has a different durational reality.

Berlant's objects of study are very different from those considered in this book. She concentrates on film and novels from the United States and Europe, both of which formerly enjoyed wealthy welfare states. Thus, most of her subjects suffer under the demise of formerly functioning infrastructure, a luxury of loss many Latinx Americans know little about. Berlant does not consider cultural production by U.S. Latinx persons or Latin Americans nor does she wrestle with the particular legacies of colonialism they render. She also does not engage theater in any way in the book. In fact, her grasp on theatricality is metaphorical rather than methodological. When she uses the language of method acting it is outside of the realm of theatrical production. That said, despite the differences between Berlant's subjects of study and mine, her link between the aesthetics of affect and the neoliberal condition is productive for investigating Cuban American dramas of the Special Period. Her conceptual frame also helps illuminate the way severe deprivation is rendered temporally and kinesthetically within them. In combination with registering a departure from revolutionary teleology discussed in the previous chapter and a penchant for queering time, the plays I consider here create affective environments that articulate a mode of processing experience that contrasts with exilic paradigms of the past, which trafficked in nostalgia, distance, and paralysis as ways of coping while waiting for Cuba's communist regime to fall. These new travelogues feature inhibited but constant motion, unsuccessful trips home, and new modes of waiting that have nothing to do with outlasting Castro. Their dramaturgical innovations are met with theatrical techniques that immerse audience members in the contemporary experience of neoliberal life, including precarious trips across the ocean *and* quotidian modes of migration and movement. This combination of features was seemingly confusing to critics who wanted what they did not find: consistent characterization, independence from ideological debate, normative representations of straight and gay sexuality, linear plot development, and, of course, more *action*. I argue that the very problems that these reviews decry are by and large the political and aesthetic strengths of the work I consider. A short history of Cuban migration to the United States, including the shifts in immigration policy that made Cubans economic migrants rather than welcomed exiles, is necessary to understand the changing shape of these representations.

Cuba in the Special Period

> In recent weeks the Castro regime has encouraged Cubans to take to the sea in unsafe vessels to escape their nation's internal problems. In so doing, it has risked the lives of thousands of Cubans, and several have already died in their efforts to leave. This action is a cold-blooded attempt to maintain the Castro grip on Cuba and to divert attention from failed communist policies. He is trying to export to the United States the political and economic crises he has created in Cuba, in defiance of the democratic tide flowing throughout the region.
> —Bill Clinton[3]

Bill Clinton's speech came at the pinnacle of the Balseros (Rafter) Crisis of 1994, which he was desperate to resolve. Although Cubans had been risking their lives by attempting to cross the sea between the island and Key West for some time, the number of people who made the attempt escalated in 1993, as the Cuban economy worsened. In 1994 the exodus was even more severe. Some 30,000 left by August of that year, causing domestic and international crisis. Responding to the unrest in the streets of Havana and perhaps trying to "bleed his country of dissidents," on August 13, 1994, Castro announced on Cuban television that he would "allow" Cubans to leave Cuba for the United States.[4] Given that the Cuban government did not let its citizens travel to the United States easily—visas were difficult to obtain and the government forbade illegal exits, often violently detaining those who attempted them—Castro's gesture was as dramatic as the rafters' crossings were.[5] Six days after Castro's order, Clinton stemmed the tide of Cuban rafters coming to the United States by ordering that rafters caught at sea by the U.S. Coast Guard would be sent to a safe haven in Guantánamo to await repatriation to

Cuba.⁶ While Clinton ultimately accepted many of the rafters into the United States as part of a compromise made with the Cuban government, if they were rescued at sea outside of Cuban controlled waters this policy ultimately denied them the automatic status of political refugees that they had previously enjoyed under the 1966 Cuban Adjustment Act.⁷

The Balseros Crisis was the culmination of a desperate situation in Cuba during the era Castro named the Special Period in Time of Peace (1990–ca. 2005) when malnutrition was endemic and the country came to rely on the dollarization of the economy to survive.⁸ Once dollars became legal tender in Cuba, Cubans drove cabs, gave tours, and engaged in prostitution to make those dollars, which could allow them to survive in the midst of the crumbling economy. Those who did not have dollars continued to suffer. It is no surprise that desire to leave Cuba escalated around this time. Called "Mariel II" by the U.S. press, the mass exodus on rafts by Cubans during 1993 and 1994 replayed the 1980 exodus from the port of Mariel during which the United States accepted 10,000 Cubans from the island. In 1980, President Jimmy Carter agreed to find space for those who left (despite their categorization as "entrants"), and it was a costly political move.⁹ Unlike those who left during the Mariel exodus, however, the *balseros* left not only on large boats, but also on rafts made of scavenged materials with various degrees of resilience.¹⁰ It has been estimated that only one of three rafters made it to the other shore during the journeys undertaken in 1993–94.¹¹ To make things worse, after August 1994, the *balseros* had to make it to shore to apply for citizenship. From late 1994 to 1995, when they were released from Guantánamo, the *balseros* were literally adrift—facing persecution if they went back to Cuba, horrible living conditions if they ended up at Guantánamo, and an uncertain fate if they managed to make it to the United States.¹²

While scholars disagree about the extent to which Clinton's legislation represented a break with previous policies, the new categorization of Cuban Americans as entrants or migrants instead of exiles was a perceptible and real paradigm shift.¹³ For the rafters, who often identified as *balseros* rather than as Cubans, this experience constructed their identities by their mode of travel rather than by their national origin, marking mobility as a mode of self-definition.¹⁴ This form of self-definition, affected but not completely circumscribed by the regulations mentioned above, made the *balsero* into a literal and figurative border crosser.¹⁵ Their experiences were not that different from their Mexican and Central American counterparts. For example, at Guantánamo, the border between the United States and Cuba was on land. Some desperate rafters crossed the line to go back to Cuba rather than waiting for entry into the United States. The strange combination of the liminality of identity and place (especially within the camps at Guantánamo) and the clearly wrought violence of the nation-state made the borderlands' *herida abierta* (open wound) the heritage of Cuban *balseros* as well as Mexican *mojados* (an often derogatory term for Mexican migrants). In addition, as many of those who left were fleeing not only political oppression but also malnutrition, poverty, and impossible living conditions brought on by a near collapse of the Cuban economy after the fall of the Soviet Union, they shared more with the "illegal immigrants" of the Americas than ever before.[16] Indeed, many U.S. citizens viewed the *balseros* in much the same way as they did migrants: as unwelcome intruders.[17]

It is no coincidence that the 1994 passage of the North American Free Trade Agreement (NAFTA) and the Balseros (Rafter) Crisis occurred within months of each other. Although trade liberalization and the emergence of market economies in formerly socialist states had been occurring throughout the '70s and '80s, the expression of these movements in North America as a factor of mobility came to fruition in the mid-1990s. Both NAFTA and the Balseros Crisis marked immobilities and mobilities as part(s) of a global (and globalizing) neoliberal project—whose architects promoted free trade and privatization as the cure-alls for economic development. And, as Bill Clinton's comments about "exporting" political crisis unwittingly reveals, the discourse of trade had infiltrated all aspects on international policy, including migration, exposing its contradictions along the way. NAFTA, of course, allowed goods to travel more freely between Mexico, the United States, and Canada, while the militarization of the U.S.-Mexico border continued, inhibiting the movement of Mexicans over their northern border.[18] Xenophobic measures such as California's Proposition 187 (1994), which denied social services to undocumented workers, followed soon after. Meanwhile, travel restrictions for U.S. citizens going to Cuba were briefly relaxed in 1993 and 1999, allowing many Cuban Americans to travel to the island for the first time in their adult lives.

The dramatic conditions of the Balseros Crisis and the complementary opening up of travel to Cuba for Cuban Americans in the 1990s mobilized many Cuban American playwrights to encounter contemporary Cuba for the first time, or for the first time in a long time. While U.S. politicians encouraged said travel in the interest of "spreading democracy" on the island through human-to-human contact, Cuban American playwrights used the opportunity to confront the reality of contemporary Cuba.[19]

This was not the first time that Cuban American theater had taken on the return to Cuba. The openness of the late Carter presidency also allowed many Cuban Americans to go back to the island. The plays that resulted from these contacts depict homecomings in which Cuban and Cuban American family members confront each other and their respective ideologies head on.[20] Nonetheless, the emphasis on travel in plays written during Cuba's Special Period makes them quite different from their predecessors. Unlike the plays from the 1970s, the more recent works always depict the travel to and from Cuba—whether or not the characters' destination is reached. And they theorize that travel as a crucial part of Cuban American imagining of Cuba and Cuban (American) identities. In fact, many of these plays function as travelogues that document their authors' movement to and from Cuba during the 1990s. I see these late 1990s plays as a watershed movement during which Cuban American authors also became border crossers. Their ability to traverse national and cultural borders within greater Cuba make them foils to the *balseros*, whose border crossing was much more difficult and dangerous. How these playwrights depicted this travel onstage reimagines the idea of the travelogue. Rather than following the formula articulated by Michel de Certeau, where the circular journey through difference is enacted in order to establish the self, these plays displace self-knowledge.[21] The narration of how a Cuban American becomes oneself more fully through contact with mainland Cuba is left by the wayside in the face of the actual experience of Cuba. This departure is also one that veers from a standard trope of Latinx drama in which Latinx subjects learn their identity as Latinx (as opposed to Latin American) through such a journey.[22] The decision to depict travel is in some sense controversial for an audience for whom one's Cuban-ness or Cuban American-ness is predicated on not traveling to the island as a matter of political principle. In plays staged within a strictly exilic frame, Cuba remains frozen in earlier era, its authors refusing to acknowledge what has happened since the revolution as anything other than a betrayal. The inability to move in the earlier plays—used metaphorically and literally—is an impasse, but not the impasse that Lauren Berlant describes. The exilic impasse enacts what Alex Vasquez calls the "cynical stasis" that haunts Cuban exilic literature, including some of Machado's earlier plays.[23] The new impasse, more in concert with Berlant's, depicts constant motion without forward movement—anxiety without nostalgia—a form of kinesthetic embodiment that resonates deeply with the larger set of difficulties faced in the neoliberal Americas. This type of motion is rendered theatrically to great effect because of, rather than despite, the limitations of the stage.

Theatrical Depictions of the *Balseros*: Rehearsing Ambiguity and Failed Motion

> He, who goes out to sea
> on a raft
> risks his life.
> And the life
> of his children,
> of his wife.
> —María Irene Fornés, *Balseros/Manual for a Desperate Crossing*

Theatrical depictions of the Balseros Crisis first appeared in 1996 and continued ardently through 2005. *Rites of Passage*, the first English-language play about the Balseros Crisis, was written by Loretta Greco, a Miami native.[24] The *balseros'* journeys also captured the imagination of María Irene Fornés, who used a similar technique to create *Manual for a Desperate Crossing (Balseros)*, which premiered at the Florida Grand Opera in Miami in 1997. Other plays soon followed. After a workshop production as part of the Brown University New Plays Festival, Jorge Cortiñas's *Sleepwalkers* premiered at Area Stage in Miami in 1999, later moving on to Atlanta; Caridad Svich's *Prodigal Kiss* premiered at the Key West Theatre Festival in October 1999; Nilo Cruz's *A Bicycle Country* premiered in December 1999 at Florida Stage and went on to the Coconut Grove. In addition, Eduardo Machado's *Kissing Fidel*, set in Miami but featuring a *balsero*, was produced by New York's INTAR theater in fall 2005 (although Machado began writing it in 1997). It is notable that workshops aside, all of these plays except for *Kissing Fidel* were performed in South Florida before traveling elsewhere—a point I will return to later. The plays themselves take place at different points in the crisis and have various vantage points and settings. *Balseros* is an opera that takes place almost entirely on the sea and has no marker of time in its stage directions. *Prodigal Kiss* also has no marked time frame. Although it begins on the sea, it soon moves to land, crisscrossing its way from the southeastern United States to the West Coast and back. Two of these plays stage action before the official Balseros Crisis of 1994, although after the rafters began to take off from Cuba in rafts. *Sleepwalkers* takes place in Havana in 1993; Nilo Cruz's *A Bicycle Country* occurs on land and at sea "before the U.S. intervention on the Cuban rafters."[25] Machado's play *Kissing Fidel* takes place during the height of the Balseros Crisis in August 1994. Machado's subsequent play, *Havana Is Waiting*, involves protests in Cuba demanding the return of rafter Elián González, who arrived in the United States in November 1999. Neither the U.S. intervention on the rafters nor their confinement in Guantánamo is ever shown in any of the plays. What are shown, however, are difficult crossings and stalled travel, complete with renderings of the borderlands of the Florida Straits. The cumulative power of these early plays is their representation of the move away from Cuban exceptionalism and toward an understanding of the *balsero* as migrant.

The plays that were first produced largely center on travel itself. *Balseros/Manual for a Desperate Crossing* depicts the journey to the United States, admittedly unidirectionally, so as to expose the violence of the Cuban American borderlands. The play followed the *balseros* across the sea, documenting their methods of survival. *Balseros*'s set, designed by Jorge Alberto Fernandez Suarez, included a large platform in the middle of the stage designed to rock back and forth like a raft, with a motion so violent, according to a feature article on the play, that the singers had a hard time performing on it.[26] The motionless motion of the raft that rocks in place but does not move forward created the seemingly vertiginous feeling of the ocean: the feeling of being adrift. Even when motion of the raft was violent, it seemed as if one were going nowhere because the raft largely moved side to side. The very labor of performing the play was a difficult crossing for the actors as well as the characters. More material than metaphorical, this simple set portrayed the limited mobility of both the *balseros* and those who played them, evincing a general sense of unease.

This unease is echoed at the end of the play when the image of the blurred boundaries is taken in by the *balseros* who made the crossing. When describing colors they see, the rafters recall being in the middle of the sea:

> It's not the blue
> It's a blue green
> Which can only be seen
> in the calm of the sea.
> It's
> a transparent green
> almost white
> White-green.
> And it's difficult to tell
> where the sea ends
> and the sky begins.[27]

The liminal area between sea and sky embedded in Fornés's characters' recounting of their travel experience suggests that the fearfully blurred realities of their trip across the sea, often referred to in plays and novels about *balseros*, isn't completely erased by their having made it to Key West and drinking a cold Coke (a symbol of American dominance and capitalist pleasure par excellence) even though that liminality is displaced to a poetic description. This liminality would remain in subsequent depictions as well.

Like *Balseros*, Nilo Cruz's *A Bicycle Country* functions as a travelogue of limited mobility. Infused with Fornésian sensibility, the play also follows a journey across the ocean, but with more attention to the borders of the sea. Its title references the imported Chinese bicycles that took over the island when gasoline shortages were rampant and alternative forms of transportation were necessary. The play follows three Cubans who decide to leave the island. Broken into four parts, titled after the elements land, water, fire, and air, *A Bicycle Country* is also bifurcated. The first half of the play takes place on land, before the group of three leaves; the second half of the play is at sea. Each of the characters has a different relationship to the possibility of leaving. Pepe was left by his lover, who went to the United States on a raft; Ines wants to leave herself, having tried before; Julio, having recently had a stroke, cannot leave at all. When the characters are on land, they have long conversations about going or staying, whether by bicycle, raft, or on foot.

A Bicycle Country is predicated on the gradual relinquishing of mobility on land to gain mobility at sea. Ines takes Pepe's bicycle in scene 3, and although she returns riding it in scene 4, it is gone by scene 5. We never see Ines sell the bicycle, but we assume she bartered it to get a raft. Cruz also foregrounds (im)mobility in other scenes. The first stage direction introduces Julio, "standing, strapped to a wooden board with a rope," an image which recalls an image of a raft while also underscoring his inability to move.[28] Julio's description of his lack of mobility due to his stroke mixes metaphors of land and sea to suture his practical and psychic impediments. Using disability as metaphor for the Cuban situation, Cruz, in a squarely Fornésian vein, has Julio explain his predicament:

> JULIO: You want me to throw myself to the sea—look at me! How can I put myself in a little raft, of a truck tire, when I can't walk well enough?
>
> Can't you see I am drowning! I am sinking in my own body. I am sitting here on solid ground and I am drowning.
>
> (*Julio wheels himself out of the room. There is a pause. Ines looks at Pepe.*)
>
> PEPE: (*Taking his bag*) I'll come by later. (*He starts to exit.*)
> INES: Pepe, what is this thing he has that won't allow him to move forward?
>
> (*Lights change.*)[29]

If the play does indeed question Julio's inability to move forward as a character flaw vis-à-vis the conventions of psychological drama, his literal immobility as well as the theatricalized immobility of others undermines this simple reading. For example, when the trio moves to the sea, limited mobility is again highlighted. After five hours of rowing, Ines claims that she feels like they "haven't moved a bit."[30]

Notably, *A Bicycle Country* marks the rafters' passage as a traversal of the borderlands, with the blurring of reality, identity, and truth common to that experience. Yet like crossings within the U.S.-Mexico borderlands, the liminality that living in the U.S.-Cuba borderlands affords is constructed and constricted by the violence of the nation-state. It is important to note that the play takes place before the U.S. intervention, and thus once Pepe, Ines, and Julio leave land they are simply *balseros*—not migrants as they would be after August 1994, or exiles or refugees as they would be if they reached the other shore before that date. Cruz is also careful to point out that there are clear borders in the sea as well as on land, both before and after the crisis. When Pepe tries to keep Ines rowing by telling her that she needs to pass the "picket line" after which "[t]here'll be ships, the American Coast Guard.

Balloons . . . ," he references an expired borderline.[31] In reality, when the play was written, the borders had changed such that those found in the watery expanse Ines and Pepe traveled were afforded no protections. They would not have been welcomed with open arms, as his audience in Florida surely would have been aware.

This dramatic irony exposes the present dangers of the crossing by recalling a more idyllic past; and it points to the fact that the Cubans will come to share more with border crossers by land than they might have shared with earlier generations of exiles.

Caridad Svich's *Prodigal Kiss*, in contrast to Fornés's and Cruz's plays, takes place almost entirely on land. *Prodigal Kiss* has an ugliness the other plays lack, making it less amenable to viewers who support mainstream U.S. ideologies. Svich effectively erases, rather than simply questioning, Cuban exceptionalism by framing her lead characters' journey within a transnational history of migration. Framed as a pilgrimage to Santiago, the play traces Marcela's journey to New Jersey by way of San Diego, intersecting with the paths of other diasporic Latino/a Americans looking for their own Santiagos. The protagonist begins the play on a "slim board in the middle of the ocean," singing about going to Cuba as she is moving away from it.[32] Soon, however, she is in a field of saw grass in Florida alongside Ignacio, a fellow traveler whose appearance as "poorly clothed and uncomfortably sunburnt" references the infamous conditions of the rafters.[33]

Like the actual rafters, no matter where Marcela goes she remains defined by her nomadic movements. Svich states: "Marcela, the woman at the center of this play, is *in transit*. Part of her is in Cuba, part of her in the United States. This play is an exploration of the split in her soul."[34] Writing the story of immigration through the movements of a *balsera* is a particular act, which links the *balseros*' particular identity with a larger sense of alienation and longing common to many immigrant groups. Svich's depiction interrogates the particularity of the *balsera* experience, even though she respects the material reality of Marcela's present life. The scarcity that her *balsera* character experiences references the very different circumstances that Cuban migrants to the United States in the 1980s and 1990s lived under. From the Mariel boatlift forward, Cuban migrants had a more difficult time mimicking the entrepreneurial pursuits of earlier generations of exiles. Shifts in economic possibility in combination with racial and class discrimination combined to dampen the economic advancement heralded by earlier generations and the narrative of success key to Cuban American identity.

Svich's depictions of travel, then, place all migrations under neoliberalism within the frame of a *balsera*'s journey *after* she leaves the raft. This choice disrupts the border between exile and immigrant so embedded in separating Cuban and other Latino/a migrants' experiences of the United States. This intervention is clearly personal for Svich. *Prodigal Kiss*'s appearance at a particular point in the late 1990s is no coincidence: difficult travel was constitutive of many Latinx identities at this time as was a lack of economic and social advancement. We see in Svich's play a certain mode of precariousness faced by many marginalized groups before they were felt by the U.S. middle class. Svich renders this precariousness as a form of nomadism and homelessness in the United States. While her play's mode of representation is not as purely affective as Cortiñas's and Machado's are, *Prodigal Kiss* effectively emits a feeling of displacement which is not exilic; it is rooted in trying to belong, to move through a boatless harbor, to try to enter a home on a snowy day without a coat to keep one warm. Marcela is forced to become a subaltern of sorts, as Anne García-Romero suggests; García-Romero reads her journey as a failed acculturation to Anglo norms.[35] While I acknowledge how the play traces a journey into (and out of) identity, it is also a movement into the precarious existence of the 1990s migrant who, rather than settling in, assimilating, and becoming successful, is left out in the cold by the neoliberal modes of life in the United States.[36] Finding herself amid waste, like the discarded French fries she tries to eat out of desperation, she must continually work to avoid becoming waste herself. And this requires constant movement. Even when she is at rest at the end of the play, she has not found a home. She is left standing. She simply places her red sash on the ground to mark her presence while the sound and lights fade. Her aunt's letter is recited from memory, but her aunt is now dead, so even the home promised there is gone. And, like the other *balsero* plays, we are left with a "band of blue and green laid out flatly against the sky."[37] This theatrical enactment of ambiguity is a reference and a genealogical link between the plays, resolving into a lack of resolution, embedded in all Cuban American drama about this subject. It should also be noted that Fornés's, Svich's, and Cruz's depictions of ambiguity and motionlessness set the stage for the more radical temporal and queer interventions Eduardo Machado and Jorge Cortiñas make in the works I consider in the next section, in which the authors explore the Special Period in Cuba as an affective experience that undoes both capitalist progressive and revolutionary teleological time.

Queering the Impasse: Eduardo Machado's Travelogues

"The Horizon is a Line No One Can Cross"
—Jorge Cortiñas, *Sleepwalkers*

Cuban exilic paradigms are predicated on the inability and/or unwillingness to travel to the island.[38] The opening up of travel in the 1990s, combined with the willingness of certain Cuban Americans to travel, fostered the emergence of plays about that very experience in the form of a traditional travelogue from the United States to Cuba and back. The best known of these plays, in academia, at least, is Carmelita Tropicana's biographical *Leche de Amnesia* (1993), which chronicles Alina Troyano's trip to Havana in the Special Period, during which she visits her childhood home.[39] In this section, however, I concentrate on two plays by Eduardo Machado, written after his journey home to Cuba, which reveal how the temporal condition of stalled travel functions as an epistemological tool to explain the affective experience of mobility under neoliberalism. Machado's queer (in the most multivalent sense of the term) travelogues interrogate the temporal assumptions of both exilic and Cuban revolutionary teleology. And in doing so, they sketch out the contours of Berlant's idea of the impasse with a specifically Cuban outlook. I quote her description at length:

> I offer impasse both as a formal term for encountering the duration of the present, and a specific term for tracking the circulation of precariousness through diverse locales and bodies. The concept of the present as impasse opens up different ways that the interruption of norms of the reproduction of life can be adapted to, felt out and lived. The impasse is a space of time lived without a narrative genre. Adaptation to it usually involves a gesture or undramatic action that points to and revises an unresolved solution. One takes a *pass* to avoid something or get somewhere; it's a formal figure of transit. But the impasse is a *cul-de-sac*, indeed, the word *impasse* was invented to replace *cul-de-sac* with its untoward implications in French. In a cul de sac one keeps moving, but one moves paradoxically in the *same space*. An impasse is a holding station that doesn't hold securely, but opens out unto anxiety, that doggypaddling around a space whose contours remain obscure.[40]

I gesture to Berlant here to show how Eduardo Machado extends her observations in specifically theatrical ways.

Although it did not debut until fall 2005, Eduardo Machado started *Kissing Fidel* in 1997, before he returned to Cuba for the first time in over thirty years. When Machado picked it up again after his visit in 2000 he cut five characters and rewrote it so that the man who wanted to travel to Cuba to "kiss Fidel" was Oscar Marques, the notorious hysteric from his famous tetralogy, *The Floating Island Plays*. *Kissing Fidel*'s action takes place on August 14, 1994, the night before the *fictional* burial of Oscar's grandmother Cusa, and just after Castro allowed people to leave on August 13 (notably, also Castro's birthday.)

Kissing Fidel stages the many conflicts of the Marques family over the course of one night in the lobby of a very chic Cuban funeral home in Miami.[41] Although people come and go to view the corpse offstage throughout the night, as often as not they just make their way around the lobby toward the coffee machine. As I suggested at the beginning of this chapter, director Michael John Garcés demanded this nonstop stage movement. He also asked set designer Mikiko Suzuki to create a space where lingering would be unwelcome.[42] As more coffee is consumed at the viewing of Cusa's body, the characters get more and more jittery despite the free-flowing Valium. The confrontations that occur over the course of the night reveal that the family is as dysfunctional as ever: the characters' escalating energy fuels the emergence of old family conflicts, a series of volatile confessions, and the rehearsal of more than one old love affair. After Daniel meets his uncle Oscar for the first time, he confesses his love; Oscar, in turn, makes out with his aunt. In addition, Oscar tells his relatives he is going to Cuba to kiss Fidel and thirty-year-old Daniel, freed of his inhibitions, proclaims that he is both gay and a Democrat. No one in the family can decide which is worse.

This constant movement in a confined space does more than nurture familial tension, however. It also serves to expose restlessness as a possible frame for understanding the play's contemporary moment: emotionally, historically, spiritually, and physically. The characters want to move on but they can't; their momentum is in traction, and they are left to bounce off of the walls and off of each other. On a spiritual level, Oscar is passing on to another world just as his deceased grandmother is, but they both are temporarily and intentionally delayed on their way to their final destinations. The funeral home itself signals a liminal zone between life and death—it is an in-between space where anything can happen. The juxtaposition of Oscar's impending trip to Cuba and his grandmother's to the afterlife underscores the bracketed temporality of the play. Their containment is stalled motion rather than complete stasis; they may be able to move on—literally and otherwise—if only they can get through the night.

More successful in getting where he wants to go is Oscar's cousin Ismael, who makes it to the funeral home just in time to meet his cousin, whose novels he loves. Ismael enters the room sunburned, dirty, and nearly delirious from his ninety-mile raft trip, falling asleep on the floor soon after he performs an enthusiastic hip-hop routine.[43] No longer Cuban, yet not yet American, neither emigrant nor exile, he too is in a liminal space, just like Oscar and Cusa. *Kissing Fidel* reveals the material consequences of moving between worlds. While Oscar's family is pleased with Ismael's criticism of censorship on the island, his desperate appearance, admission of having engaged in prostitution, and lack of interest in a mainstream job leaves much to be desired. By substituting an expected departure with an unexpected arrival, *Kissing Fidel* suggests the possibility of moving on without dismissing the messiness of U.S.-Cuban politics, which in this play is exacerbated by Miami's contact with Cuba rather than by its lack of it. An ironic take on this family reconciliation act—the term sometimes given to cessations in draconian travel restrictions between the United States and Cuba—*Kissing Fidel* links the Balseros Crisis to U.S.-Cuban travel to the island. The connections Machado draws show that difficult travel moves both ways, even if the consequences are greater for those who travel from Cuba.

There is also the issue of time, which begs more attention. Beyond the play's religious overtones, its temporal maneuvers revise revolutionary teleology. Ricardo Ortiz writes eloquently about this issue in relation to Machado's *Floating Island Plays*, which, in his view, articulate a kind of historical contretemps that "performs the tragic fallout of a missed historical rendezvous between the two chief forces, revolution and exile, marking Cuban time, and making (impossible) Cuban history, since 1959." Ortiz also ventures to consider how these plays, which were written in the 1980s, but revised for production in the mid-1990s, reflect upon the historiographical exigencies of the Special Period, a time that even Castro admits "could take on names other than Revolution."[44] Ortiz concentrates primarily on one of the four plays, *Fabiola*, which takes place before and after the revolution, following the Marques and Ripoll families as they deal with the death of the eponymous character.[45] Although Fabiola died in 1954, her widower, Pedro, is still full of grief, and the rest of the family is filled with anxiety, in part because her body disappeared from the family mausoleum. As Ortiz himself makes clear, one does not have to stretch far to read Fabiola as Cuba and to see the family dramas that include incest as a familial exilic set of perversions in full allegorical form.[46] *Fabiola*, after all, introduces Osvaldo and his brother Pedro's sexual and romantic relationship in the wake of Fabiola's death. This relationship haunts the rest of the plays. Fabiola's absent presence as a ghost sends erotic rumbles through the rest of the family. Although we never see the body—making it literally obscene in a theatrical sense—and only understand its sensual presence, we do learn that Fabiola's body never decomposed in the years after her death, deepening the uncanny alliance between the idea of Fabiola as a Catholic saint, a Cuban analogue, and an erotic ghost.[47] Ortiz's thoughts on this play articulate how these queer moments mark "queer moments," where temporality plays tricks on revolution, gesturing theatrically to "*Fabiola*'s play and dance, as *performance* with time and history."[48]

Here, however, I wish to return to *Kissing Fidel*, which I read as the fifth *Floating Island* play and a Special Period response to *Fabiola*. If, as Ortiz convincingly argues, the earlier plays looked critically at the idea of revolution and exile, *Kissing Fidel* assumes a post-Revolutionary and potentially postexilic paradigm in search of another way. Unlike the earlier works, the Revolution is not central to this play, nor is its mode of teleological fruition. The play pointedly moves us away from thinking revolution as well as teleology. Oscar, although he prides himself on the truth of his writing, claims that he does not have the guts to be a revolutionary. Ismael's retort, "no, you do not," also refers to Ismael himself. Even if his poetry was revolutionary in Cuba, it won't be in the United States. His family's desire to make him into a bourgeois subject will most certainly act against his fantasy. More pointedly, just as Fabiola's death/persistence can be read as the death/persistence of a *fabula*—a story about Cuba—Cusa's death and funeral could be read as the death and funeral of Cuba. This death is in effect the recognition that the Special Period marks the end of the exilic dream wherein the fall of socialism would necessitate Castro's fall. At the time Machado revised *Kissing Fidel* in 2005, ten years after the Balseros Crisis and a few more into the Special Period, this recognition was commonplace. If we take August 14, 1994, after midnight as the true time of the play, we are forced to recognize its proximity to August 13, Fidel's birthday: a day of festivity that marks the persistence of the rhetoric of revolution and Fidel's persistence. Cusa's death occurs simultaneously with the Balseros Crisis, inscribing the same persistence/demise dichotomy that Fabiola's corpse represents.

Rather than simply point out the death of the dream of a post-Castro Cuba, however, Machado calls on us to queer the Balseros Crisis and the Special Period so as to see the opportunity for new forms of relation, even in the midst of neoliberal scarcity. He does this dramaturgically by triangulating Fabiola's body not just with Cusa's but also with Ismael the *balsero*'s. Ismael, it should be noted, references a son of Abraham, who was cast out with his mother Hagar and nearly died in the desert. He was saved when his mother had a vision of water. This name is also given to the character in Herman Melville's *Moby-Dick* who must go to sea. Never one to avoid an allusion, Machado stages Ismael's journey to the United States such that it ends about two days after Castro allowed the rafters to leave Cuba, almost mirroring the time from the crucifixion to the resurrection of Christ.[49] This means that Ismael is in a liminal space and ripe for a resurrection when he arrives at the funeral home.

Kissing Fidel clearly lays out the stakes of the liminal body under the migratory disciplinary apparatus, which escalated under this era of neoliberal capital. Ismael is neither Cuban nor American; Cusa's body is neither in heaven nor on earth. Machado places them in a kind of purgatory reserved previously for Fabiola. Ismael, a wayward son, also inhabits a liminal space between death and life, like Cuba in the Special Period, and migrants stuck within and between disciplinary apparatuses in the contemporary moment. Ismael is alternately treated like the living or transformed into the dead *theatrically*, meaning that Ismael's instantiation as a corpse is literally staged, rather than gestured to metaphorically or symbolically. This process occurs when his family attempts to "clean him up" after he passes out from exhaustion on the floor of the funeral home. I quote this section at length to show this transformation from sleeping recent arrival to corpse:

> MIRIAM: Not on the floor, no! He is going to dirty the tiles.
> DANIEL: Let him sleep on the floor, Mamá.
> MIRIAM: We have to clean him up my guests cannot see a cousin of mine looking like this.
> DANIEL: But he escaped a tyrant.
> MIRIAM: That's not a reason to smell.

(Ismael is now asleep)

YOLANDA: The boys should take his clothes off.
MIRIAM: Yes.
DANIEL: So the guests can see him naked?
OSCAR: Maybe after they see the size of his cock, they will want to give him a job.
YOLANDA: Don't be vulgar.
MIRIAM: The mortician sells suits for the corpses and paper shoes. We'll dress him in that.
YOLANDA: Yes!
MIRIAM: Come with me to the mortician's office.
YOLANDA: Of course.
MIRIAM: Son. Take his clothes off. Wait 'til I get disposable gloves.

(Yolanda and Miriam exit)

OSCAR: Why would they have disposable gloves?
DANIEL: For when they touch a dead body.
OSCAR: We lost. They won. We left. They stayed. They're destroying themselves. And we have to go back and be kind. You understand that, right?[50]

The comedy of this scene comes from the combination of the Marques's hyperbolic prudery and horror—which later evolves more explicitly into casual racism and classism—and the uncanny nature of Ismael's body onstage. Ismael is unresponsive to touch while asleep in this scene and is treated simultaneously as an abject object and a potential sexual commodity. His transformation into a corpse, first by being stripped of his clothes and later by being covered again in a funeral-parlor suit, is fully staged in front of an audience. This theatrical transformation literally makes him into a corpse, rather than revealing him as a corpse. This transformation, then, reveals that the abjection and/or subjectification of the migrant body is a conscious act rather than a state of being to be passively apprehended. Gesturing to Mbembe's concept of necropolitics, Machado's theatrical corpse making shows how migrants are made part of the "vast populations . . . subjected to conditions of life conferring on them the status of the *living dead.*"[51] Within the frame of global neoliberal practice, Ismael is but one more member of a population, rather than of a people.

Strictly within the frame of Machado's larger oeuvre, Ismael is a queer body double both to Fabiola, whose body remained absent in her eponymous play even after it was recovered, and to Cusa, whose dead body is offstage for *Kissing Fidel*'s duration. Unlike Fabiola, Ismael's putrefying state is palpable, visible, and olfactory, reminding us of the true state of things in Cuba in the

Kissing Fidel. Bryant Mason as Oscar. Javier Rivera as Daniel, Andres Munar as Ismael. Photo courtesy of Carol Rosegg.

Special Period. Speaking through Oscar, as he often does, Machado offers that it is precisely through confronting the reality of this outcast Cuban son that Cuban Americans might relieve Cuban scarcity rather than relive Cuban exile. He is a walking, talking argument against the embargo. It is for this reason that Oscar continues on to Cuba at the end of the play, leaving after the sun comes up, after his "layover" in Miami, ending his impasse in the funeral home.

Yet Machado does not let us, the audience, out of this impasse so easily. He asks that we dwell in the morass of the Special Period by eroticizing Ismael's abject body so as to rethink social and familial relations. In the play, Oscar and Daniel are both attracted to Ismael, triangulating their desire for each other. While he is still unclothed, Daniel kisses Ismael and subsequently comes out to his family. Soon after, Oscar and his aunt Miriam indulge in some incestuous affection, outing past dalliances to a shocked Daniel. Oscar, inspired perhaps by Daniel's calling him a "vampire," during a subsequent tirade, acts on this incestuous circuit of desire, not only kissing Ismael, but sucking on his neck, causing him to wake up. When he rises, Ismael screams out "Fidel," linking the experience of being violated with the name of the Cuban dictator. The obvious reading of this moment equates Castro with a vampire, who sucks the blood of his people, just as Daniel claims Oscar does in his writing. The true moral of this story, if there is one, is to stand aside from such an easy equivalence. Machado dares us instead to see the stalled motion of the Special Period, shot through as it is by incestuous desire, as a respite within which to reconsider familial and political relations. Right before Ismael wakes and the characters revert to their agonistic vilification, Daniel and Oscar have the following exchange, which brings us back to the issue of movement and temporality:

> DANIEL: I wouldn't mind fucking him.
> OSCAR: You should stop trying to pick up your cousins.
> DANIEL: But you said . . . it was good to . . .
> OSCAR: *It will lead you nowhere, believe me.*[52]

This scene hearkens to the moment in the Special Period edition of *Fabiola* when Cusa asks Pedro to pick up a gun and defend the Revolution, and he answers by saying, "Mother, I can't move," to which Cusa responds, "Cubans are killing each other again. Pedro, nobody can move."[53] As Ortiz claims, the centripetal movement of Pedro's desire and the centrifugal force of revolution, "devolve into mere paralysis."[54] In the Special Period, this paralysis is more ambivalent than negative. Although Oscar ultimately propels forward to Cuba, it is this not-so-peaceful respite in the funeral home that allows his characters, if only briefly, to think outside of two rather tired possibilities—a revolutionary teleology that imagines Castro as victorious or a counter-revolutionary crisis that imagines the exiles' triumph. The lack of moving forward, then, is not only the inhibition of movement but also the stoppage of progressive time. Thus, the fact that Daniel's cousin love will "get him nowhere" might not be the harbinger of his doom, as is the case with Pedro's paralysis and subsequent suicide. Instead, it might be that loving his *balsero* cousin will open up a different relationship between Cuba and the United States, if the Marques family can extend their respite from agonistic debate a little while longer.

On the surface, then, although Machado's queer form of family reconciliation is literalized in the very idea of Oscar kissing national patriarch Fidel and his own biological father Osvaldo, *Kissing Fidel*'s family reconciliation is manifest through the material reality of kissing cousins. Sexual intimacy between cousins is a gray area for incest generally, and especially if procreation is not a possibility. Thus, I see the intimacy between Oscar, Ismael, and Daniel as an early foray into nonreproductive queer futurity and horizontal relationality. As José Muñoz claims in his larger explication of queer temporality, "queerness's ecstatic and horizontal temporality is a path and a movement to a greater openness to the world."[55] The form of relationality this temporality opens up acts similarly. *Kissing Fidel*'s form of family romance, despite its title, undoes the patriarchal excesses of exilic drama and dependence on a Fidel-led Revolution as well as a strictly matriarchal fidelity to a feminized Cuba (Cusa). Machado replaces these hierarchical relationships with an experimental alliance, with no clear end. This ambivalent potentiality is made possible in the midst of neoliberal capitalism.

If circumstances in this period forced Fidel Castro to imagine events outside of revolutionary teleology, it also forced Machado to further queer his own temporality, freeing himself from his own exilic inheritance. By doing this, Machado seems to fulfill Ortiz's desire that reading *Fabiola* can ask us to move beyond "ungenerous acts of refusal (embargo, stalemate, impasse)" and to imagine a future where "we might still, together, at once, touch."[56]

In *Kissing Fidel*, written after Machado returned from a trip to Cuba but set before Oscar leaves, less is staked upon the possibility of future than on its two presents: the liminal space of the *balsero* period—which did not, but could have, completely undone binary modes of identity construction (Cubans and Cuban Americans, exiles and migrants, and communists and capitalists)—and the play's present, which features the open-ended uncertainty of the late Special Period. Ironically, by following an Ibsenian form of the neoclassical three unities of time, space, and action, Machado avoids the progressive future-oriented teleology of the Revolution. Yet, as Alisa Solomon astutely opined, it is a real attack on the realistic family drama even as the play uses some of the same generic structures. It is for this reason that she suggests that *Kissing Fidel* "holds great promise," even though she feels that the 2005 version of the play does not quite realize that potential.[57] Machado's generic undoing is perhaps more productive than his drama of return, *Havana Is Waiting*, which more closely subscribes to the mode of the travelogue. Yet, this play also holds its own lessons for its audiences in its affective tenor and expansion of queer possibilities.

Havana Is Waiting, which debuted in October 2001, also takes on family reconciliation, but in a post-Elián universe. Set in Cuba and New York in 1999, *Havana* was started later but completed earlier than *Kissing Fidel*. One can feel the overlap in Machado's dramaturgical strategies as well as Garcés's directorial tactics. In *Havana*, Cuban American Federico and his Italian American friend, Fred, undertake a journey to Havana together despite their fears. Fred is scared of flying; Federico is scared of Cuba. Federico begins *Havana Is Waiting* seemingly suspended in midair. Actor Bruce McVittie seems to run in place or tread water during this scene—moving without directionality or forward motion.[58] During the flight there and during the journey back, the motion of the plane is depicted by stillness; Federico's agitation before the flight, however, employs the same caged rhythm that plagued *Kissing Fidel*'s Miami funeral parlor. For example, Federico runs around the bed in circles before he lets Fred talk him into going downstairs to meet the waiting taxi to the airport.

Once they are in the midst of their journey, they discover that Elián González has arrived in Miami and that there are protests to bring him home all over Cuba. Fred and Fed join one of the protests and shout alongside the Cuban protesters. As in *Fidel*, *Havana* traces two journeys under the guise of presenting only one. Parallel to Oscar and Ismael, Federico and Elián are two travelers going separate ways whose paths accidentally meet. The irony is not lost on Federico, who, after he learns the news about Elián, comments, "I wish someone would have fought to get me back."[59]

On the surface, *Havana Is Waiting* follows the tidy structure of a travelogue; the play commences with Federico and Fred's departure and ends with their return flight. The play is not as pat as it sounds, however, upending previous dramaturgical forms. Despite Ernesto's best efforts, Federico never gets into his former house. This type of entrance is reserved for Machado's *The Cook*, which stages its ideological entente with a more orthodox structure. These "travel failures" are not the only ones we see. Ernesto's car breaks down when its Russian spark plugs fail, and the plane Federico and Fred leave on starts to fall soon after they make it into the air.[60] The malfunction happens after the two shout wishes for Cuba as they leave, during which Fred suggests that Federico's desire to end imperialism and ownership culture might be unfeasible.[61] Federico blames the potential crash on Fred's cynicism. The plane starts again after its engine's temporary lapse, however, and they fly off. The transportation problems Federico and Fred experience accurately portray mechanical difficulties faced by those dependent on outdated Cuban equipment. Yet the mechanical problems also symbolize the difficulty of travel between the two sites, emotionally, spiritually, and ideologically.

Interestingly, Machado uses the word *stuck*, as if in the groove of a record, to describe many aspects of his experience of Cuba in a 2004 interview. He claims that he is stuck because his "possibility of being anything but a tourist there is stuck."[62] He says there was "no movement" the last time that he was there and that he was "stuck relating to it."[63] Later in the interview he asks how Cubans can take a step back from where they are stuck. While his comments evoke the phrase "frozen Cubans" which he used earlier in his career to describe exiles who hold on to images of Cuba pre-Revolution, Machado's use of a metaphor of mobility underscores how stalled travel articulates his experience of contemporary Cuba.[64] His rendering of stuckness, as I suggest above, is made from ineffective motion instead of stillness, perhaps at the behest of Michael John Garcés.

Yet not all is lost despite the limitations of Machado's experiences. *Kissing Fidel* and *Havana Is Waiting*, like the other plays I analyzed earlier in this essay, stage border crossings.[65] Machado's plays traverse gay and straight sexualities, pro and anti-embargo attitudes, as well as national borders. He forces his surrogate Fed to seek closure by opening himself to Fred: Fred kisses Federico passionately in front of the house, rather than going inside of the building. This queer resolution, common in Machado's plays, works here to break the tension between the characters and offers a different sort of home for Federico, who must face the present instead of chasing the past. That this queer moment comes at an impasse is notable. Yet, the queer kiss harbors the possibility of reconciliation as well. After a play's worth of banter and political and sexual tension, Ernesto kisses Fred on the lips. This kiss between two "straight" men hearkens the end of an embargo. That Federico, the openly gay character only shakes hands with Ernesto underscores queerness not as sexual identity but as a more polymorphous form of openness necessary to undo the standoff between the United States and Cuba. It is notable that both of these kisses happen in spaces that mark limited mobility: the space just outside Fed's childhood home and the Havana airport. Ernesto, of course, can't get on the plane and leave Cuba just as Federico cannot makes his way into his home.

Queer horizontality in this sense becomes a line everyone can cross theoretically, if not in actuality—it is a form of thinking otherwise that stops short of cruel optimism but does not quite cruise utopia. The impasse that the characters face, then, although often literal, opens up the possibility of doing the work Berlant asks of the impasse—by "open[ing] up different ways that the interruption of norms of the reproduction of life can be adapted to, felt out and lived."[66] In the midst of neoliberal precariousness and the prohibitions and obstacles it places on mobility, there is room to explore a different mode of being, if one steps out of tried and true narratives that bolster the very heteronormative and chrononormative gestures that are at the heart of the disciplinary regimes that bind us.

Feeling Neoliberalism: Anxiety and the End of Revolutionary Time in Special Period Cuba

Jorge Cortiñas also openly undoes revolutionary teleology and depicts limited mobility as a reality of Special Period Cuba. *Sleepwalkers*, however, more clearly articulates these conditions to the emergence of an affective state that pervades Cuba under hemispheric neoliberalism. Cortiñas wrote *Sleepwalkers* a few years after his own first trip "back" to Cuba in 1992, which he visited as a graduate student in public health.[67] This was, notably, early in the Special Period, when the practices necessary to survive the horrible conditions were still emerging. The play confines itself to Havana in the summer of 1993, following a twentysomething young man's decision to leave Cuba on a raft for the United States. Tito spends much of the play arguing with his father, rereading the same book, and hanging out with his friend Charley and the Skinny Woman next door. Many of *Sleepwalkers*'s scenes punctuate the strange combination of listlessness and low-level anxiety that surround its characters. Nothing really happens in the play other than Tito making the decision to leave. The play does not move toward this future event so much as show how the characters try to survive the present. One scene shows the Skinny Woman trying to relax herself so that she can go to sleep; another features the Soldier, Tito's father, following commands from his military past after wearily dozing off in a chair; the most attenuated scene features Charley and Tito literally sleepwalking as they talk about their lives.

This scene, which frames the very idea of the play, is a meditation on motion and affect in neoliberal Cuba. The scene starts when the two friends stand up against the back wall of the theater, acting as if the wall was a horizontal surface, and slowly sleepwalk throughout the scene. The stage directions tell us that Charley and Tito are in their respective beds as they converse about Charley's queer sex work in the tourist industry.[68] They act as if they were talking while waiting for a bus: when the first one arrives, they realize it is not the right one; the second time, the bus passes them; the third time, it never arrives. Charley and Tito's failure to catch the bus alludes to their inability to get where they need to go. As they talk, Charley and Tito move to the front of the proscenium and back again, punctuated by the headlights of the buses that never stop. The suspended yo-yoing back and forth is only interrupted once: when Tito awakes and "breaks pace" at the end of the scene, suggesting that he may in fact escape the constricted motion Charley engages in.[69]

In some sense, these moments are out of time and place, articulating an alternate reality. Director Rubén Polendo had it rain on stage during these scenes to contrast with the drought that was happening in real time in the play.[70] They are not dream sequences, however, but materializations of neoliberal time. The mens' sleepwalking reveals that linear, progressive time is a cultural construct—neoliberalism exists in temporal suspension from this forward motion. Neoliberal time, or perhaps better said, temporality, as I explore throughout this book usually is and certainly *feels* recursive. Characters often move in circles in what Lauren Berlant calls "crisis ordinariness." Here, however, the Charley and Tito's circular motion explicates their affective state in Special Period Cuba—where one moves forward only to be thwarted by failing infrastructure and misrecognition of reality as working toward linear progress. Cortiñas's critique of a standard revolutionary teleology is implicitly linked to the temporality of anxiety throughout the play. For instance, in a poignant scene, Tito imagines being able to read on an air-conditioned train in Miami all day, going around in a loop and ending up where he started. The circular journeys Tito visualizes in the United States are a release from the anxiety and anticipation of Special Period Cuba's uncertainty. Tito's reading itself suspends suspense and linear time to relieve his anxiety. As Tito explains to his sister, "When I finish a novel, I start again from the beginning. Once you have read a book seven or eight times, you don't have to worry about what is going to happen next."[71]

The more overt critique of Marxist materialist time at the end of the play is also rendered in terms of motion. When Pionera (Tito's sister) and her father try to fix their broken bicycle, her father claims that everything has a way to get fixed, to which the Pionera responds, "At school they taught us no. That historical materialism means that when the time comes for something to break, it breaks."[72] Her father, less doctrinaire than usual, retorts, "Well the time has not yet come for this Chinese bicycle to be superfluous. We still need it, material conditions dictate it."[73] The Soldier fixes the bike, and he and his daughter prepare to go to the Malecón to see if they can see Tito, who left on a raft to the United States the day before. Yet the scene ends before they move forward. This last image, with its promise but not fulfillment of forward movement, complements the scene titled "The Horizon Is a Line No One Can Cross." In that scene, the Skinny Woman and Charley, left behind, sit by the shore. They watch a tanker that seems to be sitting perfectly still in the middle of the sea. Of course, the boat is moving; she just can't see it until she looks away, which Charley convinces her to do.[74] This slow motion is a different iteration of Special Period temporality in which things happen at a macropolitical level even though they appear not to change. *Sleepwalkers*, then, is a meditation on motion which critiques ideological orthodoxy by denaturalizing linear time and space. Cortiñas makes the audience feel suspended, and in doing so, he revises the tried-and-true structure of the travelogue. We don't really see Tito come or go or experience a transformation of self during or through travel. Instead, we watch him *wait* to go.[75] Our suspension is a shared experience of neoliberal affect.

In Cortiñas's imagination, the stalled time of the Special Period revises the frozen time of exile from the Cuban side of the sea, replacing a longing nostalgia for the past or hope for a future with an injunction to deal with the present. Cortiñas delivers the message by dispensing with the valorization of teleological time and futurity, both of which fuel both capitalism and orthodox Marxism by underscoring the idea of progress. Tito's retelling of the William Tell story is a sort of anticommunist *fabula* countering the platitudinous parables of the Revolution. In the traditional tale, William Tell is captured, and he brokers a deal for release: he is allowed to go if he can shoot an apple off the head of his son without killing him. He does so, but the official finds a second arrow. Tell claims he would have used it to kill his captor if he had killed his own son. Tell is captured but later escapes, killing the official. His act of independence became a symbol of liberty for the Swiss. In Cortiñas's version, Guillermo Tell is a traveling act in small towns. He hits a potato off of his son's head with a Soviet rifle in order to earn his money until one day his son asks to shoot the potato off of his father's head. Tell agrees, but "only after one more go with the potato on his son's head, just for old time's sake. So he levels the rifle, aims, puts his finger on the trigger, and winks at the crowd. Then Guillermo Tell shoots his son. Straight through the skull. Pretty smart that Guillermo Tell. Smartest guy in the whole country."[76]

Tito's humorous but dispiriting story undermines Pionera's sense of truth and her sense of future directed justice for the nation state. Here, raw self-interest takes over. Tell is smart because he protected himself at the expense of another. This version of the tale deeply upsets Pionera. She reacts to the story by defending her revolutionary activities. Warning his half sister about the perils of ambition, Tito tells her, cleverly, just to keep her head down. The message becomes more complicated when he delivers the moral of the story—what Tell said to his son:

> He said. Son, we have a deal. I was going to protect you from the Future. I was going to keep the Future just out of your reach. That way you would always have something to look forward to, you would always have a goal. But, you wanted something else. Very well then, my dead son, meet the Future.[77]

Tito's personal sense of doom and lack of belief in the continuation of revolutionary struggle colors the moral of his story. Couched in a warning about hubris, Tito's parable is really about the state of the future, notably capitalized and personified in this speech. Tell's desire to protect his son from the future was to make sure he always had something to look forward to, to have a goal—that is, to keep him moving in a telos toward the future. Tell's son's death not only undoes progressive teleology but also the assumption of reproductive futurity: the sacrifice of the self for a future generation. Tell kills his son to save himself. Certainly conditions in contemporary Cuba might proffer a reading of this passage as evidence that an older generation kills off its youth for its own desires, despite rhetoric that makes the opposite claim. But I read Tito's words as doing more than pointing his finger at ideologues in Cuba. Instead, he is proposing a different form of thinking that quits subsuming present conditions and asking for sacrifice from a populace for a future payoff that is ever deferred. As in *The Hungry Woman*, the killing of a child, rather than the killing of a mother or father, is a brutal opening for a new way of thinking.

Like Moraga's, Cortiñas's thinking is postrevolutionary but not reactionary. *Sleepwalkers* straddles the line between describing a condition and prescribing a different possibility, between seeing lack of forward motion as dystopian—a sign of stuckness that reproduces neoliberal affect—or as an alternate possibility. The end of teleological time has many consequences, which are not limited to theorization or abstraction. In fact, one can say that neoliberal time creates large-scale affect. One must remember that anxiety, as clinically described, is a temporal disorder in its own right—a worrying about a future that has not happened but looms. To stay in the present is to relieve oneself of the burden.

Unlike the purely psychological condition, however, neoliberal anxiety is neither unfounded nor individuated; it is a social affect emergent in relation to the very material conditions that slowly grind away at people's livelihood. As Cortiñas explained to me, the anxiety his characters felt was directly related to their inability to deal with the sudden change in conditions that the Special Period brought, such as the scarcity of water, food, and medical resources that had to be bartered for on the black market in a country that abjures this form of capitalist enterprise and did not teach its citizens to navigate it. The mental machinations were incredibly taxing, especially at the beginning of the Special Period; people were simply worn out and confused by this type of work.[78] Although it seems like the characters in the play have a lot of time in on their hands, it took all of that time to get the basic tasks done that were necessary to sustain a life.[79]

The anxiety that pervades the play as a whole is both particular to 1993 Havana and diffused throughout the neoliberal Americas. As many plays I consider in this book suggest, constant low-grade anxiety is a part of everyday life for most of the world today, even if the intensity of these experiences differ according to their characters' economic means. Many of these characters attempt to mitigate their anxiety by playing with time and or sensation. Machado's upper-class Cubans and Saracho's *fresa* Mexicans pop Valium; the working class and poor characters in their plays chomp antacids and try to get sleeping pills. Although *Sleepwalkers* is not centered on the pharmacological economy of the Americas in the way that Saracho's *El Nogalar* is, Cortiñas does reveal how the pharmacological era also exists in a site seen as the exception to neoliberal capital: Cuba. This phenomenon, although pronounced in neoliberal Cuba, is linked to earlier periods of consumption. Ricardo Ortiz, for example, lovingly paints the complicated relationship of Machado's characters to café—a relationship that extends well into *Kissing Fidel*—and its role as stimulant, deflection, and reminder of a trenchant nationalism with colonial overtones.[80] In *Kissing Fidel*, café is paired with

Valium; the pills function as an affective monitoring system that keeps people on an even keel despite their caffeinated excesses. *Havana Is Waiting*, however, primarily deals with Valium and cigarettes—the latter of which, one must note, is a quite effective appetite suppressant in scarcity. In *Sleepwalkers*, this relief is offered only by the sleeping pills that come to the Skinny Woman through intense bartering. This detail, to Cortiñas's mind, ironically indexes Cuba's history of medical innovation and development.[81] Despite their particularities, together, these plays' rendering of pharmacological consumption reveal the need to anesthetize oneself from neoliberal scarcity and anxiety whatever one's class background. This consumption is a regular part of the plays I consider in this book and contributes to the affective tenor of contemporary life in the Americas.

Doing Commerce in Neoliberal Cuba

This chapter has largely concentrated on motion, queer sexuality, and temporality to gauge dramatic depictions of conditions in Special Period Cuba. One area not yet considered is the way in which commercial exchanges themselves are rendered in these plays. Scenes of commercial sexual exchange are perhaps the one common feature of most Special Period plays. Dramas from this period are riddled with German, Italian, and Spanish tourists, who can travel freely to Cuba looking for sex with men and *mulatas*. Coco Fusco and Nao Bustamante's *Stuff*, for example, takes on the issue of sex commerce directly, making parallels between *jineteria* in Special Period Cuba and the tourist industry's selling of heritage and cultural curios in mid-'90s Chiapas.[82] Alejandro Morales depicts Special Period sexual commerce by engaging the spectral presence of Federico Lorca, who comes cruising into a Havana nightclub as a modern-day Spanish tourist, alluding to queer anxieties of influence.[83] These are only a select few of the many depictions of these encounters.

Dramaturgically, scenes of exchange serve as a way to force Cuban citizen-tourist conversations about the states of capitalism and socialism, to underscore how sex tourists exoticize Cuba and Cubans (especially *mulatas* and Afro-Cubans), and to show how Cubans are forced to sell themselves to survive, betraying their own ideals and principles. These scenes gesture to the very real practice of engaging in sex work to survive on the island—a reality the plays do not exaggerate. That said, I have deferred this discussion to frame commercial exchanges through a queer lens, offering them less as documentary depiction of exigency (although they are that) and more as a representation of the complex historical and affective conditions that informal labor exchanges create in neoliberal times.

In *Sleepwalkers*, *Havana Is Waiting*, and *Kissing Fidel*, queer sexuality intersects with both queer temporality and nonsexual commerce, helping us rethink the very ends of capital exchange under neoliberal socialism. *Havana*

Is Waiting's third character, Ernesto, is necessitated by a commercial transaction: the hire of a private car to get around. His presence allows Machado to explain Cuba's shadow economy in some detail. Ernesto also literally becomes the straight man in Federico and Fred's jokes about sex traffic. In the end, however, he too is queered by commerce—revealing how affective ties of homosocial and homoerotic kinship are embedded within economic exchange. At the end of the play, Fed and Fred call Ernesto their friend.

In *Kissing Fidel*, this sex commerce is only alluded to, largely because the play takes place in Miami, not Cuba. Ismael's desperation instantiates a common representation of Special Period reality: that men, many of whom identified as straight, were forced to sell themselves sexually to both men and women in order to survive. Ismael, who claims he sold himself for a sandwich, says that it is easier to sell to men rather than women, because women want romance. In contrast, one can simply "hang out in front of the Ferrari dealership" to find men, who often simply want to know the size of one's cock.[84] This statement, in addition to inscribing a sexist stereotype, reveals that Ismael does his sex work with a mind to capitalist efficiency. It is also notable that he sells himself as a top rather than a bottom, which in much of Latin America would acquit him from being considered gay. His bracketing of sex work as labor in a play with so much attention to homosexual desire skirts close to the denial of sexual identity the family prefers for its members. In the larger scheme of things, Ismael's statement that under communism his body "was all" he "could sell" is framed within a dialogue that lets audiences know that this condition is also true under neoliberal capitalism, which helped create conditions in Special Period Cuba.[85] So, even though Oscar claims that "I sold my talent not my body," we simply can't believe the dichotomy between the United States/capitalism and Cuba/communism given the play's sexual excesses.[86] Joking aside, the fact that Ismael's penis is considered a commodity in the United States is a parallel to, rather than an exception from, his prospects in Cuba. In this regard, Ismael's sneering at the idea of computer or business school is not merely rebellion against bourgeois life but a refusal to do labor which is not predicated on selling oneself in the public sphere.

Ismael's marketing of himself as an antigovernment hip-hop artist is a performance of his own radicality as a political self; his hip-hop self is a theatrical foil to his prostitute persona who sold himself for a sandwich. Ismael's chosen career as a politically inflammatory hip-hop artist is also a form of selling blackness as alterity. Ismael, despite his tan, is a white Cuban who consumes U.S. hip-hop, making him a minstrel, or at least a minstrel-like performer, who recalls legacies of love and theft throughout the Americas.[87] As Jill Lane suggests, the long legacy of blackface was as crucial to creating national identity in Cuba as it was in the United States, and we can feel that legacy here.[88] The Marques family's discomfort with Ismael directly relates to his performance of blackness. His tanned skin exacerbates his treatment as an object, both dramaturgically and theatrically, throughout the play thus revealing the racialized nature of contemporary capitalism.

Sleepwalkers's scenes of commerce also grapple with the intersection of subjectivity and exchange, using theatrical techniques to point to the contradictions of neoliberal socialism. Consider, for example, the circuit of exchanges that occur between Charley, Tito, the Skinny Woman, and a tourist. The Skinny Woman, whose husband has disappeared, regularly visits Tito's family, with whom she shares a phone. Tito tries to get her pills so she can sleep. Tito also visits her and sleeps with her. When he is there, she reveals others have given her gifts in the past. She also saves books for Charley, who later gives her four dollars. On one hand, these exchanges simply represent a mode of bartering and getting by in the scarcity of Special Period Cuba. This scarcity was rendered theatrically through the almost talismanic use of props throughout the play. In both professional productions there were few props; the book, the pills, and the antenna stood out as both real and emblematic; they contextually represented Cuban scarcity in the Special Period and existed as exceptional objects on a stage devoid of realistic props and furniture. This made these things materialize as the actual objects they were and as props weighted with significance. Following this logic, there was also no food on the table during the dinner scene with Tito, Pionera, and the Soldier. Having the actors use empty plates in this scene referred to the theatrical illusion of miming eating on stage as well as the lack of food in Special Period Cuba offstage. In this sense the limitations of the theater conveyed the poverty of existence more credibly than realistic representation could.[89] The books on stage end up gaining the emblematic quality they have for Tito, phenomenologically and theatrically justifying his near religious reverence for them.

Books do not escape from capitalist exchanges, however. Charley procures books through the economic gain that comes from his sexual relations with the tourist; his manipulation of Special Period situations is what brings Tito his lifeblood. These exchanges also define Charley's identity as a low-level capitalist entrepreneur. His identity is in contrast to Pionera and the Soldier, who are still defined by their volunteerism, and Tito, whose intransigence cannot be categorized under any orthodox ideological template. He is quite simply confused and deeply unhappy. Cortiñas marks Pionera's and the Soldier's forms of identity construction under socialism as outmoded, in part by hailing them by their state titles rather than their names. But he also does not valorize Charley's opportunism, which he likens to a more neoliberal state of mind in contrast to Tito's malaise and disgust.[90] The relationship between them, with all of its ambiguities, ultimately reveals that capitalism, socialism, and whatever Cuba is experiencing in the Special Period are affective experiences as well as economic realities.

This affective aura and ideological agnosticism extend to even the most basely commercial sexual relations in the play. Charley's description of his relations with a European tourist has a surprisingly different tone than

Ismael's in *Kissing Fidel*. Tito paints the tourist rather stereotypically—as being loud, taking more air in than he exhales, and traveling with a lot of things—evidence of his conspicuous consumption. Charley sees the tourist as physically vulnerable. His skin bruises but does not rip, and he is less greedy with resources than Tito thinks he is. The tourist also seemingly trusts Charley. He falls asleep after they have sex, because he feels spent and relaxed. The tourist's affective experience is the exact opposite of the Skinny Woman and the other characters in the play, who never get a good night's rest and thus sleepwalk throughout their lives. Cortiñas's juxtaposition of the two reveals the reality of sex commerce as immaterial labor, wherein First World citizens can buy relaxation and pleasure through the sexual labor of the disenfranchised. Nonetheless, Charley does have some power. The upshot of Tito's inquiries, after all, is convincing Charley that he might be able to use his relationship with the tourist to leave Cuba. He also has power over Tito. In the midst of this sleepwalking conversation the following exchange occurs:

> TITO: If he had a book, would you get it for me?
> CHARLEY: How long have you known me?
> TITO: Just tell me.
> CHARLEY: Can't believe you are actually asking me that.[91]

This moment in the conversation is a plaintive one; Tito seems to realize that money will trump friendship with Charley. And he is clearly also disturbed that books are only a mode of commercial exchange for his friend, which they clearly are not for him. Realizing this may in fact be the final motivator for him to leave the island and his friend Charley.[92]

There is something undeniably romantic (even if nonsexual) in this exchange. Tito is financially tethered to Charley for all of his needs above the threshold of pure survival. These include emotional needs. Although Tito is depicted having heterosexual relations with the Skinny Woman, there is something a little bit queer about his and Charley's friendship. Combined with their triangulated exchanges there is the fact of their parallel sleep against the back wall of the theater. Charley and Tito's simultaneous walking forward together makes this conversation into a kind of pillow talk, where two men exchange information about sex with an absent lover. When Tito breaks pace with Charley, it feels as much like a lover leaving a bed as a friend leaving Cuba. Thus, Cortiñas's play highlights how new modes of exchange in Cuba, such as the selling/giving of oneself to survive, have emotional and erotic consequences that exceed the transactions themselves. That these are theatrically rendered in ways that are legible as theatrical action but slightly off-kilter replicates the state of capitalism in Special Period Cuba. His unorthodox take on exchange suggests a historical shift as well as being a theatrical departure from common wisdom about Cuban realities.

Jorge Cortiñas explains his particularity in his discussion of the play's reception. He claims that *Sleepwalkers* caused a "cognitive dissonance" for Miami audiences who "take it for granted that they know" what Cuba is like.[93] As he states,

> particularly in the context of North American stages and movie screens, representations of things Cuban, often, it is worth pointing out, by Cuban or Cuban American writers, seemed to have coalesced around three different strategies: they'll only deal with pre-1959 Cuba, or they'll present this polemical, I think one-dimensional, condemnation of the current regime and socialism in general; or they'll engage with the Cuba of today but always through these folkloric flourishes, you know with lots of references to café and rumba dancing. Not surprising then, that Miamians of my parents' generation who saw *Sleepwalkers*, a play that eschews these tactics, would respond by saying, "That's not Cuba." More recent arrivals to Miami, those who had come since the Mariel boatlift or during the Balseros Crisis, however, almost always responded by saying, "How did you so accurately portray conditions and the mood so accurately?" And this in the context of a nonrealistic play.[94]

(Both plays were done in black-box theaters and neither used realistic staging.)[95] In Miami, the humor was, overall, clear as a bell, without any need for theatrical adornment to make the jokes "land."[96] Cortiñas's departure from realism and documentary modes of depicting commerce, then, allow him to capture a more accurate reality. This reality, however, was not always recognized by his, or many other playwrights', critical reception in the U.S. press.

Critical Misrecognitions, or Making the Audience Uncomfortable

Rather than concentrating on the impossibility of traveling between the two sites as much exilic drama does or depicting the difficulty of crossing the ocean by raft as do the plays I consider at the beginning of the chapter Machado's and Cortiñas's plays concentrate on the affective properties of inhibited motion. The directors of their plays seem to register this anxiety and frustration as an active stasis, an agitated waiting, a movement without forward motion, uncomfortable for spectators and actors alike. Perhaps this is why *Sleepwalkers* is the one play by Cortiñas that is not being solicited for productions outside the United States.[97] Reviews of the works bear out the difficulty these plays pose for audiences outside of South Florida. Christine Dolen's Miami review of *Sleepwalkers* was unequivocally positive, complimenting the play's formal qualities and its depiction of Cuba.[98] Curt Holman's review in Atlanta, however, was less congratulatory:

With *Sleepwalkers*, the whole may be greater than the sum of its parts, as the individual scenes lack the strength of the play's cumulative effect. The production's watery stage devices are unforgettable and help to build to a haunting resolution (or lack thereof). But much of *Sleepwalkers* leaves you feeling restless.[99]

Reviews of other playwrights' works are equally bifurcated. In South Florida, Marta Barber battled the inundation of representation of *balsero* experience in the late 1990s, asking:

> How can anyone find lyricism in the recurring stories of Cuban balseros? Where does one find beauty in the tales of "smuggled migrants" when their stories of scarcity of food and freedom sound like a broken record? Is there poetry to be found in one more raft, one more run-down boat?[100]

Yet she answered in the affirmative, lauding the play for its poeticism.[101] Reviews of *A Bicycle Country* in Los Angeles and Portland, Oregon, were less kindly disposed and made more of concerns about the play's plot.[102] Interestingly, New York reviewers were sympathetic to *Havana Is Waiting*.[103] They were less kind to *Kissing Fidel*, however. The purpose of its frenetic energy and dramaturgy was missed in its entirely by everyone but Alisa Solomon.[104] These reviews reveal how difficult it is for the playwrights' depictions of a crisis largely felt in South Florida to travel to other parts of the United States. For example, although Holman sees *Sleepwalkers*'s restlessness as a detriment, the feeling he describes is exactly what makes the play effective as a meditation on conditions in Special Period Cuba. The intransigence of these plays, their discomfort, is a sign that they are doing the political work that theatrical representations of neoliberal conditions must do: disrupting our comfortable relationship with immigration narratives with clear and happy endings.

Cuban American writers traveling to Cuba replaced distance with proximity. This shift asked them to abandon nostalgia for frustration and replace longing with grinding low-level anxiety. More plainly, their plays register the end of an exilic paradigm predicated on memory and nostalgia that hovers over Cuban American experience as well as its dramaturgy. As Eduardo Machado deftly suggests: "I used to have more memories until I went back to Cuba."[105] The reality of the 1990s articulated a new spatial and temporal experience of Cuba for Cuban American playwrights, largely registered in the formal confines of staged travelogues. These plays reveal that apprehension, difficult travel, anxiety, and the paradoxically present and liminal borders that frustrate travel are always present in our current era.

Looking carefully at this phenomenon, one might say of the set of plays considered in this essay what Curt Holman says of *Sleepwalkers*: the whole may be greater than the sum of its parts. The stolen bicycles, broken-down and gasless cars, faulty legs, stuttering airplanes, dangerous trains, and boatless harbors, as well as their theatrical manifestations such as rocking platforms and frenetic actors running in place or walking to the edge of the stage and back are all crucial to understanding Latinx American mobility in the 1990s. The plays connect *balsero* struggles to those suffered by Mexican and Central American migrants, realizing the conditions for migrants of the neoliberal Americas. The open theatricality of the plays reveals the ways in which the violence these migrants experience is consciously created by active agents, including but not limited to the state.

Chapter 3

Neoliberalism Is a Serial Killer

> Lina: The last chapter of the 20th century,
> The last decade—
> Which starts for us in 1993
> The year when men found
> Angelica Luna Villalobos dead—
> Has been sketched on desert sand
> —Victor Cazares, *The Dead Women of J-Town and Smiley*

Victor Cazares's *The Dead Women of J-Town and Smiley* (2008) features a chorus of dead women of J-Town (Juárez) greeting the newly killed Mayra, who still has the glow of life on her. Together with Lina and Mariana, the curators of the Museum of the Dead Women of Juárez, a charismatic drag queen named Smiley, and a pair of less than charming border patrol agents, they traverse a border landscape called the "necropolis of sand."[1] The ambiance of the play is clearly post-9/11—the *migra* are busy looking for terrorists when they run into the dead women instead. But the full force of the killings does not become clear until a darkly comic scene in a McDonald's restroom late in the play when one of the dead women, Jessica, compliments Lina's shoes:

> JESSICA: I like your shoes, Lina.
> LINA: Oh, Thank you, is that—
>
> *(Lina checks to see Jessica's shoes)*
>
> LINA: Jessica, very nice of you—But they are ruined, all bloody and—
>
> *(Jessica shows Lina her shoes: they're much worse and they weren't that much better in life.)*
>
> JESSICA: These were my favorite.
> I got them because the protagonist from my favorite telenovela wore some like mine.

CHELA: Which telenovela was it?
JESSICA: MariMar—ow. Haha, I still remember the theme song. I love Thalia. I wanted to be just like her.
CHELA: Oh, MariMar was a good one.
LINA: MariMar—That aired in 1994, almost two decades ago—
The grand finale was good—one of the best I remember.
CHELA: Ay, no, no no not at all!
I hated it.
JESSICA: What happened?
LINA: You did not watch it?
JESSICA: No.
LINA: How did you miss it? I thought it was your—
JESSICA: I was killed a couple of days before the finale.²

The punch line of Cazares's joke, of course, makes light of a death come too soon—before the finale of a popular telenovela with a rags-to-riches story for María, played by a very young Thalía Sodi. The disparity between María's miraculous fate and Jessica's as a femicide victim is an especially painful form of irony that underscores the disjuncture between reality and the popular entertainment forms that infuse the play. Yet, Cazares's reference to the 1994 sensation *Marimar* does other critical work by linking the rise of the telenovela as a transnational product to the killings in Juárez. With this juxtaposition Cazares implicitly argues that they are both transnational, sensationalized products of neoliberalism. Both industries flourish around the time of NAFTA and are eerily copresent as part of the intensification of free trade.³ *The Women of J-Town*'s juxtaposition of *Marimar* and the Juárez killings also makes a temporal intervention because it pairs the seriality of femicide to the telenovela's formal mode of presentation. Indeed, the author subtitles the play as "chapters of a global telenovela." Following Cazares's lead, I meditate on seriality as form of temporality under neoliberalism.

The use of the term *seriality* is a risk and will require some unpacking. The *Merriam-Webster* definition simply denotes a "serial quality or state." The larger definition of *serial* is quite wide-ranging, including "appearing in successive parts or numbers" or "belonging to a series maturing in installments periodically rather than a single maturity date." The term is used colloquially to talk about broadcasts of radio, television, or digital media that are presented in this manner. Feminist scholars, following Marion Iris Young, have used seriality as an alternative designation for a group of individuals perceived to have common qualities, who do not self-identify or organize as a group, that is, "women."⁴ Chillingly, this term fits the victims of the femicides; the young Mexicans killed in Juárez were perhaps killed because of how they were perceived—as female, poor, unimportant, or even disposable. They are in fact only defined as a group by what Young calls their common interaction with particular material conditions. Today, of course, the crimes' seriality is most directly linked to serial killing—a form of murder, that, in contrast to genocides or mass murders, is usually committed by one deranged killer, often rootless, who "can't control himself" when faced with a victim with particular physical features.[5] Developed in the neoliberal period as a concept, a serial killer's compulsive killing conveniently makes him the embodied other of the rational actor who is the ideal model of neoliberal citizenship.[6] He (the serial killer is almost always male) is a threat to the state and the family because of the brutality and constant threat of his crimes.[7] In the case of Juárez, however, even after several arrests of suspected serial killers the femicides did not end, suggesting they represented a different mode of serial neoliberal violence. This form of violence unleashed a greater threat than the admittedly overblown threat of the single serial killer impervious to rationality. This time, an entire battery of several social groups, each bolstered by impunity, has become, in Sergio González Rodríguez's words, a "femicide machine."[8] Unlike *Marimar*, which like most Mexican telenovelas ended after an intensive run over the course of a year, the femicides did not end. They continue to the present day. In this sense, they are much more like some U.S. soap operas, which emerged in the 1960s and '70s, and ran for forty or more years, making them of the same duration as hemispheric neoliberalism.

The historical memory of Cazares's play has a shorter timeline, coinciding with the first recognized femicides in the 1990s. Although they have a beginning in this play, as the epigraph clearly suggests, Cazares theorizes them as an ongoing condition. The strength of Cazares's play and others that I analyze here is precisely their assertion of the femicides as a condition with a profound genealogy and a durational obstinacy that refuses to end rather than as a bounded historical event to be reflected upon; more plainly, the plays in this chapter gesture toward the longer history of neoliberalism, which abetted the production of femicide in the Americas. These plays take on the instrumentalization of misogyny (including its manifestation within homophobia) as a state-sponsored project embedded in every level of society.

At the formal level, these plays are a meditation on *testimonio*, and more broadly on the ethics of how to represent violence, death, and subjectivity in relationship to the brutality of the crimes themselves. The playwrights in this chapter often embrace an open theatricality in contrast to documentary forms and testimonial forms that seek to convey unvarnished truth about the crimes. Their use of nonrealistic representations perform a more efficacious critique of neoliberal violence and a more ethical mode of audience engagement in the current era than *testimonio* is often able to achieve. It can also be said that these plays are coexisting durational performances that produce serial rememberings and dismemberings affected by the mechanisms of capitalism, which thrives on the intensification of violence to sustain itself.

Femicide as Representational Practice

Before I continue on with the plays, I will address the crimes, their coverage by the media, and their modality as a representational practice. Although some investigators have argued for an earlier start date, the femicides are largely believed to have begun in 1993, with the discovery of the first corpses of young women in Juárez. Over two subsequent years, thirty girls and women were found killed, many of them also having been raped. The killings continue to the present. Between 1993 and 2010 there were an estimated 878 femicidal murders in Juárez.[9] After a very short-lived reduction in frequency, 2010 saw a record 304 murders. In the last few years, which include the late years of Calderón's narcoguerra, the numbers are even higher. Yet they are difficult to label as *femicide* given the general escalation of violence against people of all genders in the area.[10] The victims in the 1990s were often slender young women with long dark hair in their teens and twenties. Some of the recovered corpses had distinguishing marks on their backs; most were raped and sexually violated in brutal ways, including having their nipples bitten off. Some of the bodies were dumped naked, or nearly naked, in the desert.[11] At times, only clothing and bones were found, making identifications difficult. Police have often misidentified victims or found items belonging to one victim near another—suggesting that they are being dumped in groups in a premeditated way, especially in recent years. Some women were missing for days or years before their bodies were found. Combined with the sexual nature of the early killings, these kidnappings suggest that the women may have been held captive and brutalized for some time before they were murdered. Theories abounded: Were the women sexually trafficked and forced to perform in snuff films? Were their organs trafficked? No hard proof exists for any of these possibilities.

The similarity in appearance of the early bodies led authorities to suspect a serial killer. Mexican authorities brought Robert Ressler, a U.S. expert on serial killings, to Mexico to help solve the crimes. Arrests followed. In 1995, Mexican police arrested Abdul Latif Sharif, an Egyptian national with a history of sexual violence. Accused of two of the murders and found guilty of one, he was sentenced to sixty years in prison. He died there in 2006 after unnecessary pancreatic surgery, despite numerous appeals and a lack of evidence that he had committed the crime. With his broken English, very limited Spanish, and foreign status, he became the perfect scapegoat. When the crimes continued despite his being locked up, authorities alleged that he was orchestrating the killings from prison with a gang called Los Rebeldes. Over three hundred men were rounded up and arrested shortly thereafter. Later, most of these suspects were released because of lack of evidence linking them to the crimes. In 1999, a group of bus drivers were arrested and charged with the murders. One died under mysterious circumstances in prison. Another, like some of Los Rebeldes, confessed to crimes.[12] Both men later testified to the fact that they were tortured into confessing to the crimes. The killings continued.

The early victims shared certain conditions as well as looks—almost all of the victims were poor or of modest means. Some were migrants from other parts of Mexico. Many did not have wide (or influential) support networks in Juárez. That said, the victims have ranged greatly in age and occupations over the years, and some had substantial family in Juárez. One needs to be wary of the sentimental migration narrative that draws sharp contrasts between naïve young women from the south and poor women from the north, the latter of whom were also victimized. In recent years, there have been many male victims of this type of violence, leading some to believe that the label "femicide" is a misnomer. In addition, there is variation in how and from where the women were abducted. Some worked in maquiladoras where they had to take buses late at night or in the early morning, making them vulnerable to attack. Others were disappeared in broad daylight in downtown Juárez near popular retail outlets, suggesting a different kind of impunity. The women were often blamed for inciting the crimes themselves by dressing provocatively or going out dancing alone. In response, in 1998, the Juárez police published a list of recommendations for women to protect themselves. This list, which appears verbatim in two plays I consider in this chapter, reveals the extent to which responsibility for staying alive was made the responsibility of the victims:

> If you go out at night, try to go with one or more than one person.
> If you do go out alone, avoid dark, desolate streets.
> Don't talk to strangers.
> Don't dress suggestively.
> Carry a whistle.
> Don't accept drinks from strangers.
> If someone attacks you, shout "FIRE," so people will pay attention to your call for help.
> Have your car keys and house keys out and ready.
> If you are sexually assaulted, make yourself vomit, so your attacker will be disgusted and run away.[13]

This ridiculousness was coupled with complete disregard when it came to investigating the crimes. Because most of the murders were left uninvestigated, activists, many of them family members of the victims, created organizations to garner media attention to the crimes and handle investigations on their own in the wake of the state's failure. (One such organization is tellingly named Nuestras Hijas de Regreso a Casa.)

Given the coincidence of the crimes with the intensification of free trade and other modes of neoliberal governance, academics and journalists have chosen to investigate the conditions that produced this violence and impunity.

Some have investigated the relationship of brutal labor conditions and poverty to the violence, suggesting the parallel between femicide victims and the maquila workers as disposable women who are "used up" by global capital and discarded without regard for their human worth.[14] Other scholars have pointed more narrowly to Mexican machismo—to the particular threat that female laborers pose to men as earners—or the more general disregard for women's rights to live a life free of violence in Mexico.[15] Jane Caputi has even gone so far as to see these women's death as a gynocide with links to Mesoamerican mythologies that dismember the female to maintain patriarchy.[16] State authorities, in turn, have blamed a culture of violence related to narcotrafficking where civil society is frayed, conveniently absolving them of naming names or admitting that narcotrafficking is, in fact, a state-sponsored crime. All of the explanations that center on Juárez as an exceptional site, it should be noted, obfuscate the fact that these femicides occur throughout Mexico and much of the hemisphere.[17]

The best scholars looking at these issues show how complex relations between globalization, state-sponsored violence, narcotraffic, misogyny, and impunity combine to make the femicides possible. Sergio González Rodríguez's 2012 *The Femicide Machine*, an extended essay that expands on his analysis of the crimes in *Huesos en el Desierto* (2002), is but one example.[18] As he claims, "in Ciudad Juárez, a territorial power normalized barbarism. This anomalous ecology mutated into a femicide machine: an apparatus that didn't just create the conditions for the murders of dozens of women and little girls, but developed the institutions that guaranteed impunity for those crimes and even legalized them."[19] He argues that U.S. militarization of the border and the drug war created this machine. Rosa-Linda Fregoso, meanwhile, has urged her readers to move beyond a simplistic reading of the killings as the result of globalization because it ignores the state's role in the crimes, incorrectly distancing the Juárez killings from the longer history of femicide in the Americas that began with the military dictatorships of the Southern Cone.[20] Diana Washington Valdez underscores Fregoso's claims by tracing the links between contemporary members of the police force to those trained in Argentina to disappear people in Mexico's 1970s dirty war.[21] Her book *The Killing Fields*, published in English in 2006, was finished before the narcoguerra under Felipe Calderón. Yet recent events, such as the massacre in Ayotzinapa, Guerrero, only strengthen her argument about the long history of neoliberal violence.

For others, these killings are evidence of necropolitics.[22] As conceptualized by Achille Mbembe, contemporary necropolitics "account for the various ways in which, in our contemporary world, weapons are deployed in the interest of maximum destruction of persons and creations of *deathworlds*, new and unique forms of social existence in which vast populations are subjected to conditions of life conferring on them the status of *living dead*."[23] Although Mbembe focuses on the African continent, the conditions he describes also pertain to the U.S.-Mexico border, as Rosa-Linda Fregoso suggests in her research on femicide.[24] Sayak Valencia posits the violence created by economic hegemony in border regions as "capitalismo gore," a genre of gratuitous and brutal violence "often intermingled with organized crime, the predatory use of violence and issues of gender."[25] For her, this violence is a form of necro-empowerment that gives subalterns a mode of taking power through dystopian and violent means: through deciding who lives and who dies.[26] Valencia revises Mbembe's mode of necropolitics by linking it more directly to the hyperconsumption of a market that desires certain modes of death as commodities. With her emphasis on feminist critique, Valencia follows Rita Laura Segato, who theorizes the crimes as a form of sovereignty in which men claim absolute power over territory, making the killings a form of regional microfascism that form a "second state."[27] Ileana Rodríguez, meanwhile, argues for a total collapse of political and criminal societies within which maquilas are a form of legitimate (albeit exploitative) labor that harbors illegitimate, sexually violent trafficking of bodies in snuff films and other displays of violated bodies. For Rodríguez, these phenomena are "an organic part of the new state of capitalism, yet another example of necropolitics."[28] She analyzes the killings as art after examining *El silencio que la voz de todas quiebra*—a book of *testimonios* about the murders. Her decision to think about the killings as art is unnerving—especially to herself—yet, her willingness to go there attests that representational aesthetic practices are key to thinking about the relationship between neoliberalism and violence in Ciudad Juárez. Rossana Reguillo's theorization of narco-violence as expressive violence, which engages Segato's formulation, is also relevant here in that it frames violence as a language rather than evidence of its exhaustion.[29] All of these feminist scholars link the desire for sovereignty to expressive violence, ultimately questioning if and when the representation of the crimes is in fact different from the execution of the crimes themselves. The plays I consider also trouble the lines that separate representation and reality, largely through theatrical means. In doing so, they highlight the larger ethical conundrums inherent to representing gendered violence in the contemporary neoliberal era.

These ethical issues come to the fore in cultural production about femicides in Juárez, because the repertoire about the crimes is so extensive. Artists and activists from the mid-1990s to the present have created a plethora of films, novels, journalistic accounts, and artworks about the phenomenon at the local, national, and international level. Cultural production about femicide includes U.S. and Mexican telenovelas, documentaries, feature films, novels, plays, and performances. In the United States, the most famous are the feature films *Bordertown* and *The Virgin of Juárez*, the documentaries *On the Edge: The Femicide in Ciudad Juárez* and *Señorita Extraviada*, the novels *Desert Blood* and *If I Die in Juárez*, as well as the recently cancelled FX series *The Bridge*. In Mexico, the most famous are the films *El Traspatio/*

Backyard and *Espejo Retrovisor*, the telenovela *Tan infinito como el desierto*, Sergio González Rodríguez's piece of investigative journalism *Huesos en el Desierto*, mentioned above, and perhaps most famously, Chilean-Mexican author Roberto Bolaño's epic *2666*. A collection of Mexican plays about the femicides, *Hotel Juárez: Dramaturgia de feminicidios*, showcases the many dramas written in the same period.[30]

This proliferation of media is in part reparative, meaning that testimonials and fictional forms such as novels, films, and artworks are a mode of speaking the truth in the absence of truth in official publications. Scholarship about these works, predictably, is quite extensive and covers a variety of concerns including a critique of masculinist and/or sexist modes of representing the gender of the victims/characters, assessments of their failure or success at indicting transnational structural forces, and interrogation of the ethics of cultural production about the Juárez killings by artists not directly affected by them or by those who might profit from publication or production of these works.[31] I echo many of these critics' concerns, while paying more careful attention to the formal analysis of theatrical production. This is important because although many scholars mention plays or theater as part of these activist ventures, almost no U.S. or Mexican scholarship has been written about theater or theatrical representations of the femicides.[32] One exception is Christina Marín's reflective essays about her productions of Rubén Amavizca's *Las Mujeres de Juárez*, Humberto Robles's *Mujeres de Arena: Testimonios de Mujeres en Ciudad Juárez*, and Marisela Treviño Orta's *Braided Sorrow*. Marín, like her academic counterpart Jimmy Noriega (who toured Mexican playwright Cristina Michaus's *Mujeres de Ciudad Juárez* from 2014 to 2016), sees her work as a form of theatrical advocacy as well as a subject of research.[33] This focus is justified given the fact that readings and performances of these plays have not only brought attention to the femicides in Juárez but have also helped female audience members confront misogyny and violence in their own lives, including incidents of domestic violence.[34] Yet a focus on advocacy alone, as in Marín's scholarship, while excellent, leaves many questions about form and dramaturgy not discussed. It is with this concern that I approach the plays I analyze in this chapter, which range from testimonial plays that extensively use documentary evidence to fictional plays that work largely outside of realism. What is interesting about all of them is that despite their differences, few are invested in the investigatory work that the films and novels privilege. They quite simply are not concerned with solving the mystery of the crimes. Instead, the plays care more about restoring the stories of the victims or tracing transnational complicity in trade, both of which are more fruitful avenues for exposing neoliberal violence than the films. As Jean Franco points out about Gregory Nava's *Bordertown*, the mobilization of the crime drama paradigm is "unconvincing," in part because "it is an example of the inadequacy of a plot device that requires a single heroine and villain to tell a story where murderers and victims are a multitude."³⁵ This critique is extended and complicated by Marissa López, who critiques *Desert Blood* because of the way that the protagonist's "solving" of the crime oversimplifies the multiple factors that create their conditions. She argues that it is only when the protagonist loses control of the narrative and is "disabled as a rational actor" that the book achieves its goals.³⁶ Latinx playwrights are, for the most part, not interested in using detective work as a quest for self-identity in the alienation of the post-nationalist world, as do the authors of the Chicano/a detective novels considered by Ralph Rodriguez.³⁷ Nor do they articulate Latina subjectivity and identity through Chicana/Mexicana recognition (or, perhaps, misrecognition) as potential victims of the femicides.³⁸ In fact, most playwrights largely avoid the problem Claudia Sadowski-Smith sees in cultural production when authors stage the misrecognition of middle-class Chicanas for poor Mexicans by engaging fantasies based on phenotypical similarity that obfuscate rather than obviate the class privileges of middle-class Chicanas.³⁹

This is not to say that Latina playwrights can be entirely removed from understanding the Juárez murders by realizing their own phenotypical similarity with the victims. Christina Marín states, "I began to realize that if my picture were placed side by side with the photograph of any of the hundreds or young women whose faces were plastered all over Ciudad Juárez, one would be hard pressed to differentiate between the maquiladora worker and the doctoral student. Why was my life worth more than theirs?"⁴⁰ Marín's horror was converted into a mission: "to stand up and testify for the victims of this phenomenon, I needed to bear witness."⁴¹ Marín's choice of words—"to testify"—alludes to the Latin American form that informs the ethnodramas or docudramas that she directs: *testimonio*. Ultimately, it is a form she tests rather than accepting wholeheartedly.

Testimonio, as defined by Marc Zimmerman is, "generally defined as a first-person narration of socially significant experiences in which the narrative voice is that of a typical or extraordinary witness or protagonist who metonymically represents others who have lived through similar situations and who have rarely given written expression to them."⁴² *Testimonios* were especially popular during the 1970s and '80s, when a series of revolutionary movements and civil wars occurred throughout the hemisphere. They accounted for a history not being told by other media sources. As John Beverley has suggested:

> The word *testimonio* in Spanish carries the connotation of an act of truth telling in a religious or legal sense—*dar testimonio* means to testify, to bear truthful witness. Testimonio's ethical and epistemological authority derives from the fact that we are meant to presume that the narrator is someone who has lived in his or her person, or indirectly through the experience of friends, family, neighbors, or significant others, the events and the experiences that he or she narrates.

What gives form and meaning to those events, what makes them *history*, is the relation between the temporal sequence of events and the sequence of the life of the narrator or narrators, articulated in the verbal structure of the testimonial text.[43]

The complication with testifying in the theater is that theatrical representation compromises these modes of establishing ethical and epistemological authority because theater often openly admits that the onstage narrator is not the person who has experienced the events she or he is testifying about. Rather than seeing this as a deficit, I see this disjuncture as an asset, even when the plays themselves do not openly theorize their distance from the truth. It is through rendering language as fraught, ironic, and material rather than transparent that many of these plays make their claims about the violence of the state, which is also discursive. My exploration centers on two transnational forays by U.S.-born Latinx artists who theatrically (and in one case, literally) translate Mexican plays about femicides into U.S. theatrical productions and modes of production, interrogating simplistic notions of truth and exploring the traversal of Latin American forms into U.S. spaces: Christina Marín's readings of Robles's *Mujeres de Arena*, and Jimmy Noriega's production of *Women of Juárez*.

The Problem with *Testimonio*, or Theatricalizing *Testimonio*

Humberto Robles, in *Mujeres de Arena: Testimonios de las Mujeres de Juárez*, attempts to convert the *testimonio* directly into theatrical form. The play generously employs direct address to deliver exposition, biographical testimonials of the victims, poetic laments, and a reading of the absurd recommendations made to women so as to avoid being attacked and killed. Each of the women has a candle that is eventually snuffed out to represent their deaths. There is little overt staging in the text (a point to which I will return). Not surprisingly, the play's form lends itself to minimally produced presentations and readings which are economically feasible to support on a limited budget and in a variety of venues; it has been performed in the United States, Mexico, other parts of Latin America, Europe, China, and Australia. This extensive production history attests to *Mujeres*'s utility as a form of advocacy and awareness over the last several years. Robles created his work from testimonies of surviving relatives of those killed, including Antonio Cerezo Contreras, Marisela Ortiz, Denise Dresser, Malú Garcia Andrade, Maria Hope, Eugenia Muñoz, and Juan Cantú. Despite his intentions to make the women's stories heard, however, Robles's play carries a number of hegemonic discursive maneuvers, including a male narrator who refers to the femicide victims as "our women," duplicating the patriarchal gestures of the state. The fact that the male actor is the last person to speak runs the risk of reasserting the state as a male (a supposition the play indulges) who has the final say.

A more complex interaction with gender ideology is embedded within Robles's conscious use of the testimonial form within a perhaps unwittingly theatrical play. As he describes his project: "The idea for this play was the result of watching the mothers and relatives of the victims of femicide giving talks and conferences on the subject; they sit on a panel and begin to give testimonies in order to educate, denounce, and give information about these crimes. This is what the play intends to reproduce."[44] Robles, then, unlike the other authors who incorporate *testimonios* into the plays, makes the claim that he is intentionally reproducing oral testimony as a *presentational* style. Marín picks this up when she says the play "calls for ten presentational scenes in which the actors deliver a text without any formal production staging."[45] For the most part, she writes, "the words tell the stories, the actors deliver these scenes from behind music stands."[46] As written, the play features four women and one male actor who introduces many of the scenes. Robles outlines an ideal order of placement for the actors onstage: "from left to right, Woman 3, Woman 1, Woman 4, Woman 2, and the Actor (if there is a musician, he/she should be seated at the extreme left of the stage)."[47] He also adds: "It is suggested that the actors wear black and white clothing," and he lays out a plan whereby the four women and actor or actor/musician should be "on two benches" and there should be "five lit candles."[48]

These stage directions are more complex than they seem. Although the stage directions gesture to a minimalist (and low-cost) set, the spare details suggest a rather complicated attitude toward theatricality: the musician is far away from the actors, but onstage, creating a differentiation between the musician as a performer and the actors as performers. This is significant because if Robles wanted the text to be scored invisibly, without being openly framed as performance, recorded music could have been used. Robles's description of the performers, which suggests that the female performers are women and the male performer is an "actor" has greater implications. Although it is true that the male actor has a more expository role—he never takes on any of the characters of the play (femicide victims or their female relatives)—the differentiation is overstated because all of the women also employ direct address and deliver expository material out of character. Robles's differentiation inscribes a gender ideology within which female witnesses are authentic subjects and/or persons and the male witness is an actor. One tells the truth while the other lies, or at least pretends. While it is true that the state apparatus is often primarily composed of males who lie and pretend and it is also true that many of the witnesses who are correcting these lies publicly are women, when enmeshed within representation, Robles's categories create an elision between female subjectivity and truthfulness, erasing the actresses' own distance from the texts. This choice reifies the trope of the brown woman as a guileless truth teller who provides authentic content to an audience. This reification erases elite female complicity with the state, while cutting close to supporting simplistic ideas about testimonial *as truth* that have allowed scholars like David Stoll to discount Rigoberta Menchú Tum's *testimonio* as a failed objective report of the events rather than recognizing it as a generic form with its own conventions and veracity.[49]

The docudrama form, of course, upends this effect by continually reminding the audience of the distance between performer and role in Brechtian and non-Brechtian ways. What is productive about the disparity between realism and truth in theatrical representation is that it absolves theatrical *testimonios* from formal authenticity, even when espousing them as truth. This distance is, in some sense, truer to the spirit of *testimonio* than forms that do not interrogate their narrative frame. Theatrical renderings, then, open up productive ways to think about *testimonios* as conscious acts of advocacy deeply engaged with form and aesthetics. Although Christina Marín does not engage historical debates about *testimonio* openly, it is clear that even in minimally produced readings, she has chosen to veer away from a purely documentary style. In the scene where the recommendations to young women to keep themselves safe are read, for example, she had each of the actresses declaim the recommendations and reenact them using a Barbie doll. At the same time, another actress stood behind the speaker and blinded her by wrapping a cloth around her eyes.[50] The uncanny presence of the Barbie dolls alongside human actors in combination to the allusion to blind justice was powerful, revealing the absurdity and untruth of the language of the state.

Marín's intervention aside, in the case of the women of Juárez, whose bodies are often mutilated beyond recognition and/or absented entirely, the actors' bodies have a third purpose: standing in for the absent young women who have been killed and, at the same time, pointing to the impossibility of the substitution. Ethically, one might say no one can ever stand in for what is lost—a truth the play conveys through its casting choices. Marín had an international multiracial cast, meaning that while some of the actresses and actors could be read as phenotypically Mexican, many of them would not be—departing from a simple one-to-one equivalence in which a U.S. Latina body stands in for a Mexican body. The actresses' youth underscores the uncanny nature of playing an older female survivor while memorializing young women closer to their own age.[51] This doubled surrogation—outside the frame of a traditional play with characters and a fictionalized plot—prevents the elision of one set of bodies with the other, proving that theatricality's shortcomings are more effective than its success.[52] In this sense, then, Marín radically reimagines Robles's play, and its gender ideologies.

Jimmy Noriega's translation of Cristina Michaus's *Women of Juárez* relies more openly on Brechtian techniques and powerful symbols, acting in counterpoint to Robles's play. Michaus gives producers the following directions, which are, in one sense, incongruous and in another, complementary. She states: "The best method for acting this play should resemble the work of a medium: truly quieting the ego in an effort to represent the women. It is also necessary to understand Brecht and the alienation effect."⁵³ The actors are meant to erase themselves so as to give voice to the people that they represent (perhaps giving up their own desire for virtuosity), while also simultaneously creating a play where the audience is not entirely seduced into the illusion of the play. This doubled direction inherently asks that actors work against reliance on empathy as the mode through which to consume and/or engage the play. Michaus's Brechtianism tempers her direction to let the work pass through them as "a medium" without becoming the characters themselves through empathizing at the level of creating character. This type of acting refuses substitution and simplistic ideas of representation even as it delivers truth.

Form is on Michaus's side. She wrote the play as "monologue for many voices," such that one actor would play all of the characters, thus preventing the submerging of actor into character. The conceit of the play is that an actress who learns about the killings created it because she feels she needs to do something. This structure parallels the choice Michaus, herself an actress, made to be an advocate by writing the play. Michaus has performed the play as a solo performer. This performance, alongside her other forms of activism in Mexico, resulted in death threats that caused her to shelve the play for many years.⁵⁴

The flexibility of the script, however, allows for a cast of many. In 2013, Noriega cast the play with five students, including three Latinas, who played all of the parts despite their age disparity. Michaus's play, like Robles's, begins with the testimony of a mother who has lost her daughter. Yet, Michaus's piece does not center on mothers as a category of designated mourner/activist that anchors the memory of those killed. Instead, Michaus includes monologues by prostitutes and others who do not define themselves in terms of patriarchal family relationships—as being daughters, mothers, or sisters—thus avoiding the prescribed gender roles valorized under Latin American neoliberal states that exploit the mores of mainstream Catholicism in their rhetoric. For example, she includes a monologue by Abeja, a prostitute, undoing the virginal martyr stereotype key to making the murdered women ethical victims. Most importantly, Michaus theorizes prostitution within a frame of economic necessity by having La Abeja talk about sex work *as work* while openly resenting the maquila workers, who have a more comfortable life, making Mexico's complex class dynamics apparent.

Notably, *The Women of Juárez* includes monologues by female officials who are part of the impunity machine. One character makes a hair dryer for another to use, referencing maquila labor focused on creating household electronics. Michaus exposes this work as part of the complex of neoliberal networks of consumption participated in by middle- and upper-class women and men. Thus, her staging forces audiences to recognize that female officials imputed to speak for working and poor mestizo and indigenous women are often affluent women who profit from maquila labor in quotidian ways, making their "speaking for" a fraught proposition in neoliberal Mexico. That the female officials are shown acting out their speeches, such as rehearsing them in the mirror, "almost as if they were sincere" questions the veracity of fiery rhetoric in general, marking public protest of the crimes as potentially false performance.

Yet Michaus does not take an easy slide into antitheatricality when explicating neoliberal networks of harm. Instead, she employs theatrical irony thoroughly and effectively. Perhaps the most disturbing section of the play is the monologue by the forensic examiner, who details the many theories about the murders. She delivers her theories while performing a striptease dance, "contorting her body" throughout her monologue. The result is "the song of the hypothesis" that serially lists possible suspects including:

> Perverse gringos.
> Spring breakers.
> Human smugglers and coyotes.
> Assembly plant foremen.
> Pimps, stepfathers, and bosses.
> We have the jealous husband,
> the unruly yuppie,
> and the privileged and spoiled sons of money.
> All of them, very very manly.
> Certainly one or another is guilty,
> but he's free
> and watches cable TV.
>
> (*She puts on a grotesque dildo.*)[55]

The sarcastic tone of this monologue is not unlike the choral reading of the safety recommendations in Robles's play. Here, however, the rather grotesque nature of machismo/misogyny is embodied by the actress who enacts fantastic imaginings of hypersexualized men and women while singing of impunity. Her parodic enactment of gender denaturalizes any possibility that the actress playing the part can either stand in for the dead women or the officials by phenotype and gender expression alone. In this sense, the play functions as an antitestimonial.

Michaus's play echoes many nondocumentary Mexican plays about the femicides that stage the brutality of the killings within a nonrealistic frame.[56] Michaus's character Celia's comment about the voices of the dead "sounding like the wind" engages with the sonic presence of femicidal women in Mexican dramaturgy, where they have been transformed into slightly menacing sirens, or the sound of current going through power lines.[57] The risk of aestheticizing or metaphorizing violence runs high in these texts, but their break from testimonial form and the reproduction of individuated ethical victims allows one to think about the femicides as an immersive situation from which one cannot exempt oneself. Michaus's reading of the names of victims at the end of the play is a case in point. Unlike in most other plays about Juárez, in Michaus's work this reading lasts a full seven minutes, forcing an audience to endure a list of names they cannot possibly humanize on an individual basis.[58] The Mexican production was more aggressive in exposing the violence during this section; the actress often yelled or screamed these names, rather than memorializing them as a more placid form of mourning.[59] Theatrically, Michaus pairs this reading with a mixture of metaphor and stark realism when she has the victims be visibly represented by empty clothing often found near their slain bodies.

The final moral of the story makes neoliberalism the cause of the murders. The actress in her play states:

> . . . With Plan Puebla-Panamá, a new Juárez is beginning to form in each State of the Republic. Should we wait for fate to catch up to us, bringing us the bodies of our own sisters, daughters, or wives?
>
> *(She wipes away her tears and puts on the raincoat that she first came in with.)*
>
> In the end, why does it all matter? Soon the play will be over, we'll leave the theatre, and you can all go enjoy a peaceful dinner. Juárez is only an "experiment of our future" and that of our children.
>
> *(She takes out a Mexican flag and places it, upside down, on the empty container. On top of the shield of the flag, she places one of the masks, very delicately. She begins to leave.)*
>
> *(Returns. Sweetly.)*
>
> Oh, and please, avoid falling into the stupid trap of always asking:
> Who is guilty?
> The Serial Killer—
> the Collective Killer—
> is called Impunity . . .
> And when you walk up to the sink and look in the mirror, don't be surprised to see an accomplice staring back at you.
>
> *(She smiles and walks away slowly, as if she carries on her shoulders the pain of all the women violently murdered.)*[60]

Michaus's indictment of impunity in Mexico is transnational but largely aimed at the authorities in power, as her use of the Mexican flag suggests.

(Noriega did not add a Mexican flag when he staged it for a U.S. audience. He was asked in Arizona not to use the Mexican flag for fear it would incite anti-Mexican sentiment in the midst of many anti-immigrant initiatives present in the state at the time. He substituted a white flag instead.)[61] Michaus's accurate description of the path of neoliberalism in contemporary Mexico—particularly the Plan Puebla Panama, an extension of NAFTA-like free trade policies, first inaugurated in 2001 by former President Vicente Fox—places economic violence on the table, rather than naming misogyny or machismo as the sole causes of the murders.[62] *Women of Juárez* places structural inequality front and center, making an indignant dig at the idea of Juárez as an "experiment of our future," in Charles Bowden's apocalyptic phrasing.

Michaus's desire to point the finger at the audience may be met with some skepticism. Her adversarial stance to the audience is unusual in these plays, upsetting simplistic empathic response to the play. (This attitude is, notably, a feature many critics defend in a male-authored novel: Roberto Bolaño's *2666*.)[63] If the reading of the names of the dead could potentially ossify into a mode to extract simplistic modes of pity or sentimentality, the jarring conclusion short-circuits such a response. In contrast to Robles's play, which continually asks us how we might feel if this happened to our relatives, Michaus's play asks that we confront female characters with whom we do not necessarily empathize and who have no familiar role or relation to us. We are not made surrogate mothers, sisters, or fathers. We are asked to remain ourselves as the actress does. Thus, although structurally similar, I see *Mujeres de Arena* and *Mujeres de Juárez* as quite different plays. One work ends in a secular prayer; the other ends in an indictment of the heteronormative aims of the state.

The dissemination of both these texts, as well as Amavizca Murúa's more formally conservative play, which I do not discuss here, begs other questions—namely, when and how do the serial productions of these plays intersect with the continual murders of women in Juárez? Amavizca Murúa's play has run intermittently in Los Angeles at the Frida Kahlo Theater for years and has also traveled to academic venues throughout the country. Noriega's production of Michaus's play has been to Quito, Ecuador, various academic venues throughout the United States, including the Kennedy Center American College Theater Festival in 2015. Robles's play has traveled throughout Mexico, Latin America, and Europe.[64] The transnational circuit of testimonial femicide plays deserves attention as a mode of seriality in itself. One must think critically about the temporal reality of both the femicides and the circulation of media about them.

The popularity of these testimonial plays is in sharp contrast with U.S. Latinx-authored plays about the events that use testimonial forms or make testimonial claims. Marisela Orta's *Braided Sorrow* has never had a professional production; Coco Fusco's *The Incredible Disappearing Woman* has rarely been produced; and Victor Cazares's *The Dead Women of J-Town and*

Smiley has had one professional production. Svich's *Iphigenia Crash Land Falls* has had more airtime, but her work is notably framed as an adaptation of a Greek original rather than a play about femicide. Perhaps, then, as in the case of Olmos's *so go the ghosts of méxico, part 1*, packaging a play as testimonial, even when it is very theatrical, ensures a work's circulation more readily than marketing a play that openly addresses its constructed nature. This may be because audiences are uncomfortable with theatricalized fictional representations of egregious crimes. Or perhaps viewers want to excise humor when they speak about violence. Whatever may be the case, while I admire the work of the artists involved, and stand behind their desires to use theater to raise awareness about the crimes, the presumed transparent relationship between the real, the serial, the authentic, and the truth projected onto these theatrical productions is at times discomfiting to me. In the rest of this chapter I move to the work of the playwrights mentioned above, who are less dependent on the *testimonio* form and more openly critical of the idea of the real. I begin with Marisela Treviño Orta's *Braided Sorrow*.

Braided Sorrow, or, How to Betray Transnational Capital

Braided Sorrow's protagonist, Alma, moves from rural Mexico to work at a maquila to make money temporarily while her sister-in-law, Yadria, helps her find better paid work in El Paso as a maid. A supervisor sexually harasses her upon arrival at the factory; Alma is then attacked on the way home by a group of low-rent security guards whose clutches she escapes because an older woman gives her body over to save Alma's. Nevertheless, Alma is ultimately killed in the desert. The play ends with her brother claiming her body at the police station. *Braided Sorrow* is not only a family drama, however. The play includes several members of Alma's family, neighbors, and the older woman, La Llorona.

The presence of La Llorona, the famous weeping woman of Mexico, adds a mythic element to the play that collapses time and space. La Llorona seems to live in both the sixteenth and late twentieth centuries simultaneously. Her inclusion underscores Orta's overt comparison between the violence of the Spanish Conquest and the violence in present-day Juárez. Her playbill note reads: "One of the omens of doom that foretold the coming of the Spanish and the fall of the Aztec empire was a woman dressed in white wandering the streets of Tenochtitlan, wailing."[65] The set registers both times by including "an Aztec pyramid made out of junk, a patchwork of corrugated tin, wire and tires: the discarded and scavenged artifacts of a border town."[66] Over the course of the play, this pyramid is undone and slowly crumbles. This overt reconstruction is not the only Brechtian aspect to the mise-en-scène. Characters announce scene titles that underscore major themes and lessons of the play, such as "a matter of economics" and "supply and demand." A "matter of economics" lays out the personal economics of the family, while "supply and demand" lays out the economics of the factory—underscoring the profitability of the enterprise in contrast to the maquila workers' inability get ahead financially.

These titles also showcase the economic frame for describing the violence in the play by revealing how the subjugation of humanity to profit is linked to sexual harassment and violence. It is in "supply and demand" that Mr. Fillmore first suggests to Alma that she can get ahead by knowing her worth, that is, being willing to acquiesce to his or others' desires for her.[67] His brutal economic rationale culminates in a sexual assault, revealing the deep relationship between both forms of exploitation. Fillmore's name evokes the idea of filling more, recalling the requirements of factory piecework labor. It is also the name of the vice president to President Zachary Taylor, who fought in the Mexican-American war, and although he did not share his predecessor's military history against Mexico, Fillmore did end up brokering the Compromise of 1850, which annexed California and made New Mexico a territory, marking a rather passive role in U.S. imperialism and the retention of slavery in the South. The fact that he is described in the play as "neither Mexican or American" and that it is suggested he be cast as a "fair-skinned Latino" makes apparent his role as part of an oppressive transnational complex.[68] While Yadria claims U.S.-Mexico jurisdiction will stop Fillmore from acting on his lecherous leering, the opposite is the case, underscoring that a different set of laws exist for transnational operators of capital. Nonetheless, the play does not suggest that Fillmore orchestrates the subsequent attack on Alma. Instead, it is a random act of street violence perpetrated by people hired to protect others. This randomness points to a more widespread misogyny in Juárez. Alma, to protect herself, cuts off her braid, removing one of the signifiers that would mark her as a likely victim of the murderers. In fact, the first scene of the play, which is out of chronological order, features her giving herself a haircut. We only later learn her specific motivation although it is foreshadowed by her comment, "I thought it might be better if I didn't have long hair.[69] The title of the play refers to this act; this ghost braid becomes a prosthetic reminder of her lost innocence and eventually the loss of her life. The attention given to the development of the character, especially her love for poetry, her ambition, her love for her family, and her willingness to voice discomfort with the rigors of maquila work, remind the audience of what is destroyed (*almas*, or souls) under neoliberal capital. Orta counters the inhumanity of the murders by creating a fully realized character—a soul—we relate to and sympathize with throughout the play, a tactic other playwrights in this chapter reject.

Other female characters, however, have more emblematic and ambivalent role, replicating complicated complicities within neoliberal Mexico. La Llorona, for example, embodies the feminized labor of truth telling often performed by female relatives of the disappeared, as well as being an agent of violence. As Christina Marín suggests, La Llorona carries the moral burden of truth telling throughout the play, making her an allegorical rendering of a *tranfronterista* activist who stands in as a mourner, supporter, and protector and as a feminized, particularized embodiment of Mexico *herself*.[70] She first appears as an older woman who points out the more sinister aspects of the desert. Later, she becomes the classic weeping woman of Mexican myth, claiming that "they're hunting my daughters."[71] She also saves Alma from sexual attack by substituting her body for Alma's at the beginning of the play.

Later in *Braided Sorrow*, however, we find out that this act came at the expense of saving Blanca, a relative of her aunt's *comadre* (close friend). This revelation comes after La Llorona's sinister request that Alma go to the desert, dig up a rosebush, and bury her braid there so that the blood underneath it can flow and bear witness to the murders in the desert. The weeping woman claims that Alma has the power to do this act because she has the "song" (the poem Alma writes over the course of the play). La Llorona says she will save Alma if she encounters danger; all she has to do is call. Although apprehensive, Alma agrees. While she is in the desert, however, she is killed, albeit obliquely. After she finishes reciting the poem, "there is a sudden crash of sound spotlights fix on her silent form. She tries to scream, but like before she begins to panic, choking on air. She sits holding her braid, terrified. Lights shift."[72] Although Marín registers La Llorona's multiple cultural roles within the play, acknowledging that she is "an evocative spirit who teaches, frightens, mesmerizes, tricks and betrays," she does not confront La Llorona's role in Alma's death.[73] Orta reads the relationship between La Llorona and Alma in a more classically tragic manner. For Orta, Alma's failure to accomplish her task is her tragic flaw, and La Llorona's lament is that she has chosen the wrong person to carry out the task. Alma, then, is a sacrifice, just as Iphigenia is in Svich's tragedy. Thinking of her audience and the need to connect them to the tragedy and feel a loss, Orta "knew Alma had to die."[74] And, she also seemed to know that a woman would be complicit in bringing about her death.

This tragic structure, in combination with Catholic iconography, offers a complex rendering of Alma's demise. Although the description of her murder in the final scene suggests Alma was the victim of a sex murder, this is not represented onstage. Instead audiences are presented with a verbal description that links her demise to her failure to perform without freezing up. La Llorona's failure to save Alma is a consequence of the fact that Alma did not call or cry out like she did when she was fighting off her attackers earlier in the play. This is, of course, one natural reaction to repeated violence or trauma. La Llorona, however, is not remorseful and blames Alma for not calling her. Additionally, La Llorona's role as a device to lead Alma to the desert displaces the fact that most women are taken there rather than journeying there on their own. The reference to roses in the desert recalls the Virgin of Guadalupe. In contrast, La Llorona acts as an anti-intercessor; within this frame Alma becomes a martyr rather than a Juan Diegan saint. In Orta's mind, however, Alma is more like Bernadette of Lourdes, who is mentioned earlier in the play as Yadria's saints' name.[75] Bernadette was an illiterate nineteenth-century French peasant who saw a Marian apparition numerous times at a grotto now believed to have holy water. She was, notably, a victim of the industrial revolution: a steam mill put her father, a miller, out of business, leading them to a life of a very limited means. The parallel with Alma is striking but does not extricate her from more orthodox Catholic framings of womanhood. Combined with Alma's sartorial virginity, underscored by her donning of a white communion dress recrafted from Yadria's wedding dress earlier in the play, this deus ex machina reifies various feminine symbols of traditional Mexican Catholicism that render Alma as an ethical victim. The fact that Alma was experiencing her body sensually (although without recourse to sexual activity) for the first time before being killed raises the specter of danger that comes with womanhood. This Catholic frame, compounded with references to the Conquest, makes her death seem inevitable, if horrific, for those versed in Mexican cultural narratives. If it is this inevitability that codes the play as tragic, one wonders about the efficacy of hailing the allegorization of Mexican history (in Marín's terms) to explain neoliberal violence.[76] It might be too easy for some audiences to blame the victim here.

A reading of Alma's fate in light of neoliberal labor may let us think about her in a different way. Alma seemingly has three essential personality qualities that make her exceptional in contrast to Blanca, who indexes femicide as a generic rather than a particular act. One is Alma's independence and ambition; the second is her love for poetry; the third is her tendency to freeze up in unfamiliar situations. This strange combination makes her both an ideal liberal subject on dramaturgical level and an un-ideal neoliberal laborer on the other. The first two qualities garner audience sympathy within a liberal humanist framework, making her relatable, likable, and perhaps even ebullient. They also mark her as someone who does not take to neoliberal discipline of the maquila easily. She is not a "disposable woman" because she is an exceptional person; yet her failure to perform smoothly in the maquila and in the face of violence are what ultimately do her in, making her exceptionality truly ambivalent in the face of neoliberal capital. This ambivalence exposes a persistent myth at the center of neoliberal capitalist discourse—that a classically liberal self is the ideal subject for the neoliberal world; yet, as this play makes clear by killing Alma, neoliberalism's disciplinary procedures ask for the exact opposite set of traits from all but the most elite entrepreneurs. Neoliberalism needs a docile body that imagines itself as singular, but only enacts submission to disciplinary order. Alma's refusal to play the game is what fills Fillmore with rage and motivates his desire to do sexual violence to her. Although Alma does not fully comprehend this lesson over the course of the play, audiences do, making this the most fulsome contribution of this play to neoliberal critique.

The play also exposes the need to respond to fine-grained changes in modes of neoliberal violence. *Braided Sorrow* depends upon unrealistic modes of representing violence, largely, I argue, to avoid reanimating gruesome violence against women while pointing to everyday violence, affective terror, and impunity in neoliberal Mexico. The pricking of fingers on nopal and the bleeding pomegranates are visceral but not literal ways to reveal the violence ignored in everyday Juárez. These images are clearly part of a representational system that culminates in the revelation of blood in the desert that La Llorona desires to be seen. The same could be said for the heartbeats under the earth that La Llorona tells Alma to listen to and the ominous dripping of water that accompanies many scenes. These representations are modes of remembrance of the dead, which disallow the play's public from ignoring the violence of everyday life. La Llorona's concentration on the visible (although the play also instantiates the aural) is a double-edged sword given how dead bodies have come to represent the wielding of power. On one hand, the femicides that have occurred since Orta wrote her play have increasingly depended upon a mode of hypervisibility of corpses rather than their erasure. On the other, given the recent disappearances in Ayotzinapa, the index of visuality as a mode of fighting impunity has again become relevant. It is notable that both Orta and Sergio González Rodríguez, author of *The Femicide Machine*, decide to forgo images of the bodies in their work, offering textual (González Rodríguez) or highly allegorized (Orta) descriptions of the images, pointing to the contemporary ethical dilemma of staging femicidal violence. Victor Cazares, rather than interrogating the representation of violence, questions our reliance on reliable narrators, effectively undoing the idea of the ebullient and ethical victim and its opposite, the well-meaning savior who desires to give voice to the voiceless.

The Dead Women of J-Town and Smiley, Transnational Violence, Consumerism, and the Power of the Anti-Testimonial

Victor Cazares's *The Dead Women of J-Town and Smiley* abandons the allegorical for the phantasmagoric while performing a different critique of the neoliberal condition. Rather than trying to illuminate how neoliberal conditions lead to the femicides in Juárez, Cazares point out how the femicides represent part of a continuum of violence in greater Mexico, which includes consumerism, poverty, and the militarization of the border. He asks what the killings can tell us about the conditions of the neoliberal bordersphere instead of asking how these factors "cause" the killings.

The action of the play is simple. The dead women of Juárez want to reunite with their families and escape from their oppression by crossing the U.S.-Mexico border. This task brings them into contact with the curators of the National Museum of the Dead Women of Juárez and a pair of border patrol agents who try to thwart their plans. Chaos ensues. When we arrive in the desert where Mayra, a recently killed woman discovers herself, we meet a chorus who tell us:

> The Dead Women of Juárez stand/walk/run/die/live/exist in the desert. They wait for rain, wait for their children. a Mexican economy boom, justice, money, the bus—they wait for everything that will not come. Nothing ever comes to the desert. Everything leaves us. Abandoned here we lie.[77]

The murders in this play are in the past; the present is about the condition of being left behind. The fact of being abandoned articulates desire rather than ends it. The pronoun switch is important too. The "we" above does not refer only to the dead women of Juárez, but to all of us who are watching and listening. This transnational abandonment is the condition for the action of the play rather than its moral punctum.

Cazares's play draws inspiration from the telenovela and Christian eschatology rather than the well-made play. The telenovela determines the histrionic tone of the play's characters' conflicts and informs its absurdity and seriality. The plot of the play is, however, eschatological, literally representing the end of the world as we know it. The joining of the everyday world and the divine is represented as a journey north by bus into the United States—an ambivalent heaven if there ever was one. The trip is undertaken in the now, making us part of this exodus of the dead. This is no selective apocalypse. The stage direction that opens the final scene tells us as much: "We are all inside the bus now. There is no division between us and its passengers."[78]

The Dead Women of J-Town and Smiley brings us—as U.S. audiences—into the story Cazares tells about desire, abandonment, and the U.S.-Mexico border by eliminating our spectatorial distance, ironically undoing the work of his museum's curators of death. The play begins with a pretext that performs this hailing. Josefa, Paco's mother and reigning matriarch, starts the play by addressing her audience as "dear American child, Dear American citizen, Dear Uncle Sam," asking the audience members to "make yourself ready for the helicopter that comes in the night, with a searchlight, with a gun with hate. America, you will cross your own border in haste. And as you do, remember us, remember me, Josefa, Matriarch of the Dead Women of Juárez. Flee this nation that never was and never will be, and don't look back. You won't turn into a pillar of salt if you do—you will turn into me."[79] The monologue is a threat even if Josefa is "genuinely concerned for us," as the stage direction suggests.[80] By implying that U.S. citizens will be subject to their own violence by crossing their own border in haste she suggests that we too can be victims of the violence the United States enacts; the results might look a lot like Juárez. Following this speech is a video installation of the National Museum of the Dead Women of Juárez which underscores this point. Lina and Mariana, the curators of the museum, erase the separation between the victims and the audience. In contrast to Josefa, they address the audience as potential women of Juárez rather than as U.S. citizens. The process by which this happens is gradual, developing over the course of the scene. At first the "you" is Angelica Villalobos, who is directly addressed as the first femicide. Next the "you" becomes all of the women of Juárez, who "became you (Angelica) forgotten." Soon, however, the audience is addressed as "you" by extension, when Lina and Mariana tell us that they bring "your bodies here to the Museum of the Dead Women of Juárez."[81] Because the video plays in the theater, the lobby, and the bathroom, one cannot escape their welcome. We are vulnerable spectators. This clarion call hails us as perpetrators and victims of violence on both sides of the border, erasing any differentiation that could secure a spectator's identity as exterior to the events of the play.

The museum's exhibits link femicidal violence in Juárez to that more generally enacted by the Mexican and U.S. nation-states. Women's bodies and their possessions flash upon the screen: "stretchers with dead women, dresses, tampons, purses, food, a McDonald's Happy Meal, a stroller, a Bible, various Mexican paraphernalia."[82] Other screens show the macrocosm they live in: "photographs of the border, of women, of Juárez, of Mexican patriotism and drugs."[83] By combining transnational consumerism items, gender specific belongings, and remnants of allegiance to the nation with the bodies of the victims, Cazares infuses the crime scenes with the presence of a state that allows savage capitalism, structural inequality, and misogyny to thrive.

By emphasizing the state's presence, Cazares counters one of the prevailing (and deeply untrue) myths of neoliberalism: that it is the absence of the state rather than the state's strengthening that is responsible for neoliberal conditions. Much of Cazares's critique engages the politics of the U.S.-Mexican border, U.S. imperialism, and post-9/11 militarization. The presence of *la migra* brings this point home. Revisiting and revising a trope in Chicano drama, Paco, Josefa's son, is a border patrol agent who denies his own mother entry into the country. His partner, Sam, who loves Paco and the United States a little too much, decides to become more militaristic in order to discourage terrorism. In a queer moment, the two men (in the absence of the baby's birth mother) names Paco's new son James Polk after the president who started the Mexican-American War. By the time Sam and the women have their final confrontation, the baby is outfitted in a stroller tank, absurdly mimicking the increased militarization of the border. Paco, on the other hand, abandons his former stance, which caused him to deny his own mother entry into the country. After getting caught in the border fence himself, he attempts to help his mother and the other dead women cross "legally" into the United States.

The women's attempts to move north—all of which are violently thwarted—are riven with black humor. First, Gloria/o, the homophobic trans woman, gets stuck in a border fence because she has no idea how to cross.

Then, after escaping the border patrol, the women happen upon an abandoned McDonald's where, starving, they scarf rancid food. After they destroy the McDonald's following a killer sandstorm, they are forced to move on. In a moment of desperation, they come up with a brilliant plan to get over the bridge in a truck filled with maquiladora goods. Because Paco, a U.S. citizen, will drive them, the trip will be legal. This barrage of physical, environmental, and economic violence leads them to Sam, who is staking out the U.S.-Mexico border. When Sam catches them he derisively dismisses their plan which he sees as "thinly disguised as a liberal critique of border policies" that would never work.[84] Their attempt fails, but the critique succeeds: NAFTA makes it easier than ever to bring goods to and fro but more difficult for people to make the same journey.

The border, of course, is not a clear boundary in this play. It is a purgatory space—a space in between—as it is in Cazares's other plays. As he tells us: "The space is a deathtrap and a prison. There is a line that designates America. There is a line that designates Mexico. They are in the space in between." The limbo of the border mirrors the limbo between earth and heaven that his characters also inhabit. They need a messiah to help them out of limbo, and he comes—in the form of Ms. Mary Masochrist, Smiley's drag persona. Sam's shooting is to no avail in the face of his power—Smiley and the women are already dead after all. They simply walk across the border once he arrives. As Ms. Mary Masochrist explains: "Borders don't work Sam. You can't contain the human spirit and that is what borders try to contain."[85] Rather than fall into a puerile form of liberal humanist rhetoric, however, Ms. Mary Masochrist continues on: "Tomorrow or sometime thereafter, despite myself, I see the day when America will be America for all. And then the world. Yes. The world will be for everyone, not just Americans."[86] Thus, the future is a nationless future, based on a more equitable global distribution of resources. That world, Cazares suggests, might be as efficacious in helping the women of Juárez to follow their dreams as catching the killers would be. By making this claim, Cazares breaks most radically with narrative and filmic forms dedicated to solving the crimes.

Unlike other authors I have thus considered, Cazares concentrates on thinking about the problem of transnational capitalism and its murderous excesses through the lens of consumption rather than production. Yet he also avoids a romanticization of the Mexican nation-state prior to capital. Cazares's irreverence is most clear in the fourth scene of the play, titled "Day of the Dead." In Mexico, the Day of the Dead persists in the face of its diabolical double—Halloween. Over the course of the three days of celebration, October 31, November 1, and November 2, many Mexican families offer food and gifts to their dead relatives either where they are buried or at home altars. This practice is a syncretic form of honoring one's ancestors equally infused with indigenous practices and European pagan celebrations. Although a quotidian practice, the state has latched onto Day of the Dead celebrations as emblematic of national culture. Cazares's characters are not part of these proceedings. The scene opens with each of the dead women waiting for their relatives and talking about the food they bring (or don't).

> JESSICA: My mom and dad come. They never wake up early, so they come at around noon. They bring me McDonald's. I love la Big Mac. And las french fries. Except that . . . last year, I bit into one and blood oozed out. And I thought I was biting into someone's fingers but I wasn't.
> GLORIA: I never liked that stuff. Las hamburgers and French fries.
> JESSICA: Well, it's not like I am offering you any.
> CHELA: She never shares.
> JESSICA: It's not like they bring me two Big Macs! I just get one. I offer you all my ketchup and salt packets. Besides none of you like fast food.
> CHELA: It tastes like a maquiladora. Made by a machine. Nothing like what my family brings—a feast. I taught them all how to cook—all the secret recipes of the Enriquez clan. I taught them how to make molé, enchiladas rojas, enchiladas verdes, frijoles refritos, gorditas, tamales, flautas, tortillas,—todo, todo, todo. . . .[87]

This nationalist-consumerist dyad is a staple of Mexican/Chicano discourses of authenticity. Tellingly, these women's stalwart resistance to fast food breaks down as they become desperately hungry and end up in a McDonald's begging for scraps. Concomitantly, their discussion of telenovelas reveals the link between desire for consumer goods, mass-produced television, and subjectivity. Cazares's translation of the serial murder into the serial television drama is more than clever association. Temporally the serial, of course, places us in a constant state of consumption and deferral without plot resolution from which we cannot escape, just as the victims of Juárez cannot. The fact that Jessica bites into a burger that bleeds and *keeps eating* is an example par excellence of the violence imbedded in transnational capitalist production, which includes narcotrafficking alongside fast-food franchising. It is also through this lens that the play takes on the narcotics industry. It is no accident that Smiley's drug consumption peaks when he is in the McDonald's and that he is particularly cruel in this scene. (Cazares's *Ramses* and *Religiones Gringas* address the dealing side of narcotraffic more openly.)

The murder of the women is also a form of consumption, as Jessica's breakout monologue shows us.

> JESSICA GARZA
> JESSICA GARZA
> Fuck this shit
> Blood blood blood

> And Shit
> Mixed
> And fucked
> Because of the Fucking
> And now I am onstage
> Display this
> Display that
> Display your own fucking
> Blood and shit,
> Rape your own bodies
> And stop treating
> Us like
> Fucking
> Happy Meals.
> I'm always lowering my prices.
> I'm marked down, marked down,
> Just pay the price.[88]

This monologue launches a stinging critique of the *representation* of the Juárez murders in the media, particularly our consumption of the victims as abject objects themselves. Jessica's references to being displayed are crucial as is her choice to scream her own name, pointing out that she is not nameless at all—despite the curators' fetish for collecting the unclaimed unnamed bodies in the desert. Her outrage reveals that the museum, despite its founders' intentions, participates in this consumption. Lina and Mariana, our "macabre, burlesque hosts," *perform* a form of consumption by bringing the bodies of the dead and their consumable items into the museum.[89] In this process, the dead women's bodies become literal commodities for the curators, who become desperate to obtain and contain these bodies for their museum. For example, when Paco goes to the museum to try to find his mother's corpse, he takes one of their bodies, and rather than being glad the body is being identified, Lina and Mariana fight him for it, leaving Mariana with a bloodied lip. After the incident Lina tells Mariana the next course of action: "I'll put some ice on your lip, we'll clean up. And we'll go find another dead body in the desert and pretend this never happened."[90] In the midst of this struggle, they decide to create a Museum of Dead Illegal Immigrants and almost end up bringing Paco back into the museum as an exhibit. The curators, who serve their communities by creating a site to remember the dead, ultimately fail. It is only when they give up their U.S.-based NGO rhetoric and the othering process it entails and actually listen to dead women of Juárez that they are able to get anything done.

> JOSEFA: We need to do this now for my grandson—
> PACO: For Chela's children, too—He'll be after them soon. Your dad too, Jessica. Sam's planning on sifting out all of the illegals—

LINA: I think the word you are looking for is undocumented.
MARIANA: No human being is illegal.
LINA: You know, it sickens me to think about how dehumanized your undocumented family members must be in the U.S. right now.
MARIANA: To think that the inanimate things that you all made in your maquiladoras are treated more humanely than they—
LINA: And thanks to NAFTA allowed to cross into America without problems.
JESSICA: I always wished I could become one of the jeans I made at the maquiladora so I could get shipped into the U.S.
MARIANA: Oh my god that is so genius![91]

Cazares's humor and irony reveal migrant perseverance in the face of impotent self-righteous sloganeering even as he exposes the modes of exotification that NGO practice can enact. He also points to how we as audience members participate in this process: we re-victimize the women of Juárez and deny them agency through our consumption of their representation. Cazares restores this agency when he has Mayra take revenge on her attackers by running them down in a maquila bus. That the women end up crossing the border in that same bus underscores his critique. The bus, which is the site of victimization for so many of the women in films, plays, and novels about Juárez, becomes a vehicle of vigilante justice, a place to take power rather than to be rendered powerless.[92]

Although Cazares is mostly concerned with economic violence, he does not discount the influence of misogyny and homophobia that predates, extends, and is transformed in the neoliberal era. He examines how contemporary Mexico as a cultural entity remains dependent on harmful religious ideology as an embodied practice perpetuated by people of all genders. Many of the women of Juárez are homophobic and transphobic toward Smiley, whose non-cis-gendered body causes them to lash out at him repeatedly. Smiley's mother, we learn, killed him when she discovered him being raped by her boyfriend. She justifies her actions by claiming that Smiley provoked her boyfriend in much the same way as the authorities blamed the women killed in Juárez for their deaths because they were wearing scanty clothing.

It is true that many transgendered people are victimized on the U.S.-Mexico border, particularly sex workers, who are targeted because of the lack of respect they receive in society.[93] Cazares, however, uses non-cis-gendered characters in a less documentary way by denaturalizing sex and gender so as to underscore how Christianity traffics in internalized misogyny, homophobia, and transphobia that aid and abet the conflation of deviance, sexual pleasure, and destruction. The dead women of Juárez are culpable for this violence as well as being victimized by it. Smiley, of course, is no saint either. He has a drug problem; he screams at dead Iraqi children; he is mean to his sister. But he is still the messiah. This choice interrogates the latent form of Marianismo that infiltrates representations of Juárez.[94] Cazares's view here contrasts with representations of the victims, who privilege their real and apparently female Catholic virtue in the mode Rosa-Linda Fregoso finds problematic in her review of *Señorita Extraviada*, a film she otherwise champions.[95]

There is also a wilier formal innovation at play: *The Dead Women of J-Town and Smiley* is an anti-testimonial that turns the dramaturgy of Juárez representation on its head. Cazares has his curators, Lina and Mariana, tell the audience that the crimes are unsolved, that the victims are poor, and that they are largely forgotten. Mayra's testimony about how she actually dies—by being killed by a gang of men, not her lover or husband—performs the setting straight of the record many plays and movies perform. Yet Cazares's dramaturgical strategy differs from the ones used by other playwrights discussed in this chapter. His narrators are not always reliable. For example, Smiley gets the facts wrong about Mayra's death; Gloria/o lies about her gender identity while being violent to Smiley. They are both untrustworthy performers who make their own realities. There is also no reverence in representations of the grotesque aspects of ritual sexual violence, as there was in the other plays considered here. Jessica's death, which involved porn production, is staged as a "snuff film translated for the stage" that starts out erotic and becomes horrific.[96] That Jessica is a sexual being who initially participated in a non-normative sex act is radical. And the staging of the film as a consciously theatrical act (which many S/M practices arguably are) underscores *J-Town*'s awareness of itself as a performance that comments on the very problem of testimony as truthful. By interrogating the valorization of the women as subaltern truth tellers whose bodies and words simply reveal rather than consciously articulate the violence done to them, *The Dead Women of J-Town* undoes the othering of the women of Juárez as abject, voiceless, or guileless, while never erasing their disenfranchisement.

Cazares largely achieves his critique through theatricality rather than by stripping away theater's artifices. Smiley, as Ms. Mary Masochrist, is aware of herself as a performer and acknowledges that her role as a messiah is performative. The first time we see her is during an act in a club, after which she is absurdly removed on a stretcher. She begins her act by entering in full glory, selling CDs, and then detailing her death. This is not a standard testimonial. The narration occurs in the middle of a performance that ends with the revelation that Ms. Mary Masochrist is pregnant with a child, a fantastical possibility at best. When Mary speaks, we are hailed as the audience of a drag show, not as a witness to the crimes in a traditional sense. The choice of the drag show is crucial because it is a performance form that acknowledges, engages, and flirts with its audience while registering the theatricality of the intervention.

Chela's description of her own death when she was the last passenger on the bus is alienating in a different way, exposing Cazares's reimagination of the audience's relationship to these testimonials. The dead women in the desert constantly interrupt Chela when she details the crime, never giving her or the audience an opportunity to have a catharsis or even be immersed in her story. Cazares's refusal to let his audience be overtaken by sympathetic attachment to these women's dehumanization and destruction during their testimonials forces his audience to reflect on the affective manipulation of straight testimonials that impute a certain kind of sympathy from the audience. He asks that we reject this mechanism and be aware of ourselves as audience members so that he can later take away our ability to stand aside, which he does when Lina and Mariana are stripped of their curatorial privilege as observers of atrocity. Both of them end up dying in the desert and become part of the crew of the dead in the bus as it crosses the desert. One could simply read this as a statement that cultural production about femicides is always exploitative. The eschatological resonances of the final scene indicate a more world-historical implication: that privileged citizens of the Americas will not always be safe under the aegis of transnational capitalism. Lina and Mariana clearly stand in for the audience within the frame of the play. Their fate is also ours. The play is the process by which we as spectators all get on the bus, as though we are the dead women who pretended to be things to survive. It is through refusing to empathize in a traditional sense—by performing as things ourselves or, at least, imagining ourselves as things—that we articulate our ethical relationship to the Juárez femicides and to the dangers of transnational capital.

Cazares's mode of alienation contrasts with Bolaño's strategy in "The Part about the Crimes" in *2666.*[97] Bolaño's political critique is made through highly formal means.[98] For example, as Sebastian Ferrari claims, the listing of crimes in the near but not quite documentary fashion of a catalogue never allows the dead to speak, ultimately refusing liberal subjectivity.[99] Denying the separation of public and private spheres so crucial to that subjectivity's construction forecloses the very possibility of witnessing.[100] Cazares's undoing of empathic identification or witnessing works through hypertheatricality rather than through emotionless documentary serial description. In Cazares's work, then, theatricality is the most successful mode of gesturing to the real. Cazares's revelation is not lost on Coco Fusco.

Theatricalizing Performance: *The Incredible Disappearing Woman*

Fusco's *The Incredible Disappearing Woman* is dedicated to tracing the history of sexualized violence against Latin American women over the course of the last forty years, from the emergence of the first traces of neoliberal hegemony in the hemisphere. Her play juxtaposes contemporary violence against brown women in Mexico and Central America with two incidents in the 1970s—the torture of young leftists under Pinochet's rule in Chile and a

U.S. art project from the 1970s that involved a white male conceptual artist having sex with a female corpse he paid for in Mexico.[101] Her performative genealogy creates an alternate historiography of neoliberal violence that parallels Diana Washington Valdez's claim that the femicides are rooted in the policing practices of Latin American dictatorships in the '60s and '70s.[102] Although Fusco never refers to the murders in Juárez in her play, it is clearly at the forefront of her thinking. She dedicates *The Incredible Disappearing Woman* to "the memory of 220 women, most of whom were maquila workers, who disappeared in the city of Juárez from 1993 to 1999."[103]

Rather than memorialize the dead, however, Fusco creates a play that writes art-making practice, particularly performance art, into the creation of a neoliberal hegemony that devalues Latinx women. For this reason, *The Incredible Disappearing Woman* takes place entirely in a museum where three Latinas work: a Chilean security guard, Magaly, and two janitors, Dolores, a very Catholic working-class Salvadoreña in her fifties, and Chela, a thirtysomething Mexican Norteña. An upper-class Mexican female curator appears on-screen to introduce the conceptual art to the audience when the play begins. Docents and a set of supernumerary male characters of Chilean and Mexican descent also appear at the margins. Chela and Dolores need to prepare the exhibition room for an audience, while Magaly stands guard. In the midst of their work they collaborate on a plan to surprise the artist who will appear at the exhibition. They decide to replace the mannequin with whom he plans to reenact "the act" with a live person, shocking him. In the process of setting up their theatrical trick, they deliver *testimonios* about their own experiences of violent situations. We learn that Dolores, who was systematically abused by her husband and raped by her priest for years, often faints on the job and Chela continually covers for her. Chela, meanwhile, was previously fired after a bizarre sexual liaison with a maquila boss which led her to come to the United States. Magaly was tortured under Pinochet and is in the United States to escape the torturers, who followed her to Mexico City after she left her home country. Labor-related, sexual, and political oppressions live side by side and occupy the same space. By recognizing each other's painful pasts, they are moved to drop their adversarial attitudes, which are fueled in part by the class tension between the women. The Chilean guard is in a hierarchically superior position in the museum (she actually seems to get breaks, for example), enjoying a privileged class position and educational background (she used to be a teacher) in comparison to her Central American and Mexican coworkers.

Their working together is traditional form of grassroots political collaboration that constructs a lie in order to expose the truth; what they work on, after all, is the elaboration of a theatrical trick, linking their confessions to theatricality from the outset. Their confessions come in the midst of deciding which one of them should play the role of the corpse, standing in for the defective mannequin; their stories attest to their suitability, or lack of it, for the job. At first, it seems like Dolores should do it because she can just pretend she is having one of her fainting spells, but given her fear of having Donald Horton, the artist whose work they are restaging, look at her naked, this seems like a bad choice. This leads Chela to explain why she can't play dead effectively but also why she wants someone else to do so. Chela, who worked at a Mattel maquiladora before she came to the United States, has a hard time holding still. She learned this after she had a strange sexual encounter with a supervisor from the factory, during which he offered her a drink which had drugs in it that knocked her out. When she awoke, she saw him in her clothes, dancing around, and she laughed rather than playing dead and pretending the drugs were still working.[104] Humiliated, he later gets her fired, causing her catastrophic financial hardship. Eventually, Chela tells Magaly that she needs to be the *muertita* because the other two will fail. At first, Magaly refuses, but then she agrees.

> MAGALY: Chela! Chela, you're right. I should be the one.
> CHELA: (*Walking back into the diorama.*)The one what?
> MAGALY: The one on the table when that man comes in. La Muertita.
> (*She slides the mannequin under the table again.*)
> DOLORES: (*Walking back in*) Porque habla de muertas?
> MAGALY: I'm the only one here who is alive because I knew how to play dead.
> DOLORES: Que dices?
> MAGALY: I was very convincing. I was dead for years. Some people say I'm dead.[105]

Magaly then describes how she was raped and tortured by the Chilean army. On the advice of an unknown man, she played dead during a rape and was left for dead afterward without being killed. Eventually rescued, she left Chile for Mexico City and later for the United States.

That all of the women go unconscious and play dead—successfully or not—links them with the unnamed dead woman the artist defiles. Their traumas are spoken, if not relived, in the process of encountering the art object and its history. And it is through reliving these experiences that they work through their own violations together. The punch line, of course, is that the artist simply ignores the reality of what is before him: a live woman playing dead. When he enters the room he "stands alone and still for a moment, listening to the tape. When it ends, he looks at Magaly briefly but does not get close to her. Instead, he pulls out a comb and runs it through his hair, then hoists up his jeans and leaves the projection."[106] Magaly, Chela, and Dolores "look at each other sheepishly" and eventually come together under the sheet Magaly covered herself with, sharing a brief moment of solidarity.[107] They are revivified in much the same way as Magaly was when she escaped death in Chile. In contrast, Horton tries to revive a part of himself through his contact with a dead woman before he mutilates himself. He explains that he could not obtain a corpse in the United States, so when he was in a porn store, he "turned around and saw this Mexican guy who was looking at some pretty gruesome snuff videos, so I went up to him and asked, did he know about that kind of thing? And he said sure, I can put you in touch with someone in TJ, if you're willing to pay. I said sure, how much. And he said, oh maybe 70 or 80 bucks an hour."[108]

Horton's actions expose the illicit sexual economies of the Americas under neoliberalism. The value of a corpse is quantified here, although a dead body cannot reap a profit. In the context of the play, however, one is stunned by the translation to the hourly wage, considering the wages of maquila labor. Horton, as an artist whose performative acts are modes of expression, has sex with a corpse as a mode of expressive violence just like the Juárez killers do. He participates in the same transnational trade in bodies. By telling Horton's story in the midst of her larger critique of the romanticization of the dead Latina body, Fusco inducts the abjection of the brown female body in the Americas into U.S. art history and labor history simultaneously. Merely condemning the artist is not Fusco's point. Her goal is remembering the anonymous Mexican woman who, after all, was part of the artwork, even without her consent.

Fusco restores the unnamed dead woman's presence through the aliveness of the three women characters/actors of the play, literally making the bodies that do not matter into matter *theatrically*. It is for this reason that I wish to concentrate on the formal choices Fusco makes in rendering these real events as a doubly theatrical event (the characters stage a play within a play) that makes the play function as an anti-testimonial testimonial. What is most curious about *The Incredible Disappearing Woman* for those who know Fusco's oeuvre of performance art is that it is a traditionally structured play with a beginning, middle, and end. And it has characters.[109] Unlike Fusco's performance art that renders the body as a site of direct violence for/by the audience, *The Incredible Disappearing Woman* displaces that violence onto characters and is rendered verbally. While these monologues take the form of *testimonio*, the play argues against the direct relation of experience as a transparent mode of restoring truth to the public sphere or healing the women involved. Fusco's characters are too self-conscious about the very act of storytelling as a performance for this to be true. And none of the characters really have a denouement after telling their stories. Dolores does not come out of what Magaly calls her "delusion." Chela is no less angry about what happened to her than she was at the beginning of the play. Magaly gains nothing from playing the corpse; she is just the best person for the job. What remains at the end of the play is a stagy tableau of theatrical failure. What is effective in this play, then, is its critique of the representation of violence through theatricality: the staged doubling of the real women who suffered violence and the characters who portray them which gestures to the real bodies that mimic the mannequin that mimics the real body of the woman in Tijuana. That the entire play documents what happens backstage—both in terms of setting up the exhibit and in terms of showing the often invisible labor of Latina workers within art spaces—makes its theatricality even more apparent. That the women *stage* their own abjection consciously reframes their testimonials as something more than simple transparent truth telling. Dolores's body may speak in ways she cannot control, but Chela and Magaly control their own bodies when they create a spectacle.

Although there have been productions where actors played the parts separately, it is perhaps most interesting to consider the piece as a text for reading. Fusco has read the piece (as opposed to performing the piece) on more than one occasion, presenting the script and the stage directions as herself, without fully submerging herself into the characters.[110] This strategy is different from creating personae that are not characters. The phenotypical difference between Fusco and the characters works against the audience submerging themselves in the reality of the play (a feature of her work that is often elided rather than recognized). At the same time, her narration of the play via a reading, which she does seated at a table, deemphasizes the body as a site of the exposition of violence. What is staged is the rhetorical and theoretical iteration of truth by a brown woman whose body is not theirs. The verbal rendering of the theatricality of the play doubles our distance from the truth. Fusco, in contrast with her other performance works, does not become the other. She does not even try.

This form of reading rubs strangely against the first play I considered in this chapter, *Mujeres de Arena*. Robles, in his urgency to tell the truth, stages a play in the form of testimony delivered at a conference. Coco Fusco reads the play at a conference and in doing so exposes the very theatricality that only an oral reading of a play can render. She directly dictates stage directions and indexical references to characters not fully embodied by the reader, so that the audience can follow the play ("So Magaly says . . . ," "then Chela says . . ."). Even the least theatrically realized reading of the play exposes violence successfully, creating successful bonds between the three female characters while simultaneously rendering their control of theatrical representation apparent. By refusing to let us submerge into these characters—and feel for them in more traditional ways—Fusco asks her audience to retain their critical distance. Yet she avoids conflating the theatrical with the inauthentic. Horton, in contrast, in his desire to experience something real, emerges as a violently inauthentic subject complicit with neoliberal hegemony. Theatricality's exposure of its constructedness can counter the naturalization of violence under neoliberalism. Caridad Svich, whose work I consider next, not only embraces theatricality but also relies heavily on the power of dramatic irony. Through employing these techniques, Svich shows how state practices of misogyny manifest differently throughout the hemisphere for elite and nonelite subjects, whose fates are tied together in unexpected ways. Svich's exploration is crucial to understanding how neoliberal practices in the Americas induct classism (and racism) within their violent gestures, inside and outside of media representation.

Engaging Dramatic Irony: Svich's *Iphigenia Crash Land Falls on the Neon Shell That Was Once Her Heart*

Caridad Svich's *Iphigenia Crash Land Falls on the Neon Shell That Was Once Her Heart (A Rave Fable)* (2000) takes place in the present in "an unnamed country in the Americas during a time of unrest."[111] Iphigenia is a young rich white (of European descent) girl used to the public eye—as many members of ruling families in Latin America are. Her father, Adolfo (association fully intended), is a typical military dictator qua president; her mother, Camila, is a "narcotized prop wife." Achilles, Iphigenia's lover, is an HIV-positive androgynous rock star. Although the play could in fact be anywhere in Latin America, the description of the country as "the ass of the continent" signifies the Southern Cone. Yet once Iphigenia moves "to the northernmost point of the city" to find a rave, she clearly moves into a Juárez-like environment replete with pink crosses on the walls and factory workers in the dance halls.

Echoing its classical counterparts, Iphigenia begins with a problem. President (and General) Adolfo is at war on the verge of an electoral loss. There is only one possible way out of this mess: empathy from the populace he disenfranchises daily. As the TV anchor projected onstage puts it:

> The general will need a miracle to stay in office. . . . But if some personal tragedy were to befall him, it is possible the country would embrace him again. No one can resist the tug of the human heart. One senseless death of a rich girl and we will be united in grief, sorrow and peace. Do you hear me, Iphigenia? Do you hear me?[112]

Svich's play, by blending different versions of the Iphigenia story, creates a double sacrifice embedded in a critique of the tug of the human heart.[113] In *Iphigenia Crash Land Falls*, Iphigenia's and Achilles's deaths happen simultaneously, in a conflagration of sex transmogrified into a satyr play that Iphigenia dreams in Achilles's arms. In this dream, the general's ass, played by the actor playing Adolfo, describes how Iphigenia should be murdered: "Lead her to a quiet house off the main road. She will follow you if you tell her her lover waits for her. Then close the door, blind her and pierce her with a knife. She's not my daughter anymore. She has abandoned me."[114] A few scenes later Soldier X, a mercenary, goes after Iphigenia, and she tells him exactly how to kill her using these same directions. In this sense, Iphigenia sacrifices herself. The news media reports her death promptly, and Adolfo asks for the country to be united just as we expected. Iphigenia becomes the rich daughter martyred for her war-torn country. Simultaneously, she escapes her circumscription as a virgin by having ecstatic sex with Achilles and leaving the earth. At the play's culmination, Iphigenia looks down on the airplane hangar in Juárez where the rave is held and its inhabitants, the factory workers who frequent it. She is physically and psychically divorced from the state family drama.

In Svich's own account, her decision to adapt Iphigenia to the contemporary Americas was an effort to let Iphigenia speak.[115] In Euripides's version of the story, upon which Svich's play is based, Iphigenia says little, largely playing the silent victim to her father without much agency. In Svich's play she talks a lot and owns her own death—choosing a mode of perishing that disrupts the state narrative. In this sense, one can say, as Chiori Miyagawa does, that Iphigenia is an attempt to "give voice to the voiceless" evidenced in Svich's other work.[116] However, Svich largely rejects modes of *testimonio* that force the subaltern to speak in the frame of nongovernmental organization (NGO) discourses and mise-en-scènes. After all, Iphigenia is not a subaltern even if she is suppressed under patriarchy. And she is not guileless. Svich's Iphigenia is *acting* the role of dutiful daughter throughout and is very aware of her role as a performer in the state drama.

Svich's exploration of gender, violence, and the neoliberal condition, unlike the others in this chapter, gives substantial space to revealing the connections between how elite women are trafficked in national symbolism in relation to the way working-class women are destroyed by it. This linkage is a unique and important one that often goes unexplored in Latinx drama (although Tanya Saracho also explores it in *El Nogalar* in a different context). The sacrifice of the (white, rich) virgin daughter and the control of female sexuality more generally has been crucial to military dictatorships and to the integrity of their ideological renderings of the nation as woman, as Diana Taylor and others have argued.[117] The play spells out the equation between female worth and sexual purity at all levels of society, a construct that continues into the neoliberal era. For example, when describing a previous kidnapping attempt, Iphigenia tells Violeta what her captor said when he handed her over: "Don't worry. She is still a virgin, cabrón."[118] This control of female sexuality is every bit as toxic—although often not as purely physically threatening—as those enacted on young working-class, and usually nonwhite, women in Juárez. Yet Svich does not move toward a solidarity paradigm; she even stops short of the shared misery Fusco's characters exhibit in *The Incredible Disappearing Woman*. Instead, Svich concentrates on the inability to bridge the gap, even as she points out the apparatus of state violence. This portrayal recognizes the class politics of hemispheric neoliberalism with full use of dramatic irony that asks us to question Iphigenia's actions at every step.

Svich employs this irony when she stages Iphigenia's quest as an attempt to lose her body in order to find it. Her desire to escape her image is also an attempt to abject herself as a mode of (un)self-making. This unmaking is only partially successful and intentionally so. After all, Svich has Iphigenia float in the air and look down on the factory girls as a goddess looks upon mortals at the end of the play. Yet, even if Iphigenia never fully understands the implications of what she sees, she opens up the possibility that the audience can. *Iphigenia Crash Land Falls* enacts a social critique of neoliberalism precisely through Iphigenia's failure to fully inhabit the space of the other. In a classical sense, then, Iphigenia engenders irony as she compels the audience to learn what she cannot. Iphigenia's archness is often lost on audiences who look to Iphigenia to be an earnest heroine. She is not. Iphigenia is in fact "a little vapid" by design and thus allows a different kind of opening for thinking about her failures.[119]

The unbridgeable gap between the haves and have-nots is articulated in Iphigenia's relationship to Violeta Imperial. When the two women share their stories of violence, Violeta recognizes Iphigenia as the general's daughter. Violeta shows her scars to the young scion and tells her how she got them—for kissing a woman who worked for the police. Called a *pata*, Violeta was cut open and later dumped beside the dead body of the policewoman. Iphigenia, naïve, offers to talk to her father about the incident before Violeta cuts her off and demands that she interrogate her father for the crime instead. In response, Iphigenia shares her own story of having been kidnapped, relating her fear and anger at her father, who never acknowledged the crime. By denying Iphigenia's pain, Adolfo hid his own inability to stop violence against her, thus avoiding telegraphing his weakness as a (patriarchal) leader of the state to the public. As their dialogue reveals, Violeta and Iphigenia are both victims of the father state. Yet their class positions and sexualities lead them to different fates. The integrity of Iphigenia's elite body was valued as a symbolic resource, so she was rescued rather than being left for dead; Violeta's body needed to be disintegrated in order to render state power over her sexuality. Thinking about these bodies in relation to Juárez asks us to admit that control of women's sexuality is intrinsic to rather than lying outside of or being a supplement to the state's instantiation of neoliberalism.

Despite their common oppression as women, for most of the play, no solidarity comes out of Iphigenia's and Violeta's testimonial sharing. Iphigenia does not want to acknowledge the connection Violeta makes between them.

> IPHIGENIA: Here and into the trash with you, remnant of the mutant underclass.
>
> (*Iphigenia throws dollar bills at Violeta Imperial and starts to walk away.*)
>
> VIOLETA: I am only speaking the truth.
> IPHIGENIA: What truth is that? To think I almost believed you when said all that about being cut up by my father's men . . .

> VIOLETA: I've the scars . . .
> IPHIGENIA: Put there by someone else.
> . . . .
> IPHIGENIA: I gave you money. I don't want to hear anything else. I hear things all the time, voices, screams . . .[120]

At the beginning of her conversation, Iphigenia retains her elite class position and her understanding of herself as an independent subject by abjecting Violeta as "a remnant of the mutant underclass." When challenged by Violeta's testimony, she oscillates between willful blindness to the truth and admission of violence, echoing the selective knowledge of torture brandished by elite characters in Southern Cone plays and novels such as Roberto Bolaño's *By Night in Chile*. Despite her qualms, Iphigenia retains herself as self in relation to Violeta's other and soon leaves her to go to the rave. The complicated negotiation of self and other speaks to the operations of abjection crucial to the continuation of violence throughout the hemisphere.

Iphigenia has a very different reaction when she stumbles upon a factory that holds the ghosts of the *fresa* girls, the "ripe girls, like strawberries who come from the deep country to work in the factories," played by male actors.[121] Unlike her revulsion for Violeta, she has only admiration for the Juárez dead, as her ecstatic utterances that conjure them suggest.

> IPHIGENIA: Names upon names
>   Foreign to my tongue
>   I move them around in my mouth
>   As I run my hands against the smooth surface of these factory walls.
> FRESA GIRL 1: Is that where we are? I haven't been near the factory in a long time.
> FRESA GIRL 2: The last thing I want to be is near a sewing machine.
> FRESA GIRL 3: We're here because of her.
> FRESA GIRL 1: Who?
> FRESA 3: Iphigenia.
> FRESA GIRL 1 AND 2: That bitch.[122]

Iphigenia exoticizes the *fresa* girls—their names are "foreign to her tongue," and she consumes them, moving them around in her mouth. Her perception of reality is distorted. Although the *fresa* girls are "ghosts inhabited by male bodies," Iphigenia references their warm touch against her skin.[123] Although they suffer, she enters an ecstasy in their presence, exclaiming, "I could be one of these girls. Who says I have to be Iphigenia?"[124] Her romanticization of these girls gestures to the romanticization of the women's destruction in the media more generally.

Iphigenia's attempt to erase herself by becoming one with the factory girls is equally fraught with peril and ignorance. As the *fresa* girls contend, "she doesn't know about us."[125] Employing dramatic irony, the *fresa* girls tell the audience what Iphigenia does not know or does not let herself know: that the disappeared women come from the rural areas to work in the factories; they work twelve hour days; they have their throats slit, they scream, and no one cares. These facts mark the reality of the women killed in Juárez in contrast with Iphigenia's fantasies of freedom. The *fresa* girls decide to scare Iphigenia by showing her their scars. Unlike her revulsion at Violeta, Iphigenia calls the girls beautiful. Willfully ignorant, she eventually loses herself in the throes of the dance: "The names of all of these girls enter my brain / I take them on and undulate / Oh, I am losing myself."[126] After losing herself she tries to become the other. But of course she cannot be a *fresa* girl. Nor can anyone in the audience, which was made to mirror Iphigenia's actions in Lance Gharavi's media-heavy immersive rave production.[127] Although the play's stage directions transform the space to reflect Iphigenia's misguided perception of what is going on—Iphigenia spins among pink crosses projected on the walls—the *fresa* girls' reality ultimately wins out. As their sartorial reality makes clear, Iphigenia cannot recede into their material conditions. They wear fake Prada; she wears the real thing. Her death will matter; theirs never will. In an interesting reversal, the *fresa* girls take their revenge by assaulting Iphigenia. In this assault they prove that while the presidential daughter fails to be a *fresa* girl, the *fresa* girls do get to play Iphigenia. Stripping her of her Prada suit before she leaves with Achilles, wearing only a slip, they put on her designer clothes in grotesque fashion. This charade reveals the violence of wealth and privilege in the conspicuous consumption of the upper classes.

It is also here that Svich's engagement with the complicated history of the *fresa* is most visible. In the 1960s, *fresa* was a term used to classify the rich or the well-bred, many of whom wore—because they could afford it—U.S. designer clothing. For Carlos Monsiváis, these are the young people who pretended at protesting on the weekends. They are the "squares," those who belong to the social order.[128] By the 1980s and '90s, an apex of the neoliberal era in U.S.-Mexico relations, *fresas* described a group that imitated U.S. fashion and taste from a wider swath of the population. Because U.S. labels were available as knockoffs, middle- and working-class youth could afford them, allowing them to imitate a form of vacuity alongside their sartorial choices.[129] The *fresa*, then, historically and presently is an actor/actress, one who pretends in their assumption of cultural identity. That these *fresa* girls are also performers, but distinctly not drag performers as classically understood, bears note. Svich is adamant that the roles be cast with men, meaning that the men's bodily inhabitation of the female ghosts of femicide victims is arguably a queerer, less campy, more haunted mode of performance. This play at playing, shot through with the presence of the dead, invigorates many of the plays I consider in the following chapter. Here, however, I note that the undoing of gender is consistent throughout the play, complementing Achilles's Bowie-like performance of the androgyne, who lip-synchs throughout.

Svich's choice to call these characters *fresa* girls mixes misogynist and classist metaphors in ways that may be confusing for those unfamiliar with the cultural specificity of the term. Yet in a broader theatrical critique, with full knowledge of Latin American cultural production, the *fresa* girls' presence frames Iphigenia's desire to become other as something put on that perhaps cannot be taken off.

This failed mimesis is the location of Svich's critique of neoliberalism, and it is at the heart of neoliberal (maquila) factory production that creates the *fresa* girls' products, which both try and fail to be real luxury items. The high demand for these fakes and the conditions of producing them allow women to be killed at the U.S.-Mexico border. This failed mimesis is thus linked to the consumerist side of late capitalism's promise—the idea that the democratization of luxury and eroticization of product purchase will be liberating. It is telling that Iphigenia's sense of disquiet when trying to become other happens not during her straight sex act with Achilles, but through her erotic experience of a garment. As Iphigenia passes Violeta on the road on the way home, Violeta offers Iphigenia a dress made of Queen Anne's lace. The lace is made from the clothing of one of the dead girls, whose presence Iphigenia senses. She asks Violeta to hold her: "I can feel the dead girl's breath inside this dress. I feel all the dead through me."[130] Iphigenia not only rejects the cheap dress, she finally understands the death the women face. This time, however, she does not reject Violeta—she moves toward her. Faced with this truth, the general's daughter decides instead that she wants to mourn these women; she "wants to free them of their pain."[131] She also wants Violeta's scars on her. Moving from self-abnegation to surrogation, Iphigenia still fails at her mission. Her body is incontrovertibly different from her father's other victims; it renders representation differently. Soldier X shows up promptly after this exchange, taking her to be killed so that her body can signify for the state. Svich's dramatic irony shows that Iphigenia's imagination of her sacrifice cannot come to be. In the neoliberal Americas, violence against the rich and poor will always be different; wealth is a form of violence in itself. Concomitantly, this failed substitution revises the doubling in Euripides's rendering of Iphigenia's story, which literalizes the idea of sacrifice. *Iphigenia in Aulis* ends with a messenger arriving, letting Clytemnestra know that Iphigenia's body was replaced by a deer on the altar at the moment of her sacrifice. In short, Iphigenia has gone to the gods.[132]

Here, Svich engages the idea of the obscene with a hemispheric twist that shows the conundrums of representation in the neoliberal Americas. In Svich's play, Iphigenia floats above the airplane hangar after she is killed, but instead of substituting her body with an animal, Svich leaves only her blood behind. In classical Greek times, this theatrical trick kept violence offstage, as was expected within the religious paradigm of the theater.[133] In the context of Juárez, the disappearance of the body is neither a miracle nor the sign of obeying religious precepts. It is a quotidian reality that forces families, friends, and spectators to mourn a body, a person who is no longer present. In contemporary reality, disappearance is the sign of a disposable body, a corpse sent elsewhere, buried instead of elevated. The bodies of the maquila workers are without symbolic relevance in the state family drama, but they proliferate nonetheless. Although familial (and heteronormative) discourse about the disappeared, especially as utilized by nongovernmental organizations such as Nuestras Hijas de Regreso a Casa, attempt to reanimate these structures of belonging for the poor, their actions do not disrupt the patriarchal discourses that undergird neoliberal governance in the Americas. Svich's play makes this abundantly clear.

Dramaturgically, the absence of Iphigenia's corpse at the end of Svich's play gestures to Iphigenia's circulation as *image* within a patriarchal and mediatized culture. In Lance Gharavi's production her appearance at the end was completely virtual. She was projected onto an as yet unused surface on the stage, which was actually recorded in a closet offstage.[134] Notably, in Iphigenia's virtual appearance, her body is intact so as to be perceived and mourned as a proper victim (however ironically) within the representational economy of the play. Today, the richer and poorer victims of neoliberal violence are often subjected to an equally mediatized demise, but without any attempt to keep them whole. Those who circulate images of the dead expose decapitated and mutilated bodies. These bodies in fragments telegraph the abject horror that comes with dehumanization of a corpse. These images garner not sympathy or allegiance to a nation but serve as a threat that it could happen to you next. As Reguillo reminds us:

> In a radical way, and citing Sontag, these messages encrypted in the space of a finite and forever-broken body may be read as *memento mori* ("remember you will die"); you will die three times: when you are tortured (the torture that precedes death is almost always unimaginable), when you die, and when your death is converted into data reported in the media (for example, "five heads were found in front of the Attorney General's office"). The signifying chain of expressive *violencias* could not be more eloquent.[135]

Today, Svich's tactics might have to change to accommodate the escalation of neoliberalism's modes of violence outside of the Southern Cone. At the time that *Iphigenia Crash Land Falls* emerged, however, a critique of the efficacy of empathy exacted by these patriarchal discourses was deeply necessary. The problem of the play is, after all, that Adolfo has to gain empathy from an audience—the populace—who is being oppressed by him daily. His ploy employs a classic empathic relationship between audience and characters. The audience is to be coerced (in Boal's sense) into pity and fear when imagining Iphigenia's demise primarily through the big screen. Svich makes us critical of this empathy by using sardonic performances in the video coverage of Adolfo's plight, which she aims directly at us as audience members. If and when we learn something from this play, it is when we break this televisual bond. Although Svich abjures the proscenium and the emotional discipline embedded in Aristotelian modes of audience identification, she does not reject the theater or the idea that an encounter with the other can change one. Iphigenia's ability to understand Violeta at the end of the play is in some sense an attempt at body-to-body transfer rather than a practice of feeling for exemplified by testimonial performances. She has to touch the wounds. Iphigenia interprets her desire as a desire to wear scars; and, in a rather misguided way, she chooses to die, falling into the national narrative of mourning despite her best efforts (which are, of course, still tinged with minor self-aggrandizement).

Perhaps rather than accusing Iphigenia (or even Svich) of bad faith, we might think less about who is disappeared and spend more time considering who is left behind. Even if Violeta is an "apparition" as Svich suggests, she is also "earth-bound." Her embodiment onstage as a live character enacted by an actor (she is one of the few characters who does not show up on video) does not allow us to think that she comes from another world or that she is telegraphed from elsewhere. Violeta Imperial is ours, and her scars remain. Rejected, but not fully abject, she wanders the world selling chicken parts and the clothes of dead to give violence material form, evidence of destruction. She is, in her own words, "a remainder," a "walking warning for others who wish to speak up against anything or simply live in peace."[136] She is the fleshy presence of the dead. She is both an ageless woman and a prematurely aged woman, an archetype that skirts close to the crone. Unlike Camila, she is nonreproductive, queer, and a caretaker for the dead, not (quite) a mother. Violeta portends the end of reproductive nationalism as much as the death of a virgin can fuel it.

In sum, over the course of the play, Svich demonstrates that violence against women in Juárez is a mode of expressive violence exemplified throughout the hemisphere. She remixes signifiers from throughout the Americas to make her point. Achilles, for example, speaks with a border polyglot tongue, breaking from his Bowie ventriloquism to talk about *la migra*. Orestes is both the muralist who memorializes the girls with pink crosses and a coca baby from the south. These multiple signifiers are vertiginous for spectators. After all, material and cultural specificity is crucial to understanding the vicissitudes of neoliberal violence. One might risk moral hazard in thinking about the violence of Juárez without the specificity of the gendered mestiza body.

In our political moment, and in our representational economy, one must ask: Does replacing the Juárez femicide victims with non-ethnically marked male actors distance and aestheticize the violence in ways that make the social specificity of the crimes hard to read? Perhaps. But production choices could certainly exacerbate or minimize this potential misreading.[137] Svich's play can be a conduit for revealing the complex relationships of violence in the Americas exactly because of how *Iphigenia Crash Land Falls* eschews realism. The wounds left on the bodies of the *fresa* girls echo Violeta's, linking torture by the military police and the extinction of women's bodies at the Mexico border.

The preponderance of drug consumption in Svich's play links pleasure, subjectivity, and capital in uncomfortable ways. Iphigenia's escape, after all, is a journey into the pleasures of Ecstasy and chemical self-loss; she is a '90s club kid reminiscent of Michael Alig and his crew, a crew that emerged with the intensification of Mexican drug trafficking. The play makes the relationship between narcotrafficking and governance explicit. When Svich creates a standoff between corporations, the Zero gang drug traffickers, and the government, she links governmental and nongovernmental actors throughout the hemisphere. When she introduces Camila's and Orestes's drug-induced hazes, she articulates the connective corridor of narcotics from the site in which coca is grown (presumed to be Colombia, South America) and where it often ends up, in the narcotrafficked border of Mexico on its way to the United States. Today, after six years of the Calderón's narcoguerra and two years of Enrique Peña Nieto's war on the left, we could push harder on these representations, revealing that the government and the traffickers are complicit with each other rather than in an adversarial relationship. In the next chapter, I will explore these entanglements in the work of Octavio Solis, Tanya Saracho, Victor Cazares, and Matthew Olmos. Each of these playwrights confronts the complex economic and social history of narcotrafficking throughout the hemisphere while gesturing toward different modes of thinking about how the dead might rise among us.

Chapter 4

✦

Swallowing the '80s (W)Hole: Millennial Drama of the Narcoguerra

Narcotrafficking is a primary contributor to the transnational American imaginary, in part because of the role of U.S. and Mexican films. In the United States, the most famous of these films are *Scarface*, whose poster graces the walls of many a narcotrafficker's home, and *Traffic*, a film that collated a series of famous rumors about 1980s and '90s narcotraffic into a moralistic parable aimed at preserving the heteronormative family—as nation—as the defense against drug consumption.[1] An inadvertent, more recent meditation is also relevant here: *Dallas Buyers Club*, which clumsily and unintentionally reveals the deep relationship between U.S. neoliberalism and transnational drug commerce.[2]

For most viewers, *Dallas Buyers Club* is not a movie about narcotraffic; it is a movie about AIDS, the inefficiency of the federal government, and the bravery of an HIV-infected man who figures out how to use alternative drug regimes, often in addition to azidothymidine (AZT) to make a cocktail, and how to get these non-FDA-approved drugs into the United States. Based on the life of Ron Woodroof, *Dallas Buyers Club* was wildly successful. To the consternation of many viewers, myself included, this film effectively erased the collective forms of DIY medical research and distribution enacted by queer persons and their allies that characterized most buyers' clubs and advocacy organizations. Critics such as A. O. Scott, who praised the acting in the film, juxtaposed *Dallas Buyers Club* with *How to Survive a Plague*—an award-winning documentary that follows ACT UP's activism in the 1980s. *How to Survive a Plague* convincingly argues that this activism led to legal dispensation of the cocktail and the effective end of an HIV-positive diagnosis as death sentence.[3] Scott and others also rightfully criticized the film's portrayal of trans characters and its stubborn insistence on employing a straight white male protagonist with homophobic tendencies as a hero in the AIDS struggle.[4]

What was virtually unremarked upon was the way in which *Dallas Buyers Club* valorized entrepreneurship as an individualistic mode of activism, encased within this white male body as an ideal conduit. While Woodroof certainly has a staff that helps him, including a trans friend and a butch black woman, most of the research about the disease and trips to fetch the drugs are solo treks by Woodroof, who works with doctors around the world to obtain portions of the cocktail. Nothing in any review I have found mentioned the political implications of his trips to Mexico—the primary place he purchased drugs—or the role of Latinx persons in the film. But they are everywhere, hidden in plain sight. The first appearance by a Latino is when Woodroof ends up being diagnosed with AIDS after a workplace accident. After indulging in the requisite racialized insults, Woodroof tries to help this undocumented (and never named) Latino worker to escape from an oil drill by cutting the power. This solution is the only possible one as the supervisor in charge is unwilling to call for medical help because of the worker's immigration status. When the surge he tries to stymie knocks Woodroof out, he ends up in the hospital, linking an act of supposed generosity toward a Latino subject to his own self-discovery. The first person to get Woodroof the contraband AZT is a nameless Latino orderly, who dumps pills for him behind the hospital for pay. And finally, there are Woodroof's trips to Mexico to obtain many of the drugs he needs for the club. The footage in Mexico is nondescript, featuring a fairly standard border crossing by car into the desert, tapping into standard dramaturgies of crossing. Yet the doctor from whom he is obtaining drugs is supposedly in Mexico City, a megalopolis in the mountains never seen on film. This elision reveals a certain U.S. imaginary of Mexico which erases Mexican modernity and cosmopolitanism in its desire to preserve an idea of Mexico as less civilized or advanced than the United States; not surprisingly, this trope underscores the lack of regulation in Mexico, allowing Woodroof his entrepreneurial virtuosity.

Dallas Buyers Club betrays a racial unconscious in which the business of narcotraffic is a Latino affair. Brown bodies are everywhere in the background of the film, reminding us of the traffic in bodies and goods between Mexico and the United States, and particularly Mexico and Texas in the neoliberal '90s. The twist is that the Mexican bodies are not associated with the copious cocaine Woodroof snorts in the early scenes of the movie but with the antiviral drugs usually considered to be part of the licit economy of medical institutions. The film, despite its nationalist essentialism and casual state-o-phobia, exposes a more complex relationship between the biomedical industry, narcotraffic, and the emergence of the antistatist entrepreneur as hero. The film backwardly admits that the 1980s inaugurates a form of entrepreneurship deeply embedded in the business of drugs—the period critic Hermann Herlinghaus calls the pharmacological era.[5] Viewers of *Breaking Bad* will also be familiar with these figures. They lurk within our romance of the (straight) white male entrepreneur, who stands out in a sea of lesser Latino luminaries.[6]

This detour into film to introduce a series of Chicano/a plays on narcotraffic highlights their dramaturgical and political difference from mainstream, even critical mainstream, representations of drug trafficking. In contrast to their filmic companions, the plays by Cazares, Saracho, Olmos, and Solis consciously take on the idea of the entrepreneur and the specters of the narcoguerra as a state-sponsored war. Rather than remaining in an apolitical present, these plays track the current moment in a much longer history of Mexico and the United States. In doing so, they show the trenchant links between the dominance of drug trafficking and the deep history of neoliberalism, including its inducement of everyday performances of self. It is often the theatricality of these works—the impossibility of representing horrors within the frame of narco-realism—that harbors their most trenchant critiques. This issue becomes most crucial when thinking about the visibility of violence under the current narcoguerra.

I learned this lesson firsthand when I directed a student play about drug trafficking and Santa Muerte titled *En las Manos de la Muerte*, by Alexandra Bernson.[7] Bernson, a student of Latino/a descent, became interested in the recent history of drug trafficking and its relationship to Santa Muerte while taking a playwriting class. Muerte is a folk saint, associated with both death and the Virgin, who is known as a patron saint of those outside of cultural norms, including drug dealers, prisoners, and queers.[8] Bernson's play followed the lives of two young men, Benecio and Incenio, who decide to dedicate their lives to the business and to Santa Muerte to escape the very limited opportunities of their northern Mexican pueblo. The play plays at the edge of narco-realism. As in many movies, successful and unsuccessful performances of masculinity function as harbingers of possibility in the narco world. The moral centers of the play, not surprisingly, are women: Benecio's girlfriend and Incenio's mother, neither of whom convinces their male loved ones to leave the business. Santa Muerte's seduction is too great.

Although the play largely replicates many of the genre expectations of narco-realistic films and their gender politics, there were openings in the script to show the queer everyday worship of Santa Muerte and to depict the real violence of narcotraffic without sensationalism. The violence was not made metaphorical; I staged the scenes somewhat realistically so as to avoid aestheticization of violence. At the same time, I underscore the playwright's attempts to avoid abjecting or heroizing narcotraffickers or their victims. The importance of reproducing images of these killings within the media was staged by showing the murderers taking pictures without actually reproducing the images of the dead themselves. In addition, a great deal of context was provided to the audience to underscore the geopolitical realities of narcotraffic, which were not in the script itself: U.S. complicity with the regime, the increased brutality of Calderón's narcoguerra, and the post-NAFTA economic situation in rural communities.

This context is also the backdrop for the plays I consider here. The passage of drugs on land through Central America and Mexico escalated after the crackdown on water transport to Miami, whose heyday is chronicled in

Miami Vice and other forms of early '80s narco-realism. In the older regime, Colombian cocaine was transported by boat to the United States. After this pathway was blocked in the 1990s cocaine began to be transported through Mexican intermediaries who were not producing or controlling product but being paid as employees to carry it for the Colombian cartels. Soon, however, the Mexicans created cartels of their own, with their own regional differences and rivalries, which were often managed rather than eradicated by the police, military, and politicians from the United States and Mexico. The Mexican cartels also began growing heroin and marijuana in much larger quantities, while also displacing many of the Colombian cartels as controllers of cocaine. Refusing to be complicit with the system, at least ostensibly, was Felipe Calderón, the Mexican president from 2006 to 2012, who called for a war on drugs at the beginning of his term. His desire to attack narcotraffickers directly has led not to their eradication or loss in profits but to an ever more violent Mexico with more entrenched acephalous networks. For many in Mexico, Calderón is as much of an assassin as the drug lords. In fact, he might have simply favored certain traffickers rather than others instead of eradicating them. There is, of course, a much longer history of drug trafficking and production between the United States and Mexico that goes back to the Porfiriato—an issue I will address later in the chapter in relation to Cazares's work. At this point, however, I wish to trace the history of narcotraffic as depicted in work by Latinx playwrights, beginning with Octavio Solis. Solis's *Santos y Santos* (1993) and *Dreamlandia* (2000), which take on the business of narcotraffic before the narcoguerra, suggest the dramaturgical innovations necessitated by the changing practice of drug trafficking and the performative gestures embedded within narcoentrepreneurship. Together with plays by Saracho, Cazares, and Olmos, Solis's works articulate a neoliberal pharmacological economy in the Americas, the emergence of an entrepreneurial form of selfhood necessitated by economic conditions, and a particular form of movement between the United States and Mexico which undoes the unidirectional northward migration narrative. In exploring these playwrights works together, I explore how Latinx dramaturgical thinking can complicate the historiographical geography of neoliberalism.

Solis's *Santos y Santos*: Past as Prologue

One could argue that the genealogy of narco-dramas on the U.S. Latinx stage emerges with Octavio Solis's *Santos y Santos*, a play that interrogates the boundary between licit and illicit transnational business in a pre-NAFTA era of neoliberalism.[9] First produced at the Dallas Theater Center in 1994, this play, set in "the heady mid-eighties," revolves around two Chicano brothers, Fernie and Mike Santos, who supplement their law firm earnings with drug trafficking.[10] The entrance of a third brother, Tomás, who disapproves of this practice and rats on them to the police, sets off a series of events that violently ends the brothers' business as well as many lives, including that of a federal judge. Written around the time of NAFTA was being passed (1994), and with acute hindsight regarding labor practices, the play hearkens to the era in which Mexican and U.S. traffickers were intermediaries for the Colombian cartels, when conspicuous consumption of cocaine was at its height in the United States.

From this temporal distance, Solis underscores shifts in labor made more striking in the later neoliberal period—the move from material to immaterial labor among the Latinx middle classes. The Santos brothers are the sons of a furniture maker. Although their role as lawyers registers a standard narrative of upward mobility in which manual labor is replaced by brain work or immaterial labor for subsequent generations, the play also documents the move away from making one's living from the production of material objects for consumption to the transport (but not production) of consumable pharmacological products. I believe that this contrast is more important than the juxtaposition of licit and illicit activity that the morality of the play ostensibly hinges upon: the conundrum created by the fact that Latinx lawyers who do good in the community also use and sell drugs.

Like many of Solis's plays, *Santos* is haunted by white men's abjected love for Mexican culture, particularly Mexican women, underscoring the erotic relationship underneath transnational transits. This attraction/repulsion threatens his Anglo characters' clean ties to belonging exclusively to a white U.S. nation, exposing a more complicated history. Judge Benton, whom the Santos men eventually kill, is a case in point. Early in the play, Benton approaches Tomás at a banquet to convince him to work for him, tapping into Tomás's discomfort with his brothers' "dirty work" (which may or may not tap into some form of Chicano self-hatred). Tommy, as he is often called in the play, rejects the offer, but the judge admits that he has a child with a prostitute in Juárez whose eyes remind him of Tommy's, which makes Tommy a sort of a son to the judge. The judge's ode to Tommy, while framed within an act of heterosexual sex, nonetheless resounds with a certain homoeroticism. The judge confesses the following in his encounter with the prostitute: "but this santos runt, this beautiful boy, he pierces my soul, with a message deep, dark."[11] Crossing the border, for the judge, is an intimate and eroticized act as is his paternity of Tommy, queering what seems to be a very orthodox paternal relation. Tomás's relationship to Judge Benton is the background against which other forms of legacy, futurity, and family appear. In the most literal sense, Tommy survives by killing Benton, after Tommy has already betrayed his own family. Yet Tommy has no legacy because his progeny does not survive. His child with his brother's wife, Vicki, dies when she miscarries after her husband beats her up. In relation to the other plays I consider in this volume, however, Tommy's form of "no future" (in terms of reproductivity) feels more dystopic than liberating. Constant references are made to characters' anxiety about providing for their family as a form of futurity and the bleak world that does not allow for the survival of the Latinx family within the rubric of the American dream.

Solis, however, avoids individualizing this plight, that is, making the Santos family's foibles the cause of their failures, by carefully undoing the idea of the American dream in rapturous dystopian speeches. These ecstatic dialogues and speeches ironize both U.S. exceptionalist rhetorics of justice and self-congratulatory paeans to cultural hybridity endemic to the era. Consider, for example, the prose poem, for which I use the term *reverie*, delivered by the judge and Tomás:

> TOMÁS: *LA VIRGIN DE JUSTICIA*
> JUDGE: appointed by the people for a drug-free America
> TOMÁS: our *sierra madre oriental*
> TOMÁS: ROPA PARA TODA LA FAMILIA
> . . .
> JUDGE: *MOLE* WITH YOUR METHODONE
> TOMÁS: DUTY-FREE GOODS
> JUDGE: FREE TRADE AGREEMENTS
> TOMÁS: AND ALL THE REHAB PROGRAMS, CITIZEN PATROLS, THE INTERDICTION AND STIFF SENTENCING, THE DEATH PENALTIES WILL BE OBSOLETE
> JUDGE: DRUG-TURF CRIME WILL VANISH ACROSS THE COUNTRY
> TOMÁS: AND THE RACE OF MOCTEZUMA WILL AT LAST ACHIEVE FULL CITIZENSHIP
> JUDGE: YES YES YESSSSSS
> TOMÁS: DON'T GET ME WRONG, I LOVE MY PEOPLE
> JUDGE: IT SHOWS IN EVERY FIBER OF YOUR BEING.[12]

The near orgasmic rhythm of their exchange, resolves into equivocation about and recrimination of Mexican people ("DON'T GET ME WRONG I LOVE MY PEOPLE"), undoing the possibility of liberation through U.S. judicial paradigms. Tomás's line, in fact, is repeated after appearing earlier in the conversation when he tries to explain that Mexicans are in "a cycle" they can't get out of and thus "it is not our fault," echoing the desultory discourse of the Moynihan Report. The elision between the men's voices allows rhetoric to perform outside of an agonistic relationship between characters with opposing points of view. In this regard, Solis's use of the reverie formally undoes the autonomy of individual subjectivity and dialogic debate by blurring the voices of seemingly disparate characters. By disrespecting these borders, Solis undoes the very bedrock of U.S. American Aristotelian dramaturgy and liberal democracy—the autonomous subject—as he denaturalizes the rhetoric that holds this form of subjectivity in place. This formal innovation begs us to rethink the dramaturgy of liberal democracy itself. Here, as in *Dreamlandia*, the reverie also undoes the self in a productive way, even when the content of the speeches is ironic.

While the play remains within U.S. borders, Solis's critique of the coming transnational pharmacological regime is eerily prescient, forming a precursor for other works I consider in this chapter. Written on the eve of the passage of NAFTA, their riff on the false hope of free trade is scathing. In retrospect, of course, this passage is even more barbed: rather than building the Mexican economy, NAFTA debilitated it, except, of course, for a few northern businesses, including narcotrafficking, which it greatly bolstered. Judge Benson and Tommy's reverie encapsulates Solis's larger critique of the transnational drug industry throughout the play. Everyday dealers are portrayed as victims of the larger system. The overarching critique comes from Fernie, who says of the judge: "He's just a little *moco* in the bigger conspiracy! I'm talking ongoing colonial imperialism for our *pinchi* souls, man. Drugs are the twenty-first century conquistadores. Mikey is a victim of the International Narcotics Trade! A huge motherfucking enterprise that cannot be done without the CIA, the FBI the DEA, the INS, and even the Holy Church who has realized that the opiate of the people is OPIUM."[13] The indictment of the system here does not play into the phobia of the state espoused by many U.S. movies about narcotraffic. Instead, Solis's play reveals how drug trafficking exploits and extends earlier historical modes of domination.

Solis's invocation of the border is equally revisionist. Rather than fetishize the border as a site of crime, he thinks of El Paso-Juárez as a node in a larger geographical network that implicitly gestures to the history of commerce throughout greater Mexico. The Santos brothers' father's origin in Concordia, Sinaloa, is worth noting. Concordia, as the play tells us, is an area known for furniture production: a famous licit business. Yet, for most readers today and perhaps even in the '90s, Sinaloa brings to mind the Sinaloa cartel. Although this cartel was ascendant around the time *Santos y Santos* was written, there is a longer history of trafficking in the area. Sinaloa harbored some of the first attempts at mass production of marijuana and its distribution from the '60s onward.[14] The areas where the furniture and drug enterprises originate are at opposite ends of the state, yet their juxtaposition gestures to narcotraffic as a form of transnational commerce, rather than just being a crime. Like furniture building, narcotraffic is intimately related to the upward mobility of Mexicans on both sides of the border. Rather than remaining an amorphous evil sited at an abjected location, as in U.S. filmic dramaturgy, in *Santos*, narcotraffic is a ruthless business, but a business nonetheless. Solis's evocation of narco-masculinity, the performance of masculinity so key to this genre, is less stringently critiqued as performance than it will be in *Dreamlandia*. Nonetheless, he clearly sees how the desire for cultural nationalist belonging, masculinity, violence, and consumption work together: one only needs to watch the Santos brothers bond over a cocaine-laden painting of Pancho Villa while verbally undressing the secretary to see the full majesty of this complex. That the brothers are forced to murder soon after this scene presages the new mode of violence Sayak Valencia describes as "capitalismo gore." As Valencia explains,

> We propose that the term *capitalismo gore* as reinterpretation of an hegemonic and global economy in geographical border spaces and those that are economically precarious. We take the term *gore* from the cinematic genre that describes extreme, "slasher" violence. With capitalismo gore, then, we refer to the explicit and unnecessary spilling of blood (the price the Third World pays to hold onto the logic of capitalism, which is always becoming more extreme), the high percentage of dismemberments and disembowelments frequently involved with organized crime, the binary division of gender and the predatory use of bodies, all within the medium of a most explicit violence as a tool of narco-empowerment.[15]

The post-NAFTA version of this violent complex of capitalism is more clearly delineated in *Dreamlandia*, which I will consider next.

Solis's Switch-Up: Revising the Border, Undoing the Organism

Dreamlandia updates and retells Pedro Calderón de la Barca's Golden Age play *La vida es sueño* (*Life Is a Dream*) on the U.S. Mexico border at El Paso/Juárez.[16] Produced in 2000, the play concentrates on the struggle between a narcotrafficker and maquila boss, Celestino, and his son, Lazaro, whom he banished to an island in the Rio Grande between the United States and Mexico to prevent being usurped by him in his drug business. As in Calderón's play, a son forgives his father for his sins, which include not taking his mother to a hospital when he was born so as to prevent his relationship with the drug-addicted Vivian and his larger participation in the drug trade from being exposed. The curse that Lazaro carries in this play comes from the midwife, Dolores, who saved him by pulling him out of his mother's stomach. Blanca, the midwife's child with Frank, unravels the mystery of her U.S. bicultural identity of the course of the play. Along the way to these revelations and resolutions, the play allows audiences to see a panorama of scenes in maquilas, roadside hotels, and border patrol stakeouts at the Juárez-El Paso border. By linking exploitive labor in the maquilas, the 1990s drug trade, femicides, and the militarized borderlands, *Dreamlandia* registers the effects of the decade of history after *Santos y Santos*.

When Celestino is educating Lazaro into his new role in the business, he explains his transnational empire:

SONIA: Crown your head with knowledge. Everything a worldly man needs to know.

(*Lazaro is fed data via headphones and reading material.*)

FRANK/CARL/SETH: Texas History, Texas Monthly, Austin City Limits, Dallas Cowboys, price of oil per barrel, EDS, Bill Moyers, Wall Street Journal, Beemer 500 series.
SONIA: This is El Paso, gateway to the North, city on the cusp of Time.
FRANK: And this Juarez, back door to the Third World, to all parts Mexican.
CELESTINO: This is Rio Bravo, Rio Grande, Rio Polluted . . .
SONIA: The river that separates and binds cities to el Organismo.
CELESTINO: And this is my grand enterprise, the NexMex Maquiladora. Our fine addition to the two-plant system of the U.S. and Mexiconomies.
SONIA: One factory in El Paso for assembling parts by robotics. One factory in Juarez for assembling parts by hand. Together these plants collaborate to bring to America its finest contribution.
CELESTINO: Television.
FRANK: This is the US Border Patrol, an arm of the Immigration and Naturalization Service, sovereign protector of America's boundaries, watching out for illicit goods and persons. This agency stems the flood of narcotics threatening the Great Organism.
CELESTINO: But to keep pace with *traficantes*, we bargain with the Devil. A number of select cartels find safe passage north for a special toll and secret information on rival groups.
SONIA: This fee is funneled through the NexMex account where it is recycled as clean money.[17]

This passage reveals the interweaving of licit and illicit businesses as well as the selective discipline of border policing. Celestino not only launders his money from his drug smuggling scheme through the maquiladora's accounts but, as we learn later, sends the drugs over the border packed in TV boxes. Unlike the business in *Santos*, however, drug running is not a side business to a legitimate one. The maquila and the drugs are one business. Celestino's tactics imitate forms of trafficking that NAFTA facilitated by deregulating inspections on Mexican business vehicles, which allows the cartels to transport drugs through legitimate vehicles. The heightened militarization of the border is to no avail; they may stop laborers from moving, but they allow as many narcotics to come in as they stop, often by design. In *Dreamlandia*, Frank and Celestino's business relationship represents this collusion. Interestingly, Celestino's new wife, Sonia, basically runs the company, doing the feminized work of supervising staff while Celestino's everyday existence is taken up with manipulating officials, drug smugglers, and the like. Like many Juárez businessmen who run maquilas, he lives in El Paso. His house, with its twenty-two rooms, resembles a narco-mansion.

Celestino is not what he seems. What we do not know until the end of the play is that Celestino's performance as patriarch and boss is also a performance of United States identity. Celestino is also "illegal," having had the same hardscrabble life as Pepín. His double performance—made explicit during a scene where he performs as the street clown he once was in manic fashion—deepens a theme that runs through Solis's plays: that the erasure of one's history as a poor Mexican is necessary to assimilate into U.S. culture. In a sense, then, the assimilation to U.S. culture is assimilation into capitalist success. This allegiance to U.S. capitalism often occurs as much through consumption of U.S. products as through acceptance of U.S. ideology. Yet, unlike its depiction in Solis's earlier plays, in *Dreamlandia*, Mexico ceases to become a marker of a more ethical past heritage for its Chicano characters. The characters in *Dreamlandia* cross over and back across the border regularly and are deeply mired in Mexico's present violence. Sonia, in an interesting twist, grew up poor in the United States before ascending to power by running a Mexican maquiladora. Sonia's upward mobility by consumption, aided and abetted by her learned poise in selling and using high-end cosmetics in a U.S. mall, lands her in Juárez rather than in the United States, delineating new modes of transnational upward mobility. The discomfort Frank feels in going to Juárez parallels Judge Benton's, as does his sexual activity, but he does eventually go there rather than staying away.

Celestino's aversion to Mexico is not that he has to confront his past but that he no longer has control of his business in the present, which is a time of escalating complexity and violence in narcoentrepreneurship. Bustamante, the female drug lord, bothers him, as does the everyday business of the maquila. He is getting tired and wants to start thinking about an heir, gesturing to the need for an ever-regenerating set of young men to replace those destroyed by the business—a form of capitalismo gore, of disposable selves. Celestino's training of his son, Lazaro, for this role radically transforms the conflicts caused by rules of royal succession in the seventeenth-century play into a battle to discipline a young man to thrive in a world ruled by transnational capitalism at the verge of the twenty-first century.

Celestino hopes to make Lazaro a modern narcoentreprenuer in his own image, channeling Lazaro's violent nature strategically. Blanca, dressed as a male named Alfonso, is hired as his tutor. Rather than doing Celestino's bidding, however, she urges Lazaro to see the truth about the narco life and follow a more ethical path. Solis concludes his play with logical actions that come of this journey. Following a self-consciously theatrical reconciliation where Lazaro forgives his father, the play ends with Lazaro's turn away from his inheritance. After Celestino jails himself in his son's former hovel out of shame, Lazaro rejects becoming the new kingpin of his father's drug and maquila empire. He wades into the water with Blanca, leaving the narco life behind. Lazaro links himself with Blanca as family (they are cousins through Vivian, Frank's sister and Lazaro's mother), abandoning capital accumulation, consumerism, *and* patrilineal kinship and inheritance. Lazaro's choice stops him from becoming the organism his father wanted him to become. As individuated a choice as it is, Lazaro's decision to not become a monster, a "junior" (son of the powerful) who can combine his propensity for violence with the impunity given to Mexicano/Chicano upper-class sons of prominent statesmen and business owners, opens the possibility of ending the perpetuation of the narco system.

A historiographical reading of the play might cast the organism not just as Lazaro but as neoliberalism itself. This doubleness is embedded within the play. Celestino's first mention of the organism is in reference to how the stars determine the fate of the earth. He says "everything moves for the food of the organism. There, the great bear, the Bull and Dow Jones arrow between them and over here Sun Microsystems. This is your Mundo Comerciante." Soon after, he claims that the Rio Grande "separates and binds the system to El Organismo."[18] Later, he states: "We tolerate some parasites and some we don't. Some lies valued highly as truth, some truths dismissed as idle dreams, all for the sake of the Organism."[19] Finally, after he calls for fire, Lazaro asks, "Who is the organism?" to which Celestino replies, "You" (ibid., 46). This sequence suggests that the organism is both a system and a person: a mode of violence that will stabilize the transnational commercial world and that mode of violence personified. Given the period of the play and the character's age, it makes sense that Lazaro would have been born in the '80s, making his transformation into adulthood the maturation of neoliberalism into the organism at the cusp of the twenty-first century. Given the term's first definition as "a living system that can reproduce itself" and its second definition as a single living thing, the organism can be both Lazaro and the neoliberal. Only death can stop the system from reproducing, which Lazaro's ethical act instantiates, effectively ending the neoliberal regeneration of violence in the play.

Solis stages Lazaro's failure to become the organism as an increasingly self-conscious performance of narco-masculinity—the very performance of the gender binary Valencia sees as so important to *capitalismo gore*. At the beginning of the play, Blanca/Alfonso, notably as an undocumented laborer from Mexico, is hired to teach Lazaro basic comportment. Her job is to transition him to the social world, while taking the brunt of his early missteps. Celestino, after imparting the historical and contextual information about border politics he needs to survive, has to help Lazaro do something harder: learn to order rival smugglers killed and to classify undocumented migrants as inhuman. At first Lazaro balks at this violence, but ultimately yells "Fuego!" spurring the death of so-called smugglers. He later claims that he did not want to kill those men but understands that "it's what men do.

They Kill."[20] Blanca/Alfonso, after handing him his new documentation, convinces him of two truths. One, that his memory of being imprisoned was not a dream: he really was chained up on an island by his father. Two, that the land across the border is full of real people whose lives matter. Lazaro, because of his affection and attraction to Alfonso/Blanca, hears her, and his response is first to kiss her tenderly and then to knock her on the ground and try to kiss her again. Celestino intervenes but not for the purpose of quelling Lazaro's violence. Instead, he wants to prevent his son from kissing another man. Blanca/Alfonso is promptly deported at this moment, linking the desire to banish queerness with the desire to deport undocumented labor.

This scene also reveals how being a *maricón* (gay male) is conflated with failing to perform narco-masculinity. Although Celestino does not connect the two, the audience does, because it is precisely at the moment when Lazaro second-guesses his father's ideology that he acts on his romantic and sexual feelings for Alfonso/Blanca. However much his exile with fashion magazines and TV guides has inhibited his social abilities, his lack of socialization in heterosexual normativity allows him to explore attractions not based on a traditional alignment of gender and sex. After Alfonso/Blanca is deported, however, he hurls himself into a performance of hypermasculinity out of confusion and spite toward his father. Ultimately, Lazaro needlessly injures Pepín because he is an illegal alien, regaining his father's trust. Thus, Lazaro's performance of masculinity, enacted vis-à-vis violence against the undocumented, erases his status as a *maricón*. After he injures Pepín, he enacts a more exaggerated performance of heterosexuality by sleeping with his father's lover, Sonia, and flirting through a drug deal with Bustamante, displacing his queer past. Solis's revision of Calderón's play contrasts the relationship of violence to narco-rule with the role of violence to royal sovereignty. In monarchical seventeenth-century Spain, physical violence and domination was to be sublimated or transformed into benevolent, nonviolent rule. Violence against the king's employees was not tolerated. This is why Sigesmundo has to be sent back to the tower. At the turn of the twenty-first century at the U.S.-Mexico border, physical violence is only to be directed against people categorized as inhuman. Lazaro's frightening embodiment of masculinity is self-consciously theatricalized. On one hand, Lazaro is consciously performing his violence as the transference of his rage toward his father. On the other, Lazaro is quite frankly putting on a show for his father that the audience should recognize as performance. This heightened doubleness denaturalizes the performance of narco-masculinity so key to many media representations, showing its horror and its ridiculousness.

Yet, this self-conscious performance does not make his behavior any less threatening. For those versed in the development of narcotrafficking, Lazaro's performance is a reality that comes into play just a few years later. At the end of the play, one realizes how close one lives to the fantastical monster Lazaro almost becomes. How many Lazaros are at the heart of the continuing femicides? How many have found their way into the Knights Templar or are performing beheadings and dumping bodies in mass graves? Notably, by concentrating on a child of privilege, Solis reveals that the complex of violence and misogyny is fueled not only by economic desperation but also by a culture of impunity for the elite. As Valencia explains in *Capitalismo Gore*, this form of masculinity was deeply embedded in the Mexican nation-state's creation, revealing a longer history between state building, machismo, and violence. Although it is hard to argue that narco-violence is getting worse, the escalation that came with Felipe Calderón's narcoguerra constituted an intensification of the violent tactics that Solis gestures toward. In the last decade, there has been a shift away from a world in which the Celestinos hire others to do their violence, holding onto a certain gentlemanly distance from sheer brutality, toward one where there is no such concern. Celestino begins this transition himself when, rather than simply letting his employees meet their fate in the desert, he actually drives Sonia there and leaves her after he learns of her cocaine use and affair with his son. Sonia is closed in on by "shadowy presences" and found "half-buried in the desert" just like the early femicides.[21] In the Thick Description Theatre Company's production of the play, directed by Solis himself, Sonia literally disappeared as the light focused on her tightened and dimmed into darkness.[22]

The way Celestino killed Sonia strips of her not only of her class status but of her subjectivity: she is converted from character to corpse. Solis does not use the desecration of Sonia's body as a form of language as killers do in the subsequent narcoguerra; instead he stages her death purely as evidence of the brute misogyny of the culture in which his characters are living. The murdering shadowy presences detect Sonia by her smell, the smell of woman, rather than by the scent of the beauty products she consumes to cover it up. No performance of class or privilege can save her from her fate as a brown woman at the U.S.-Mexico border. However oedipal the framing of her killing, her demise is clearly a social commentary on the femicides in Juárez and the misogyny that allows them to thrive. Solis, as he confided to me, included this killing even if that meant "putting too much" in the play.[23] Solis was indeed accused of putting too much into the play—as have been other playwrights and television writers who include depiction of multiple forms of border violence within one work.

Instead of seeing this as a fault, however, I argue that *Dreamlandia*'s inclusion of commentary on NAFTA, femicides, and drug cartels in the midst of a deeply theatricalized depiction of a father-son conflict imbued by fate is an explicit strategy to show the deep interconnectedness of all forms of neoliberal violence. By having the same characters or the same actors show up in different places (we see Blanca in the maquila as a worker and in El Paso; the actress who plays Sonia also plays Vivian) and be subjected to parallel but not identical violent acts, Solis undergirds the networks of gendered harm in greater Mexico. His appropriation of the trope of mistaken identity in Calderón's play is crucial. For example, when Lazaro sees Blanca in the maquila and recognizes her, he accords her a particular subjectivity that the conditions in his father's factories erase. Seeing his former lover in everyday Mexican women, meanwhile, forces Frank to quit thinking about Dolores as different from the other Mexican people who he harms as a border patrol sector chief. The moment where he deports his own daughter, Blanca, before recognizing her consciously, revises a trope within Chicano/a drama where family members deport their own relatives, such as in his subsequent work *Lydia*. The messiness of *Dreamlandia*'s ending, however, curtails narrative resolution via such moral recognition, leaving a murkier mess for its audience to swim in.

Life Is a Dream's final allegiances uphold the rightful rule of the Hapsburg monarchy. In *Dreamlandia*, the characters' lack of clear allegiances combines ethical hope with a somber acknowledgment of the impossibility of revolution in the current age of neoliberal capital. Bustamante and Lazaro's reverie during his first and final drug deal describes the new order of the transnational narco world, whose rulers are "Los CEOS de multinational corpse and Citibank executives on Telemundo, a silicon breast in each hand" who work with "cops moonlighting as narcobodyguards . . . laughing at the drug war, the legislation, the just say nos" and the "Founding Fathers of the DEA—"[24] After making it clear that Lazaro is Bustamante's bitch and not the other way around, Bustamante and Lazaro spell out the dystopian present, inverting the possibilities of Cherríe Moraga's indigenous eschatology. Their exchange is worth quoting at length.

> BUSTAMANTE: We are the best export, the true ambassadors.
> LAZARO: The real Zapatistas of these twisted times.
> BUSTAMANTE: 'Cause the real narcotic is hope, smuggled in body cavities they will NEVER reach muthafukkah.
> LAZARO: And one awesome apoca-lipstick day
> BUSTAMANTE: All the cell phones, yours and mine
> LAZARO: Gonna wail on the very same line.
> BUSTAMANTE: Solidarity.[25]

The new regime, then, promises the culmination of "these twisted times" in an ironic mode, which twists many of the keywords of the left into a monstrosity which is the present. The story this reverie tells is that of the decline in possibility for mass action from 1994 to the play's present. For Solis and many others, 2000 marked a moment when hopes for the Zapatista rebellion as national insurgence, as opposed to a model of localized democratic practice, were dashed. That Lazaro hears this insurgence and its demise over a Mexican cell phone is an ironic comment on how monopolistic capitalism owned all means of communication under Mexico's so-called democracy under neoliberal rule. Carlos Slim, the third-richest man in the world, owns

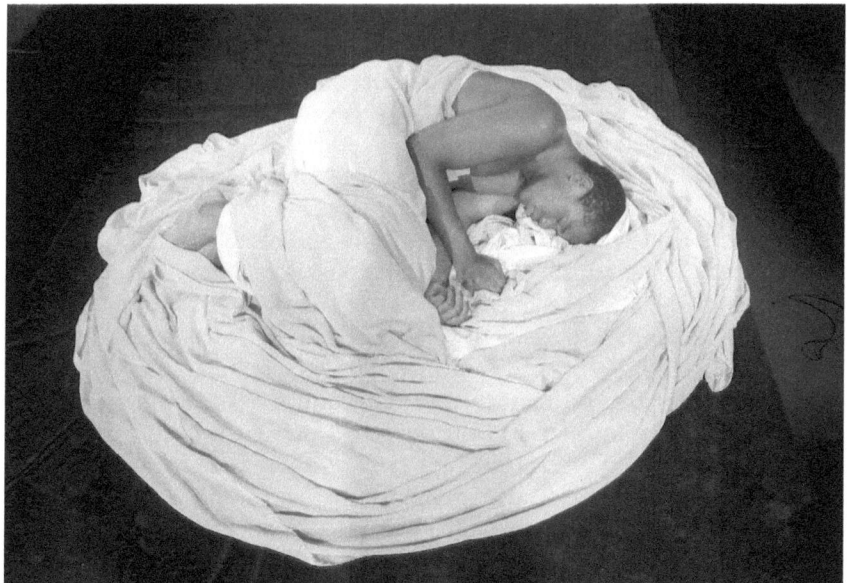

Dreamlandia. Directed by Monica Sanchez. Lazaro played by Elijah Bradford. Photo courtesy of Working Classroom.

a monopoly on Mexican cell phones, part of the *New York Times*, as well as having undue influence in the Mexican state apparatus.[26] Instead of having his characters start, join, or reanimate such an insurgency, as *The Hungry Woman*'s characters do, Solis has Lazaro simply decline the allures of narcoentrepreneurship. And this perhaps is the conservative move in Solis's dramaturgy: the reaching for the possibility of individual change rather than revolution.

It should be noted, however, that neoliberal conditions forced Solis to dispense with the "Mexico as past" dramaturgy he inherited from the Chicano/a canon. In *Santos*, Tommy opposed his brothers' trafficking because his imagination of his father's unidirectional migration to the United States as an act of social betterment rejects drug trafficking as an appropriate mode of wealth accumulation and self-making. In contrast, in *Dreamlandia*, Celestino's crossing provides no moral object lesson for his son, either positive or negative. After learning who he truly is, Lazaro ends the play by stepping into the flux of the river with another character, Blanca, ultimately "let[ting] the water decide" where they will end up.[27] I do not read this scene as a return to Mexico, which would secure his identity, but as a refusal of his father's form of the transnational world. Lazaro's walk into the river has no sure outcome. Thus, this scene upends the standard dramaturgy of male Chicano subjectivity that depends upon the violent unidirectional traversal of the border into the United States (his, his parents, or even his grandparents) as the primarily subjectifying force that articulates cultural identity ready to be cannibalized by liberal humanism. Although he has not eliminated the liberal subject, Solis has destabilized the ground on which the liberal subject walks.

El Nogalar and the Affective Labor of Narcoentrepreneurship

Dreamlandia and *Santos y Santos* stand alongside the works of Saracho, Cazares, and Olmos, which articulate a later phase of narcotrafficking: Felipe Calderón's post-2006 narcoguerra as manifest in northern Mexico. I begin my exploration of these plays with Tanya Saracho's *El Nogalar* (2011). A riff on Chekhov's *The Cherry Orchard*, the 1903 Russian play that staged the decline of the Russian aristocracy at the beginning of the twentieth century, *El Nogalar* chronicles the Galvan family's loss of their hacienda and pecan orchard in Nuevo León. Saracho cut the cast to just five characters, which parallel Chekhov's: Maité, the matriarch (Ranevskaya); her daughters Anita (Anya), who lives with her in the United States, and Valeria (Varya), who has been trying to hold on to Maité's crumbling estate in Mexico; Dunia (Dunya), their housekeeper; and López (Lopahkin), the son of the groundskeeper who becomes the owner of the estate. The plot of the play tracks their journey from Anita and Maité's return to Mexico to López's purchase of the orchard and subsequent celebration. At the end of the play, however, Saracho adds a twist. Once López buys the orchard, he hooks up with Dunia, suggesting a new order where, with allusion to Chekhov, the trees fall "along with the upper class."[28]

The backdrop for the end of the upper class in northern Mexico is the ascension of narcotrafficking cartel activity in this formerly pastoral paradise. In the play's view, those who ascend are people of the lower classes, such as López, who become kingpins and middlemen for the *maña*. Saracho describes the state of impunity in Mexico by pointing both to the impotence of the state—one can now sit in open air and criticize the government—and to the violence in formerly peaceful areas of Mexico. Her characters refer to their current conditions as "an occupation," describing narco-rule with the terminology of encampment by military force.[29] The loss of the estate to country houses for the middle class is Chekhov's characters' horror; for the Galvans it is the loss of their estate to this new regime—the "nacos," rich young men of a lower class, and the "good boys" alike who plan to convert their secluded rural paradise into a landing strip or a growing site for marijuana or heroin. This is a new occupation in a doubled sense of the term.[30] Thus, it is not so much who occupies the house that is at issue here—in fact, López is able to strike a deal with his *maña* superiors to let the Galvans stay in the house—but how the land around it is used. If the Galvans were to stay, they would probably be trapped inside because the world around them is no longer safe. Saracho's decision to focus on the women in this world, her avowed entry into adapting Chekhov's work, makes the gendered terror of narco-rule all the clearer. In the offstage world of Saracho's play, as opposed to the play itself, most of the women are gone. The Galvans are a very visible exception. As Maité remarks when she tries to throw a party and only men, notably all offstage, arrive: "What, don't we know any women?"[31] Of course, for those who know the usual politics of rural migration this is a reversal of the often remarked upon situation in which females remain alone or with nonlaboring loved ones in rural towns while loved ones migrate to the United States to find work. Here, the scarcity of women seems to escalate the possibility of terror for the Galvans. The only people left are the (mostly male) narcos. Constant references are made to the danger posed by their vacations at the cascade, where Pedro tries to get them out of the visual field of narcotraffickers.[32]

Perhaps more dangerous, as Marci McMahon eloquently points out, is the culture of "narco silence" created by a culture of fear and threats of death that cause witnesses to constantly see violence but not saying anything, "walking around moving their mouths like a TV on mute."[33] As McMahon suggests, protesters have strategically used the silent protest as critique to underscore silence's role in impunity; she also convincingly argues that Saracho draws attention to narco silence for the purpose of denaturalizing it through her and her production team's innovative use of sound design. Within the text itself, Dunia threatens her livelihood by refusing this silence—even within closed doors—when she mentions the *maña* and describes their killings. López explains this to Dunia, who he assumes does not understand:

> LÓPEZ: This is not a game.
> DUNIA: I know this is not a game! Why do you always think I am so stupid? I know it's not a game. But people have to do something.
> LÓPEZ: Dunia!
> DUNIA: I am not trying to be a hero. I don't mean something like that! Believe me I'm not trying to end up dismembered by a landfill. All I'm trying to do is learn to swim in it like you. Without drowning.
> LÓPEZ: Understand that in all of *this*, there is no way for girls like you to "figure it out." Women are zeros, you understand me, zeros to the left. I don't want to have to start worrying about you, you hear me Dunia? I already got these fucking women coming in today. I'm going to have enough with making them get that they can't just come in here and parade about the way they used to. I'm going to have a hard time making them understand that we are under an occupation.[34]

López's suggestion that women are zeros to the left suggests that women like her, women without great social and class privilege, are as insignificant as zeros to the left of a number. Yet given the number of femicides in Mexico, the zeros to the left also recall the zeros to the right, the great number of women whose deaths have become numerical statistics. Dunia, although she considered going to work in the maquilas before the play, is now trying to come up with another plan to escape the present and become something else. This is why her pairing with López is so essential.

In *El Nogalar*, Dunia *and* López both emerge as a new class of entrepreneurs. Dunia strives to learn how to get online so that she can be in touch with the world and place herself in that world. She sees this act as an extension of telling her story, of narrating herself. As Saracho herself points out, Dunia's whitening of herself with cosmetics undergirds her desire's racial unconsciousness, which equates whiteness with class and social mobility. Dunia's racially charged refraction of Sonia's use of cosmetics in *Dreamlandia* directly links entrepreneurial selfhood and consumption. Dunia's actions are the beginning of her transformation into an entrepreneur of the self, a subject who produces her own satisfaction and subjectivity through consumption.[35] It is notable that the example López comes up with when imagining her as "too dangerous for the Internet" is her selling herself as a mail-order bride.[36] Dunia's power on the Internet (as López imagines it at least) is her staging herself as human capital rather than marketing her skills as a laborer for hire (although admittedly this form of existence, like sex work, confounds traditional definitions of labor). Spatially, this articulation of self in the media world substitutes for migrating north to work in a maquila, indicating a spatial shift in labor practices and self-making possibilities. Engaging the power of "Facebook money" she attempts to opt out of her material constrictions.[37] Yet, as a woman of her class and skin tone in Mexico, this form of entrepreneurship comes to a rather mundane end at the end of the play. Despite her attempts to get out of town, or into the world, her hope seems to ride on her liaison with López, whom she seduces after he acquires the orchard. If one imagines her future in terms of narco-culture, this will make her his girlfriend, a result wholly unsatisfying for Dunia. Her reading of the moment as an opening up of the possibility of true class mobilization in Mexico may be a form of cruel optimism. If she fights against such a limiting role, which she might, the consequences could be fatal.

López's upward mobility is equally fraught. Buying the orchard may hold promise for him becoming a capitalist stakeholder, but it seems unlikely he will gain any independence from the *maña*, indicating that he too will remain an affective laborer for someone else rather than being autonomous. When the play begins, his primary job in the cartel seems to be managing his narco superiors' emotions through consumption and care (buying them iPads, calming them down). López's job is affective—he does not produce anything. In his own words, using a pointedly performative metaphor, he claims that he is just "the court fool trying to keep the balls up in the air."[38] López is never seen transporting or selling drugs or enacting physical violence, though he packs a gun for protection. Instead he manages people endlessly much like

Sonia does in the maquila. His role as a self-conscious performer alludes to narco-masculinity as performance, while also being a clever joke about the gun on the wall that must, but never, goes off.

In contrast with other media representations of narcotrafficking, Saracho's play is notable for refusing to show violence; rather we hear its threat just offstage. What we see instead is a world where affective laborers work hard to stave off that violence from the "nacos" who run the place. This type of labor has replaced taking care of the aristocracy as well as the creation of and care for their material goods. López's tinkering with the bookcase in *El Nogalar* is a clever displacement of Gaev's "useless" attachment to a hundred-year-old object. López's craft work is now an avocation rather than a vocation. His manual labor, his skill at it, is linked to nostalgia for a past era of Mexico, which he does to appease the Galvans emotionally rather than to earn his keep. It is no accident that López gets interrupted from his tinkering to "teach" Dunia "the Internet."[39] The substitution of one form of labor by another forms a major tension at the heart of the play, which parallels its anxiety about class politics. Maité points to this tension when she expresses disgust at the new economic order filled with "new money," "Facebook money."[40] On one level, one can read this as another instance of Maité's denial of the reality of narcotraffic as the new wealth generator in the area. On another level, however, the juxtaposition aligns Facebook money and new money because they separate capital accumulation from the accumulation of property, in contrast with land wealth or rustic crafts (such as the pecan candies coveted by Dunia), which combine the two. The Goodman Theatre in Chicago's production of *El Nogalar* openly linked the Galvans' nostalgia with the practice of manual labor by having López repairing a huge dollhouse over the course of the play.[41] That said, it should be noted that repurposing the Galvan estate for drug cultivation is an act of mass manual labor and agricultural toil and that drug cultivation is an act dependent on conceptions of property and turf, as narco disputes over plazas suggest. As Sayak Valencia points out, the move to cultivating rather than simply moving drugs is an ironic re-vindication of agricultural production, albeit one that impoverishes small farmers rather than sustaining them.[42] Yet, for women of Maité's generation, Facebook money is a kind of unrecognizable virtual entrepreneurship, which sells experience in the same way that narcotics do. For Maité, at least, this is a form of capitalism she imagines herself as being both above and outside of because of her (soon to disappear) land wealth.

Maité's denial of her complicity in narcotrafficking is a more willful ignorance, which is ironized in how she consumes drugs to cope with the affective reality of neoliberalism. Neither she nor anyone else in this play is outside of the pharmacological regime. López consumes cocaine, alcohol, and antacids to manage his anxiety so he can manage others' needs. He and Pedro's offstage negotiations with Maité are, after all, done over a bottle of tequila. Even before she arrived, Maité drugged herself with a "little pill" at the airport on her way back to Mexico to calm herself down. When she touches down, she demands caffeine, an often unacknowledged participant in effectuating colonial and industrial work regimes.[43] Clearly, drug consumption is key to the world Saracho created; as she remarks in an interview, although she cut the character of Yasha, Ranevskaya's ne'er-do-well servant, he "could have been a cokehead."[44] Saracho's sinister adaptation of Chekhov's vodka- and champagne-drinking camaraderie reveals how recreational intoxication and the necropolitical world are intertwined in the affective experience of everyday life.

Ultimately, her upper-class characters have to try to escape the scene and enter the new economic and social regime with mixed results. Chekhov's characters return to Moscow; Saracho's go to Monterrey. Known for its technical schools and business climate, Monterrey is a commercial capital. Going there is a decision to enter contemporary capitalist culture. In direct contrast to expectations, Valeria does not get married but adopts the tactics of her economic inferiors by migrating to the city for work, just as her Russian counterpart went to the city to be a governess. Valeria decides to use her knowledge of four languages and accounting skills to get an office job, an opportunity in Mexico usually reserved for the middle class, not the upper class or, notably, the truly impoverished. For the less-privileged Mexicans in the play, the sale of the orchard also opens up a future within rather than outside of the bounds of the Mexican nation-state. As Dunia says after López buys the estate, "Memo, maybe the idea right now is not to leave up north anymore. We keep looking up, in hope of miracles, but maybe the miracles are right here beneath our feet. No one ever thought you would be the owner of Los Nogales, not in a million years!"[45] Despite the somewhat fantastical nature of Dunia's musings in relation to reality, her thought experiment dislodges crossing into the United States or heading to the border as the primary mode of subject making for her characters. Unlike many of the other plays in this chapter, *El Nogalar* plots migration *back* to Mexico as a possible solution to the family's ills. This decision is no doubt exacerbated by the poor health of the U.S. financial markets as much as any squandering of resources by the Galvans. (As I write this, immigration to Mexico has exceeded immigration from Mexico for the first time in years. This may soon be more extreme, given President Trump's proposed policy changes.) Whether or not these characters' reinvestment in Mexico will reanimate a reproductive nationalism is open to interpretation, but López and Dunia's making love in the open field, a known fertility ritual to bring about good crops, suggests a link between the fruits of the union and the fruits of their fields, and perhaps of the future of the nation as well. Given that both characters are mestizo or indigenous identified, their copulation restages *mestizaje* in its post-neoliberal mode.

The play's ending contrasts with Chekhov's, engaging with Mexican national narratives in surprising ways, which underscores extreme modes of dispossession in contemporary neoliberal capitalism. *El Nogalar*'s complete absenting of the event that was supposed to free López and Dunia from oppression a hundred years earlier—the Mexican Revolution—is notable, especially given the historical synchrony between it and the Russian Revolution. Chekhov's play was written on the eve of this event, which overthrew an old order to create a socialist nation. *The Cherry Orchard* looks to that future, marking a major shift in social, cultural, and economic structures. Saracho's play, if taken as a true adaptation of Chekhov's, anticipates not revolution but a realignment of class relations based on an emergent form of capitalism. Setting the play exactly one hundred years after the beginning of the Mexican Revolution, the absence of even a mention of the event is striking. Has *El Nogalar* given up on the idea of revolution? Is the play a commentary of the failings of the revolution in line with standard Mexican national dramaturgy? Or does the absence of the revolution in *El Nogalar* simply reveal the event's lack of traction in the rural north where powerful families retained huge swaths of land even after the revolution? I suspect all of these may be true.

But what looms larger than the lack of revolution in this play is the presence of the Porfiriato, the era of Porfirio Díaz's dictatorship (1876–1911) that preceded the revolution, which is scarcely engaged in Chicano/Mexicano dramaturgy. This presence opens up the possibility that the current narco-regime reenacts the Porfiriato's social and economic relationships, which relied upon repressive actions against poor laborers and farmers by a strong-arm leader (and his cronies) so as to pacify the nation and thus accelerate foreign investment. The Porfiriato is visible from the first moments of the play when Saracho introduces the most talked-about set piece in the show, an old bed that Díaz may or may not have slept on. Certainly, the Galvans' possession of the bed registers their class position as haves rather than have-nots. However, its prominence as an onstage set piece in a theatrical production underscores its historiographical importance. That the bed induces sleep and forgetting for López in particular suggests the bed's role in causing the new class of entrepreneurs to forget where they are and thus refuse to understand one's history. The bed is not simply a piece of obsolescent period furniture that signifies the Galvans' romantic nostalgia for the past. Instead. López's physical link to the bed for a significant portion of the play suggests that the new regime of narcotraffickers may be an extension of the elite concentration of power under the Porfiriato rather than a break with its reign. López will now help run a system that depends upon large swaths of agricultural land controlled by a few and worked by the many. Today's peasants can harvest marijuana for wages but do not get to grow sustainable crops for their own *milpas* (Nahuatl for "maize field"), making López a future hacienda owner. In this sense, the fall of the Galvans may be a reformist gesture rather than a revolutionary one. It is for this reason that I put special pressure on Saracho's final stage direction:

An interpretive sound of trees falling. Now don't go cueing chainsaws because it's not literal. Just make me feel trees are falling. Along with the upper class. Ting. Ting. TONG. Good-bye to the bed of Porfirio Díaz. Good-bye to the bed of Porfirio Díaz.[46]

The play as a whole attests that we might instead be saying hello to a new Porfiriato, even if the traditional landowners are displaced. Saracho's play also opens up a conundrum in terms of temporality. On one hand her dramaturgy gestures toward progress for Dunia and López, who look to Mexico's future as a chance to escape from past failures. The falling tree signals the transition. At the same time, the playwright's seemingly critical attitude toward teleological progress and her erasure of the Mexican Revolution from the play charts a course that breaks as radically with Mexican historiography as it does with U.S.-centric Latinx dramaturgy. Her choice suggests a strange complicity with Chekhov. Maybe it won't get better, after all. This conscious historiographical meditation is more overt in Cazares's plays on transnational drug trafficking, which spend less time with the Mexican upper classes and more with *los de abajo*.

Queer Historiography, Recursive Time

Two of Victor Cazares's plays deal explicitly with narcotraffic—*Religiones Gringas*, a comedy that follows the travails of a family split by geopolitical borders and the Seventh-day Adventist Church, and *Ramses contra los monstruos*, an epic play about a liaison between a cartel employee hired to dissolve bodies and a young grad school dropout from the other side of the border. Both, however, play with time and borders in a more radically queer way than Cazares's predecessors. *Religiones Gringas*, which I will consider only briefly, takes place in El Paso and northern Mexico, before and after the death of the family's matriarch, an important figure in the town of San Lorenzo, Chihuahua. Her grandson Epi, although a college-educated U.S. citizen, is working for the cartel, a fact that his family is slower to catch on to than the fact that he is gay. His cousin Nene, who is undocumented, is also gay and works in a porn store as a clerk and custodian, but without Epi's privileges. In *Religiones Gringas*, we learn about Epi's profession largely because it allows him to transport his grandmother's corpse across the border to his sisters, who cannot cross back into Mexico because of their immigration status. The violence he suffers from is placed within a comic frame, even though the business is deadly serious. The signifiers of narcotraffic lurk in the shadows—in Epi's SUV, in the pickup trucks that park and disappear, and from the gunshots that come out of nowhere.

In *Religiones Gringas*, Cazares, like Saracho, invokes the Porfiriato rather than the Mexican Revolution when addressing his characters in northern

Mexico. Güe Güe, Nene's aunt and his mother Chayo's sister and lover, comes back over the border from her mother's funeral with a collection of gravestones from the San Lorenzo cemetery. Extracted from a recently disemboweled plaza, the metaphorical power of these gravestones is that they came from the section of the cemetery reserved for souls in limbo, namely, babies and children who were not yet baptized. Like these babies, Cazares metaphorically argues, all of his border-crossing characters live suspended, betwixt and between recognizable states. All of the gravestones Güe Güe steals are from the Porfiriato, a period often left un-exhumed in Mexican national history because it is at odds with the idea of the modern revolutionary state upon which Mexican nationalism depends. The Porfiriato's appearance here is less a critique of the Mexican Revolution's failure than a temporal disjuncture that makes us aware of the failure of teleological time to explain northern Mexican history. It is worth noting that one of the gravestones is from October 22, 1844, the Great Disappointment, which created the Seventh-day Adventist Church. Cazares has Epi retell their grandmother's version:

> EPI: Yeya used to tell us this story. "All the way up there in the land of the gringos—a group of people believed Christ would come on October 22, 1844. And they sold all their belongings, said goodbye to everybody. And waited the whole day. But He didn't come. But they kept on waiting. We keep waiting."[47]

By evoking the history of the Seventh-day Adventists, which has a small set of adherents in northern Mexico and Texas, Cazares engages not only his own family history (he was raised as a Seventh-day Adventist) but an eschatological mindset in which waiting for the Messiah forms the affective everyday of his character's lives. This liminal state is parallel to the one experienced by people with undocumented status or whose residence in one country or another is deemed to be temporary, as is the liminal state of Chayo and Güe Güe's cohabitation. That Nene's Anglo lover, Taylor, is Branch Davidian, a form of Adventism, only underscores the strange coexistence of the U.S. eschatological view of salvation with the affective state of transnational migration. Underneath the play's utilization of traditional comic structure—it starts with a funeral and ends with a marriage, with plenty of Plautine slamming doors in between—is a depiction of the affective experience of neoliberalism as a suspended and confounding hope for a future that will not come.

Although darkly humorous, Cazares's *Ramses contra los monstruos* departs from *Religiones Gringas*'s comic structure. Instead, it runs with the eschatological present to make a more pointed political critique about the transnational pharmacological industry under neoliberalism. The presence of corpses is also key to this play, revealing not only how neoliberalism "re-makes death" but how reanimating death can speak the truth about the

Ramses contra los monstruos. Directed by Ryan Purcell. Amanda Dolan as Chema, Rudy as Rudy. Photo by Mark Turek.

regime's violence. Cazares has written two significant versions of *Ramses*, in 2011 and in 2013. Elsewhere, I have read the first version of the play as a mode of queer eschatology, largely concentrating on its dramaturgical articulation of historiographical principles.[48] Here, I engage Cazares's eschatology but primarily concentrate on the significantly revised 2013 version, staged at Brown University's New Plays festival, as a mode of rethinking the pharmacological era.[49] Briefly summarized, *Ramses* centers on the eponymous character, a *pozolero* who has been cursed by an avenging migrant, Lidia. Kidnapped by the cartels and made their laundress, Lidia gets her revenge by thwarting Ramses's recipe for dissolving human flesh. Consequently, the bodies that Ramses disappears for the cartels are no longer dissolving, threatening his job security and his life. This story is intercut with the story of Amelia, whose daughter, Chema, has been killed in an act of narco-violence. Amelia, who seeks to avenge her daughter's death by not letting her body rest, ultimately decides to kill Felipe Calderón, the Mexican president from 2006 to 2012, who designed the recent drug war in Mexico. The linchpin of these two stories is Tito/ Titus, a lover of Ramses and good friend of Chema's. Acting as the audience's Virgil, he guides us through the inferno, bringing his characters together at a crossroads: a long-shuttered movie theater in Juárez named El Egipcio.[50] Over the course of the play, we meet a series of narco-villains, including a misguided priest, Padre Alonso, the brutal La Barbie, and a Robomascota art project remade from the very real Rudy the Border Patrol Robot.

Unlike *El Nogalar*, which tracks the very recent escalation of the drug war, *Ramses* contains scenes from the 1980s to the present. Also unlike Saracho's play, *Ramses* is transnational, moving fluidly between Ciudad Juárez and El Paso. Cazares's dramaturgical choices argue that the period between the 1980s and the present is a continuous transnational cultural moment. *Ramses* helps its audiences rethink the implicitly nationalist histories that separate U.S. and Mexican histories of neoliberalism and their attendant violence, forcing them to confront the transnational nature of contemporary necropolitics and its representational practices.[51] Cazares centers on queer relations as the primary lens through which to view the time period. He depicts time queerly in Elizabeth Freeman's sense.[52] As Freeman writes: "Queer temporalities . . . are points of resistance to this temporal order, that in turn propose other possibilities for living in relation to indeterminately past, present, and future others: that is, of living historically."[53] For her, this movement is a departure from nationalist time that depends not only on "empty homogenous time" but also the proper temporality of movements such as "coming out, consummation, development, domesticity, family, foreplay, genealogy, identity, liberation, modernity, the progress of movements," which all "contribute to a vision of time as seamless, unified and forward moving."[54] Ramses's particular location and its open engagement with U.S.-Mexican neoliberalism particularizes Freeman's queer temporality in the borderlands. By eschewing the chrononormativity and heteronormativity of border discourse and migration narratives, he, like many other playwrights in this chapter, undoes the particular unidirectionality that still haunts Latino/a American dramaturgy and U.S. narratives of belonging. This queering of the border is in part necessitated by the particularities of the El Paso-Juárez region and its long history.

As Lara Nielsen, Claire Fox, and others have pointed out, in terms of the U.S.-Mexico region, the neoliberal process begins in 1964–65 with the border industrialization program that commenced the creation of maquiladoras (factories) in northern Mexico.[55] The escalation of maquilas continued throughout the 1970s, through the Mexican oil boom and bust and the beginning of Mexico's economic debt difficulties in the 1980s. As a result, Ciudad Juárez became a boomtown: from 1970 to 2000 the population quadrupled without requisite expansion of infrastructure.[56] The emergence of Juárez as megacity did not come with NAFTA, but much earlier. Thus one might think of the neoliberal period as a fifty-year-long trajectory with an intensification that occurred some thirty years ago.

Ramses (2013) marks the high points of the neoliberal calendar—1982, 1988, 1994, and 2006—by employing a Mexican *sexenio* history (referring to the six-year term the Mexican president serves) rather than a decadal one, so as to unhinge neoliberal historiography from a strictly U.S. timeline. In the play, these dates mark life cycles and crossings—Chema was born in 1988 along with election fraud; she and her mother cross and are deported in 1994, the year of NAFTA; the first maquiladora nights she shares with her friend Alex are close upon the 1982 debt crisis; and the contemporary action of the play is in the narcoguerra *sexenio* (2006–2012) led by Felipe Calderón. Cazares's use of Mexican periods transnationalizes history. Pointedly, the neoliberal period brackets Tito/Titus's entire life and Ramses's life cycle as "Ramses." An orphan, Ramses is named by a lover, not a parent. His new life begins when Alex, Amelia's friend, meets him on the road one night. After an act of sex in public and more at Alex's place, Alex christens his lover with his new name:

> RAMSES: Never do heroin.
> ALEX: Why?
> RAMSES: It's more dangerous.
> ALEX: Really?
> RAMSES: Yes. Only do coke.
> ALEX: In this house, only coke-a-cola. Like in all of Mexico.
> RAMSES: I'm serious.
> ALEX: Do you sell it?
> RAMSES: Not yet. But soon.
> ALEX: What's your name?
> RAMSES: If I tell you, I'll have to kill you.
> ALEX: Don't tell me then. Better I tell you. Your name is Ramses.[57]

I quote this scene at length because it manifests Cazares's linkages between the AIDS crisis and narcotraffic while also sketching out the contours of his historiography of neoliberalism more broadly. The name Ramses recalls both the Egyptian pharaoh and the condom brand, linking procreation, violence, and latex protection in the era of AIDS. Note that the title of this scene is "The First Dose"—which seemingly refers to Tito/Titus's ingestion of antiretrovirals earlier in the scene as well as to Alex's first dose of Ramses and of cocaine. The era in which the scene occurs might also be said to be the one that contained the first dose of the effects of neoliberal economic shock therapy in Mexico. The title is prescient given that this first dose becomes the "dose without end" by the end of the play, a state one might refer to as a chronic neoliberal project.

Cazares stages this neoliberal penetration as a set of cross-temporal and queer intergenerational encounters. It is notable that Tito/Titus has sexual and romantic relationships with lovers (Ramses, Profesora Alonso) who were young adults when he was born. It is through these relationships that the fold between the 1980s and the present coexists. This eroticization of the relationship between past and present veers away from straight time as well as straight sex. Untethered to a progressive teleological history with clear demarcations between past and present, the scenes between Alex and Ramses and

Alex and Amelia and Tito/Titus and Ramses coexist rather than follow each other. There are no flashbacks. Many of the scenes change times within their courses. For example, the aforementioned scene between Alex and Ramses follows a scene between Ramses and Tito/Titus where Tito/Titus in the present asks his lover about his past: "What were you doing in the 80s?" Ramses responds with the comment, "I was just a kid, Tito. I was just a kid, Tito. Trying to survive in Juaritos. I don't want to talk about it."[58] The structure of the scene militates against the idea that the movement between the scenes is the result of any one character's memory. The scene with Alex happens when Ramses is sleeping and Tito/Titus is awake, so that the prompt for the scene does not come from the person whose past it documents. Dramaturgically, these conjugal connections represent a shared history of the Americas that joins what has happened and what is happening. The swallowing of the pill lets Tito/Titus ingest the entire history of the era as well as facilitating our consumption of the same period. This scene is emblematic of many others in the play: relationships coexist in the present and past worlds and between the living and the dead. To this end, many of the early scenes of the play were described in an earlier draft as "hauntings"—a word that describes the copresence of spectral visitation.[59] The implication, however, is not that the past haunts the present, although it is clear that the play is invested in exposing how actions in the 1980s impact contemporary narcopolitics in Mexico.

Instead, Cazares reminds us that the neoliberal era is a continuous present, whose crises are variations on a theme. Ramses's dissolving of narco-victims is juxtaposed with the disappearances of the maquila workers with whom Amelia and Alex work. In a sequence of 1994 scenes in the middle of the play, we find out that the bodies that Ramses dissolved in the '90s were maquila bodies that he was forced to disappear after he did too much of the cocaine he was supposed to be selling; that Amelia is about to escape a Juárez she foresees will become a ghost town just as the femicides start to escalate; and that Ramses has begun to question why Alex gave him his name. Ramses leaves Alex in the desert, presaging the vulnerability of the bodies that will soon be found there. While the two do not discuss HIV transmission, their conversation is haunted with its possibility.

Through the journeys of his character, Cazares theorizes the neoliberal era as chronic and recursive, mimicking both the daily regime of antivirals and the seriality of sexual encounters. Just as Mexican and U.S. financial crises repeat themselves (1982 and 1994, 1987 and 2008), scenes repeat themselves or nearly do with only the slightest of revisions. Ramses and Alex's scene in the car echoes the scene where Ramses is named, recursively reminding us of Ramses's origin story. And the scene that brings Ramses and Tito/Titus together after what is supposed to be their last encounter occurs twice. In that scene, Padrecito Alonso picks Tito/Titus up in a car, offering him money and cocaine to have sex with La Barbie. Alonso chloroforms Tito/Titus, masks him, and gets him into the car. The first time, the scene occurs at a normal speed and dissolves into a consensual sex scene between Ramses and Tito/Titus; the second time, the action is accelerated and dissolves into a scene where La Barbie rapes Tito/Titus and asks Padre Alonso to dispose of the body of his victim, which Alonso refuses to do. (The actor who plays Padre Alonso also plays Profesor(a) Alonso and Doctor Alonso, linking them together.) The cyclical nature of the violence reveals the recursive nature of sex and violence in the narco world, placing temporally disjunctive moments together on the same plane. Tito/Titus and Ramses register these temporal confusions when they meet for breakfast at McDonald's soon after Chema's death.

> RAMSES: I feel like I have been here before.
> TITO/TITUS: You have, they are all the same.
> RAMSES: No. Here. With you.
> TITO/TITUS: Devil dreams, I'm sure.
> RAMSES: What do you want?
> TITO/TITUS: Nothing. I do not eat at McDonald's.
> RAMSES: Fine. What happened to you there?
>
> (*He points to a scrape on Tito/Titus' face.*)
>
> TITO/TITUS: The scrape that saved my life. I hit the ground hard when I was caught in between a narco shootout a couple of weeks ago while I was waiting for a hamburger last night.[60]

The actor playing Tito/Titus registers his confusion, but the play never tries to rectify or resolve his conclusion, dramaturgically or theatrically. The disjuncture remains unexplained. This lack of resolution allows the neoliberal era to live on uncannily throughout the play, giving untimeliness to the play as a whole. To this end, the play ends not with its chronological end, the scene that documents Tito/Titus's death and the beginning of Amelia's crusade for justice, but with the repetition of a sex scene between Tito/Titus and Ramses in one of the many houses he uses for his liaisons.

Space can be just as liminal in *Ramses* as time, making space durational. The movements of Cazares's characters make the border not just contiguous but continuous, by moving between spaces without scene changes. The link between these scenes is associative, all linked to moving in and out of El Paso, but we do not see Chema actually move across the border at all. The fluidity between the scenes suggests that these places are on the same plane despite the very different living conditions opposite sides of the border. The depiction of the crossing of borders in the play also works against the idea of unidirectional (and seemingly chrononormative) movement over them as an end goal for labor or love. The actual border is never depicted on stage; that is not where the trauma lies in this play. And no one crosses in order never to return. In contrast, we see lovers and friends crossing into Juárez and El Paso in a quotidian manner. Ramses crosses into the United States to see Tito/Titus, only to show up late at McDonald's and miss breakfast. Tito crosses into Juárez to see him as well. Chema goes to school in El Paso during the day but goes home to her mother in Juárez at night.

Cazares's lack of investment in the border as a threshold space defetishizes it as an epistemological and geopolitical boundary that demarcates self-contained experiences (a binary Solis, however ambivalently, still maintains.) Instead, Juárez and El Paso are deterritorialized sites on the same plane differentially affected by transnational commerce. Who crosses and when is still of importance, of course, as it is clear that some people simply can't cross, such as Amelia and Lidia. But by and large the characters' movements argue that circulations of transnational commerce articulate the lived experience of the space, rather than unidirectional migration. As such, the historiography of the area is equally circulatory—moving back and forth and folding inward. Yet, this play harbors no late '90s era inflected utopian discourse of the hybrid or the nomad. The complex vectors of movement in this play not only depict a transnational reality, but also revise the temporal conception of the borderlands—a conception that often still sometimes functions on a teleological timeline even when rejecting spatial bifurcation.

The conjunction of cospatiality and cotemporality is best exemplified in El Egipcio, the grand 1920s era theater that closed in the '80s, where many of the play's scenes take place. The theater's obsolescence marks the dashed dreams of Mexico's nationalist period that began with the centralization of the socialist nation state under President Lázaro Cárdenas (1934–1940) and ended somewhere between the peso crash of 1982 and the Mexico City earthquake that exposed the country's lack of infrastructure in 1985. Inside the theater, movies from the golden age are projected on the walls as Rudy the Border Patrol robot is being re-created as a sort of monstrosity. Reoccupied and transformed into Chema's studio, El Egipcio harbors the nationalist past, the post-nationalist past (the 1980s), and Titus's present (now). By collapsing past, present, and future, Cazares creates a space illuminated by the spectral light of 1940s celluloid and the surveillance lights of the '80s and '90s, retrofitted into a contemporary border patrol Frankenstein. So, even if the theater is a "tomb for a Mexico that never came," it is also a safe house, a respite that suspends the progressive time of the plot and a place where one can temporarily imagine a future even if it never happens.[61] Cazares's depiction of the theater both engages and undoes the drug safe house of filmic dramaturgy whose utopian promise is read as dystopia by a knowing, sober audience. This safe house is a transformation of the theater as cruising site—a purpose referenced when Tito/Titus is introduced in the play. An indelible pre-AIDS queer space, popular in gay literature of the '60s and '70s, the darkened movie theater looms large in the sexual imaginary. Cazares's theater was specifically inspired by a Gil Cuadros poem, "Conquering Immortality,"

Ramses contra los monstruos. Directed by Ryan Purcell. Drew Ledbetter as Ramses, Brandon Vukovic as Tito/Titus. Photo by Mark Turek.

which describes a shuttered but glorious theater in downtown LA becoming a double for a still majestic body ravaged by AIDS. The transformation of the movie theater from pre-epidemic cruising zone to post-nationalist safe house marks it as both a refuge and a ruin. The palimpsest nature of the space combines Mexican national and U.S. queer memories, joining past, present, and imagined future in one space.

In the 2013 production, the entire stage becomes El Egipcio for the second half of the play—transforming before our eyes right before the intermission. This is the only major scene change in the play, and it is consciously staged in front of the audience, making us keenly aware of the space itself. All further action in the play, then, happens "in the theater." Cazares's stage directions ask actors to do what cannot be staged, such as sleeping on a row of red theater seats, and designers to do the near impossible—making a shower of rain and sand. These impossibilities underscore El Egipcio's biggest failure—its refusal to resolve into a stable domestic space for the characters who inhabit it. Chema, who uses it as a studio, is adamant that she does not live there. When Ramses and Tito/Titus try to make themselves comfortable, the theater fails to be a home sweet home. Ramses vomits up the hot chocolate that Tito/Titus makes him, undoing any hope the audience may have of their liaison resolving into monogamous cohabitation. This safe house ultimately becomes an unsafe house violated by the very violence that it tries to keep at bay. It is where Rudy kills Tito/Titus in a freak accident and where La Barbie is killed. Because the movie house becomes the entire set for the second half of the play, the theater ceases to be a discrete place, preventing it from becoming a place set apart from the world of the play. This scenic decision necessitates that the rest of the play occur there, making the entire world an (un)safe house. History is no refuge in this regard; it is no time or space apart. *Ramses*'s set also incorporated the coexistence of hell, heaven, and purgatory in a way inspired by and departing from Reza Abdoh's formulation in *The Law of Remains*.[62]

Because of the limits of *Ramses*'s stage space, heaven, hell, and purgatory are not stacked vertically but remain on a largely lateral stage plane. The exception is a hollow created by a shallow trapdoor downstage center. Used as a cauldron, the site of some of Ramses and Tito/Titus's best sex and of his subsequent rape by La Barbie, the bowels of the El Egipcio as trapdoor literalizes the rectum as grave and glory.[63] Leo Bersani's return is through the floorboards. This space harbors the incomplete dissolution of self and other during the sexual act and the incomplete dissolution of personhood under extreme neoliberal violence—be it rape or Ramses' stew making from the bodies of the dead. This shallow grave extends to envelop Chema when she throws herself into the pot some time after her death, prompting her mother to move on to vengeance. The underground of *Ramses*'s stage space is also a literalization of the catacombs Padre Alonso mentions as the space underneath the church that is ideal for a clandestine lab. Yet, unlike many catacombs, everything that disappears in the underspace in *Ramses* reappears, much like the secret histories of neoliberalism that the play exposes.

Theatrical Obsolescence as Critique

The appearance and reappearance of bodies, of course, engages with the theatricality of the theater, notably, the recognition that dead and dying characters always return to live again as actors taking their bows at curtain call. This uncanniness, explored so fully by Herbert Blau, haunts the play.[64] Yet, unlike a more generic formulation of the actor as dead and undead, in Cazares's play these bodies reference the materiality of the narco-dead specifically. The play theatricalizes and depicts a refusal to be disappeared. The premise that drives the plot, after all, is Ramses's inability to dissolve the bodies and souls of those killed in the narcoguerra.

Cazares's disappearances are the latest in a long (neoliberal) series of disappearances emergent in the 1970s in the Southern Cone, where bodies of those who opposed military dictatorships (and the economic shock doctrines that came with them) were thrown from planes and absented from view by the state. In the 1990s in Juárez, assassins first disappeared women, then buried or dissolved them. Later, they placed their corpses in the open air for display as they do male cadavers, writing a violence that expresses absolute power over territory and consciousness. As Rosanna Reguillo argues, these killings are a language that replaces utilitarian violence with expressive violence.[65] They were meant to be *seen* and apprehended by spectators. In some ways, then, Cazares's choice to have the erasure of narco-violence be the play's spectatorial index is anachronistic given the events of the most recent narcoguerra. On another level, however, this erasure more accurately indexes the procedures of death under Mexican-U.S. neoliberalism (and, it should be noted, El Pozolero, the inspiration for Ramses, worked throughout the narcoguerra, suggesting that there are multiple modes of dealing with the fallen).

Chema's treatment in *Ramses* best exemplifies Cazares's mode of making death material. Her long-limbed body remains onstage after she is killed, first spilling awkwardly out of a makeshift refrigerator, then in subsequent scenes being led around the stage clumsily by her mother, whom she towers over. The uncanny appearance of the very tall, living actress who plays Chema being awkwardly dragged around the stage refuses her character's erasure or naturalization as a corpse. Chema remains, not by standing and exiting the stage as actor after the performance but by remaining on stage as a character, sutured to her mother's side. Her mother's mourning is not of her daughter's absence but her very (un)real undead presence. Amelia's act is political. As she explains to a friend who tries to help her comes to terms with Chema's death:

> I'm not burying her! She's mine. I won't let her leave my house. Chemita, don't worry. I won't let anybody take you, bury you underneath. Don't you understand, comadre? Our fucking son of a bitch president wants us to feed our dead to the earth so they're forgotten. So it's easier to not have justice. So that her death is *normal*.[66]

The embodied presence of the character also refuses the spectrality of the deceased, in a way echoed by Olmos in *so go the ghosts of méxico, part 1*. Chema's presence is joined by the corpses that emerge from the body bags Ramses brings into the Egyptian safe house; for example, La Barbie sits up after Tito/Titus opens the body bag to look at him. The corpses of La Barbie and Lidia cease to be docile bodies or even corpses, forcing Tito/Titus to mourn Chema's death openly for the first time in the play.

While these reappearances recall the Mexican monster movies whose undead border on camp, Cazares's undead remain monstrous, rather than zombielike. This distinction is important to make in the age of zombie capitalism. In Haitian culture zombies are beings raised from the dead by an external force; in contemporary culture they stand in for dead labor, or mindless adherence to capitalistic norms. The performative zombies we often see in protests, movies, and flash mobs remind us of dead labor by taking over public space in the First World, even when speaking against the mobilization

Ramses contra los monstruos. Directed by Ryan Purcell. Sophie Netanel as Lidia, Alston Brown as La Barbie. Photo by Mark Turek.

of finance capital elsewhere.[67] Cazares's monsters neither participate in so-called legitimate operations of finance capital nor do they make mass public appearances in finance capitals. Instead Cazares's monsters are from the Global South, enacting the violence in their own backyards. This cannibalism is necessary to accumulation by dispossession throughout the Global South. The everyday destruction of human beings is anything but dead labor; it is the labor of remaking death. These monsters represent the deformation of the world in the flesh. The monsters we see on stage take over: Ramses consumes them, they consume Ramses, they both consume Tito/Titus. And, I think it is fair to say, they also consume us.

An early version of the play suggests that Cazares imagined an army of the dead as zombies (a voodoo resurrection) that would fight a war against narcotraffic. In the final draft of the play, however, this large-scale war has become a very human strategic strike, not against the narcos, but against Felipe Calderón. With the help of Lidia's curse, Amelia, one of the few characters left alive, vows to assassinate the former president. So while the play is ostensibly about Ramses and the monsters, the true avenging angel is Chema's mother, who remains unconsumed—a situation reversed in Olmos's play, whose female hero is ambivalently replaced by a mass protagonist.

This is not to position Amelia as a neoliberal hero, however, or Calderón as a singular melodrama villain. The biopolitical machinations of the narcomachine are not simply the work of one man, but of an entire economic system, as Cazares well knows. His dramaturgy underscores his point. An early lecture by Profesora Alonso states it plainly, cheekily revising Charles Bowden's famous dictum: "El Paso/Ciudad Juárez is neoliberalism's patient zero. But this is not a laboratory. This is a battleground. And the drug war raging on the other side of the border right now is a crisis of neoliberalism, of accelerated economic stratification."[68] This professor, who teaches at the University of Texas at El Paso (UTEP), is no mere innocent bystander or moral guardian. S/he is complicit in the regime as a consumer. As S/he claims near the end of the play: "By now, as I am sure you all know your classmate Chema Carrasco was gunned down in Ciudad Juárez the night after our last class. I asked my dealer if it was somehow my fault. If I somehow, by consuming illicit drugs, was complicit in her death. If I was a narco too."[69] The look on the actor's face when delivering the monologue tells us the answer is yes.

The final scene of the play, where Tito/Titus tries to offer Ramses some mushrooms in exchange for the coke Ramses usually provides him, literalizes this violence:

> TITO/TITUS: There's a note inside.
> RAMSES: Ramses, the next time we fuck, we'll eat these, teononancatl, flesh of God, the divine mushroom.
> TITO/TITUS: No wonder the Aztecs were fucked up and sacrificed people. Their gods were hallucinogens.
> RAMSES: It's no different now, m'ijo.
> TITO/TITUS: Right. From now on, every time I snort some coke or take a pill, it'll be an offering to you, all those souls going into my bloodstream.
> RAMSES: I'd rather not think about you as I do my job. It's been too sweet. Get dressed. We need to leave before anybody gets here. We're fucked if we get caught.
>
> (*Tito/Titus gets dressed. As he does, a bottle of pills falls out of his pocket. Tito/Titus scrambles to pick it up.*)
>
> RAMSES: What's that?
> TITO/TITUS: . . . Pills. Meds.
> RAMSES: Are you sick?
> TITO/TITUS: . . .
> RAMSES: Are you sick?
> TITO/TITUS: What if I were?
>
> (*Ramses kisses Tito/Titus.*)[70]

The marked relationship between consumption and death literalizes Profesora Alonso's concerns. Ultimately, however, this scene goes beyond making a claim about complicity and consumption to making a more complex claim about the false distinction between licit and illicit drugs. By bringing antiretrovirals, mushrooms, and cocaine into the same scene, and into the same body, Cazares reminds audiences that legal prescription drugs and illegal drugs are both part of the contemporary pharmacological regime that defines the experience of everyday life. Although there is a pill bottle in this scene, in others, Tito/Titus carries his HIV meds in a baggie much like the one the mushrooms are in and like those in which cocaine is usually sold. The presence of the baggies as props onstage is a constant signifier of drug consumption and purchase as a quotidian habit, much like carrying just enough meds with you for a short trip. La Barbie mistakes Tito/Titus's meds for Tylenol carried by a nobody, misunderstanding Tito/Titus's identity as Ramses's lover and an HIV-positive individual. This juxtaposition, aided by a prop, reveals a more intimate link between identity and consumption. Additionally, Ramses's intimate relations with Tito/Titus and Alex make it clear that the intensification of neoliberal practices in the United States and Mexico—such as the rise of the maquila, the emergence of narcotraffick, and the onslaught of the AIDS crisis—share the same cultural time and space. The AIDS crisis is not usually thought to be a symptom of the neoliberal; certainly, I do not posit causality here. Yet, as Cazares notes, that crisis and its pharmacological supplement, antiretrovirals, are not isolated from capitalistic networks of violence throughout the hemisphere. It is no coincidence that during Alex and Ramses's first night together, when Ramses outs himself as a narcotrafficker, Coca-Cola is mentioned. This is not only a joke about U.S. market saturation of Mexico but also a crucial part of the play's genealogy of a transnational pharmacological regime. After all, Coca-Cola did actually begin its life as a drug (it contained cocaine).[71] Thus, this scene inaugurates and theorizes an era of pharmacological violence that has existed from the 1980s to the present, but whose roots span the entirety of the twentieth century.

The play marks an extended biopolitical moment, when the creation, sale, and distribution of pharmacological products becomes the capitalist venture par excellence, licit and illicit, in the United States and Mexico. In the '80s, the cost of HIV medications kept them out of the hands of all but the most affluent users. Those who could not afford the drugs were left to die, connecting capitalism and physical violence at the most basic level. Today, Gilead Sciences, the company that owns most of the patents on single-dose HIV regimens (and Truvada) is one of the most profitable businesses in the world.[72] In this way, the Sinaloa cartel and Gilead Sciences are not so different: they are organizations that control the distribution, sale, and price point of pharmacological products. By exposing this connection, however obliquely, *Ramses* performs as the anti-*Dallas Buyers Club*. Instead of romancing the straight white male entrepreneur as savior racing toward a more democratic distribution of drugs leading to a clear teleological end to the AIDS crisis, Cazares's queer lovers reveal how the experience of antiretroviral therapy and quotidian work for the cartels in and across the U.S. border underscore a chronic and recursive state of being within transnational capitalism from which there is no escape even in (or around) death.

In a more extreme way than Saracho, Cazares shows how neoliberal affective experience is deeply pharmacological. López and Maité medicate themselves to stave off their apprehension of neoliberal precarity. Tito/Titus takes his antiretroviral drugs to stay alive. Ironically, like the Aztecs' *teonanácatl* (Nahuatl for "sacred mushroom"), the antivirals also evince a mode of experience filled with hallucinations and devil dreams—a radical reordering of the world that structures the entire play. The jumps in time and space, the move between nightmares and reality so crucial to Cazares's dramaturgy, mimic the effects of antiretroviral drugs, so painstakingly detailed by Doctor Alonso in a darkly comic scene where Tito/Titus first learns of his HIV status. His and others' recreational drug use may or may not exacerbate or enhance these experiences.

The greatest moral hazard in this play, however, is not consuming drugs or performing low-level labor in narco networks. After all, Ramses and Tito/Titus are not described as monsters in the prologue to the play. The moral hazard is remaining actively ignorant of the history and present reality of neoliberal violence. Consider Tito/Titus's confession, which ends the play:

> TITO/TITUS: When I take the pill,
> I feel that I'm swallowing the 80s.
> I learned love from Enrique Iglesias songs.
> The ones that played at the beginning of telenovelas—
> telenovelas made in a Mexico made for export.
> Clear images of love.
> Clean images of blood.
> Never real.
> Never ending without resolution.
> When I take the pill,
> I'm swallowing the 80s whole hole.
> The 80s never happened.
> It's a decade we only dreamt of.
> Goodbye Ramses, I love you.
> RAMSES: I love you too, Chiquito.[73]

The play, unlike Tito/Titus, does not even try to forget. And it does not even try to resolve. Resolution here, it should be noted, is paired with forgetting.

This final scene upends the idea of national progress as well as the possibility of escape from the violence of neoliberal narcoentrepreneurship. In the wake of these failures, Cazares offers eschatology. Although he theorizes the play as the end of the world, the play actually does not end, indicating that Cazares's investment is in thinking about the future as a present event. He shows how the end of one era and the emergence of the next coexist and also meld with empires past. That Cazares references both the Egyptian era and the Aztec past suggests a palimpsestic relationship to cosmology as well. Chema's painting references the ritual of the new fire, the same ceremony of renewal Moraga does. Here, however, the cycle of destruction and renewal seems more chronic than revelatory. Ramses's failure, particularly his failure to dissolve bodies, can bring about the end of the world. But we don't know if he has yet, and we still won't by the end of the play. If Tito/Titus feels that he is being reinfected "with the 80s" every time he and Ramses fuck, then we, as audience members are reinfected as well, with a sort of antiretroviral historiography that reveals how time binds.

Following Elizabeth Freeman's imperative, Cazares unbinds the future from reproductivity, effectively rejecting both U.S. and Mexican investments in progressive teleology and the child as future. The avenging angel of this play, Amelia, is effectively un-mothered in this play. It is her child's death and her refusal to nurture the living that allows her to imagine the violent act that will create a radical break with the present order: killing the former Mexican president. Amelia, given her age, cannot have another child. Her relationships in the future will be allegiances with young male queers and outlaws with whom she will not procreate. The future then, is queer kind of regeneration.

This queer regeneration, however, rejects a hallmark of mainstream gay dramaturgy: monogamous heteronormative coupling as post-revelation resolution. Cazares's play refuses to hinge on the double confession of Ramses's relationship to the cartels and Tito/Titus's HIV status—an important revision to the 2011 version of the play. Ramses's and Tito/Titus's confessions are beside the point. Given the intimate relationship between reproductive futurity and nationalism in the United States and Mexico and the importance of gay marriage to the domestication of queer threats to said nationalisms, Cazares's dramaturgical choices represent a radical critique of neoliberalism at the level of dramatic structure, suggesting the importance of form as a mode of political critique in contemporary Latinx drama.

Enter the Mass Protagonist: *so go the ghosts of méxico, part 1*

Matthew Paul Olmos shares Cazares's resistance to easy resolution, despite *so go the ghosts of méxico, part 1*'s more orthodox structure. Partly biographical, the play tells the story of Marisol Valles García, a Mexican woman, who at age twenty, became the police chief of Práxedis G. Guerrero, Chihuahua, a small town besieged by cartel violence. Sick of the violence she was seeing, the criminology student and mother of a small child took office in November

2010, when no one else applied.⁷⁴ Their reluctance was not surprising, as her predecessor was killed and beheaded by the cartels. In her short time in office, Valles García hired a number of female officers, who were mostly unarmed, and implemented a number of social reforms aimed at making life livable in Juárez. These included getting kids back to school, creating neighborhood watch communities, and going door to door offering support to communities. She also instituted a free lunch program, which she took particular pride in.⁷⁵ Despite the nonviolent tactics she used to discourage young people from getting involved in the cartels, Valles García began receiving death threats a few months into the job. She fled over the U.S. border in March 2011 with her family and sought asylum.

In *so go the ghosts of méxico, part 1*, Valles García is called "a brave woman in Mexico," a sobriquet that echoes the one given to her by the Spanish newspaper *El País*, which was quickly disseminated by the U.S. press: the bravest woman in Mexico.⁷⁶ The Valles García character, Mari, is the sole woman onstage in *so go the ghosts of méxico, part 1*, surrounded by four men and no one else, which is notable considering that Valles García expressly hired many women to be on her police force. Mari's orders are given to invisible coworkers, who by default largely leave her alone onstage to defend herself against visible and invisible forces. The chilling reality of abandonment is made clear by Mari's work in the police station, where she hands off tasks to imaginary employees. Their absence is noted by El Morete when he jokes that a busy police station should be, well, busy—not empty and quiet as it stands. That this emptiness is acknowledged theatrically suggests that these invisible workers were consciously used to render absence rather than simply being a production exigency (that is, absent to avoid the cost of casting actors to play such small roles).

Mari's primary psychological conflict is with her husband, who badgers her for taking the job, pointing to the damage that it will cause a not yet conceived daughter, who becomes another absent presence onstage. The attention to procreation is present from the play's inception. It opens with Mari and her husband having sex in their car; they are arguing about having a child when they are interrupted by static, which puts an end to their intercourse and any possibility of impregnation. This failed reproductivity, an issue to which I will return, culminates with the emergence of a different presence, a mass mobilization, which brings with it a detour away from psychological realism and from representational mimesis. This transformation occurs when Mari's husband checks out the car, which is not running, to see where the noise is coming from. When he does this Mari turns the dial on the radio, only to have "sounds of music burst from the static."⁷⁷ Eventually, the music takes over, harassing El Morete, the minor cartel lieutenant, with a song he refers to as "my sister's ass."⁷⁸ Over the course of the play, the music functions as Mari's tool and companion in idealism. She is the only one who can hear its siren song. Eventually she uses it to save her life, summoning the dead police chief with it at a crucial moment. The 2013 production used music much as Marci McMahon describes Saracho's sound design for *El Nogalar*, as a mode to break the narco silence created by fear in many Mexican communities. El Morete's and Güero's reaction to the music as a threat argues that this sonic presence endangers their domination of the world. Güero, the white U.S. interloper—who also is part of the business in a way we don't quite understand—claims late in the play that he can't do his work with "all . . . this noise."[79] As the last stage direction tells us, within a cacophony of confusion after Mari disappears, "music goes in strength over the voices, silencing them. Deafening in beauty before spilling over the sort of serenity that just does not exist anymore."[80] The music, then, is a sonic imagining of the world as it should be but is not. Olmos couples this aural utopia with the threat of a rising army of ghosts just outside the play's doors, mixing beauty and terror, horror genre and dreamscape, so as to render the possibilities of the true ends of the drug war theatrically. This combination materializes Olmos's thesis that it is a collective of souls and voices that can change the situation in Mexico rather than recourse to individual agency and the protection of the nuclear family. (Here, Olmos departs from Valles García's own public discourse, where she often refers to the nuclear family, albeit strategically).[81]

Perhaps ironically, this claim is embedded in a play that ostensibly hinges upon the idea of a singular hero: the so-called bravest woman in Mexico. The complexity of this bait and switch is challenging, as is Olmos's tone which moves between eerie, lyrical, and darkly comic. Both the 2013 production directed by Meilyn Wang and the 2014 Spanish-language production at Repertorio Español attempted to navigate these dramaturgical challenges while rendering Olmos's vision into theatrical language, revealing the conundrums of staging neoliberal violence.[82] For most of the play, the dead police chief, who returns to help Mari, represents the ghosts of Mexico. In the 2013 production at New York City's La Mama Experimental Theatre Club, this figure was a stagy undead creature complete with stage blood, whitened face, and a removable head. His first entrance is through a door made of plastic strips, much like those popular in butcher shops, a site allusively rendered when seeing the bloody corpse enter the stage. Until Mari's husband dies, this door is the portal between the ghosts and the living. Mari's husband, in contrast, resurrects himself onstage, reminiscent of *Ramses*'s Chema.[83] In the 2014 production at Repertorio, the dead police chief was similarly attired but emerged from within the set itself, not from an offstage exit, making his ability to appear consistent with the dead husband. The Mexican production, perhaps because of lack of resources, costumed the dead police chief less forcefully, using white makeup and tattered clothing—a choice that Olmos himself found quite affecting in its minimalism.

Yet Olmos clearly has a theatrical and self-referential imagining of how the dead are resurrected onstage. In the scene in which Mari's husband rises from the dead after being killed by El Morete, Güero admits he is freaked out by the dead husband's presence. He references the theatrical conceit by which the actor rises from the ground in the dialogue:

> GÜERO: Alright, alright.
> DEAD HUSBAND: Is it, alright? You don't look alright.
> GÜERO: I'll give you that. The fact that you're standing there talking, but at the same time you're sort of lying on the floor over there . . . bleeding—[84]

Güero's sarcastic demeanor masks his horror and lets the audience in on the absurdity of his rise. Referencing both the actor's movement onstage and the separation of the ghost and corpse of Mari's dead husband's, Güero's comment uncannily forces audiences not to make invisible the victims of narco-violence. Notably, this maneuver echoes Chema's rise from the dead in *Ramses*. Wang and her design team's costuming and makeup choices for these two figures, however, made the characters legible as zombies rather than ghosts to audience members such as the *New York Times* critic who reviewed the production.[85] While the critic only noted the "cheesiness" of this aspect of the production, reading the ghosts as zombies has another potential effect: encouraging one to read the end of the play as a zombie apocalypse. Within U.S. cinema, this apocalypse often symbolizes a large-scale dystopia run by invisible forces, spreading contagion.[86] That event is quite different from Olmos's rising up of the ghosts, even if it is also dependent on the power of the collective. Olmos's ghosts' Lazarus-like resurrection is meant to remind audiences of those killed in the narco wars and to materialize the permeability of national borders by said ghosts, literalizing transnational complicity and the possibility of recognition. The spectral other of undocumented laborers who populate the paranoid U.S. mind, these ghosts are both material and not, made invisible by U.S. failure to recognize them. They are not trying to eat or infect the living so much as to open up the possibility of a new tomorrow. An exchange between the dead police chief and Güero, the American interloper, lays out the stakes of the situation, soon after dead husband rises from the stage:

> DEAD POLICE CHIEF: You Americanos, you see ghosts on all your days, but you never look at them. (*Güero has to hold his hand up as it is so bright.*) There is nothing little about it, Americano.
> DEAD POLICE CHIEF: On the streets, in your home. But pretty soon, there will be no more homes, there will only be ghosts. And tell me Americano, what will you look at then? (*Güero moves away from the window.*)
> GÜERO: That's uh . . . quite a view. (*El Morete quietly dials his phone.*)
> DEAD POLICE CHIEF: Don't worry Güero, soon you will be surrounded by so many of us, that my heart cannot even understand it how

surrounded. But maybe tha's okay, huh. It's not my heart that needs to understand it.[87]

In both New York productions, at Repertorio Español and at La Mama, this scene asked the actors and audience to do the work of imagining the masses that are not represented onstage, either by sitting behind Güero and the dead police chief and imagining them behind the plastic door (as at La Mama) or by occupying the space of the ghosts as the dead police chief and Güero look out at the audience (at Repertorio).

By the end of the play, Olmos abandons any attempt to have the actors embody the ghosts materially onstage. Olmos concedes that he had no particular image in mind for the last stage direction of the play and has questioned whether or not this stage direction adds one too many endings to the play. In the 2013 La Mama production, when "several hundred ghosts appear" we are confronted with a blackout and the rustle of the narcos looking for the missing Mari—a simplification of the play's ending.[88] Without the burden of having to represent the ghosts' invasion of the world Olmos and Wang can abandon the woefully inadequate door that the dead police chief enters through at the beginning of the play, opening up borders through aural means instead. Certainly, the permeation of the soundscape modeled this form of expansion. In the Repertorio production, the last scene was handled differently: the ghosts were represented by a handful of sets of empty clothing raised on tie line which appear to float upward to the sky. El Morete shoots at these ghosts as the play ends. This interpretation of the ghosts more clearly marked the present absence of the narco-dead, alluding to the femicides throughout Mexico—which are often represented in performance art and theater by empty and discarded clothing, performing a certain memorial function, as in Cristina Michaus's *Women of Ciudad Juárez*.

In Olmos's play, I argue, we are to think about the ghosts as a collective, rather than as evidence of individual casualties—and it is here that the impossible stage direction becomes most productive for rethinking the problem of the transnational drug trade. The impossibility of staging Olmos's hundreds of ghosts underscores the near impossibility of staging collectives and transnational forces irreducible to emblematic characters within a theatrical frame. This conundrum is not confined to the stage but penetrates the political imaginary as well. We struggle to imagine mass mobilization against neoliberalism in ways that acknowledge the necropolitical world without being unduly cynical. In *so go the ghosts of méxico, part 1*, Olmos's ghosts suggest that they might return as a spectral yet fleshy mob becoming a multitude. A curious version of Hardt and Negri's utopian imagining of democracy after (E)mpire, this "multitude" is less a new form of democracy in the secular political tradition than an eschatological return, echoing with Moraga's and Cazares's understanding of end times with its presence of past, present, and future at once.[89]

More mundanely, the conflicted legacy of ghosts as absence or presence is shot through the process of developing the play. As Olmos claims in an interview, his early conception of the play was fueled by his interest in the idea of ghost towns at the U.S.-Mexico border.[90] It is notable that the town where Valles García was sheriff is one of these towns. Prádexis de Guerrero's 2010 census showed a population of under 5,000, about 60 percent of its population in 2000.[91] This absence corresponds with one of the initial influences for the play—the idea that if everyone left towns that were riddled with narco-violence, the violence would necessarily stop, marking the unsustainability of the current situation. Of course, in reality, the abandonment of these towns has had dire effects on nonurban economies and the survival of the current residents. As a theatrical allegory, however, we are asked to remember who is not present at every step of the play. Thus, these ghosts, those who are not there, are as much Olmos's protagonists as Mari is. That the ghosts will almost inevitably dominate Güero and other U.S. citizens is the play's threat and hope.

Fascinatingly, the hope and threat of these ghosts is untethered from Mari's singular success or failure at stopping violence in her town. Mari brings the music—the sonic presence of that same staged absence—that symbolizes a different way forward, but her personal crusade does not matter so much in the end. She ultimately fails to stop the violence and comes to the United States instead. Consider the penultimate scene of the play (the last one with text), when Güero tries to convince Mari to come to the United States:

> MARI: Es a simple question, Americano, what happens to la música if I go with you.
> DEAD HUSBAND: And imagine what can happen to la música if you doesn't go with him.
>
> (*Güero pulls out his mobile.*)
>
> GÜERO: Look I've made my offer. It's your life to take or let go of. Just say the word. And if you don't say the word . . . well . . . then good luck to you, you best be on your way and me on mine.
>
> (*They stare. A moment. He dials, lights darken over him. Music bursts through, it crosses countries and expands borders. Mari and husband look at each other as they listen in awe at the vibrations of the music. White out.*)[92]

Given that the music ultimately prevails and ends the play, rather than an individual act of heroism, *so go the ghosts* proffers the possibility of a new order that depends more on the power of the collective, the surround sound of the dead, rather than Mari's heroism. This ending is at odds with the agonistic demands of the dead husband and Güero—the former of which tries to convince her she needs to stay to change things, and the latter of which urges her to save herself. In addition, Mari's exchange with Güero about crossing the border lays out the problem with heroism.

> GÜERO: . . . You'll be in the papers: online and off. News anchors will want to interview you about you. About what happened to your husband. How did this twenty-two year old with a family of her own decide to . . . well, we know the story.
> MARI: And I'll get to go with you across . . .
> GÜERO: Look, I've got no shot of quieting whatever all this is in this country, but I've got a pretty good chance of making you famous in mine. And well, my country is, if nothing else, somewhat louder than yours.
> DEAD HUSBAND: Did you hear him, he can't quiet you, Mari. Nobody can. Not him, not los narcos, not los soldados, not—
> MARI: And what do you get?
> GÜERO: Mari, your "husband"'s right. I can't have all this . . . noise. In the business sense of it. And while I know the business is the opposite of what you care about, if you don't come with me, your entire family, will be . . . just like him. Which, I am sorry might sound like music to you now, but we're talking Grotesquely. Fucking Torturously.[93]

Meaning that the music does not need a hero. In addition, the play claims that being a hero is, in some sense, being complicit with the neoliberal machine. Güero effectively silences Mari in Mexico by making her a hero in the United States. Güero's comments make visible the reality that the staging of the liberal subject/hero within the media foments the continuance of cartel activity rather than representing a way out of its procedures. His U.S. identity drives the point home that his nation houses both powerful pharmacological and media industries, exhuming the link between the valorization of the maverick liberal hero and the furtherance of neoliberal capital. Equally political is Olmos's critical self-awareness about his own desire, as a U.S. citizen, to make Mari a hero. In this sense, his labeling her "the bravest woman in Mexico" is not without irony, a point largely ignored in critical reception of the play. Olmos himself does see the real Mari as heroic for standing up against violence, but he does not reproduce a hero narrative uncritically. While Olmos's dramaturgy may also have been an attempt to wrestle with the rather ambivalent ending of the Valles García's story, his maneuvering undoes the audience's ability to valorize Mari as a singular heroine. In doing so, he frustrates the conventional desire to valorize the individual crusader as the best potential agent for ending the violence of the narco war. That said, the hero narrative was exactly what drew the press to the show—including many non-arts journalists who would not usually attend an off-Broadway show.

Olmos's critique of the singular protagonist, and by extension the liberal subject, is met by critique of the rhetoric of family so important to rhetorical defense of the Mexican nation and to many neoliberal mobilizations throughout the Americas. Mari attempts to widen the scope of care, pointing out that all Mexican citizens are her family, even when she links her concerns to her own future childbearing. Notably, Olmos's fictional Mari is a mother even though the real Marisol Valles García already had a child—notably a son—at the time she took office. Mari's husband's shortsightedness in understanding her motivations to help Mexico is critiqued throughout the play; his rants about Mari's maternity read as deeply sexist and ridiculous on the page and on the stage. Yet the amount of stage time given to this discourse and the reference to Mari's potential maternity in the United States as a motivating factor for her crossing reveal the persistence of heteronormative futurity, even as it is being rejected. For Mari, in life and onstage, the extinction of narcotraffic comes in stopping future generations from participating. Her success could be tied to a lack of procreation that would prevent a future generation of narcotraffickers. This is a project to which the ghosts, as well as Mari's social reforms, are essential.

On Rejecting Narco-Masculinity, Narco-Realism

Olmos links his critique of U.S. imperialism to a critique of masculinity. U.S.-born Güero is also the one who is most clearly threatened by the dead police chief, who blames the United States for much of the problem. The police chief points out to Güero that his own death was "one of your conquests," and he goes on to think through the consequences of these conquests. He says:

> How do you think the world will look at you when back outside there we all are, in the thousands upon thousands, with our un'dead hands all pointing straight at you. My guess: you'll shit yourself worse than he just pissed himself, Americano. And maybe one day you'll be an empty too. Just like when bullets cross La Linea. Oh, Los Estados Unidos will de' flate. Do you hear me what I'm tellin' to you, you fuckin' memory.[94]

The ex-police chief's emasculation of Güero is similar to Güero's own humiliation of El Morete, who is easily disarmed, literally and figuratively. When they first meet, Güero accuses El Morete (in English: the bruise) of cruising him—as a queer and a bottom. It is clear that Olmos is depicting Güero, the white U.S. citizen, as a potential top who tries to subordinate his Mexican counterpart. Their homophobic banter underscores the ridiculousness of narco-masculinity, echoing *Dreamlandia*'s critical appraisal of the easy conflation of queerness and failure to dominate. Yet one does wonder if the naturalness with which we encounter these forms of machismo makes the critique less legible than it could be, despite Olmos's intentions. According to Olmos, in the Mexican production in San Miguel de Allende, El Morete was scary rather than bumbling and the critique of narco-masculinity did not read.[95] While his scariness may have been largely attributable to the reality of narcotrafficking in Mexico, the banter between El Morete and Güero may not have been as much a part of a cultural self-critique in Mexico as it was in urban New York theater circles. In the La Mama production, the actor playing Güero was over the top, and it was not always clear whether the audience was laughing with Güero or at him. In the Repertorio production, the link between the ridiculousness of narco-masculinity and imperialist history was borne out with a more self-conscious performance in the first scene where they meet. These production choices included the scene's accompaniment by spaghetti western music, red lights, and allusions to the trappings of the western genre, features that are often associated with duels between macho men for popular audiences. That Olmos's sequel to this play is described as exploring "the ridiculous machismo of narco culture as shown through a cast of all women" suggests he might be conscious of the difficulty in portraying this critique with male bodies onstage.[96] That said, the fact that Mari is the sole woman onstage surrounded by archetypical male characters in *so go the ghosts* underscores the fact that she is constantly fighting a masculinist mode of being as much as she is trying to hold off the traffickers. Olmos's escalation of the personal manifestations of patriarchy calls attention to the feminist, and arguably feminine, way Valles García herself chose to fight narcotraffic: through hiring unarmed women to go door to door, doing social work with area youth to prevent them from entering the cartel industry in the first place. This form of attack on *narcomenudeo* (the everyday effects of narcotraffic not related to the trade) is a hopeful one, but one not often represented in traditional media about narcotrafficking and transnational capitalism, perhaps because of its antidramatic and feminine nature.

In my interview with Olmos, he made it explicit that he links femininity with compassion and the hope for changing the dominance of narcotraffic in the future. He views the music in the play as a feminine force that battles openly with more masculine forces throughout the play. This music is deeply incorporated in the rest of the trilogy, including the third play, which is inspired by the story of Javier Sicilia, the Mexican poet turned activist whose son was killed in a club in 2010. As a leader of peaceful protest, he has become a lightning rod figure in Mexican protests against the current drug war. Interestingly, at this point, the second play also centers on female characters, namely, a mother who loses her daughter in narco-violence. Although Olmos admits that he struggles with showing the rather epic reality of transnational complicity in his plays, his attempt to think through the gendered aspects of the drug trade and focus on *narcomenudeo* in *so go the ghosts, part 1* distinguishes his work from Hollywood narratives that valorize law enforcement solutions to the end of transnational narcotrafficking. His sound design works to the same end. Consider the sound design embedded in the play's last stage direction:

> EL MORETE looks up at the sky as it brightens, as the music soars. Several hundred ghosts appear. He pulls his gun and aims it in all directions. Lights drown over him. Inside the home is messed; drawers are opened, clothes strewn about. It is vacated and looks exactly like the sort of house you would see a decapitated man laying in a pool of blood. From outside, the sounds of tires crushing onto gravel are heard. Headlights flash the window. Several car doors open and shut. The music swells, drowning out the sounds of footsteps on gravel moving closer and the clocking of automatic weapons.
> When the stage has hit to black, we hear men's voices entering the home, shouting through it. Fragments of phrases such as: "¡¿Donde están?!" "¡No están aqui!" can be heard. The music grows in strength over the voices, silencing them. Deafening in beauty before spilling over into the sort of serenity that just does not exist anymore[.] Curtain.
>
> END OF PLAY.[97]

The sound of cars driving up and engaging in gunfire is replaced by music displacing sound as a document of individualized forms of violence. This literally performs the death of the sound effects linked to filmic narco-realism, a form that reifies violence as entertainment. The choral, undifferentiated mode of music that ends the play instead offers up what bodies onstage cannot do themselves: render palpable the hundreds of ghosts Olmos asks to enter the stage. A literal reading of this direction would simply drown out what is going on stage. A more careful reading would suggest a more choral collaboration, upending the narco-realistic solution—a crime solved (or not) ending in heroic capture, assassination, and or redemptive death for a singular hero.

This chapter has revealed how the performance of entrepreneurship, violence, and heroism are best critiqued through overt theatricality and innovative dramaturgy rather than narco-realism. These plays' successes (and constructive failures) suggest that the theater may be the likeliest unlikely place to think through the necropolitical performances of hemispheric neoliberalism. In the conclusion, I will review and advocate for the efficacy of theatricality and dramaturgical revision as important tools to rethink politics in the neoliberal Americas.

Conclusion

So Go the Ghosts of . . .

> But this is a course on Religions of the World, and even though I have tenure now, I don't need any of you writing your evaluations about how I always talk about politics. But the war on drugs is about death and religion begins with death. So here's your assignment, don't leave without hearing your assignment. I want you to write two pages about how war remakes death. What do I mean? Think about the ways in which the current crisis is remaking death—how are the victims of this drug war being mourned? How are the missing buried? Who gets mourned? In the current war, who deserves to die?
>
> —Profesor(a) Alonso, *Ramses contra los monstruos*[1]

Over the course of this book, I have considered how Latinx playwrights have exposed the violence of neoliberalism throughout the hemisphere. Their painstaking thick descriptions of the transnational transit of bodies and goods reveal the ways in which economic violence affects the quotidian lives of citizens of the Americas. In many ways the playwrights whose works I have considered here have done exactly what Cazares describes above: they have "remade death" by staging it with overtly theatrical means. In doing so, Latinx playwrights have rallied against the naturalization of the condition that Rebecca Schneider calls "'late-late' capitalism" and the obfuscation of violence in which proponents of its methods engage.[2] Certainly, these conditions affect almost everyone in the hemisphere. Yet there has been a special toll paid by indigenous, poor, female, queer, and gender-nonconforming people who have not instantiated themselves within capitalist regimes of resource and capital accumulation. There have been dire consequences for those who have dared to speak out, or at least not silenced themselves, in the face of neoliberal death machines. Many of these brave souls, in the scheme of things, in being destroyed, have become less than persons. They have been transformed into bodies that do not matter. Latinx plays render these conditions apparent in visceral and explosive ways. The ways in which the playwrights construct their critiques through theatrical means, making a bold contribution to thinking neoliberalism and the future of political subjectivity, is more interesting than the accuracy of their descriptions of current conditions.

First and foremost, Latinx playwrights have rendered those injured or killed by neoliberal economic violence present in a society which tries to obliterate them. Some playwrights have done this literally, by materializing the dead onstage as characters that refuse to exit, embodied by actors who stubbornly remain, despite their nonliving condition. Consider Amelia's refusal to bury her daughter Chema, first dragging her dead body around the stage and then seeking revenge by threatening to murder the former president of Mexico. Although Chema eventually jumps into the cauldron below the stage to acquit her soul of the earth, she does so on her own terms. And we know that things can return from under the floorboards. A trapdoor always has the possibility of opening again. The very exposure of the trapdoor as a trapdoor—there was no obfuscation of its theatrical mechanics in the 2013 production—makes us aware that Cazares is overtly using theatricality to critique violence as a mode of representation without material consequences. In contrast, he shows the materiality of violence in theater. Chema's obsolescence is met by that of La Barbie and Lidia, who literally unzip themselves from body bags after Ramses drags the bags, with the full weight of the actors in them, onstage. Raising the dead raises the possibility of violence being forgotten. That the audience experiences the actor's labor in lifting these bags is also important, making their corporeality real for the audience. In contrast to his failed attempts to dematerialize the fallen with acid, Ramses's struggle to drag bodies shows the difficulty of making the world forget, exposing the burden of death on our societies. Watching Ramses work does not allow us to dismiss the presence of the dead, or their weight in the world. Olmos, in contrast, gestures to ghosts who can't enter the stage—making them a present absence on stage. The impossibility of their entrance is made manifest through sound rather than obsolescent actors. Nonetheless, like Cazares, he questions the border between the living and the dead. By engaging the analogue possibilities of sound design, Olmos rejects a clean line between diegetic and nondiegetic sound as a mode of disturbing the line between the living and the dead, embracing a very theatrical mode of auditory intervention that troubles the agency of the sonic insurgency. Who is controlling whom? The presence and power of Olmos's ghosts reveals that the dead could rise up in an anti-neoliberal insurgency completely independently of our own wills, a threat (or promise?) best understood through the theatrical rendering of sound.

Olmos's embrace of theatricality is met by his refusal to make his characters good liberal heroes through dramaturgical revision. There are many tactics for doing this. One is the bait and switch Olmos offers by placing a mass protagonist alongside a hero. If we give up Mari as a singular liberal subject, the social worker who introduces new forms of sociality in her hometown to quell a culture of violence, and instead give in to the idea of the ghosts as the true harbingers of this change, could we not come to the new forms of democracy and communism that so many of us strive for? Moraga's emblematic mode of creating a composite indigenous female subject that cannot be individualized, meanwhile, counters the idea of a singular liberal subject; Solis's hailing of the Organism also does this work, by pointing not only to how neoliberalism creates subjects, but to the very mechanisms of subjectification. In contrast, Caridad Svich employs a dramatic irony that interrogates our desire to give voice to Iphigenia or the dead factory girls she fetishizes, suggesting a radical rethinking of subjectivity, in addition to ending our dependence on decrying violence through staging ethical victims. Garcés's *points of departure*, meanwhile, makes us work as hard as his characters do to make sense of the fractured lives we see before us. His fragmented language, incomplete characterization, and minimalist staging are surprising to many. His interventions do not allow us to feel for another in ways that collude with neoliberal practices of empathy. Garcés asks that we interrogate ourselves and our spectatorship constantly by experiencing the labor of (not) understanding. We are, quite simply, forced to quit depending on the stable liberal subject as a point of identification under neoliberalism. Giving this up is a form of recognition that contemporary conditions have eliminated the sovereign subject while also being a realization that letting go of this construct is key to fighting these conditions.

As the title of this book portends, Latinx authors also illuminate how the times of neoliberalism feel. Their use of theatrical copresence and its impossibilities make the crises of neoliberalism's ordinariness (Berlant's "crisis ordinariness") and its temporal machinations perceivable. This is realized in *Ramses contra los monstruos*, where the dizzying repetition of sex scenes, rapes, and murder under the trapdoor reminds us of the recursivity of neoliberal crisis. The speeding up of the scenes over time, meanwhile, references the acceleration of violence. The haunting copresence of the '80s and the present in the juxtaposition of Tito/Titus's affair with Ramses and Alex's affair with Ramses makes the neoliberal experience palpable. The young mens' energies pass through a circuit of erotic energy between actors, a circulation that is both pleasurable and painful. Cortiñas's sleepwalkers, meanwhile, by moving back and forth to the limits of the stage and away from their stagy beds, show how the stuckness particular to crisis ordinariness feels like perpetual motion. This theatrical invocation complements the play's antiteleological discourse by making its theoretical intervention palpable. Bumping up against the literal limits of the stage, Charley and Tito expose the limits of life.

I argue, then, that it is theatricality, rather than realism—filmic or otherwise—that most accurately depicts and explains the possibilities of neoliberal life, including the experiences of immobility, anxiety, and terror persons in the Americas feel. The theater is successful because of what it can do (awkward copresence, uncomfortable corporeality, analogue theatrical machinery and machinations) and because of what it cannot do (find a way out, materialize the masses without imagination, render large-scale death real).

Perhaps more disappointing to audiences is the extent to which these plays fail to proffer solutions to the problems they engage. Many of them end on an ambivalent or unresolved note. Characters jump in the river or into a cauldron; they walk into the ocean or wait before it, listening to what the world tries to tell them. Would-be reformers disappear in blackouts, perhaps to appear on the other side of *la linea*. Would-be entrepreneurs collaborate with the *maña*, dispose of their corpses, often opting to stay rather than leave *narcolandía*. Others, in the face of the fall of the revolutionary hope, try to kill or heal themselves out of the psychic and physical pain they feel in its aftermath. We have to imagine the way out, instead of seeing it represented before us.

For many playwrights, the consequence of their intractable commitment to theatricality and dramaturgical innovation has been a lack of critical understanding or appraisal. There is something not quite legible to mainstream critics about these plays' strategic acts of refusal. Many of the playwrights, however, would concede that this is a small price to pay for the opportunity to expose the cost of the necropolitical regimes that affect Latinx and Latin American people under neoliberalism. I can't help but contrast critical engagement of these plays with the widespread acclaim given to Lin-Manuel Miranda's *Hamilton*, the hip-hop musical that reimagines the biography of Alexander Hamilton. To be sure it is a formally innovative and virtuosic musical. That said, Alexander Hamilton—as a figure—is an ideal immigrant entrepreneur of exactly the sort the plays I write about here reject, partially or entirely. At this time of crisis, it is easy to get behind a musical that valorizes rather than demonizes immigrants, gives over the stage to actors of color, and seems invested in knowing U.S. history. That said, the extent to which *Hamilton* leaves unexamined the relationship between liberalism and capitalism or fails to mention chattel slavery or indigenous presence in the Americas deserves to be interrogated, as Patricia Herrera and Donatella Galella, among others, have pointed out.[3] We also must scrutinize the romance of the male immigrant entrepreneur as the ideal American. Hamilton's story is complete with a unidirectional migration story, a self-made crucible of struggle, and the emergence of the modern capitalist financial system. That this figure enacts Afro-diasporic/Latinx cultural forms cannot undo its reliance on an ideology that disenfranchises all but the most elite members of our society. Could one say that on some level *Hamilton* manifests a kind of unhealthy attachment in the times of neoliberalism? Sing along as we will, we must also think harder and better about said attachments and our cruel optimism(s) in the times of neoliberalism. To let go of this attachment is less pleasurable than retaining it, but perhaps it is a more ethical decision. In this sense we must heed Tito/Titus's ambivalence as he swallows a bitter pill:

> When I take the pill,
> I feel that I'm swallowing the 80s.
> I learned love from Enrique Iglesias songs.
> The ones that played at the beginning of telenovelas—
> telenovelas made in a Mexico made for export.
> Clear images of love.
> Clean images of blood.
> Never real.
> Never ending without resolution.
> When I take the pill,
> I'm swallowing the 80s whole hole.
> The 80s never happened.
> It's a decade we only dreamt of.[4]

We must vow not to forget recent history in our desire to write ourselves into an older one which gives us the veneer of national belonging at the expense of transnational truths. At this moment, after the election of Donald Trump as president of the United States, I feel more strongly than ever that our dependence on individual liberalism and our ignorance of the violence of neoliberalism are destructive and dangerous. While I cannot predict the future, it is clear that an understanding of the recent past in the Americas is crucial to thinking our way out of our current situation.

NOTES

Preface

1. Cherríe L. Moraga, *The Hungry Woman* (Albuquerque, N.Mex.: West End Press, 2001). I refer here to the 2006 immigration reform protests.
2. Cherríe L. Moraga, *The Last Generation: Prose and Poetry by Cherríe Moraga* (Boston: South End Press, 1993), 145–74.
3. Alexandra Bernson, *En Las Manos de la Muerte*, produced at the Rites and Reason Theatre, Brown University, Providence, R.I., October 27–November 1, 2010.
4. Tiffany Ana López, "Violent Inscriptions: Writing the Body and Making Community in Four Plays by Migdalia Cruz," *Theatre Journal* 52, no. 1 (2000): 51–66.
5. When this term proves unwieldy, I defer to Latino/a to deemphasize the naturalization of the male pronoun as a neutral as it is often used in the Spanish language.
6. Lila Abu-Lughod uses the term *halfie* in her essay "Writing against Culture," in *Recapturing Anthropology: Working in the Present*, ed. Richard Fox (Santa Fe, N.Mex.: School of American Research Press, 1991). Abu-Lughod attributes the term to Kiran Narayan.
7. See Lindsay Goss, "Tactical Acting Jane Fonda, GI Resistance, and the FTA" (Ph.D. diss., Brown University, 2014), for an excellent theorization of solidarity. Dr. Goss was my advisee.
8. See, for example, Spencer Golub, *Infinity (Stage)* (Ann Arbor: University of Michigan Press, 2001); Bert O. States, *Great Reckonings in Little Rooms: On the Phenomenology of Theater* (Berkeley: University of California Press, 1987); Alice Rayner, *Ghosts: Death's Double and the Phenomena of Theatre* (Minneapolis: University of Minnesota Press, 2006); Herbert Blau, *Take Up the Bodies: Theater at the Vanishing Point* (Urbana: University of Illinois Press, 1982).

Critical Introduction

1. Jon D. Rossini and Patricia Ybarra, "Neoliberalism, Historiography, Identity Politics, Toward a New Historiography of Latino Theatre," *Radical History Review*, 112 (Winter 2012): 163.
2. For a debate about these terms, and in particular how we might think of the post-neoliberal coming after neoliberalism, see Laura MacDonald and Arne Ruckert, eds., *Post-Neoliberalization in the Americas* (Houndmills, U.K.: Palgrave Macmillan, 2009); John Burdick, Philip Oxhorn, and Kenneth M. Roberts, eds., *Beyond Neoliberalism in Latin America? Society and Politics at the Crossroads* (Houndmills, U.K.: Palgrave Macmillan, 2009); and Richard Snyder, *Mexican Politics after Neoliberalism* (Cambridge, U.K.: Cambridge University Press, 2006).

3. Rossini and Ybarra, "Neoliberalism, Historiography, Identity Politics."

4. As I will argue more fully in chapter 1, this postrevolutionary feeling is especially felt in Moraga, *The Last Generation*.

5. Walter Mignolo, *The Idea of Latin America* (London: Blackwell, 2005), 1–50.

6. See Michel Foucault, *The Birth of Biopolitics: Lectures at the Collège de France 1978–1979* (Houndmills, U.K.: Palgrave Macmillan, 2008); and Wendy Brown, "Neoliberalism and the End of Liberal Democracy," *Theory and Event* 7, no. 1 (2003), doi: 10.1353/tae.2003.0020.

7. Foucault, *The Birth of Biopolitics*, 217–18; 225–26.

8. See F. A. Hayek, *The Road to Serfdom*, ed. Bruce Caldwell (1944; repr. Chicago: University of Chicago Press, 2007); Gary Becker, *Human Capital: A Theoretical and Empirical Analysis, with Special Reference to Education* (Chicago: University of Chicago Press, 1964); and Milton Friedman, *Capitalism and Freedom* (Chicago: University of Chicago Press, 1962).

9. Juan Gabriel Valdés, *Pinochet's Economists: The Chicago School in Chile* (New York: Cambridge University Press, 1995).

10. Naomi Klein, *The Shock Doctrine: The Rise of Disaster Capitalism* (New York: Henry Holt, 2008).

11. Klein, *The Shock Doctrine*, 86–87.

12. Ibid., 89–94.

13. For an excellent critique of China's enterprise zones see Aihwa Ong, *Neoliberalism as Exception: Mutations in Citizenship and Sovereignty* (Durham, N.C.: Duke University Press, 2006), 97–120.

14. For more on this periodization, see David Harvey, *A Brief History of Neoliberalism* (London: Oxford University Press, 2005). Despite the timeline within, the photographs of '80s leaders on the front cover of the paperback edition marks the transition with these leaders rather than with earlier policies.

15. See Lara D. Nielsen, "Introduction: Heterotopic Transformations: The (Il)liberal Neoliberal," in *Neoliberalism and Global Theatres: Performance Permutations*, ed. Lara D. Nielsen and Patricia Ybarra (Houndmills, U.K.: Palgrave Macmillan: 2012), 1–24.

16. See, for example, Peter Andreas, *Border Games: Policing the U.S.-Mexico Divide* (Ithaca, N.Y.: Cornell University Press, 2000), 74–84.

17. See, for example, Mark Cameron Edberg, *El Narcotraficante, Narcocorridos and the Construction of a Cultural Persona on the U.S.-Mexico Border* (Austin: University of Texas Press, 2004); Elijah Wald, *Narcocorrido: A Journey into the Music of Drugs, Guns and Guerillas* (New York: Rayo, 2001).

18. See Luis Astorga, *El siglo de las drogas: El narcotráfico, del Porfiriato al nuevo milenio* (Mexico City: Plaza y Janés, 2005).

19. See Sayak Valencia, *Capitalismo Gore* (Santa Cruz de Tenerife, Spain: Melusina, 2010).

20. Rosa-Linda Fregoso and Cynthia Bejarano, *Terrorizing Women: Feminicide in the Americas*, (Durham, N.C.: Duke University Press, 2010); Alicia Gaspar de Alba with Georgina Guzmán, *Making a Killing: Femicide, Free Trade and La Frontera* (Austin; University of Texas Press, 2010); Melissa W. Wright, *Disposable Women and Other Myths of Global Capitalism* (New York: Routledge, 2006).

21. Max J. Castro, ed., *Free Markets, Open Societies, Closed Borders? Trends in International Migration and Immigration Policy in the Americas* (Miami: North-South Center Press, 1999); Felix Masud-Piloto, *From Welcomed Exiles to Illegal Immigrants: Cuban Migrants to the U.S., 1959–1995* (Lanham, Md.: Rowman & Littlefield, 1996).

22. For more on the long history of narcotrafficking, see Curtis Marez, *Drug Wars: The Political Economy of Narcotics* (Minneapolis: University of Minnesota, 2004); and David T. Courtwright, *Forces of Habit: Drugs and the Making of the Modern World* (Cambridge, Mass.: Harvard University Press, 2001).

23. Arlene Dávila, "Locating Neoliberalism in Time, Space and Culture," *American Quarterly* 66, no. 3 (2014): 552.

24. See Ileana Rodríguez, *Liberalism at Its Limits: Crime and Terror in the Latin American Cultural Text* (Pittsburgh, Pa.: University of Pittsburgh Press, 2009); Mignolo, *The Idea of Latin America*; Aníbal Quijano, "The Coloniality of Power, Eurocentrism and Latin America," *Nepantla: Views from the South* 1, no. 3 (2000): 533–80.

25. Achille Mbembe, "Necropolitics," *Public Culture* 15, no. 1 (2003): 11.

26. Ibid., 34.

27. See Valencia, *Capitalismo Gore*, 139–72; Rosa-Linda Fregoso, "'We Want them Alive!' The Politics of Culture and Human Rights," *Social Identities* 12, no. 2 (March 2006): 109–38, and Rodríguez, *Liberalism*, 197–205.

28. I use the word *Chicano* in its masculine specific form here advisedly, as the movement did not cede equal rights to Chicanas. On the 1974 Quinto Festival de los Teatros Chicanos y Latino Americanos, which brought this issue to a head, see Yolanda Broyles-González, *Teatro Campesino* (Austin: University of Texas Press, 1994), 117–27; and Alma Martinez, "*¿Un continente, una cultura?* The Political Dialectic for a United Chicano, Mexican and Latin American Popular/Political Theatre Front, Mexico City, 1974" (Ph.D. diss., Stanford University, 2005). I will further consider this event in chapter 1.

29. I borrow the term *tropicalization* from Frances R. Aparicio and Susana Chávez-Silverman, *Tropicalizations: Transcultural Representations of Latinidad* (Hanover, N.H.: University Press of New England, 1997). See Coco Fusco, "The Other History of Intercultural Performance," *TDR* 38, no. 1 (1994): 143–67, for more on audience reactions to *Couple in a Cage*.

30. María Irene Fornés, *Conduct of Life*, in *Plays* (New York: PAJ, 1986), 65–88; Lynne Alvarez, *Tales of Revolution*, in *Lynne Alvarez: Collected Plays, Volume 1* (Lyme, N.H.: Smith and Kraus, 1998), 213–62; Ariel Dorfman, *Death and the Maiden* (New York: Penguin Plays, 1994).

31. Much of this discourse has taken place at theater conferences and in informal conversations.

32. For examples of this violence in Argentina in relation to spectacle, see Diana Taylor, *Disappearing Acts: Spectacles of Gender and Nationalism in Argentina's "Dirty War"* (Durham, N.C.: Duke University Press, 1997).

33. *Death and the Maiden* was written by Ariel Dorfman, an Argentine-Chilean citizen. That said, he wrote the play in the United States some twenty years after he was exiled following the 1973 coup in Chile, and thus, I think of the play as Latina/o American.

34. Caridad Svich, *Iphigenia Crash Land Falls on the Neon Shell That Was Her Heart (A Rave Fable)*, in *Divine Fire: Eight Contemporary Plays Inspired by the Greeks*, ed. Caridad Svich (New York: Backstage Books, 2005), 329–74.

35. Compare for example Solis's *Dreamlandia* (New York: Samuel French, 2010) from 2000 with his earlier plays such as *El Otro* and *El Paso Blue* from the '90s, published in *Plays by Octavio Solis* (New York: Broadway Play Publishing, 2006). I will discuss this distinction further in chapter 3.

36. Victor I. Cazares, *Ramses contra los monstruos*. Unpublished play script, 2013.

37. See Rossini and Ybarra, "Neoliberalism, Historiography, Identity Politics," 170.

38. See Jon D. Rossini, *Contemporary Latina/o Theatre: Wrighting Ethnicity* (Carbondale: Southern Illinois Press, 2008), 150–58.

39. Eduardo Machado, *The Floating Island Plays* (New York: TCG, 1993). The last play of this tetralogy, *Broken Eggs*, takes place in the '80s in Los Angeles and features the family's legacy as exiles in the United States.

40. Eduardo Machado, *The Cook* (New York: Sam French, 2004).

41. Her travels are referenced throughout *The Last Generation*.

42. María Josefina Saldaña-Portillo, "Who Is the Indian in Aztlán? Re-Writing Mestizaje, Indianism, and Chicanismo from the Lacandón," in *The Latin American Subaltern Studies Reader*, ed. Ileana Rodríguez (Durham, N.C.: Duke University Press, 2001), 402–23.

43. María Josefina Saldaña-Portillo, *Indian Given: Racial Geographies across the U.S. and Mexico*. (Durham, N.C.: Duke University Press, 2016).

44. Jon D. Rossini, "José Rivera, Neoliberalism and the Outside of Politics," *Latin American Theatre Review* 43, no. 1 (Fall 2009): 49–51. Interestingly, Rossini suggests that the West Coast production seemed less felled by this political discourse, perhaps because of its production in a Latinx cultural space at San José's Teatro Visión.

45. Tanya Saracho, *El Nogalar*, *American Theatre* 28, no. 6 (2011): 69–87.

46. Michael John Garcés, email correspondence with the author, October 2014.

47. Brown, "Neoliberalism," para. 32.

48. Ibid., para. 42.

49. Hardt and Negri's *Empire* famously references the Zapatistas as a key theorization of insurgency while making specious claims about their communicative strategies; Michael Hardt and Antonio Negri, *Empire* (Cambridge, Mass.: Harvard University, 2000), 54–58. For more nuanced understandings of Zapatistas, subjectivity, and insurgency, see José Rabasa, *Without History: Subaltern Studies, the Zapatista Insurgency, and the Specter of History* (Pittsburgh, Pa.: University of Pittsburgh, 2010); and María Josefina Saldaña-Portillo, *The Revolutionary Imagination in the Americas and the Age of Development* (Durham, N.C.: Duke University Press, 2003): 191–258.

50. For a more complete history of the Latin American subaltern studies movement, which is outside of the scope of this introduction, see Ileana Rodríguez, ed., *The Latin American Subaltern Studies Reader* (Durham, N.C.: Duke University Press, 2001).

51. Coco Fusco, *Incredible Disappearing Woman*, in *The Bodies That Were Not Ours and Other Writings* (London: Routledge, 2001), 202–20.

52. This periodization of *testimonio* is taken from John Beverley, *Testimonio: On the Politics of Truth* (Minneapolis: University of Minnesota Press, 2004).
53. Ibid., 36.
54. Ibid.
55. This change can be traced over the course of the essays in *Testimonio: On the Politics of Truth*, which contains essays written from 1989 to 2004. See also Georg M. Gugelberger, *The Real Thing: Testimonial Discourse and Latin America* (Durham, N.C.: Duke University Press, 1996).
56. Alberto Moreiras, *The Exhaustion of Difference: The Politics of Latin American Cultural Studies* (Durham, N.C.: Duke University Press, 2001), 208–38.
57. Josette Féral, "Foreword," and "The Rise and Fall of Theatricality," in *SubStance* 31, nos. 2 and 3(2002): 10. For a historical genealogy of the term, see Tracy C. Davis and Thomas Postlewait, "Theatricality: An Introduction," in Tracy C. David and Thomas Postlewait, eds., *Theatricality* (Cambridge, U.K.: Cambridge University Press, 2003).
58. Lib Taylor, "The Experience of Immediacy: Emotion and Enlistment in Fact-Based Theatre," *Studies in Theater and Performance* 31, no. 2 (2011): 223–37.
59. Ibid.; and Rossini, "José Rivera," 42.
60. Patricia Stuelke, "The Reparative Politics of the Central American Solidarity Movement," *American Quarterly* 66, no. 3 (2014): 768.
61. Nelly Richard, *The Insubordination of Signs: Political Change, Cultural Transformation and the Poetics of the Crisis*, trans. Alicia Nelson and Silvia R. Tandeciarz (Durham, N.C.: Duke University Press, 2004), 82, 94–96.
62. See, for example, Sergio González Rodríguez, "Epilogue: How to Take Textual Photographs," in *The Femicide Machine* (New York: Semiotext(e), 2012), 99–128; Violeta Luna, *Requiem for a Lost Land*, and Fernando Brito, *Tus pasos se perdieron con el paisaje* available in the NarcoMachine, *e-misférica* 8, no. 2 (2010).
63. Rodríguez, *Liberalism*; Fregoso, "'We Want them Alive!'"; and Rossana Reguillo, "The Narco-Machine and the Work of Violence: Notes Toward Its Decodification," *e-misférica* 8, no. 2 (2010).
64. Reguillo, "The Narco-Machine," para. 21.
65. Hermann Herlinghaus, *Violence without Guilt* (Houndmills, U.K.: Palgrave MacMillan, 2009), 8–19.
66. Sergio González Rodríguez, *The Femicide Machine*, trans. Michael Parker-Stainback (New York: Semiotext(e), 2012), 9–10.
67. Fusco, *Incredible Disappearing Woman*.
68. Valencia, *Capitalismo Gore*.
69. Sayak Valencia, "NAFTA: Capitalismo Gore and the Femicide Machine," trans. Irmgard Emmelhainz, *Scapegoat* 6 (2014): 133. I use this essay here to supplement Valencia's longer monograph because she openly engages with González Rodríguez's book, which was published after *Capitalismo Gore*.
70. Solis, *Dreamlandia*. Saracho, *El Nogalar*.
71. Jorge Cortiñas, *Sleepwalkers* (unpublished play script, 1999); Eduardo Machado, *Havana Is Waiting* (New York: Samuel French, 2008).
72. Catherine Kingfisher and Jeff Mavkofsky, "Introduction: The Limits of Neoliberalism," *Critique of Anthropology* 28, no. 2 (2008): 115–26; and Kathy

Powell, "Neoliberalism, Solidarity and the Special Period in Cuba," *Critique of Anthropology* 28, no. 2 (2008): 177–97.

73. Mary Pat Brady, *Extinct Lands, Temporal Geographies: Chicana Literature and the Urgency of Space* (Durham, N.C.: Duke University Press, 2002), 171–201.

74. Marez, *Drug Wars*, 8.

75. José David Saldívar, *Transamericanity: Subaltern Modernities, Global Coloniality and the Cultures of Greater Mexico* (Durham, N.C.: Duke University Press, 2012), xxiii.

76. I thank Jorge Cortiñas for helping me clarify this point; interview with Jorge Cortiñas, December 31, 2014.

77. Lauren Berlant, *Cruel Optimism* (Durham, N.C.: Duke University Press, 2011). The TDR's special issue on performance and precarity, offers a battery of essays helpful to my thinking, including Nicholas Ridout and Rebecca Schneider, "Precarity and Performance: An Introduction," *TDR* 56, no. 4 (2012): 5–9; Shannon Jackson, "Just in Time: Performance and the Aesthetics of Precarity," *TDR* 56, no. 4 (2012): 10–31; Tavia Nyong'o, "The Scene of Occupation," *TDR* 56, no. 4 (2012): 136–49; and Rebecca Schneider, "It Seems as If I Am Dead: Zombie Capitalism and Theatrical Labor," *TDR* 56, no. 4 (2012): 150–62. See also Nicholas Ridout, *Passionate Amateurs: Theatre, Communism, and Love* (Ann Arbor: University of Michigan Press, 2013).

78. José Muñoz, *Cruising Utopia: The Then and There of Queer Futurity* (New York: New York University Press, 2009); Elizabeth Freeman, *Time Binds: Queer Temporalities, Queer Histories* (Durham, N.C.: Duke University Press, 2010); Judith Halberstam, *In a Queer Time and Place: Transgender Bodies, Subcultural Lives* (New York: New York University Press, 2005).

79. Rafael Pérez-Torres, *Mestizaje: Critical Uses of Race in Chicano/a Culture* (Minneapolis: University of Minnesota Press, 2006), 15–19; and Alicia Arrizón, *Queering Mestizaje* (Ann Arbor: University of Michigan Press, 2006), 61.

80. Román de la Campa, *Latin Americanism* (Minneapolis: University of Minnesota Press, 1997).

81. I take the notion of "long thought" from Jonathan Kalb, who used it at the 2009 No Passport Conference in New York City.

82. María Irene Fornés taught workshops for playwrights at INTAR from 1981 to 1995. Many of the playwrights mentioned or whose work is analyzed in this volume studied with her, including Caridad Svich, Jorge Cortiñas, Eduardo Machado, Cherríe Moraga, and Migdalia Cruz. The Latino Theatre Commons was founded in 2012. I am an active member. The 2013 Encuentro in Boston gathered many of the playwrights discussed in this volume.

Chapter 1

1. Michael John Garcés, *points of departure* (unpublished play script, 2006). The date in the text refers to the date of production, not the final script.

2. Guillermo Bonfil Batalla, *México Profundo: Reclaiming a Civilization*, trans. Philip A. Dennis (Austin: University of Texas, 1996).

3. See Saldaña-Portillo, *The Revolutionary Imagination*.

4. For a good history of the Chicano nationalist movement, see Carlos Muñoz, *Youth, Identity, Power: The Chicano Movement* (New York: Verso, 1989).

5. Alurista was a name that Alberto Baltazar Urista Heredia took. He is often credited as the main author of the Spiritual Plan. As Sheila M. Contreras suggests, the preamble to the "Spiritual Plan de Aztlán" was redrafted in 1972 with references to a "red" rather than a "bronze" nation so as to include coalition with U.S.-based Native American movements. See Sheila M. Contreras, *Blood Lines, Myth, Indigenism and Chicana/o Literature* (Austin: University of Texas, 2008), 98–100.

6. See Juan Bruce-Novoa and Carlos May-Gamboa, "El Quinto Festival de Teatros," *De Colores* 2 (1975): 65–72, as cited in Martinez, "¿*Un continente, una cultura?*" 236; and Yvonne Yarbro-Bejarano, "From *Acto* to *Mito*: A Critical Appraisal of Teatro Campesino," in *Modern Chicano Writers: A Collection of Critical Essays*, eds. Joseph Sommers and Tomás Ybarra-Frausto (Englewood, N.J.: Prentice Hall, 1978), 176–85 and Saldaña-Portillo, *Revolutionary Imagination*.

7. Yvonne Yarbro-Bejarano defines this term in "*Teatropoesía* by Chicanas in the Bay Area: *Tongues of Fire*," in *Mexican American Theatre Then and Now*, ed. Nicolás Kanellos (Houston: Arte Público Press, 1983), 79.

8. See Contreras, *Blood Lines*, 85; Broyles-González, *Teatro Campesino*, 116; and Jorge Huerta, *Chicano Drama: Performance, Society and Myth* (London: Cambridge University Press, 2000), 37n42, for the importance of the Popol Vuh, especially Domingo Martinez Paredes's interpretation of that text.

9. Theodore Shank, "A Return to Aztec and Mayan Roots," *The Drama Review* 18 (1974): 56–70; Martinez, "¿*Un continente, una cultura?*" 191–234; Huerta, *Chicano Drama*, 37.

10. Martinez makes this point through the comments of an anonymous viewer and participant; Martinez, "¿*Un continente, una cultura?*" 253–55.

11. See Martinez, "¿*Un continente, una cultura?*" 203–10, for Valdez's version of *carpa*'s relation to Marxism, which Martinez stands behind. See also Yarbro-Bejarano, "From *Acto* to *Mito*," 180–85.

12. Broyles-González, *Teatro Campesino*, 79–127.

13. There are different opinions of Segura's influence. Martinez claims that Segura's influence came indirectly through the influence of company members who studied with him rather than in workshops with El Teatro Campesino; Martinez, "¿*Un continente, una cultura?*" 41. Broyles-González calls him, along with Domingo Martinez Paredes, one of their maestros, but without details as to the relationship. Huerta does the same in *Chicano Drama*, 37.

14. Barclay Goldsmith, "Brecht and Chicano Theatre," in *Modern Chicano Writers: A Collection of Critical Essays*, eds. Sommers and Tomás Ybarra-Frausto (Englewood, N.J.: Prentice Hall, 1978), 171.

15. See Ridout, *Passionate Amateurs*, 9.

16. Ibid., 8.

17. Ricardo F. Vivancos Pérez, *Radical Chicana Poetics* (New York: Palgrave Macmillan, 2013), 70. Notably, Vivancos Pérez writes before the Rite to Remember project/Cihuatl theater project, a set of developments that would only deepen his analysis.

18. Sita Venkateswar and Emma Hughes, eds., *The Politics of Indigeniety: Dialogues and Reflections on Indigenous Activism* (London: Zed Books, 2011), 1–3.

19. Jodi Melamed, *Represent and Destroy: Rationalizing Violence in the New Racial Capitalism* (Minneapolis: University of Minnesota Press, 2011), xvi.

20. Ibid., xvii.

21. Chela Sandoval, *Methodology of the Oppressed* (Minneapolis: University of Minnesota Press, 2000); Quijano, "The Coloniality of Power"; Walter Mignolo, *The Darker Side of Western Modernity: Global Futures, Decolonial Options* (Durham, N.C.: Duke University Press, 2011); Linda Tuhiwai Smith, *Decolonizing Methodologies: Research and Indigenous Peoples* (London: Zed Books, 1999).

22. Sonia Saldívar-Hull, *Feminism on the Border: Chicana Gender Politics and Literature* (Berkeley: University of California Press, 2000), 46–48.

23. Cherríe L. Moraga, *Giving Up the Ghost: Teatro in Two Acts* (Boston: West End Press, 1986), 46.

24. Ironically, this area is now the queer neighborhood in Mexico City.

25. Cherríe L. Moraga, *Giving Up the Ghost*, in *Heroes and Saints and Other Plays* (Boston: West End Press, 1994), 25.

26. Moraga, *The Last Generation*, 18.

27. Huerta, *Chicano Drama*, 63; and Yvonne Yarbro-Bejarano, *The Wounded Heart: Writing on Cherríe Moraga* (Austin: University of Texas Press, 2001), 27.

28. Cherríe Moraga's use of *neoliberal* is found in "An Irrevocable Promise: Staging the Story Xicana," in *A Xicana Codex of Changing Consciousness* (Durham, N.C.: Duke University Press, 2011), 44.

29. Sandra K. Soto, *Reading Chican@ Like a Queer: De-Mastery of Desire* (Austin: University of Texas Press, 2010), 17.

30. Vivancos Pérez, *Radical Chicana Poetics*, 62.

31. I refer here to Johannes Fabian's famous work, *Time and the Other: How Anthropology Makes Its Objects* (New York: Columbia University Press, 2002).

32. Moraga, *Giving Up the Ghost* (1994), 5.

33. Ibid., 19.

34. Moraga, Giving Up the Ghost (1986), 52.

35. Yarbro-Bejarano, *The Wounded Heart*, 43.

36. Moraga, Giving Up the Ghost (1994), 29.

37. Freeman, *Time Binds*, xiii.

38. Ibid.

39. Moraga, *Giving Up the Ghost* (1986), n.p.

40. On temporal drag, see Freeman, *Time Binds*, 59–64.

41. Rebecca Schneider thinks through these questions in terms of reenactment, but her theatrical take on temporal drag is helpful here as it points to Corky's enactment of Marisa's past, notably by an actor for whom this era is gone—as it was for Moraga herself. See Rebecca Schneider, *Performing Remains: Art and War in Times of Theatrical Reenactment* (London: Routledge, 2011), 16–17, 35.

42. Sara Warner, *Acts of Gaiety* (Ann Arbor: University of Michigan Press, 2013).

43. Vivancos Pérez, *Radical Chicana Poetics*, 62.

44. See Yvonne Yarbro-Bejarano's chapter "Whiteness in the Last Generation: The Nation, the Half-Breed and the Queer," in Yarbro-Bejarano, *The Wounded Heart*, 107–26; and Sheila M. Contreras's chapter "From Malinche to Coatlicue: Chicana Indigenist Feminism and Mythic Native Women," in Contreras, *Blood Lines*, 105–32, among many others.

45. Moraga, *The Last Generation*, 1.

46. Nineteen ninety-two was a threshold year for many Latina/o artists, as much of the world was keen on celebrating the five-hundred-year anniversary of Columbus's discovery of America. María Irene Fornés, one of Cherríe Moraga's mentors, responded with her wryly critical *Terra Incognita*, which chronicles the musings of U.S. tourists in Spain. The tourists encounter, among others, a friar modeled on (and with text from) the historic Chiapas-based Fray Bartolomé de las Casas (a defender of Indian rights during colonization) and a derelict beggar who recites events from Columbus's life. In the midst of their own estrangement from their surroundings they are forced to face the truth of America—that it was created through violent conquest and colonization. The exposition of the atrocities suffered by indigenous people, however, are voiced entirely through a Spanish Christian lens. Moraga concentrated more pointedly on indigenous history and moved toward a mode of history making that breaks with the colonial tradition.

47. Moraga, *The Last Generation*, 55.

48. Ibid., 55, 56.

49. Ibid., 60.

50. Ibid.,.61

51. Ibid.

52. I refer here, a bit ironically to Moraga's essay, "The Breakdown of the Bicultural Mind," in *The Last Generation*, 112–31.

53. Ibid., 165.

54. Ibid., 171.

55. Ibid.

56. Priscilla Solis Ybarra has written elsewhere about Moraga's environmentalism; see "Longing and Belonging in Cherríe Moraga's Ecological Vision," *New Perspectives on Environmental Justice: Gender, Sexuality, and Activism*, ed. Rachel Stein (New Brunswick, N.J.: Rutgers University Press, 2004), 240–48.

57. Eva Bruné, Grant Proposal, INTAR Archives (1993). I thank Lou Moreno for access to this document.

58. Moraga, *The Hungry Woman* (2001), 6.

59. Ibid.

60. Ibid.

61. Cherríe Moraga, *The Hungry Woman* (2001), 3; Moraga, *A Xicana Codex*, 28.

62. Moraga, *The Hungry Woman* (2001), 23.

63. Moraga, *The Hungry Woman* (2001), x.

64. Moraga. *The Hungry Woman* (2005), 6. See Patricia Ybarra, "The Revolution Fails Here," *Aztlán: A Journal of Chicano Studies* 33, no. 1 (2008): 63–88, for an extension of this argument about cultural specificity.

65. Moraga, *The Hungry Woman* (2005), 2.

66. Ibid., 3.

67. Moraga, *A Xicana Codex*, 33.

68. She compares her decision here to the one made by Sherman Alexie, who claims he made a conscious decision to marry an Indian woman. Discussed in "A Xicana Dyke Codex of Changing Consciousness," in Moraga, *A Xicana Codex*, 6–7.

69. Moraga, *The Last Generation*, 192.

70. Ibid.
71. Ibid., 174.
72. Ibid., 185.
73. See Vitor Westhalle, *Eschatology and Space: The Lost Dimension in Theology Past and Present* (New York: Palgrave Macmillan, 2012); and Patrick S. Cheng, *Radical Love: An Introduction to Queer Theology* (New York: Seabury Press, 2011), for more on queer eschatology.
74. Paul Vanderwood, "Millenarianism, Miracles, and Materialism," *Mexican Studies/Estudios Mexicanos* 15, no. 2 (1999): 396.
75. Rabasa, *Without History*, 57.
76. Ibid., 47.
77. Ibid.
78. Carlos Monsiváis, *Mexican Postcards* (London: Verso, 1997), 146.
79. Ibid., 139.
80. Moraga, *The Hungry Woman* (2001), 23.
81. Moraga, *A Xicana Codex*, 37.
82. Ibid.
83. Ibid., 39.
84. Ibid., xv-xvi, xviii.
85. Ibid., xvii.
86. I viewed a video of the production at Theatre Bravo, 2012.
87. Cherríe L. Moraga, *New Fire* (unpublished play script, 2012), 3.
88. Cecelia Klein, "The Devil and the Skirt: An Iconographic Inquiry into the Pre-Hispanic Nature of the *Tzitzimime*," in *Ancient Mesoamerica* 11 (2000): 1–26.
89. Moraga makes a claim for using the word *tribe* in "Queer Aztlán." She explains: "'Tribe,' based on the traditional models of Native Americans, is an alternative socioeconomic structure that holds considerable appeal for those of us who recognize the weaknesses of the isolated patriarchal capitalist family structure" (166).
90. Tuhiwai Smith, *Decolonizing Methodologies*, 160.
91. Moraga, *New Fire*, 2.
92. Flor Crisótomo, in a letter addressed to Felipe Calderón, http://americanhumanity.wordpress.com/2008/03/04/nafta-whats-it-really-good-for.
93. Moraga, *A Xicana Codex*, 89.
94. Moraga, *New Fire*, 22–23
95. Ibid., 22–24.
96. Robert Hurwitt, "Healing Burns," review of *New Fire*, *San Francisco Chronicle*, January 16, 2012.
97. Interview with Kelly Anderson, *Voices of Feminism Oral History Project Sophia Smith Collection*, (Northampton, Mass.: Smith College, 2005), http://www.smith.edu/libraries/libs/ssc/vof/transcripts/Moraga.pdf.
98. Tuhiwai Smith, *Decolonizing Methodologies*, 142–62.
99. Jorge Huerta, "Introduction," in *Mummified Deer and Other Plays* (Houston: Arte Público Press, 2005), x.
100. Victor Payan, "An Interview with Luis Valdez during the Writing of *Mummified Deer*," May 21, 1999, http://web.archive.org/web/20070208040740/http://www.flyingserpent.net/justwords1/mummydearest.html.

101. Luis Valdez, *Earthquake Sun* (unpublished play script, 2003).
102. Valdez, *Earthquake Sun*, 48–49.
103. This is a shout-out to his former teacher, Domingo Martinez Paredes, who appears as Domingo Martinez Solar.
104. Valdez, *Earthquake Sun*, 61; Huerta, "Introduction," ix. The year 2012, of course, was said to be the end of the world according to Mayan prophecies, a gross oversimplification of Mayan cosmological texts.
105. Rubén González, *La Esquinita, U.S.A.*, directed by Kinan Valdez, Encuentro 2014 Festival, Los Angeles Theatre Center, November 6, 2014. The play was developed and first performed at El Teatro Campesino in 2010.
106. Interview with Kinan Valdez, Los Angeles Theatre Center, Los Angeles, Calif., November 8, 2014.
107. Rosa-Linda Fregoso, "For a Pluriversal Declaration of Human Rights," *American Quarterly* (Special Issue titled Americas Quarterly) 66, no. 3 (2014): 583–603. Her earlier article on El Teatro Campesino is Rosa-Linda Fregoso, "The Representation of Cultural Identity in *Zoot Suit*," *Theory and Society* 22, no. 5 (1993) 659–74.
108. Fregoso, "For a Pluriversal Declaration," 597. In a note on this page she points the reader to her work *The Bronze Screen: Chicano and Chicana Film Culture* (Minneapolis: University of Minnesota Press, 1993), 60n57: "for a critique of the masculinist use on this term [sic]." Her critique, however, is centered on the film of *Zoot Suit*, not on theater productions. Her critique is valid, but I would argue that ETC's practices as a collective might complicate her suggestion here.
109. Fregoso, "For a Pluriversal Declaration," 592–95.
110. Robert Laughlin, *Monkey Business Theatre* (Austin: University of Texas Press, 2008), 261.
111. Ibid., 272. The term *wetback* here, at least in its Spanish iteration, is not the insult it is in the United States.
112. Ibid., 20–22.
113. Eisa Davis, "Michael John Garcés: A Point of Departure," Loggernaut Reading Series, http://www.loggernaut.org/interviews/michaeljohngarces/.
114. Garcés, *points of departure*, front matter.
115. Ibid., 87.
116. Garcés, email correspondence with the author, September 2, 2014.
117. Garcés, *points of departure*, 49.
118. Ibid., 99–100.
119. Ibid., front matter.
120. Ibid., 98–99.
121. Garcés, email correspondence with the author, September 2, 2014.
122. Joy Goodwin, "Victims in an Unnamed Land," *New York Sun*, March 20, 2006, http://www.nysun.com/arts/victims-in-an-unnamed-land/29403/.
123. Patricia Ybarra, "Young Jean Lee's Cruel Dramaturgy," *Modern Drama* 57, no. 4 (2014): 516–17.
124. Garcés, email correspondence with the author, September 2, 2014.
125. Ibid.
126. Jacques Rancière, "Ten Theses on Politics," in *Dissensus: On Politics and Aesthetics*, ed. Steve Corcoran (New York: Continuum, 2010), 33.

127. Ibid., 32.
128. Gareth Williams, *The Mexican Exception: Sovereignty, Police and Democracy* (New York: Palgrave Macmillan, 2011), 35–40.
129. Rancière, "Ten Theses on Politics," 33.
130. Ibid., 38.
131. Garcés, *points of departure*, front matter.
132. This quote from Aristotle seemingly comes from a translation used by Kierkegaard in *Fear and Trembling* (1985; repr. London: Penguin, 2005), 100.
133. Aristotle, *On Poetry and Style*, trans. G. M. A. Grube (1958; repr. Indianapolis: Hackett, 1989), 21.
134. Goodwin, "Victims in an Unnamed Land."
135. Ana Puga, "Migrant Melodrama, Human Rights, and Elvira Arellano," in *Imagining Human Rights in Twenty-First Century Theatre*, ed. Florian Nikolas Becker, Paola Hernandez, and Brenda Werth (Houndmills, U.K.: Palgrave Macmillan, 2013), 155–78.
136. Ibid., 160.
137. Ibid.
138. Stuelke, "Reparative Politics."
139. Stuelke, "Reparative Politics," 769.
140. See Augusto Boal, *Theatre of the Oppressed* (New York: TCG, 1993), chap. 1.
141. Stuelke, "Reparative Politics," 770.
142. Garcés, email correspondence with the author, October 2014.
143. Garcés, *points of departure*, 120.
144. Goodwin, "Victims in an Unnamed Land."
145. Michael John Garcés, "Los Illegals," *Theater* 41, no. 2 (2012): 104.
146. Ibid.
147. Ibid., 114.
148. Ibid., 118.
149. Ibid., 114.

Chapter 2

1. Michael John Garcés, Talkback for the production of *Kissing Fidel*, October 9, 2005.
2. Berlant, *Cruel Optimism*, 9–10.
3. Bill Clinton, "The President's News Conference," August 19, 1994, http://clinton6.nara.gov/1994/08/1994-08-19-press-conference-by-the-president.html.
4. Castro's response was also a response to escalating violence in Havana where protests ended in a riot on the Malecón on August 5, 1994.
5. For more on this violence, see Alfredo A. Fernández, *Adrift: The Cuban Raft People*, trans. Susan G. Rascón (Houston: Arte Público, 2000), 6–33.
6. For an excellent depiction of the human cost of these crossings, see Carles Bosch and David Trueba, *Balseros*, directed by Carles Bosch and Josep Maria Domènech (Barcelona: Lauren Films, 2002), DVD.
7. Kelly M. Greenhill, "Engineered Migration as Coercive Instrument: The 1994 Cuban Balseros Crisis," *The Rosemarie Rogers Working Paper Series #12* (Inter-University Committee on International Migration, 2002), http://web.mit.edu/cis/www/migration/Greenhill_rrwp_12.html; United States General

Accounting Office, *Cuba: U.S. Responses to the 1994 Cuban Migration Crisis* (Washington, D.C.: Author, 1995).

8. Formerly, U.S. dollars were illegal in Cuba. With the U.S. dollar came the creation of convertible peso. The regular Cuban peso was nonconvertible—meaning that it could not be exchanged for other currencies. U.S. dollars and convertible pesos allowed hard currency to enter the Cuban economy, propping it up at a time of crisis. This shift, largely designed to bring in remittances in dollars and convert tourist money into profit, flew in the face of previous policy. In 2004, the U.S. dollar was again outlawed as legal tender in Cuba. Economic disparity between dollar holders and those who did not hold dollars created great inequalities in Cuban society.

9. Many saw Carter's expensive solution to the crisis as anathema to fiscal responsibility, touted by his opponent Ronald Reagan. Carter himself blamed Mariel for his lack of success in the 1980 election. See Greenhill, "Engineered Migration," 10n67, for details. Bill Clinton also blamed the Mariel situation for his loss in his run for reelection as governor of Arkansas in 1980 after the Mariel refugees rioted at Fort Chaffee and Clinton brought in the National Guard. Some see this incident as showing Clinton's lack of control over the situation, hurting him in the election. See Greenhill, "Engineered Migration," 12n87.

10. Holly Ackerman and Juan M. Clark, *Cuban Balseros: Voyage of Uncertainty* (Miami: Policy Center of the Cuban American National, 1995), 2–5.

11. For a critique of the validity of these statistics, see Bert Hoffman, "Emigration and Regime Stability: Explaining the Persistence of Cuban Socialism," *Working Papers: Global and Area Studies* 2 (2005), 14n8, www.duel.de/workingpapers.com.

12. There are divergent reports on the conditions at Guantánamo. See Tomás Diaz, *Balseros in Guantánamo: Su Historia y Testimonio* (Miami: Nuevos Horizontes Internacionales, 1996); Fernández, *Adrift*, 92–138; and US GOA, *Cuba: U.S. Responses*.

13. See Ted Henken, "*Balseros, Boteros,* and *El Bombo*: Post-1994 Cuban Immigration to the United States and the Persistence of Special Treatment," *Latino Studies* 3, no. 3 (2005): 393–416; and Masud-Piloto, *From Welcome Exiles to Illegal Immigrants*, for two different views on the topic. Henken points out the obvious and shameful disparity between treatment of Haitians and Cubans during this period. Greenhill, "Engineered Migration," 16, reveals that Janet Reno first used the words *illegal immigrants*, instead of *political refugees* to refer to the *balseros* in May 1995, after the United States decided to admit those held at Guantánamo. Throughout this essay I will define the term situationally, defaulting to the term *migrants* when the context does not necessitate a particular term.

14. This identity was, for example, represented in the *balsero* art made in Guantánamo, described in Fernández, *Adrift*, 180–85. Some of this art can be accessed at the Cuban Rafter Phenomenon Site at http://balseros.miami.edu.

15. Cuban American scholars rarely use this term to describe the *balseros*. One exception is Juan León, who when discussing 1990s Miami culture refers to the *balsero* as a "tropical border crosser." See Juan León, "Tropical Overexposure: Miami's 'Sophisticated Tropics' and the *Balsero*," in *Tropicalizations: Transcultural Representations of Latinidad*, eds. Frances Aparicio and Susana Chávez-Silverman (Hanover, N.H.: Dartmouth University Press, 1997), 217.

16. Many detainees for example claim political persecution and desire for freedom as their main reason for leaving, although the material conditions are detailed at length in their testimonies, contained in Ackerman and Clark, *Cuban Balseros*. See also Felicia Guerra, *Balseros: Historia Oral del Éxodo Cubano de '94* (Miami: Editorials Universal, 1997); and Silvia Pedraza, *Political Disaffection in Cuba's Revolution and Exodus* (London: Cambridge University Press, 2007), 177–235.

17. For information about anti-immigrant bias, see Matías F. Travieso-Díaz, "Cuban Immigration Challenges and Opportunities," *Berkeley Journal of International Law* 16, no. 2 (1998): 69–70; Greenhill, "Engineered Migration," 19; and Masud-Piloto, *From Welcome Exiles to Illegal Immigrants*, 139. Although this shift in attitudes about Cubans was no doubt related to general xenophobia in the wake of Proposition 187, the impact of the Mariel Exodus, which included the emigration of some criminals, and the advent of the criminalization of the darker-skinned Cubans who entered the United States in this period, also had an impact. Cuban Americans were less likely to open their arms as well, perhaps for the same reason.

18. See Castro, *Free Markets, Open Societies, Closed Borders*.

19. In 1993, Clinton loosened restrictions for those traveling for humanitarian and educational purposes, allowing human rights organizations to travel if they got permission from the OFAC. The Balseros Crisis necessitated a stricture allowing visits only when "extreme hardship is demonstrated in cases involving extreme humanitarian need." In 1995, he loosened restrictions, "authorizing general licenses for transactions relating to travel to Cuba for Cuban Americans making yearly visits to close relatives in 'circumstances that demonstrate extreme humanitarian need.'" However, those traveling for this purpose more than once in a twelve-month period had to apply to OFAC for a specific license. These measures also allowed for specific licenses for freelance journalists traveling to Cuba. Charter flights were suspended in 1996, after the shooting down of two U.S. civilian planes in Cuban airspace. With the pope's visit to Cuba in 1998, Clinton opened up charter fights from Miami to Havana, eventually adding flights from Los Angeles and New York City in 1999, alongside the reinstatement of general travel for educational purposes and for Cuban Americans visiting relatives in humanitarian need. Tightened OFAC restrictions went into place in 2000, bolstered by the Bush presidency in 2001 and 2003. On April 13, 2009, President Obama released all travel restrictions for Cuban Americans who wanted to visit Cuba. Cuban travel to the United States was more difficult—legal travel restricting itself to moments when Castro used the threat of Cuban immigration to the United States as a negotiating tool. See Mark P. Sullivan, *Cuba: U.S. Restrictions on Travel and Remittances* (Washington, D.C.: Congressional Research Service, Library of Congress, 2007), for more details.

20. Carter did not renew the U.S. ban on travel in the 1970s, but it was reinstated by Ronald Reagan in 1982. Dramas such as René Alomá's *A Little Something to Ease the Pain* and Pedro R. Monje Rafuls's *Nadie Se Va El Todo* take place in Havana or in a number of Cuban and U.S. spaces but do not depict travel. See Pedro R. Monje Rafuls, "El Re-Encuentro, Un Tema Dramatica," in *Lo que no se ha dicho*, ed. Jesus J. Barquet and Pedro R. Monje Rafuls (Jackson Heights, N.Y.: Ollantay Press, 1994), 63–72.

21. Michel de Certeau, *The Writing of History* (New York: Columbia University Press, 1988), 209–43.
22. For example, Carmen Rivera's *La Gringa* (New York: Sam French, 2008), among others.
23. Alexandra T. Vasquez, "Learning to Live in Miami," *Americas Quarterly*, 66, no. 3 (2014): 858.
24. Pamela Gordon, "Rites of Passage," *Miami New Times*, June 6, 1996, Arts Section, http://www.miaminewtimes.com/1996-06-06/culture/rites-of-passage.
25. Nilo Cruz, *A Bicycle Country* (New York: Dramatists Play Service, 2004), 4.
26. James Roos, "Balseros Cuban Rafter's Journey to South Florida and Freedom Inspires New Opera," *Miami Herald*, May 11, 1997, Arts Section.
27. Fornés, *Balseros/Manual for a Desperate Crossing*, 136.
28. Cruz, *A Bicycle Country*, 5.
29. Ibid., 15.
30. Ibid., 25.
31. Ibid., 26.
32. Caridad Svich, *Prodigal Kiss*, in *New Playwrights: Best Plays of 1999* (Hanover, N.H.: Smith and Kraus, 2001), 243.
33. Ibid., 244.
34. Svich, "Author's Note," for *Prodigal Kiss*, 241. Italics mine.
35. Anne Garcia-Romero, "Transculturation and Twenty-First Century Latina Playwrights" (Ph.D. diss., University of California, Santa Barbara, 2009), 116–21.
36. For an alternate reading of this play, see Natalie Alvarez, "Transcultural Dramaturgies, Latina Theatre's Third Wave," in *Contemporary Women Playwrights: Into the 21st Century*, ed. Penny Farfan and Lesley Ferris (Houndmills, U.K.: Palgrave Macmillan, 2014): 82–97.
37. Svich, *Prodigal Kiss*, 299.
38. See Gustavo Pérez Firmat, *Life on the Hyphen: The Cuban American Way* (Austin: University of Texas Press, 1994).
39. Carmelita Tropicana, *Leche de Amnesia*, in *Latinas on Stage*, ed. Alicia Arrizón and Lillian Manzor (Berkeley, Calif.: Third Woman Press, 2000), 136.
40. Berlant, *Cruel Optimism*, 199.
41. Eduardo Machado, *Kissing Fidel*, directed by Michael John Garcés, INTAR Theatre, New York City, September 20–October 16, 2005.
42. Michael Garcés relayed this information during a talk back for the production of *Kissing Fidel* at INTAR Theatre, New York City, October 9, 2005.
43. Eduardo Machado, *Kissing Fidel* (New York: Samuel French, 2006), 64.
44. Ricardo L. Ortiz, *Cultural Erotics in Cuban America* (Minneapolis: University of Minnesota Press, 2007), 162.
45. Eduardo Machado, *Fabiola*, in *The Floating Island Plays*.
46. Ortiz, *Cultural Erotics*, 179.
47. Ibid., 165.
48. Ibid., 182.
49. Machado indicates that the play takes place after midnight on August 14. It is hard to know if this means that it actually takes place in the early hours of August 15 or 14, making the analogy imperfect. Considering that the trip by raft, if without great incident takes about three days, it seems possible that this date

was chosen in order to stage Ismael as a Christ figure. Of course, the length of time between death and burial is also often three days.

50. Machado, *Kissing Fidel*, 64–65.
51. Mbembe, *Necropolitics*, 40.
52. Machado, *Kissing Fidel.*, 72. Italics mine.
53. This passage is taken from the revised edition of *Fabiola* (1994) that was presented at the Mark Taper Forum. It is quoted in Ortiz, *Cultural Erotics*, 182.
54. Ibid.
55. Muñoz, *Cruising Utopia*, 25.
56. Ortiz, *Cultural Erotics*, 189.
57. Alisa Solomon, "Two Ambitious Dramas Cross Borders and Consciousness: Review of *Kissing Fidel* and *No Foreigners Beyond This Point*," *Village Voice*, September 20, 2005, http://www.villagevoice.com/2005-09-20/theater/another-country/full/.
58. Eduardo Machado, *Havana Is Waiting*, directed by Michael John Garcés, Cherry Lane Theatre, opened October 1, 2001; video of the production viewed at the Billy Rose Theater Collection, Lincoln Center, June 12, 2007.
59. Eduardo Machado, *Havana Is Waiting* (New York:Samuel French, 2008), 42.
60. Ibid., 75.
61. Ibid., 74.
62. Eduardo del Rio, "Interview with Eduardo Machado," in *One Island, Many Voices: Conversations with Cuban-American Writers* (Tucson: University of Arizona Press), 64.
63. Ibid., 64–65.
64. Quoted in Jorge Huerta, "Borders in Three Latino Plays," *Of Borders and Thresholds: Theatre History, Practice, and Theory*, ed. Michal Kobialka (Minneapolis: University of Minnesota, 1999), 164.
65. I take the idea of crossing borders in Machado's plays from Alisa Solomon's title for her review, "Two Ambitious Plays Cross Borders and Consciousness."
66. Berlant, *Cruel Optimism*, 199.
67. Jorge Cortiñas, interview with the author, December 31, 2014. I place *back* in quotation marks here because Cortiñas was born in the United States.
68. Cortiñas, *Sleepwalkers*, 79–85.
69. Ibid., 85.
70. Cortiñas, interview with the author.
71. Cortiñas, *Sleepwalkers*, 40.
72. Ibid., 89.
73. Ibid.
74. Ibid., 86–87.
75. This image is also found in Antonio José Ponte's short story "Coming," in *In the Cold of the Malecon* (San Francisco: City Lights, 2000), 11. Cortiñas's familiarity with Ponte's work suggests that this moment is an homage.
76. Cortiñas, *Sleepwalkers*, 53.
77. Ibid., 54.
78. Cortiñas, interview with the author, December 31, 2014.
79. Ibid.

80. Ortiz, *Cultural Erotics*, 134–55. Chapter 5 of Ortiz's book is called "Café, Culpa, and Capital: Nostalgic Addictions of Cuban Exile."
81. Cortiñas, interview with the author.
82. Coco Fusco and Nao Bustamante, *Stuff*, TDR 41, no. 4 (1997): 63–82.
83. Alejandro Morales, *Sebastian*, in *Collected Plays by Alejandro Morales* (New York: No Passport Press, 2007), 33–101.
84. Machado, *Kissing Fidel*, 64.
85. Ibid.,
86. Ibid.
87. I refer to the title of Eric Lott's canonical text, *Love and Theft: Blackface Minstrelsy and the American Working Class* (London: Oxford University Press, 1993).
88. Jill Lane, *Blackface Cuba, 1840–1895* (Philadelphia: University of Pennsylvania Press, 2005).
89. Cortiñas, interview with the author.
90. Ibid.
91. Cortiñas, *Sleepwalkers*, 84.
92. I owe this thought to Cortiñas, who mentioned it in his interview with me.
93. Ricardo Bracho, Jorge Ignacio Cortiñas, and José Muñoz, "Towards Translocalism: Latino Theatre in the New United States—Ricardo Bracho and Jorge Ignacio Cortiñas in Conversation with José Muñoz," in *Trans-global Readings: Crossing Theatrical Boundaries*, ed. Caridad Svich (Manchester, U.K.: Manchester University Press, 2003), 69.
94. Ibid.
95. Cortiñas, interview with the author.
96. Ibid.
97. Ibid.
98. Christine Dolen, "Sleepwalkers in Haunting Unforgettable Play at Area Stage Explores Present Day Life in Havana," review of *Sleepwalkers*, *Miami Herald*, July 1, 1999.
99. Curt Holman, "Sleep with the Fishes: *Sleepwalkers* Examines Deprivation and Desperation in Cuba," review of *Sleepwalkers*, *Creative Loafing: Best of Atlanta*, May 1, 2002, http://atlanta.creativeloafing.com/gyrobase/Content?oid=oid%3A8658.
100. Marta Barber, "Bicycle Spins Migrant Metaphor," review of *A Bicycle Country*, *Miami Herald*, December 16, 1999.
101. Marta Barber, "Thoughtful Bicycle Is Poetry in Motion," review of *A Bicycle Country*, *Miami Herald*, November 13, 2000.
102. Laura Hitchcock, "A Curtain Up LA Review," review of *A Bicycle Country*, *Curtain Up*, April 7, 2001, http://www.curtainup.com/bicyclecountry.html; Justin Sanders, "*A Bicycle Country*: Theatre Review," *Portland Mercury*, April 25, 2002, http://www.portlandmercury.com/portland/Content.
103. Ben Brantley, "Theater Review: So Many Mixed Blessings in a Life Lived Bilingually," review of *Havana Is Waiting*, *New York Times*, October 27, 2001, http://theater2.nytimes.com/mem/theater/treview.html; Elyse Sommer, "*Havana Is Waiting*: A Curtain Up Review," *Curtain Up*, October 24, 2001, http://www.curtainup.com/havanaiswaiting.html; Charles McNulty, "Southern Discomfort," review of *Havana Is Waiting* and *Thou Shalt Not*, *Village Voice*, October 30, 2001, http://www.villagevoice.com/2001-10-30/theater/southern-discomfort/21.

104. Elyse Sommer, "A Curtain Up Review of *Kissing Fidel*," *Curtain Up*, September 17, 2005, http://www.curtainup.com/kissingfidel.html; Christopher Isherwood, "Planting Big Wet Ones on the Face of Cuba," review of *Kissing Fidel*, *New York Times*, September 22, 2005, http://theater2.nytimes.com/2005/09/22/theater/reviews/22fide.html; Solomon, "Two Ambitious Dramas Cross Borders and Consciousness."

105. Quoted in del Rio, "Interview with Eduardo Machado," 59.

Chapter 3

1. Victor Cazares, *The Dead Women of J-Town and Smiley* (unpublished playscript, 2008/2011), 7.
2. Ibid., 109–10.
3. For an analysis of the privatization of media outlets such as TV Azteca, the marketing of telenovelas, and the shift in content, see María de la Luz Casas Pérez, "Cultural Identity between Reality and Fiction: A Transformation of Genre and Roles in Mexican Telenovelas," in *Telenovelas*, ed. Ilan Stavans (Santa Barbara, Calif.: Greenwood Press, 2010): 105–7.
4. Iris Marion Young, "Gender as Seriality: Thinking about Women as a Social Collective," *Signs* 19, no. 3 (1994): 713–38.
5. Phillip Jenkins, "Catch Me before I Kill More: Seriality as Modern Monstrosity," *Cultural Analysis* 3 (2002): 1–17.
6. Ibid.
7. Ibid.
8. González Rodríguez, *The Femicide Machine*, 9.
9. Diana Washington Valdez, *The Killing Fields: Harvest of Women—The Truth about Mexico's Bloody Border Legacy* (Los Angeles: Peace at the Border, 2006), 1. It was estimated that there were 878 femicides from 1993 to 2010, which is the number Moraga uses in *New Fire*. Statistics since then are difficult to parse, given the impact of the narcoguerra. The 878 figure is quoted by Chris Arsenault in "In Juárez, Women Just Disappear" (*Al Jazeera English*, March 8, 2011), where he claims the statistic comes from *El Diario de Juárez*.
10. Ibid.
11. Rohry Benítez et al., *El silencio que la voz de todas quiebra: Mujeres y víctimas de Ciudad Juárez* (Chihuahua, Mex: Ediciones del AZAR, 1999).
12. See Sergio González Rodríguez, *Huesos en el Desierto* (Barcelona: Anagrama, 2002); Valdez, *The Killing Fields*; Teresa Rodriguez and Diana Montané, *The Daughters of Juárez: A True Story of Serial Murder South of the Border* (New York: Atria Books, 2007).
13. Rubén Amavizca Murúa, *Mujeres de Juárez* (unpublished play script, 2010), 36–37.
14. For example, Wright, *Disposable Women*; and Elvia Arriola, "Accountability for Murder in Las Maquiladoras: Linking Corporate Indifference to Gender Violence at the U.S. Mexico Border," in *Making a Killing: Femicide, Free Trade, and La Frontera*, ed. Alicia Gaspar de Alba with Georgina Guzmán (Austin: University of Texas Press, 2010), 25–62.
15. Kathleen Staudt, *Violence and Activism at the Border: Gender, Fear, and Everyday Life in Ciudad Juárez* (Austin: University of Texas Press, 2008).

16. Jane Caputi, "Afterword: Goddess Murder and Gynocide in Ciudad Juárez," in *Making a Killing: Femicide, Free Trade, and La Frontera*, ed. Alicia Gaspar de Alba with Georgina Guzmán (Austin: University of Texas Press, 2010), 279–94.

17. Valdez, *The Killing Fields*; Rosa-Linda Fregoso, *Mexicana Encounters: The Making of Social Identities in the Borderlands* (Berkeley: University of California Press, 2003), 1–29; Marissa K. López, *Chicano Nations: The Hemispheric Origins of Mexican American Literature* (New York: New York University Press, 2011).

18. González Rodríguez, *The Femicide Machine*.

19. Ibid., 7.

20. Fregoso, "'We Want Them Alive!'"

21. Valdez, *The Killing Fields*, 183–96.

22. Mbembe, "Necropolitics."

23. Ibid., 40.

24. Fregoso, "'We Want Them Alive!'" 113.

25. Valencia, *Capitalismo Gore*, 15.

26. Ibid.

27. Rita L. Segato, "Territory, Sovereignty and the Crimes of the Second State: The Writing on the Body of Murdered Women," in *Terrorizing Woman: Femicide in the Americas*, ed. Rosa-Linda Fregoso and Cynthia Bejarano (Durham, N.C.: Duke University Press, 2011), 70–92.

28. Rodríguez, *Liberalism at Its Limits*, 196.

29. Reguillo, "The Narco-Machine."

30. Alan Aguilar, ed., *Hotel Juárez: Dramaturgia de feminicidios* (Durango, Mex.: Editorial Espacio Vacío, 2008).

31. See, for example, Steven S. Volk and Marian E. Schlotterbeck, "Gender, Order, and Femicide: Reading the Popular Culture of Murder in Ciudad Juárez," in *Making a Killing: Femicide, Free Trade, and La Frontera*, ed. Alicia Gaspar de Alba with Georgina Guzmán (Austin: University of Texas Press, 2010), 121–53. López critiques Gaspar de Alba's novel *Desert Blood* in particular for only concentrating on recent border history; López, *Chicano Nations*, 175–82. See Julia E. Monárrez-Fragoso, "The Suffering of the Other" (183–200), and Clara E. Rojas, "The V-Day March in Mexico: Appropriation and Misuse of Local Women's Activism" (200–10), both in *Making a Killing: Femicide, Free Trade, and La Frontera*, ed. Alicia Gaspar de Alba with Georgina Guzmán (Austin: University of Texas Press, 2010).

32. Plays are mentioned in Rodríguez, *Liberalism at Its Limits*, 175; Rojas, "The V-Day March in Mexico," 204; and Claudia Sadowski-Smith, "Imagining Transnational Chicano/a Activism against Gender-Based Violence at the U.S.-Mexico Border," in *Imagined Transnationalism: U.S. Latino/a Literature, Culture and Identity*, ed. Kevin Concannon et al. (New York: Palgrave Macmillan, 2009), 91n10. Interestingly, although Rojas mentions a play in her essay, the editors' appendix of books, film, and media about the killings does not include a section for theater and performance.

33. Christina Marín, "Staging Femicide/Confronting Reality: Negotiating Gender and Representation in Las Mujeres de Juárez," *Gender Forum: An Internet Journal for Gender Studies* 17 (2007); and Christina Marín, "Echoes of

Injustice: Performative Activism and the Femicide Plaguing Ciudad Juárez," in *Taking Risks: Feminist Activism and Research in the Americas*, ed. Julie Shayne (Albany, NY: State University of New York Press, 2014), 181–208. The plays are Humberto Robles, *Mujeres de Arena* (unpublished play script, 2010), courtesy of the author; and Marisela Treviño Orta, *Braided Sorrow* (unpublished play script, 2008), courtesy of the author.

34. Interview with Jimmy Noriega, January 14, 2015; Personal Correspondence with Christina Marín, February 13, 2015.

35. Jean Franco, *Cruel Modernity* (New York: Columbia University Press, 2013), 223.

36. López, *Chicano Nations*, 179.

37. Ralph Rodriguez, *Brown Gumshoes* (Austin: University of Texas Press, 2004), 8–9. His book was published before *Desert Blood* and is not considered there.

38. Sadowski-Smith, "Imagining Transnational Chicano/a Activism," 88.

39. Ibid., 89.

40. Marín, "Echoes of Injustice," 183.

41. Ibid.

42. Marc Zimmerman, "Testimonio," *The SAGE Encyclopedia of Social Science Research Methods*, ed. Michael S. Lewis-Beck, Alan Bryman, and Tim Futing Liao (Thousand Oaks, Calif.: SAGE Publications, 2004), 1118.

43. Beverley, *Testimonio*, 3.

44. Robles, *Mujeres de Arena*, 1.

45. Marín, "Echoes of Injustice," 204.

46. Ibid.

47. Robles, *Mujeres de Arena*, 1,

48. Ibid., 2.

49. John Beverley, "'Through All Things Modern': Second Thoughts on Testimonio," *Boundary 2* 18, no. 2 (1991): 1–21. David Stoll famously critiqued Rigoberta Menchú in his *Rigoberta Menchú and the Story of All Poor Guatemalans* (Boulder, Colo.: Westview Press, 1999), by disputing her truth claims and questioning the veracity of *testimonio* as a form.

50. Humberto Robles, *Mujeres de Arena* (trailer), directed by Christina Marín, February 25, 2013, https://www.youtube.com/watch?v=an3bNB_npq0; and Bridgit Brown, "Staged Reading Explores Femicides in Mexico," *Emerson College Today*, March 29, 2011, http://www.emerson.edu/news-events/emerson-college-today/femicides-mexico-explored-staged-reading#.VJnFXMAAw.

51. Marín has had radically different casts in terms of ethnic identity in each of the readings of the plays that she has directed. In New York, she worked with a pan-Latina cast without a Mexican cast member; in Boston she has worked with majority (but not exclusively) Anglo female casts; and in Arizona at Teatro Bravo, she worked with majority Chicana/Mexicana casts.

52. I am, of course, influenced here by Joseph Roach's conception of surrogation; see Joseph Roach, *Cities of the Dead: Circum-Atlantic Performance* (New York: Columbia University Press, 1996).

53. Cristina Michaus, *Women of Juárez*, trans. Jimmy Noriega (unpublished play script, 2013), 2. The Spanish language version of the play is available in Aguilar, *Hotel Juárez*, 171–88.

54. Personal interview with Jimmy Noriega, January 14, 2015.
55. Michaus, *Women of Juárez*, 8.
56. As Noriega suggested, Mexican audiences did not need the narrative arc at all and are not dependent on Aristotelian structures.
57. For example, see Antonio Zúñiga, *Estrellas Enterradas* (315–39), and Demetrio Avila, *Sirenas de Rio* (71–88), both in Alan Aguilar, ed., *Hotel Juárez: Dramaturgia de Feminicidios* (Durango, Mex.: Editorial Espacio Vacío, 2008). Victoria Martínez points out these features in "La Vida Vale: Once Obras Acerca de Los Asesinatos de Mujeres," ibid., 6, 11.
58. Noriega discussed this production detail with me in my interview with him, January 14, 2015.
59. Ibid.
60. Michaus, *Women of Juárez*, 18.
61. Noriega, interview with the author, January 14, 2015.
62. The Plan Puebla Panama is available at http://www.diputados.gob.mx/comisiones/asunindi/dgmxuno.pdf. For a critique of the plan, see Paulette Stenzel, "Plan Puebla Panama: An Economic Tool That Thwarts Sustainable Development and Facilitates Terrorism," *William and Mary Environmental Law and Policy Review* 30, no. 3 (2006): 555–623.
63. Hermann Herlinghaus, *Narcoepics* (New York: Bloomsbury Academic, 2013), 170–74.
64. Production histories can be found at the website for Humberto Robles's play, http://mujeresdearenateatro.blogspot.com/, and at the website for Amavizca Murúa's *Women of Juárez*, http://www.fridakahlotheater.org/#!Juárez/c1vkx; the history of Michaus's play comes from my interview with Jimmy Noriega, January 14, 2015.
65. Orta, *Braided Sorrow*, 2.
66. Ibid., 5.
67. Ibid., 29.
68. Ibid., 2.
69. Ibid., 3.
70. Marín, "Echoes of Injustice," 200.
71. Orta, *Braided Sorrow*, 13.
72. Ibid., 63.
73. Marín, "Echoes of Injustice," 200.
74. Interview with Marisela Orta, January 11, 2015.
75. Orta, interview with the author.
76. Marín, "Echoes of Injustice," 193.
77. Cazares, *Dead Women of J-Town and Smiley*, 12.
78. Ibid., 145.
79. Ibid., 2.
80. Ibid.
81. Ibid., 7–9.
82. Ibid., 6.
83. Ibid.
84. Ibid., 141.
85. Ibid., 143.
86. Ibid.

87. Ibid., 23–24.
88. Ibid., 53.
89. Ibid., 6.
90. Ibid., 38.
91. Ibid., 136–37.
92. In a frightening reversal, in 2013, a killer calling herself Diana the Huntress began to board buses to kill bus drivers who victimized women. See Rafael Romo, "'Diana, the Hunter' Slayings Frighten Ciudad Juárez Bus Drivers, Commuters," *CNN News Online*, September 5, 1993.
93. See Debra Castillo, María Gudelia Rangel Gómez, and Armando Rosas Solís, "Violence and Transvestite/Transgender Sex Workers in Tijuana," in *Gender Violence at the U.S.-Mexico Border: Media Representation and Public Response*, ed. Hector Domínguez-Ruvalcaba and Ignacio Corona (Tucson: University of Arizona Press, 2010), 14–34, for more about this phenomenon at another border site.
94. See Volk and Schlotterbeck, "Gender, Order, and Femicide," 121–54.
95. Fregoso, "'We Want Them Alive!'" 125–27.
96. Cazares, *Dead Women of J-Town and Smiley*, 53.
97. Roberto Bolaño, *2666: A Novel* (New York: Farrar, Straus and Giroux, 2008), 348.
98. See, for example, Laura Barberán Reinares, "Globalized Philomels: State Patriarchy, Transnational Capital, and the Femicides on the U.S.-Mexico Border in Roberto Bolaño's *2666*," *South Atlantic Review* 75, no. 4 (2010): 51–72; Sharae Deckard, "Peripheral Realism, Millennial Capitalism, and Roberto Bolaño's *2666*," *Modern Language Quarterly* 73, no. 3 (2012): 351–72; Grant Farred, "The Impossible Closing: Death, Neoliberalism, and the Post-Colonial in Bolaño's *2666*," *Modern Fiction Studies* 56, no. 4 (2010): 689–708. Hermann Herlinghaus—the only scholar to frame Bolaño's formal innovations in theatrical terms—suggests that he enacts a form of Brechtian alienation that forces viewers into a different relationship to the representation of the crimes. See Herlinghaus, *Narcoepics*, 170–74.
99. Sebastian Ferrari, in his dissertation "Imagining the Inoperative Community: Documentary Aesthetic in Roberto Bolaño and Alfredo Jaar" (Ph.D. diss., University of Michigan, 2012), suggests that these lists are a formal catalogue that refuses "to give us a sense of order" in Santa Teresa, which is of course a fictionalized Ciudad Juárez. The mode in which Bolaño details the crimes, in Ferrari's mind, also eliminates the idea of "private history and identity," unrelated to the description of public destruction, a conclusion that strikes at the heart of liberal ideology of subjectification, which supposedly undergirds but is actually eviscerated by neoliberal conditions (136).
100. Ferrari, "Imagining the Inoperative Community," 163–65.
101. See Lara D. Nielsen, "Institutionalizing Ensembles," *Law, Culture, and the Humanities* 4, no. 2 (2008): 176, for analysis of how the play exposes international divisions of cultural labor.
102. Valdez, *The Killing Fields*, 183–96.
103. Fusco, *The Incredible Disappearing Woman*, 202. Fusco's concentration on the maquila workers stems in part from her interviews with a maquila worker who was sexually harassed, which forms part of Chela's story in this play

and was the basis for a piece of performance art with Ricardo Dominguez titled *Dolores from 10 to 10*.
104. Ibid., 212.
105. Ibid., 215.
106. Ibid., 220.
107. Ibid.
108. Ibid., 207.
109. *The Incredible Disappearing Woman* has also been produced as a performance piece with Dominguez in which the audience directs Fusco into sexual acts. This performance piece is better known and more typical of her work. Yet, I believe it is Fusco's play version that more successfully tells the long history of neoliberalism.
110. A 2003 performance in Berlin can be found at http://future-nonstop.org/c/5ac64bade5e1be1f57b920a0f74cab1b
111. Svich, *Iphigenia Crash Land Falls*, 334.
112. Svich, *Iphigenia Crash Land Falls*, 338.
113. Like the eponymous character in Euripides's *Iphigenia in Aulis*, Svich's damsel magically disappears at the time of her murder. Taking a cue from Racine, however, Svich inserts a double for Iphigenia, who is sacrificed as well. Alluding to Calderón's *The Monster in the Garden*, this double is not another woman named Iphigenia, as it is in Racine's play, but an androgynous David Bowie–like Achilles. In Calderón's play, Achilles is dressed as a woman to avoid his fate as a warrior who will be sacrificed to win the war.
114. Svich, *Iphigenia Crash Land Falls*, 361.
115. Ali Rohrs, "Iphigenia Gets Down," *American Theatre* 23, no. 7 (September 2006): 24.
116. Chiori Miyagawa, "The Rise, Fall, and Rise of Iphigenia," *Brooklyn Rail* (September 2, 2006).
117. Taylor, *Disappearing Acts*, 76–89.
118. Svich, *Iphigenia Crash Land Falls*, 343.
119. Caridad Svich, interview with the author, January 18, 2015.
120. Svich, *Iphigenia Crash Land Falls*, 344.
121. Ibid., 346.
122. Ibid., 345–46.
123. Ibid.
124. Svich, *Iphigenia Crash Land Falls*, 346.
125. Ibid., 346.
126. Ibid., 347.
127. See Lance Gharavi, "Of Both Worlds: Exploiting Rave Technologies in Caridad Svich's *Iphigenia*," *Theatre Topics* 18, no. 2 (2008): 223–42.
128 Carlos Monsiváis, *Dias de Guardar* (Mexico City, Mexico: Biblioteca era Ensayo, 1970), 121.
129. Ramón Rivera-Servera, *Performing Queer Latinidad* (Ann Arbor: University of Michigan Press, 2012), 188–89.
130. Svich, *Iphigenia Crash Land Falls*, 367.
131. Ibid., 368.
132. There is controversy over the ending of *Iphigenia in Aulis*, as it was largely believed to be unfinished, making the peculiarity of its ending a potential mistake or the result of a subsequent author cobbling together an ending.

133. Alan Sommerstein, *The Tangled Ways of Zeus and Other Studies in and around Greek Tragedy* (London: Oxford University Press, 2010), 30–46.

134. Svich, interview with the author.

135. Reguillo, "The Narco-Machine."

136. Svich, *Iphigenia Crash Land Falls*, 341.

137. The one full academic article on a production of the play, Lance Gharavi's "Of Both Worlds," does not deal with this issue but instead concentrates on technology.

Chapter 4

1. *Scarface*, directed by Brian de Palma (Los Angeles: Universal Pictures, 1983); and Stephen Gaghan, *Traffic*, directed by Steven Soderbergh (New York: U.S.A. Films, 2000). Also see Kane Race, *Pleasure Consuming Medicine: The Queer Politics of Drugs* (Durham, N.C.: Duke University Press, 2009).

2. Craig Borten and Melisa Wallack, *Dallas Buyers Club*, directed by Jean-Marc Vallée (Universal City, Calif.: Focus Features, 2013); screenplay (2012), http://focusguilds2013.com/workspace/media/dbc_final-script_-12.02.12-.pdf.

3. For example, see A. O. Scott, "Taking on Broncos and a Plague," *New York Times* (November 1, 2013).

4. Ibid. See also Stephen Freiss, "Don't Applaud Jared Leto's Transgender Mammy," *Time* (February 28, 2014), http://time.com/10650/dont-applaud-jared-letos-transgender-mammy/.

5. This is Hermann Herlinghaus's formulation. See Hermann Herlinghaus, "Placebo Intellectuals in the Wake of Cosmopolitanism: A 'Pharmacological' Approach to Roberto Bolaño's novel *2666*," *The Global South* 5, no. 1 (2011): 101–19.

6. See Malcolm Harris, "Walter White Supremacy," *The New Inquiry* (September 27, 2013), http://thenewinquiry.com/essays/walter-white-supremacy/; and Chris Prioleau, "Walter White and Bleeding Brown: On *Breaking Bad*'s Race Problem," *Apogee* (October 3, 2013), http://www.apogeejournal.org/walter-white-bleeding-brown-on-breaking-bads-race-problem/.

7. Alexandra Bernson, *En Las Manos de la Muerte* (unpublished play script, 2010). I directed the production at the Rites and Reason Theatre, Brown University, Providence, R.I., October 28 to November 1, 2010.

8. Ginger Thompson, "On Mexico's Mean Streets, the Sinners Have a Saint," *New York Times* (March 26, 2004); Claudio Lomnitz Adler, *Death and the Idea of Mexico* (New York: Zone, 2005), 486–96; Cymene Howe, Susanna Zaraysky, and Lois Ann Lorentzen, "Devotional Crossings, Transgender Sex Workers, Santisima Muerte and Spiritual Solidarity in Guadalajara and San Francisco," in *Religion at the Corner of Bliss and Nirvana: Politics, Identity and Faith in New Migrant Communities*, ed. Lois Ann Lorentzen, Joaquin Jay Gonzales III, Kevin M. Chun, and Hien Duc Do (Durham, N.C.: Duke University Press, 2009), 3–38.

9. Octavio Solis, *Santos y Santos*, in *Plays by Octavio Solis* (New York: Broadway Play Publishing, 2006), 1–82.

10. Ibid., 4.

11. Ibid., 13.

12. Ibid., 19.

13. Ibid., 52.

14. For accounts of this history, see Diego Enrique Osorno, *El cartel de Sinaloa: Una historia del uso político del narco* (Mexico City, Mexico: Grijalbo, 2010); Andreas, *Border Games*; and Astorga, *El Siglo de las Drogas*.

15. Valencia, *Capitalismo Gore*, 15. Translation is my own.

16. In *Life Is a Dream* by Calderón de la Barca, Vasily decides to test whether or not his son—whom he has exiled to a tower because astrological signs pointed to his future as a tyrant—is civilized enough to take over the kingdom as his male heir. If not, his nephew, Aistalf, who has decided to marry Stella rather than fight against her as rival for the throne, will take over. Sigesmundo is so violent he is sent back to the tower. A group of rebel soldiers, however, wants him to be king, leading to a civil war after which Sigesmundo is made king. After admonishing his father for making him a monster, rather than preventing him from being one, Sigesmundo forgives his father and stands at his service; he then orders Aistalf to marry Rosuara, who he abandoned, after which he offers himself to Stella as a husband. In the end, blood birthright to the throne is retained and the rebel soldier is exiled.

17. Solis, *Dreamlandia*, 44–45.
18. Ibid., 44.
19. Ibid., 45
20. Ibid., 47.
21. Ibid., 78–79.
22. Octavio Solis, personal interview with the author, July 14, 2014.
23. Ibid.
24. Solis, *Dreamlandia*, 72.
25. Ibid., 73.
26. According to *Forbes* magazine, Carlos Slim was the world's richest man again as of July 15, 2014, with a personal net worth of $79.6 billion. He owns América Movil, which powers 70 percent of mobile phones and 80 percent of landlines in Mexico, and is also a minority owner of the *New York Times*. See Dolia Estevez, "Mexico's Carlos Slim Reclaims World's Richest Man Title from Bill Gates," *Forbes* (July 15, 2014), http://www.forbes.com/sites/doliaestevez/2014/07/15/mexicos-carlos-slim-reclaims-worlds-richest-man-title-from-bill-gates/ Retrieved August 15, 2014.
27. Solis, *Dreamlandia*, 86.
28. Saracho, *El Nogalar*, 87.
29. Ibid., 74, 87.
30. Ibid., 78.
31. Ibid., 85.
32. For an alternate reading of the gender dynamics of this play, see Alvarez, "Transcultural Dramaturgies, Latina Theatre's Third Wave," 89–90.
33. Marci R. McMahon, "Soundscapes of Narco Silence," *Sounding Out* (Blog), August 19, 2013, https://soundstudiesblog.com/2013/08/19/soundscapes-of-narco-silence/. She is referring to the production of *El Nogalar* at South Texas College Theatre (STC) directed by Joel Jason Rodriguez in McAllen, Texas, June 2013. The internal quote from *El Nogalar* is quoted in this blog.
34. Saracho, *El Nogalar*, 74.
35. Foucault, *The Birth of Biopolitics*, 226.
36. Saracho, *El Nogalar*, 82.
37. Ibid., 80.

38. Ibid., 72.
39. Ibid., 82.
40. Ibid., 80.
41. The dollhouse was used in the production of Tanya Saracho's *El Nogalar*, directed by Cecile Keenan, at the Goodman Theatre, Chicago, March 26–April 24, 2011. Many reviews mention the dollhouse, but they do not understand what López is doing with it.
42. Valencia, *Capitalismo Gore*, 72.
43. See Courtwright, *Forces of Habit*.
44. She mentions her interest in the female characters in an interview at the Fountain Theatre, January 10, 2012. https://www.youtube.com/watch?v=7dqIVyyIIPU.
45. Saracho, *El Nogalar*, 87.
46. Ibid., 87.
47. Victor I. Cazares, *Religiones Gringas* (unpublished play script, 2011), 78.
48. Patricia Ybarra, "Latino/a Dramaturgy as Historiography," in *Theatre/Performance Historiography: Time, Space, Matter*, ed. Rosemarie Bank and Michal Kobialka (Houndmills, U.K.: Palgrave Macmillan Press, 2015), 75–91.
49. Cazares, *Ramses contra los monstruos*, Writing Is Live Festival, February 2013, Providence, R.I.
50. Cazares, *Ramses contra los monstruos*, 10.
51. Mbembe, "Necropolitics."
52. Freeman, *Time Binds*.
53. Freeman, xxii.
54. Ibid.
55. Nielsen, "Introduction," 6; Claire Fox, *The Fence and the River: Cultural Politics at the Border* (Minneapolis: University of Minnesota Press, 1999). In brief, this program allows for the duty-free importation of goods into Mexico if made into products within Mexican factories for export. These factories, however exploitative their labor practices were, benefited both countries in that they allowed U.S. manufacturers to use cheaper labor to make products and eased the mass unemployment in Mexico that came with the end of the Bracero Program, which allowed Mexicans to do agricultural work in the United States without legal issue.
56. González Rodríguez, *The Femicide Machine*, 19.
57. Cazares, *Ramses contra los monstruos (2013)*, 118–119.
58. Ibid., 113.
59. I refer here to the 2011 version of the script.
60. Here I return to the 2013 version of the script. Cazares, *Ramses contra los monstrous*, 67.
61. Ibid., 94.
62. Reza Abdoh, *The Law of Remains*, in *Plays for the End of the Century*, ed. Bonnie Marranca (Baltimore, Md.: Johns Hopkins University Press, 1996), 9–94.
63. Cazares, *Ramses contra los monstrouos, production*, 2013.
64. See, for example, Blau, *Take Up the Bodies*.
65. Reguillo, "The Narco-Machine."
66. Cazares, *Ramses contra los monstruos*, 129.
67. See Nyong'o, "The Scene of Occupation." 146–47.

68. Cazares, *Ramses contra los monstruos*, 20.
69. Ibid., 169.
70. Ibid., 172–73.
71. Paul Gootenberg, *Andean Cocaine: The Making of a Global Drug* (Chapel Hill: University of North Carolina Press, 2008), 62.
72. See Kerry A. Dolan and Zina Moukheiber, "The Golden Age of Antiviral drugs," *Forbes*, October 27, 2003, http://www.forbes.com/global/2003/1027/090.html. The Gilead corporate history timeline is available at http://www.gilead.com/about/corporate-history-timeline.
73. Cazares, *Ramses contra los monstruos*, 174–75.
74. See, for example, Michael Sheridan and Tracy Connor, "20-year-old Student, Marisol Valles García, Made Police Chief of One of Mexico's Most Violent Towns," *Daily News*, October 20, 2010, http://www.nydailynews.com/news/world/20-year-old-student-marisol-valles-garcia-made-police-chief-mexico-violent-towns-article-1.190569.
75. Interview with Matthew Paul Olmos, September 4, 2014.
76. Matthew Paul Olmos, *so go the ghosts of méxico, part 1* (unpublished play script, 2013). The first reference to this work is in Pablo Ordaz, "La mujer más valiente de México," *El País*, October 20, 2010, http://internacional.elpais.com/internacional/2010/10/20/actualidad/1287525605_850215.html.
77. Olmos, *so go the ghosts*, 4. This play is now available in a published version by Samuel French publishers.
78. Ibid., 5.
79. Ibid., 79.
80. Ibid., 81.
81. Valles García often talked to the press about making a Mexico that was better for her son; see, for example, Ginger Adams Otis, "Marisol Valles García, 20-something Mexican Police Chief, Comes to New York for Play," *New York Daily News*, April 8, 2013.
82. Matthew Paul Olmos, *so go the ghosts of méxico, part 1* directed by Mei-yin Wang, La Mama Experimental Theatre Club, New York City, April 28, 2013; Así van los fantasmas en México, Repertorio Español, August 30, 2014.
83. Olmos admitted that he and Wang struggled with staging this moment, particularly deciding where and how the dead husband resurrected himself after he died, in his interview with me. Interview with the author, September 4, 2014.
84. Olmos, *so go the ghosts*, 75.
85. Catherine Rampell, "Facing a War Zone Rife with Cartels and Zombies: So Go the Ghosts of Mexico," *New York Times*, April 22, 2013.
86. For an excellent history, see Stephanie Boluk and Wylie Lenz, eds., *Generation Zombie: Essays on the Living Dead in Modern Culture* (Jefferson, N.C.: MacFarland, 2011).
87. Olmos, *so go the ghosts*, 75.
88. Ibid., 81.
89. Michael Hardt and Antonio Negri, *Multitude* (New York: Penguin, 2014).
90. Adam Szymkowicz, "I Interview Playwrights Part 320: Matthew Paul Olmos," February 25, 2011, http://aszym.blogspot.com/2011/02/i-interview-playwrights-part-320.html. In this interview, the play takes place in Tijuana. He obviously changed that when he began to incorporate Valles García's story.

91. Wikipedia cites a change in the population of the municipality (not just Práxedis proper) from 8,514 in 2005 to 4,799 in 2010; http://en.wikipedia.org/wiki/Pr%C3%A1xedis_G._Guerrero_Municipality. Instituto Nacional de Estadística y Geografía (INEGI) 2010 population statistics corroborate the 2010 population count. See also Christopher Loofe, "Drugs, Paramilitary Violence Create Ghost Towns in Mexico," *InSight Crime*, February 2, 2012; http://www.insightcrime.org/news-briefs/drug-paramilitary-violence-creates-ghost-towns-in-mexico.

92. Olmos, *so go the ghosts*, 80.

93. Ibid., 79.

94. Ibid., 72.

95. Matthew Olmos, interview with the author, September 4, 2014. The Mexican production took place at the Bellas Artes Theatre in San Miguel de Allende in November 2013.

96. The synopsis of the play is taken from Olmos's website: http://matthew-paulolmos.com/the-scripts/.

97. Olmos, *so go the ghosts*, 81.

Conclusion

1. Cazares, *Ramses contra los monstruos*, 21.

2. Rebecca Schneider, "It Seems as If I Am Dead: Zombie Capitalism and Theatrical Labor," *TDR* 56, no. 4 (2012): 153.

3. I refer here to two conference papers given at ATHE 2016 in Chicago: Donatella Galella, "I Want to Be in the Room Where It Happens: Neoliberal Multicultural Inclusion in Hamilton," and Patricia Herrera, "Sonic Hauntings of Blackness and Latinidad in Lin-Manuel Miranda's Hamilton."

4. Cazares, *Ramses contra los monstruos*, 175.

BIBLIOGRAPHY

Abdoh, Reza. *The Law of Remains*. In *Plays for the End of the Century*, edited by Bonnie Marranca, 9–94. Baltimore, Md.: Johns Hopkins University Press, 1996.

Abu-Lughod, Lila. "Writing against Culture." In *Recapturing Anthropology: Working in the Present*, edited by Richard Fox, 137–54. Santa Fe, N.Mex.: School of American Research Press, 1991.

Ackerman, Holly, and Juan M. Clark. *Cuban Balseros: Voyage of Uncertainty*. Miami: Policy Center of the Cuban American National, 1995.

Aguilar, Alan, ed. *Hotel Juárez: Dramaturgia de feminicidios*. Durango, Mex.: Editorial Espacio Vacío, 2008.

Alvarez, Lynne. *Tales of Revolution*. In *Lynne Alvarez: Collected Plays, Volume 1*, 213–62. Lyme, N.H.: Smith and Kraus, 1998.

Alvarez, Natalie. "Transcultural Dramaturgies, Latina Theatre's Third Wave." In *Contemporary Women Playwrights: Into the 21st Century*, edited by Penny Farfan and Lesley Ferris, 82–97. Houndmills, U.K.: Palgrave Macmillan, 2014.

Amavizca Murúa, Rubén. *Mujeres de Juárez*. Unpublished play script. 2010.

Andreas, Peter. *Border Games: Policing the U.S.-Mexico Divide*. Ithaca, N.Y.: Cornell University Press, 2000.

Aparicio, Frances R., and Susana Chávez-Silverman. *Tropicalizations: Transcultural Representations of Latinidad*. Hanover, N.H.: University Press of New England, 1997.

Aristotle. *On Poetry and Style*. Translated by G. M. A. Grube. 1958; repr. Indianapolis: Hackett, 1989.

Arriola, Elvia. "Accountability for Murder in Las Maquiladoras: Linking Corporate Indifference to Gender Violence at the U.S. Mexico Border. In *Making a Killing: Femicide, Free Trade, and La Frontera*, edited by Alicia Gaspar de Alba with Georgina Guzmán, 25–62. Austin: University of Texas Press, 2010.

Arrizón, Alicia. *Queering Mestizaje*. Ann Arbor: University of Michigan Press, 2006.

Arsenault, Chris. "In Juárez, Women Just Disappear," *Al Jazeera English*, March 8, 2011. http://www.aljazeera.com/indepth/features/2011/03/2011381423124 45430.html.

Astorga, Luis. *El siglo de las drogas: El narcotráfico, del Porfiriato al nuevo milenio*. Mexico City: Plaza y Janés, 2005.

Barber, Marta. "Bicycle Spins Migrant Metaphor." Review of *A Bicycle Country*. *Miami Herald*, December 16, 1999.

———. "Thoughtful Bicycle Is Poetry in Motion." Review of *A Bicycle Country*. *Miami Herald*, November 13, 2000.

Barberán Reinares, Laura. "Globalized Philomels: State Patriarchy, Transnational Capital, and the Femicides on the U.S.-Mexico Border in Roberto Bolaño's 2666." *South Atlantic Review* 75, no. 4 (2010): 51–72.

Becker, Gary. *Human Capital: A Theoretical and Empirical Analysis, with Special Reference to Education.* Chicago: University of Chicago Press, 1964.

Benítez, Rohry, Adriana Candia, Patricia Cabrera, Guadalupe de la Mora, Josefina Martínez, Isabel Velázquez, Ramona Ortiz, and S Taller de Narrativa de Ciudad Juárez. *El silencio que la voz de todas quiebra: Mujeres y víctimas de Ciudad Juárez.* Chihuahua, Mex.: Ediciones de Azar, 1999.

Berlant, Lauren. *Cruel Optimism.* Durham, N.C.: Duke University Press, 2011.

Bernson, Alexandra. *En Las Manos de la Muerte.* Unpublished play script, 2010.

Beverley, John. *Testimonio: On the Politics of Truth.* Minneapolis: University of Minnesota Press: 2004.

———. "'Through All Things Modern': Second Thoughts on Testimonio." *Boundary 2* 18, no. 2 (1991): 1–21.

Blau, Herbert. *Take Up the Bodies: Theater at the Vanishing Point.* Urbana: University of Illinois Press, 1982.

Boal, Augusto. *Theatre of the Oppressed.* New York: TCG, 1993.

Bolaño, Roberto. *2666: A Novel.* New York: Farrar, Straus and Giroux, 2008.

Boluk, Stephanie, and Wylie Lenz, eds. *Generation Zombie: Essays on the Living Dead in Modern Culture.* Jefferson, N.C.: MacFarland, 2011.

Bonfil Batalla, Guillermo. *México Profundo: Reclaiming a Civilization.* Translated by Philip A. Dennis. Austin: University of Texas Press, 1996.

Borten, Craig, and Melisa Wallack. *Dallas Buyers Club.* Directed by Jean-Marc Vallée. Universal City, Calif.: Focus Features, 2013. Screenplay: http://focusguilds2013.com/workspace/media/dbc_final-script_-12.02.12-.pdf.

Bosch, Carles, and David Trueba. *Balseros.* DVD. Directed by Carles Bosch and Josep Maria Domènech. Barcelona: Lauren Films, 2002.

Bracho, Ricardo, Jorge Ignacio Cortiñas, and José Muñoz. "Towards Translocalism: Latino Theater in the New United States—Ricardo Bracho and Jorge Cortiñas in Conversation with José Muñoz." In *Trans-global Readings: Crossing Theatrical Boundaries.* Edited by Caridad Svich. Manchester, U.K.: Manchester University Press, 2003: 66–70.

Brady, Mary Pat. *Extinct Lands, Temporal Geographies.* Durham, N.C.: Duke University Press, 2002.

Brantley, Ben. "Theater Review: So Many Mixed Blessings in a Life Lived Bilingually." Review of *Havana Is Waiting. New York Times*, October 27, 2001. http://theater2.nytimes.com/mem/theater/treview.html.

Brito, Fernando. "Tus pasos se perdieron con el paisaje." *e-misférica* 8, no. 2 (2010).

Brown, Bridgit. "Staged Reading Explores Femicides in Mexico." *Emerson College Today*, March 29, 2011. http://www.emerson.edu/news-events/emerson-college-today/femicides-mexico-explored-staged-reading#.VJnFXMAAw.

Brown, Wendy. "Neoliberalism and the End of Liberal Democracy." *Theory and Event* 7, no. 1 (2003). doi:10.1353/tae.2003.0020

Broyles-González, Yolanda. *Teatro Campesino.* Austin: University of Texas Press: 1994.

Bruce-Novoa, Juan, and Carlos May-Gamboa. "El Quinto Festival de Teatros." *De Colores* 2 (1975): 65–72.
Brune, Eva. Grant Proposal. INTAR Archives, 1993.
Burdick, John, Philip Oxhorn, and Kenneth M. Roberts. *Beyond Neoliberalism in Latin America? Society and Politics at the Crossroads*. Houndmills, U.K.: Palgrave Macmillan 2009.
Caputi, Jane. "Afterword: Goddess Murder and Gynocide in Ciudad Juárez." In *Making a Killing: Femicide, Free Trade, and La Frontera*, edited by Alicia Gaspar de Alba with Georgina Guzmán, 279–94. Austin: University of Texas Press, 2010.
Casas Pérez, María de la Luz. "Cultural Identity between Reality and Fiction: A Transformation of Genre and Roles in Mexican Telenovelas." In *Telenovelas*. Edited by Ilan Stavans. Santa Barbara, Calif.: Greenwood Press, 2010.
Castillo, Debra, María Gudelia Rangel Gómez, and Armando Rosas Solís. "Violence and Transvestite/Transgender Sex Workers in Tijuana." In *Gender Violence at the U.S.-Mexico Border: Media Representation and Public Response*, edited by Hector Domínguez-Ruvalcaba and Ignacio Corona, 14–34. Tucson: University of Arizona Press, 2010.
Castro, Max J., ed. *Free Markets, Open Societies, Closed Borders? Trends in International Migration and Immigration Policy in the Americas*. Miami: North South Center Press, 1999.
Cazares, Victor I. *The Dead Women of J-Town and Smiley*. Unpublished play script, 2008/2011.
———. *Ramses contra los monstruos*. Unpublished play script, 2013.
———. *Religiones Gringas*. Unpublished play script, 2011.
Cheng, Patrick S. *Radical Love: An Introduction to Queer Theology*. New York: Seabury Press, 2011.
Clinton, Bill. The President's News Conference, August 19, 1994. http://clinton6.nara.gov/1994/08/1994-08-19-press-conference-by-the-president.html.
Contreras, Sheila M. *Blood Lines, Myth, Indigenism and Chicana/o Literature*. Austin: University of Texas Press, 2008.
Cortiñas, Jorge. *Sleepwalkers*. Unpublished play script, 1999.
Courtwright, David T. *Forces of Habit: Drugs and the Making of the Modern World*. Cambridge, Mass.: Harvard University Press, 2001.
Cruz, Nilo. *A Bicycle Country*. New York: Dramatists Plays Service, 2004.
Dávila, Arlene. "Locating Neoliberalism in Time, Space and Culture." *American Quarterly* 66, no. 3 (2014): 549–55.
Davis, Eisa. "Michael John Garcés: A Point of Departure." Loggernaut Reading Series. http://www.loggernaut.org/interviews/michaeljohngarces/.
Davis, Tracy C., and Thomas Postlewait. "Theatricality: An Introduction." In *Theatricality*, edited by Tracy C. David and Thomas Postlewait. Cambridge, U.K.: Cambridge University Press, 2003.
de Certeau, Michel. *The Writing of History*. New York: Columbia University Press, 1988.
Deckard, Sharae. "Peripheral Realism, Millennial Capitalism, and Roberto Bolaño's 2666." *Modern Language Quarterly* 73, no. 3 (2012): 351–72.
de la Campa, Román. *Latin Americanism*. Minneapolis: University of Minnesota Press, 1997.

del Rio, Eduardo. "Interview with Eduardo Machado." In *One Island, Many Voices: Conversations with Cuban-American Writers*, 56–66. Tucson: University of Arizona Press, 2008.
Díaz, Tomás. *Balseros in Guantánamo: Su Historia y Testimonio*. Miami: Nuevos Horizontes Internacionales, 1996.
Dolan, Kerry A., and Zina Moukheiber. "The Golden Age of Antiviral drugs." *Forbes*, October 27, 2003. http://www.forbes.com/global/2003/1027/090.html.
Dolen, Christine. "Sleepwalkers in Haunting Unforgettable Play at Area Stage Explores Present Day Life in Havana." Review of *Sleepwalkers*. *Miami Herald*, July 1, 1999.
Dorfman, Ariel. *Death and the Maiden*. New York: Penguin Plays, 1994.
Edberg, Mark Cameron. *El Narcotraficante, Narcocorridos and the Construction of a Cultural Persona on the U.S.-Mexico Border*. Austin: University of Texas Press, 2004.
Estevez, Dolia. "Mexico's Carlos Slim Reclaims World's Richest Man Title from Bill Gates," *Forbes*, July 15, 2014. http://www.forbes.com/sites/doliaestevez/2014/07/15/mexicos-carlos-slim-reclaims-worlds-richest-man-title-from-bill-gates/.
Fabian, Johannes. *Time and the Other: How Anthropology Makes Its Objects*. New York: Columbia University Press, 2002.
Farred, Grant. "The Impossible Closing: Death, Neoliberalism, and the Post-Colonial in Bolaño's 2666." *Modern Fiction Studies* 56, no. 4 (2010): 689–708.
Féral, Josette. "Foreword," and "The Rise and Fall of Theatricality." *SubStance* 31, nos. 2 and 3 (2002): 3–13.
Fernández, Alfredo A. *Adrift: The Cuban Raft People*. Translated by Susan G. Rascón. Houston: Arte Público, 2000.
Ferrari, Sebastian. "Imagining the Inoperative Community: Documentary Aesthetic in Roberto Bolaño and Alfredo Jaar." Ph.D. diss., University of Michigan, 2012.
Fornés, María Irene. *Balseros/Manual for a Desperate Crossing*. In *Letters from Cuba and Other Plays*, 83–136. New York: PAJ, 2007.
———. *Conduct of Life*. In *Plays*, 65–88. New York: PAJ, 1986.
Foucault, Michel. *The Birth of Biopolitics: Lectures at the Collège de France 1978–1979*. Houndmills, U.K.: Palgrave Macmillan, 2008.
Fox, Claire. *The Fence and the River: Cultural Politics at the Border*. Minneapolis: University of Minnesota Press, 1999.
Franco, Jean. *Cruel Modernity*. New York: Columbia University Press, 2013.
Freeman, Elizabeth. *Time Binds: Queer Temporalities, Queer Histories*. Durham, N.C.: Duke University Press, 2010.
Fregoso, Rosa-Linda. "For a Pluriversal Declaration of Human Rights." *American Quarterly* 66, no. 3 (2014): 583–603.
———. *Mexicana Encounters: The Making of Social Identities in the Borderlands*. Berkeley: University of California Press, 2003.
———. "The Representation of Cultural Identity in *Zoot Suit*." *Theory and Society* 22, no. 5 (1993): 659–74.
———. "'We Want Them Alive!' The Politics of Culture and Human Rights." *Social Identities* 12, no. 2 (2006): 109–38.

Fregoso, Rosa-Linda, and Cynthia Bejarano. *Terrorizing Women: Feminicide in the Americas*. Durham, N.C.: Duke University Press, 2010.
Freiss, Stephen. "Don't Applaud Jared Leto's Transgender Mammy." *Time*, February 28, 2014. http://time.com/10650/dont-applaud-jared-letos-transgender-mammy/.
Friedman, Milton. *Capitalism and Freedom*. Chicago: University of Chicago, 1962.
Fusco, Coco. *Incredible Disappearing Woman*, 202–20. In *The Bodies That Were Not Ours and Other Writings*. London: Routledge, 2001.
———. "The Other History of Intercultural Performance," *TDR* 38, no. 1 (1994): 143–67.
Fusco, Coco, and Nao Bustamante, *Stuff, TDR* 41, no. 4 (1997): 63–82.
Gaghan, Stephen. *Traffic*. Directed by Steven Soderbergh. New York: USA Films, 2000.
Garcés, Michael John. *points of departure*. Unpublished play script, 2006.
———. "Los Illegals." *Theater* 41, no. 2 (2012): 69–119.
García-Romero, Anne. "Transculturation and Twenty-First Century Latina Playwrights." PhD diss., University of California, Santa Barbara, 2009.
Gaspar de Alba, Alicia, with Georgina Guzmán. *Making a Killing: Femicide, Free Trade and La Frontera*. Austin: University of Texas Press, 2010.
Gharavi, Lance. "Of Both Worlds: Exploiting Rave Technologies in Caridad Svich's *Iphigenia*." *Theatre Topics* 18, no. 2 (2008): 223–42.
Goldsmith, Barclay. "Brecht and Chicano Theatre." In *Modern Chicano Writers: A Collection of Critical Essays*, edited by Joseph Sommers and Tomás Ybarra-Frausto, 167–75. Englewood Cliffs, N.J.: Prentice Hall, 1978.
Golub, Spencer. *Infinity (Stage)*. Ann Arbor: University of Michigan Press, 2001.
González Rodríguez, Sergio. "Epilogue: How to take Textual Photographs." In *The Femicide Machine*, 99–128. New York: Semiotext(e), 2012.
———. *The Femicide Machine*. Translated by Michale Parker-Stainback. New York Semiotext(e), 2012.
———. *Huesos en el Desierto*. Barcelona: Anagrama, 2002.
Goodwin, Joy. "Victims in an Unnamed Land," *New York Sun*, March 20, 2006. http://www.nysun.com/arts/victims-in-an-unnamed-land/29403/.
Gootenberg, Paul. *Andean Cocaine: The Making of a Global Drug*. Chapel Hill: University of North Carolina Press, 2008.
Gordon, Pamela. "Rites of Passage," *Miami New Times*, June 6, 1996, Arts Section. http://www.miaminewtimes.com/1996-06-06/culture/rites-of-passage.
Goss, Lindsay. "Tactical Acting Jane Fonda, GI Resistance, and the FTA." Ph.D. diss. Brown University, 2014.
Greenhill, Kelly M. "Engineered Migration as Coercive Instrument: The 1994 Cuban Balseros Crisis." *The Rosemarie Rogers Working Paper Series #12*, Inter-University Committee on International Migration, February 2002. http://web.mit.edu/cis/www/migration/Greenhill_rrwp_12.html.
Guerra, Felicia. *Balseros: Historia Oral del Éxodo Cubano de '94*. Miami: Editorials Universal, 1997.
Gugelberger, Georg M. *The Real Thing: Testimonial Discourse and Latin America*. Durham, N.C.: Duke University Press, 1996.

Halberstam, Judith. *In a Queer Time and Place: Transgender Bodies, Subcultural Lives* New York: New York University Press, 2005.
Hardt, Michael, and Antonio Negri. *Empire*. Cambridge, Mass.: Harvard University, 2001.
———. *Multitude*. New York: Penguin, 2014.
Harris, Malcolm. "Walter White Supremacy." *The New Inquiry*, September 27, 2013. http://thenewinquiry.com/essays/walter-white-supremacy/.
Harvey, David. *A Brief History of Neoliberalism*. London: Oxford University Press, 2005.
Hayek, F. A. *The Road to Serfdom*. Edited by Bruce Caldwell. 1944. Reprint, Chicago: University of Chicago, 2007.
Henken, Ted. "*Balseros, Boteros,* and *El Bombo*: Post-1994 Cuban Immigration to the United States and the Persistence of Special Treatment." *Latino Studies* 3, no. 3 (2005): 393–416.
Herlinghaus, Hermann. *Narcoepics*. New York: Bloomsbury Academic, 2013.
———. "Placebo Intellectuals in the Wake of Cosmopolitanism: A 'Pharmacological' Approach to Roberto Bolaño's novel 2666." *The Global South* 5, no. 1 (2011): 101–19.
———. *Violence without Guilt*. Houndmills, U.K.: Palgrave MacMillan, 2009.
Hitchcock, Laura. "A Curtain Up LA Review." Review of *A Bicycle Country. Curtain Up,* April 7, 2001. http://www.curtainup.com/bicyclecountry.html.
Hoffman, Bert. "Emigration and Regime Stability: Explaining the Persistence of Cuban Socialism." *Working Papers: Global and Area Studies* 2 (2005). www.duel.de/working papers.com.
Holman, Curt. "Sleep with the Fishes: *Sleepwalkers* Examines Deprivation and Desperation in Cuba." Review of *Sleepwalkers. Creative Loafing: Best of Atlanta,* May 1, 2002. http://atlanta.creativeloafing.com/gyrobase/Content?oid=oid%3A8658.
Howe, Cymene, Susanna Zaraysky, and Lois Ann Lorentzen. "Devotional Crossings, Transgender Sex Workers, Santisima Muerte and Spiritual Solidarity in Guadalajara and San Francisco." In *Religion at the Corner of Bliss and Nirvana: Politics, Identity and Faith in New Migrant Communities,* edited by Lois Ann Lorentzen, Joaquin Jay Gonzales III, Kevin M. Chun, and Hien Duc Do, 3–38. Durham, N.C.: Duke University Press, 2009.
Huerta, Jorge. "Borders in Three Latino Plays." In *Of Borders and Thresholds: Theatre History, Practice, and Theory*. Edited by Michal Kobialka, 154–83. Minneapolis: University of Minnesota, 1999.
———. *Chicano Drama: Performance, Society and Myth*. London: Cambridge University Press, 2000.
———. "Introduction." *Mummified Deer and Other Plays*. Houston: Arte Público Press, 2005.
Hurwitt, Robert. "Healing Burns." Review of *New Fire. San Francisco Chronicle,* January 16, 2012.
Isherwood, Christopher. "Planting Big Wet Ones on the Face of Cuba." Review of *Kissing Fidel. New York Times,* September 22, 2005. http://theater2.nytimes.com/2005/09/22/theater/reviews/22fide.html.
Jackson, Shannon. "Just in Time: Performance and the Aesthetics of Precarity." *TDR* 56, no. 4 (2012): 10–31.

Jenkins, Phillip. "Catch Me before I Kill More: Seriality as Modern Monstrosity." *Cultural Analysis* 3 (2002): 1–17.
Kierkegaard, Søren. *Fear and Trembling*. 1985; repr. London: Penguin, 2005.
Kingfisher, Catherine, and Jeff Mavkofsky. "Introduction: The Limits of Neoliberalism." *Critique of Anthropology* 28, no. 2 (2008): 115–26.
Klein, Cecelia. "The Devil and the Skirt: An Iconographic Inquiry into the Pre-Hispanic Nature of the *Tzitzimime*." *Ancient Mesoamerica* 11 (2000): 1–26.
Klein, Naomi. *The Shock Doctrine: The Rise of Disaster Capitalism*. New York: Henry Holt, 2008.
Lane, Jill. *Blackface Cuba, 1840–1895*. Philadelphia: University of Pennsylvania Press, 2005.
Laughlin, Robert. *Monkey Business Theatre*. Austin: University of Texas, 2008.
León, Juan. "Tropical Overexposure: Miami's 'Sophisticated Tropics' and the *Balsero*." In *Tropicalizations: Transcultural Representations of Latinidad*. Edited by Frances Aparicio and Susana Chávez-Silverman. Hanover, N.H.: Dartmouth University Press, 1997.
Lomnitz Adler, Claudio. *Death and the Idea of Mexico*. New York: Zone, 2005.
Loofe, Christopher. "Drugs, Paramilitary Violence Create Ghost Towns in Mexico." *InSight Crime*, February 2, 2012. http://www.insightcrime.org/news-briefs/drug-paramilitary-violence-creates-ghost-towns-in-mexico.
López, Marissa K. *Chicano Nations: The Hemispheric Origins of Mexican American Literature*. New York: New York University Press, 2011.
López, Tiffany Ana. "Violent Inscriptions: Writing the Body and Making Community in Four Plays by Migdalia Cruz." *Theatre Journal* 52, no. 1 (2000): 51–66.
Lott, Eric. *Love and Theft: Blackface Minstrelsy and the American Working Class*. London: Oxford University Press, 1993.
Luna, Violeta. *Requiem for a Lost Land*. *e-misférica* 8, no. 2 (2010).
MacDonald, Laura, and Arne Ruckert, eds. *Post-Neoliberalization in the Americas*. Houndmills, U.K.: Palgrave Macmillan, 2009.
Machado, Eduardo. *The Cook*. New York: Sam French, 2004.
———. *The Floating Island Plays*. New York: TCG, 1993.
———. *Havana Is Waiting*. New York: Samuel French, 2008.
———. *Kissing Fidel*. New York: Sam French, 2006.
Marez, Curtis. *Drug Wars: The Political Economy of Narcotics*. Minneapolis: University of Minnesota, 2004.
Marín, Christina. "Echoes of Injustice: Performative Activism and the Femicide Plaguing Ciudad Juárez." In *Taking Risks: Feminist Activism and Research in the Americas*, edited by Julie Shayne, 181–208. Albany, NY: State University of New York Press, 2014.
———. "Staging Femicide/Confronting Reality: Negotiating Gender and Representation in Las Mujeres de Juárez." *Gender Forum: An Internet Journal for Gender Studies* 17 (2007): 1–10.
Martinez, Alma. "*¿Un continente, una cultura?*: The Political Dialectic for a United Chicana/o and Pan-American Popular/Political Theater Front, Mexico City, 1974." Ph.D. dissertation, Stanford University, 2005.
Masud-Piloto, Felix. *From Welcome Exiles to Illegal Immigrants: Cuban Migrants to the U.S., 1959–1995*. Lanham, Md.: Rowman & Littlefield, 1996.

Mbembe, Achille. "Necropolitics." *Public Culture* 15, no. 1 (2003): 11–40.
McMahon, Marci R. "Soundscapes of Narco Silence." *Sounding Out* (blog). August 19, 2013. https://soundstudiesblog.com/2013/08/19/soundscapes-of-narco-silence/.
McNulty, Charles. "Southern Discomfort." Review of *Havana Is Waiting* and *Thou Shalt Not*. *Village Voice*, October 30, 2001. http://www.villagevoice.com/2001-10-30/theater/southern-discomfort/21.
Melamed, Jodi. *Represent and Destroy: Rationalizing Violence in the New Racial Capitalism*. Minneapolis: University of Minnesota Press, 2011.
Michaus, Cristina. *Women of Juárez*. Translated by Jimmy Noriega. Unpublished play script, 2013.
Mignolo, Walter. *The Darker Side of Western Modernity: Global Futures, Decolonial Options*. Durham, N.C.: Duke University Press, 2011.
———. *The Idea of Latin America*. London: Blackwell, 2005.
Miyagawa, Chiori. "The Rise, Fall, and Rise of Iphigenia." *Brooklyn Rail*, September 2, 2006.
Monárrez-Fragoso, Julia E. "The Suffering of the Other." In *Making a Killing: Femicide, Free Trade, and La Frontera*, ed. Alicia Gaspar de Alba with Georgina Guzmán, 183–200. Austin: University of Texas Press, 2010.
Monje Rafuls, Pedro R. "El Re-Encuentro, Un Tema Dramatica." In *Lo que no se ha dicho*. Edited by Jesus J. Barquet and Pedro R. Monje Rafuls, 63–72. Jackson Heights, N.Y.: Ollantay Press, 1994.
Monsiváis, Carlos. *Días de Guardar*. Mexico City, Mexico: Biblioteca Era Ensayo, 1970.
———. *Mexican Postcards*. London: Verso, 1997.
Moraga, Cherríe L. *Giving Up the Ghost*. In *Heroes and Saints and Other Plays*, 1–36. Albuquerque, N.Mex.: West End Press, 1994.
———. *Giving Up the Ghost: Teatro in Two Acts*. Albuquerque, N.Mex.: West End Press, 1986.
———. *Heart of the Earth*. In *The Hungry Woman*, 101–54. Albuquerque, N.Mex.: West End Press, 2001
———. *The Hungry Woman*. Albuquerque, N.Mex.: West End Press, 2001.
———. *The Hungry Woman*. Unpublished manuscript, 2005.
———. *The Last Generation: Prose and Poetry by Cherríe Moraga*. Boston: South End Press, 1993.
———. *New Fire: To Make Things Right Again*. Unpublished play script, 2012.
———. *A Xicana Codex of Changing Consciousness*. Durham, N.C.: Duke University Press, 2011.
Morales, Alejandro. *Sebastian*. In *Collected Plays by Alejandro Morales*, 33–101. New York: No Passport Press, 2007.
Moreiras, Alberto. *The Exhaustion of Difference: The Politics of Latin American Cultural Studies*. Durham, N.C.: Duke University Press, 2001.
Muñoz, Carlos. *Youth, Identity, Power: The Chicano Movement*. New York: Verso, 1989.
Muñoz, José. *Cruising Utopia: The Then and There of Queer Futurity*. New York: New York University Press, 2009.
Nielsen, Lara D. "Institutionalizing Ensembles." *Law, Culture, and the Humanities* 4, no. 2 (2008): 156–78.

Nielsen, Lara D. "Introduction: Heterotopic Transformations: The (Il)Liberal Neoliberal." In *Neoliberalism and Global Theatres: Performance Permutations*, edited by Lara D. Nielsen and Patricia Ybarra, 1–24. Houndmills, U.K.: Palgrave Macmillan, 2012.
Nyong'o, Tavia. "The Scene of Occupation." *TDR* 56, no. 4 (2012): 136–49.
Olmos, Matthew Paul. *so go the ghosts of méxico, part 1*. Unpublished play script, 2013.
Ong, Aiwha. *Neoliberalism as Exception: Mutations in Citizenship and Sovereignty*. Durham, N.C.: Duke University Press, 2006.
Ordaz, Pablo. "La mujer más valiente de México." *El País*, October 20, 2010. http://internacional.elpais.com/internacional/2010/10/20/actualidad/128752 5605_850215.html.
Orta, Marisela Treviño. *Braided Sorrow*. Unpublished play script, 2008.
Ortiz, Ricardo L. *Cultural Erotics in Cuban America*. Minneapolis: University of Minnesota Press, 2007.
Osorno, Diego Enrique. *El cartel de Sinaloa: Una historia del uso político del narco*. Mexico City, Mexico: Grijalbo, 2010.
Otis, Ginger Adams. "Marisol Valles García, 20-something Mexican Police Chief, Comes to New York for Play." *New York Daily News*, April 8, 2013.
Payan, Victor. "An Interview with Luis Valdez during the Writing of *Mummified Deer*," May 21, 1999. http://web.archive.org/web/20070208040740/http:// www.flyingserpent.net/justwords1/mummydearest.html.
Pedraza, Silvia. *Political Disaffection in Cuba's Revolution and Exodus*. London: Cambridge University Press, 2007.
Pérez Firmat, Gustavo. *Life on the Hyphen: The Cuban American Way*. Austin: University of Texas Press, 1994.
Pérez-Torres, Rafael. *Mestizaje: Critical Uses of Race in Chicano/a Culture*. Minneapolis: University of Minnesota Press, 2006.
Ponte, Antonio José, "Coming." In *In the Cold of the Malecon*. San Francisco: City Lights Books, 2000.
Powell, Kathy. "Neoliberalism, Solidarity and the Special Period in Cuba." *Critique of Anthropology* 28, no. 2 (2008): 177–97.
Prioleau, Chris. "Walter White and Bleeding Brown: On *Breaking Bad*'s Race Problem," *Apogee*, October 3, 2103. http://www.apogeejournal.org/walter-white-bleeding-brown-on-breaking-bads-race-problem/.
Puga, Ana. "Migrant Melodrama, Human Rights, and Elvira Arellano." In *Imagining Human Rights in Twenty-First Century Theatre*. Edited by Florian Nikolas Becker, Paola Hernandez, and Brenda Werth, 155–78. Houndmills, U.K.: Palgrave Macmillan, 2013.
Quijano, Aníbal. "The Coloniality of Power, Eurocentrism and Latin America." *Nepantla* 1, no. 3 (2000): 533–80.
Rabasa, José. *Without History: Subaltern Studies, the Zapatista Insurgency, and the Specter of History*. Pittsburgh, Pa.: University of Pittsburgh Press, 2010.
Race, Kane. *Pleasure Consuming Medicine: The Queer Politics of Drugs*. Durham, N.C.: Duke University Press, 2009.
Rampell, Catherine. "Facing a War Zone Rife with Cartels and Zombies: So Go the Ghosts of Mexico." *New York Times*, April 22, 2013.

Rancière, Jacques. "Ten Theses on Politics." In *Dissensus: On Politics and Aesthetics*. Edited and translated by Steve Corcoran. New York: Continuum, 2010.

Rayner, Alice. *Ghosts: Death's Double and the Phenomena of Theatre*. Minneapolis: University of Minnesota Press, 2006.

Reguillo, Rosanna. "The Narco-Machine and the Work of Violence: Notes toward Its Decodification," *E-misférica* 8, no. 2 (2010).

Richard, Nelly. *The Insubordination of Signs: Political Change, Cultural Transformation and the Poetics of the Crisis*. Translated by Alicia Nelson and Silvia R. Tandeciarz. Durham, N.C.: Duke University Press, 2004.

Ridout, Nicholas. *Passionate Amateurs: Theatre, Communism, and Love*. Ann Arbor: University of Michigan Press, 2013.

Ridout, Nicholas, and Rebecca Schneider. "Precarity and Performance: An Introduction." *TDR* 56, no. 4 (2012): 5–9.

Rivera, Carmen. *La Gringa*. New York: Sam French, 2008.

Rivera-Servera, Ramón. *Performing Queer Latinidad*. Ann Arbor: University of Michigan Press, 2012.

Roach, Joseph. *Cities of the Dead: Circum-Atlantic Performance*. New York: Columbia University Press, 1996.

Robles, Humberto. *Mujeres de Arena*. Unpublished play script, 2004.

Rodríguez, Ileana, ed. *The Latin American Subaltern Studies Reader*. Durham, N.C.: Duke University Press, 2001.

Rodríguez, Ileana. *Liberalism at Its Limits: Crime and Terror in the Latin American Cultural Text*. Pittsburgh, Pa.: University of Pittsburgh Press, 2009.

Rodriguez, Ralph. *Brown Gumshoes*. Austin: University of Texas Press, 2004.

Rodriguez, Teresa, and Diana Montané. *The Daughters of Juárez: A True Story of Serial Murder South of the Border*. New York: Atria Books, 2007.

Rohrs, Ali. "Iphigenia Gets Down." *American Theatre* 23, no. 7 (September 2006): 24.

Rojas, Clara E. "The V-Day March in Mexico: Appropriation and Misuse of Local Women's Activism." In *Making a Killing: Femicide, Free Trade, and La Frontera*, ed. Alicia Gaspar de Alba with Georgina Guzmán, 201–10. Austin: University of Texas Press, 2010.

Romo, Rafael, "'Diana, the Hunter' Slayings Frighten Ciudad Juárez Bus Drivers, Commuters," *CNN News Online*, September 5, 1993.

Roos, James. "Balseros Cuban Rafter's Journey to South Florida and Freedom Inspires New Opera." *Miami Herald*, May 11, 1997, Arts Section.

Rossini, Jon D. *Contemporary Latino/a Theatre: Wrighting Ethnicity*. Carbondale: Southern Illinois Press, 2008.

———. "José Rivera, Neoliberalism and the Outside of Politics." *Latin American Theatre Review* 43, no. 1 (2009): 41–56.

Rossini, Jon D., and Patricia Ybarra. "Neoliberalism, Historiography, Identity Politics, Toward a New Historiography of Latino Theatre." *Radical History Review* 112 (Winter 2012): 162–72.

Sadowski-Smith, Claudia. "Imagining Transnational Chicano/a Activism against Gender-Based Violence at the U.S.-Mexico Border." In *Imagined Transnationalism: U.S. Latino/a Literature, Culture and Identity*, edited by Kevin Concannon, Francisco A. Lomelí, and Marc Priewe, 75–93. New York: Palgrave Macmillan, 2009.

Saldaña-Portillo, María Josefina. *Indian Given: Racial Geographies across the U.S. and Mexico*. Durham, N.C.: Duke University Press, 2016.

———. *The Revolutionary Imagination in the Americas and the Age of Development*. Durham, N.C.: Duke University Press, 2003.

———. "Who Is the Indian in Aztlán? Re-Writing Mestizaje, Indianism, and Chicanismo from the Lacandón." In *The Latin American Subaltern Studies Reader*, edited by Ileana Rodríguez, 402–23. Durham, N.C.: Duke University Press, 2001.

Saldívar, José David. *Transamericanity: Subaltern Modernities, Global Coloniality, and the Cultures of Greater Mexico*. Durham, N.C.: Duke University Press, 2012.

Saldívar-Hull, Sonia. *Feminism on the Border: Chicana Gender Politics and Literature*. Berkeley: University of California Press, 2000.

Sanders, Justin. "*A Bicycle Country*: Theatre Review." *Portland Mercury*, April 25, 2002. http://www.portlandmercury.com/portland/Content.

Sandoval, Chela. *Methodology of the Oppressed*. Minneapolis: University of Minnesota Press, 2000.

Saracho, Tanya. *El Nogalar. American Theatre* 28, no. 6 (2011): 69–87.

Schneider, Rebecca. "It Seems as If I Am Dead: Zombie Capitalism and Theatrical Labor." *TDR* 56, no. 4 (2012): 150–62.

———. *Performing Remains: Art and War in Times of Theatrical Reenactment*. London: Routledge, 2011.

Scott, A. O. "Taking on Broncos and a Plague." *New York Times*, November 1, 2013.

Segato, Rita L. "Territory, Sovereignty and the Crimes of the Second State: The Writing on the Body of Murdered Women." In *Terrorizing Woman: Feminicide in the Americas*, edited by Rosa-Linda Fregoso and Cynthia Bejarano, 70–92. Durham, N.C.: Duke University Press, 2011.

Shank, Theodore. "A Return to Aztec and Mayan Roots." *The Drama Review* 18 (1974): 56–70.

Sheridan, Michael, and Tracy Connor. "20-year-old Student, Marisol Valles García, Made Police Chief of One of Mexico's Most Violent Towns." *Daily News*, October 20, 2010. http://www.nydailynews.com/news/world/20-year-old-student-marisol-valles-garcia-made-police-chief-mexico-violent-towns-article-1.190569.

Snyder, Richard. *Mexican Politics after Neoliberalism*. Cambridge, U.K.: Cambridge University Press, 2006.

Solis, Octavio. *Dreamlandia*. New York: Samuel French, 2010.

———. *Plays by Octavio Solis*. New York: Broadway Play Publishing, 2006.

Solomon, Alisa. "Two Ambitious Plays Cross Borders and Consciousness: Review of *Kissing Fidel* and *No Foreigners Beyond This Point*." *Village Voice*, September 20, 2005.

Sommer, Elyse. "A Curtain Up Review of *Kissing Fidel*." *Curtain Up*, September 17, 2005. http://www.curtainup.com/kissingfidel.html.

———. "*Havana Is Waiting*: A Curtain Up Review." *Curtain Up*, October 24, 2001. http://www.curtainup.com/havanaiswaiting.html.

Sommerstein, Alan. *The Tangled Ways of Zeus and Other Studies in and around Greek Tragedy*. London: Oxford University Press, 2010.

Soto, Sandra K. *Reading Chican@ Like a Queer: De-Mastery of Desire.* Austin: University of Texas Press, 2010.
States, Bert O. *Great Reckonings in Little Rooms: On the Phenomenology of Theater.* Berkeley: University of California Press, 1987.
Staudt, Kathleen. *Violence and Activism at the Border: Gender, Fear, and Everyday Life in Ciudad Juárez.* Austin: University of Texas Press, 2008.
Stenzel, Paulette, "Plan Puebla Panama: An Economic Tool That Thwarts Sustainable Development and Facilitates Terrorism." *William and Mary Environmental Law and Policy Review* 30, no. 3 (2006): 555–623.
Stoll, David. *Rigoberta Menchú and the Story of All Poor Guatemalans.* Boulder, Colo.: Westview Press, 1999.
Stuelke, Patricia. "The Reparative Politics of the Central American Solidarity Movement." *American Quarterly* 66, no. 3 (2014): 767–90.
Sullivan, Mark P. *Cuba: U.S. Restrictions on Travel and Remittances.* Washington, D.C.: Congressional Research Service, Library of Congress, 2007.
Svich, Caridad. *Iphigenia Crash Land Falls on the Neon Shell That Was Once Her Heart (A Rave Fable).* In *Divine Fire: Eight Contemporary Plays Inspired by the Greeks,* 329–74. New York: Back Stage Books, 2005.
———. *Prodigal Kiss.* In *New Playwrights: Best Plays of 1999,* edited by Marisa Smith, 239–302. Hanover, NH: Smith and Kraus, 2001.
Szymkowicz, Adam. "I Interview Playwrights 320: Matthew Paul Olmos." February 25, 2011. http://aszym.blogspot.com/2011/02/i-interview-playwrights-part-320.html.
Taylor, Diana. *Disappearing Acts: Spectacles of Gender and Nationalism in Argentina's "Dirty War."* Durham, N.C.: Duke University Press, 1997.
Taylor, Lib. "The Experience of Immediacy: Emotion and Enlistment in Fact-Based Theatre." *Studies in Theater and Performance* 31, no. 2 (2011): 223–37.
Thompson, Ginger. "On Mexico's Mean Streets, the Sinners Have a Saint." *New York Times,* March 26, 2004.
Travieso-Diaz, Matias F. "Cuban Immigration Challenges and Opportunities." *Berkeley Journal of International Law* 16, no. 2 (1998) : 69–70.
Tropicana, Carmelita. *Leche de Amnesia.* In *Latinas on Stage,* edited by Alicia Arrizón and Lillian Manzor, 118–37. Berkeley, Calif.: Third Woman Press, 2000.
Tuhiwai Smith, Linda. *Decolonizing Methodologies: Research and Indigenous Peoples.* London: Zed Books, 1999.
United States General Accounting Office. *Cuba: U.S. Responses to the 1994 Cuban Migration Crisis.* Washington, D.C.: Author, 1995.
Valdés, Juan Gabriel. *Pinochet's Economists: The Chicago School in Chile.* New York: Cambridge University Press, 1995.
Valdez, Diana Washington. *The Killing Fields: Harvest of Women—The Truth about Mexico's Bloody Border Legacy.* Los Angeles: Peace at the Border, 2006.
Valdez, Luis. *Earthquake Sun.* Unpublished play script, 2003.
Valencia, Sayak. *Capitalismo Gore.* Santa Cruz de Tenerife, Spain: Melusina, 2010.
———. "NAFTA: Capitalismo Gore and the Femicide Machine." Translated by Irmgard Emmelhainz. *Scapegoat* 6 (2014): 131–36.
Vanderwood, Paul. "Millenarianism, Miracles, and Materialism." *Mexican Studies/Estudios Mexicanos* 15, no. 2 (1999): 395–412.

Vasquez, Alexandra T. "Learning to Live in Miami." *Americas Quarterly* 66, no. 3: (2014): 853–73.
Venkateswar, Sita, and Emma Hughes, eds. *The Politics of Indigeniety: Dialogues and Reflections on Indigenous Activism*. London: Zed Books, 2011.
Vivancos Pérez, Ricardo F. *Radical Chicana Poetics*. New York: Palgrave Macmillan, 2013.
Volk, Steven S., and Marian E. Schlotterbeck. "Gender, Order, and Femicide: Reading the Popular Culture of Murder in Ciudad Juárez." In *Making a Killing: Femicide, Free Trade, and La Frontera*, edited by Alicia Gaspar de Alba with Georgina Guzmán, 121–54. Austin: University of Texas Press, 2010.
Wald, Elijah. *Narcocorrido: A Journey into the Music of Drugs, Guns and Guerillas*. New York: Rayo, 2001.
Warner, Sara. *Acts of Gaiety*. Ann Arbor: University of Michigan Press, 2013.
Westhalle, Vitor. *Eschatology and Space: The Lost Dimension in Theology Past and Present*. New York: Palgrave Macmillan, 2012.
Williams, Gareth. *The Mexican Exception: Sovereignty, Police and Democracy*. New York: Palgrave Macmillan, 2011.
Wright, Melissa W. *Disposable Women and Other Myths of Global Capitalism*. New York: Routledge, 2006.
Yarbro-Bejarano, Yvonne. "From *Acto* to *Mito*: A Critical Appraisal of the Teatro Campesino." In *Modern Chicano Writers: A Collection of Critical Essays*, edited by Joseph Sommers and Tomás Ybarra-Frausto, 176–85. Englewood, N.J.: Prentice Hall, 1978.
———. "*Teatropoesía* by Chicanas in the Bay Area: *Tongues of Fire*." In *Mexican American Theatre Then and Now*, edited by Nicolás Kanellos, 74–90. Houston: Arte Público Press, 1983.
———. *The Wounded Heart: Writing on Cherríe Moraga*. Austin: University of Texas Press, 2001.
Ybarra, Patricia. "Latino/a Dramaturgy as Historiography." In *Theatre/Performance Historiography: Time, Space, Matter*, edited by Rosemarie Bank and Michal Kobialka, 75–91. Houndmills, U.K.: Palgrave Macmillan Press, 2015.
———. "The Revolution Fails Here." *Aztlán: A Journal of Chicano Studies* 33, no. 1 (2008): 63–88.
———. "Young Jean Lee's Cruel Dramaturgy." *Modern Drama* 57, no. 4 (2014): 516–17.
Ybarra, Priscilla Solis. "Longing and Belonging in Cherríe Moraga's Ecological Vision." In *New Perspectives on Environmental Justice: Gender, Sexuality, and Activism*. Edited by Rachel Stein, 240–48. New Brunswick, N.J.: Rutgers University Press, 2004.
Young, Iris Marion. "Gender as Seriality: Thinking about Women as a Social Collective." *Signs* 19, no. 3 (1994): 713–38.
Zimmerman, Marc. "Testimonio." In *The SAGE Encyclopedia of Social Science Research Methods*, edited by Michael S. Lewis-Beck, Alan Bryman, and Tim Futing Liao, 1118–19. Thousand Oaks, Calif.: SAGE Publications, 2004.

INDEX

Page numbers in **boldface** refer to illustrations.

Abdoh, Reza: *The Law of Remains*, 177
AIDS/HIV crisis, 19, 147–48, 172, 173, 175–76, 181–82
Alurista (Alberto Baltazar Urista Heredia), 27, 39–40, 207n5
Amavizca Murúa, Rubén, 120
anxiety, 74, 78, 84, 97, 102, 103; Cortiñas and, 20, 94–95, 97; Machado and, 86, 87; Saracho and, 20, 87, 165; Solis and, 152
Aristotelian dramaturgy, 69, 145, 152, 221n56; Garcés and, 64, 65, 66
Aztec culture, 26, 28, 38, 44, 54, 121, 180, 182–83

Balseros (Rafter) Crisis, 8, 12, 75–78, 85, 87, 103, 213nn13–15, 214n19
Barber, Marta, 103
Benjamin, Walter, 29, 45
Berlant, Lauren, 21, 95, 197; on impasse concept, 72, 73–74, 78, 84, 93
Bernadette of Lourdes, 124
Bernson, Alexandra: *En las Manos de la Muerte*, 149, 224n7
Beverley, John, 16, 113–14
Boal, Augusto, 69, 144
body art, 11
Bolaño, Roberto: *By Night in Chile*, 141; *2666*, 112, 120, 133, 222nn98–99
Bonfil Batalla, Guillermo, 34
borderlands concept, 21, 81, 171, 175
Bowden, Charles, 120, 180
Bowie, David, 142, 145, 223n113
Brady, Mary Pat, 21
Brecht, Bertolt, 20, 60, 116, 117, 121

Brown, Wendy, 14
Broyles-González, Yolanda, 28
caffeine, 166
Calderón, Felipe, 150, 170, 179, 183. *See also* narcoguerra
Calderón de la Barca, Pedro, 154, 158, 160, 223n113, 225n16
"capitalismo gore," 20, 111, 156–57, 159; defined, 154
Carter, Jimmy, 76, 213n9, 214n20
Castro, Fidel, 75, 84, 87, 90–91
Catholicism, 6, 27, 86, 117; in Cazares, 131–32; in Orta, 123–25
Cazares, Victor, 15, 22; *The Dead Women of J-Town and Smiley*, 17, 18, 105–6, 107, 120–21, 125–33; *Ramses contra los monstruos*, 12, 19, 129, 168, 169–83 (**170, 176**), 185–86, 195, 196, 197, 198–99; *Religiones Gringas*, 129, 168–69. *See also* queerness
Chekhov, Anton, 13, 162–63, 166–68
Chiapas uprising. *See* Zapatistas
Chicano/a culture, 10, 26–27, 161, 203n28; Moraga and, 33, 36, 39–41, 54
Chile: earlier drama in, 11; neoliberalism in, 6; violence in, 133–34
Clinton, Bill, 75–77, 213n9
Coca-Cola, 80, 172, 181
colonialism, 9, 30, 60, 62
Cornerstone Theater Company, 30, 71–72
Cortiñas, Jorge, 20, 22, 63, 94–98; *Sleepwalkers*, 79, 83, 94–98, 100–103, 197. *See also under* queerness
cosmetics and social mobility, 156, 164

243

Cruz, Migdalia, 12
Cruz, Nilo: *A Bicycle Country*, 12, 73, 79, 80–82, 103
Cuadros, Gil, 175–76
Cuba: body art in, 11; Cortiñas and, 20; dollars vs. pesos in, 76, 213n8; Garcés and, 23, 30; Machado and, 12; neoliberalism in, 6, 8; sex tourism in, 76, 98; Special Period in, 8, 12, 20, 23, 30, 72, 73–104; travel restrictions in, 77–78, 214nn19–20

Dallas Buyers Club, 147–48, 181–82
Dávila, Arlene, 8–9
docudrama, 17, 50, 113, 116
Dorfman, Ariel: *Death and the Maiden*, 11, 203n33

elite vs. working-class women, dramatic treatment of, 139, 140–42
entrepreneurship. *See* narcoentrepreneurship
eschatology, 22, 44–47, 55, 126, 133, 160, 169, 183, 187; queer, 170
ethnic cleansing, 54
ethnotheater, 17, 113
Euripides, 41, 121, 139, 143, 223n113, 223n132

FARC (Revolutionary Armed Forces of Colombia), 59
femicide, 3, 6, 8, 17, 18–20, 105–46, 154, 159, 163–64, 173, 177–78, 187, 218n9; cultural productions about, 111–12, 120–21; stage representation of, 52, 108, 111, 116–18, 123, 125, 130, 159, 187; scholarship on, 109–13
Féral, Josette, 16
Ferrari, Sebastian, 133, 222n99
Fillmore, Millard, 122
Fordism, 19, 21
Fornés, María Irene, 23, 206n82; *Balseros*, 78–80; *Terra Incognita*, 209n46
Foucault, Michel, 5–6, 7
Franco, Jean, 112–13
Freeman, Elizabeth, 22, 35–36, 171, 183
Fregoso, Rosa-Linda, 9, 18, 56, 110–11, 132, 211n108
fresa designation, 141–43

Fusco, Coco: *Couple in a Cage* (with Gómez-Peña), 11; *The Incredible Disappearing Woman*, 15–16, 20, 120, 133–37, 139, 223n109; *Stuff* (with Bustamante), 98

Garcés, Michael John, 23, 29–30, 56–72; as director, 72, 73, 84–85, 92, 93; *Los Illegals*, 30, 71–72; *points of departure*, 14, 17, 25, 57, 58–72 (70), 73, 197
García-Romero, Anne, 83
Gharavi, Lance, 142, 144, 224n137
globalization, 5, 110
Goldsmith, Barclay, 28
Gómez-Peña, Guillermo, 11
González, Elián, 79, 92
González, Rubén: *La Esquinita, U.S.A.*, 55–56
González Rodríguez, Sergio, 19, 107, 110, 112, 125
Goodwin, Joy, 67–68, 70–71
Greco, Loretta: *Rite of Passage*, 78–79

Halberstam, J. Jack (Judith), 22
Hamilton, 198
Hardt, Michael, and Antonio Negri, 187, 204n49
Hayek, Friedrich, 6
Herlinghaus, Hermann, 19, 148, 222n98
Herrera Rodríguez, Celia, 48
Holman, Curt, 102–3
homophobia, 33, 39, 43, 47, 107, 127, 131, 147, 190
homosexuality. *See* queerness
Horton, Donald, 134–37
Huerta, Jorge, 33, 55

indigeneity (*indigenismo*), 22, 25–68, 128, 166; Churchill's definition of, 39; Garcés and, 57–68; Moraga and, 25, 28–47, 50–53, 60, 65
indio bárbaro (term), 13
individual vs. mass (collective) protagonists, 14, 17, 27, 30; Garcés and, 64–65; Moraga and, 197; Olmos and, 187, 190, 196–97
In Lak'ech concept, 55, 56
INTAR (International Arts Relations), 23, 40, 58, 72, 79

Juárez, Mexico, 16, 18–19, 41, 51–52, 105–34, 136, 138–46, 154–56, 159, 170–71, 175, 177; Bowden on, 120, 180; El Egipcio theater, 170, 175–77

Latin Americanism, 23
Latinx (term), x, 201n5
Lee, Ralph, 40, 57
liberalism, 5–6, 14–15, 29, 56, 124, 162, 222n99; "homoliberalism," 37; racial, 29–30
living dead concept, 88, 110, 135–36, 196
Llorona, La, 121, 122–23, 125
López, Marissa, 113

Machado, Eduardo, 12, 22, 73–74, 78–79, 83–93, 97–98, 103; *The Cook*, 12, 73, 92; *Fabiola*, 86, 88, 91; *The Floating Island Plays*, 84, 86; *Havana Is Waiting*, 72, 73, 79, 91–93, 98–99, 103; *Kissing Fidel*, 72, 73, 79, 84–91 (**89**), 93, 97–100, 101, 103, 215n49. *See also under* queerness
machismo. *See* masculinity
maquiladora system, 3, 7, 8, 41, 109–10, 111, 117, 144, 171; in Fusco, 134, 222n103; in Orta, 121–22, 124; in Solis, 155–56, 160; in Svich, 141–43
Marez, Curtis, 21
Marimar (telenovela), 106–7
Marín, Christina, 112, 113, 114, 115, 116, 123–24, 220n51
Marxism, 28–29, 39, 43, 45, 95–96
masculinity, 14, 20, 36, 112, 149, 153, 157–59, 165, 190–91
Mayan culture: ancient, 22, 26, 28, 40, 44, 47, 54–55, 211n104; contemporary, 17, 40, 45–46, 54–55, 57–58. *See also* Popol Vuh
Mbembe, Achille, 9, 88, 110–11
McMahon, Marci, 163, 185
Melamed, Jodi, 29–30, 57
Menchú Tum, Rigoberta, 116, 220n49
mestizaje, 13, 22, 27, 32, 47
Mexican Revolution, 43, 167, 168–69
Mexico: Border Industrialization Program in, 3, 171, 226n55; class mobility in, 164; Day of the Dead celebrations in, 128–29; earlier drama in, 10–11; "México Antiguo," 38–39; nationalist period in, 29, 33, 175; neoliberalism in, 3, 6–7, 32–33, 41, 106, 117–20, 122, 124–25, 127–28, 171, 181; 1985 earthquake in, 32, 175
Michaus, Cristina: *Mujeres de Ciudad Juárez*, 112, 116–20, 187
Mignolo, Walter, 8, 30
migra, la (border patrol), 105, 127, 145
"migrant melodrama," 68, 103
migration, 3, 4, 6, 8, 38, 67, 88, 104; Cubans and, 75–83; shift in dramatic treatments of, 12, 150, 163, 166
misogyny, 35, 39, 47, 107, 110, 118, 131; Solis and, 159; Svich and, 137, 143
Miyagawa, Chiori, 139
Monsiváis, Carlos, 45, 142
Moraga, Cherríe, 12–13, 22, 25, 28–53, 56–57, 160; *Giving Up the Ghost*, 31–37, 52; *Heart of the Earth*, 40, 57; *The Hungry Woman*, 34, 35, 37, 40–43, 45–46, 48, 97, 161; *The Last Generation*, 37–39, 41, 44, 50; *New Fire: To Put Things Right Again*, 15, 30, 47–53 (**49**), 183; *A Xicana Codex of Changing Consciousness*, 44, 47. *See also under* queerness
Morales, Alejandro, 98
Moreiras, Alberto, 16
Muerte (folk saint), 149
Muñoz, José, 22, 91

NAFTA (North American Free Trade Agreement), 7, 13, 25, 26, 38, 39, 41, 51, 57–58, 106, 128, 131, 155; Balseros Crisis and, 77; introduction of, 151, 153, 172
narcocorridos, 7
narcoentrepreneurship, 7, 147–49, 156, 161, 164, 182, 193
narcoguerra, xiv, 21, 108, 110, 146, 149–50, 159–60, 162, 172, 178
narcolandía, 198
narcomachine, 8, 179–80
narco-mansions, 156
narco-masculinity, 157–58, 165, 191
narcomenudeo, 191
narcopolitics, 173, 187, 193, 198
narco-realism, 149–50, 192–93

narco-rule, 162–63
"narco silence," 163
"narcospatiality," 21
narcotrafficking (narco-commerce), 7–8, 19, 23, 110, 147–92; films about, 147–48, 153; governance and, 146; origins of, 150–51, 153; stage representation of, 21, 129, 149
narco-violence, 3, 7–8, 18, 173–74, 177–80, 186–88. *See also* violence
Nava, Gregory: *Bordertown*, 111, 112–13
necropolitics, 4, 9, 20, 88, 105, 110–11
neoliberalism: beginnings in Latin America, 5–9, 29, 171–72; Berlant on, 73–74; contradictions in, 20, 77, 100, 127; death and, 169–70; defined, x, 5, 17; femicide and, 107, 109–10, 119, 125, 143; heroism and, 189; as organism, 157, 197; temporality and, 4, 15, 21–22, 25–26, 94–96, 106, 169, 171–74, 197; violence and, 3, 6, 8–9, 20, 52, 111, 124–25, 133–38, 143–44, 159, 171, 182, 195–96. *See also specific countries*
Nicaraguan Revolution, 38
1992, significance of, 38, 209n46
Noriega, Jimmy: *Women of Juárez* (Michaus), 112, 114, 116–17, 120

Olmos, Matthew Paul: *so go the ghosts of méxico, part 1*, 14, 21, 121, 178, 183–92, 196–97; parts 2 and 3, 191
Orta, Marisela Treviño: *Braided Sorrow*, 112, 120–25
Ortiz, Ricardo, 86, 97

pan-indigenous movements, 4, 10
performance art, 10–11, 187; Fusco and, 136
Pinochet, Augusto, 6
Ponte, Antonio José, 216n75
Popol Vuh, 27, 40, 45, 55
Porfiriato, 43, 167–69
prostitution. *See* sexual commerce
Puga, Ana, 68

queerness: Cazares and, 168, 170, 171, 172–77, 182–83; Cortiñas and, 83, 94, 100–101; DIY medical research and, 147; intergenerational relationships, 36, 151, 172; Machado and, 83, 84–86, 88, 90–93, 98–100, 101; Moraga and, 12, 31, 36, 39, 41; Olmos and, 190; queer temporalities, 22, 35, 74, 84, 86, 91, 171–73; sexual commerce and, 85, 98–103; Solis and, 151, 158, 190
Quijano, Aníbal, 9, 30

Rabasa, José, 45
Ranciére, Jacques, 65–66
realism: departures from, 17–18, 107, 116, 121; Cortiñas and, 102; Garcés and, 57, 64; Orta and, 125; Svich and, 146; theatricality and, 197–98. *See also* narco-realism
Reguillo, Rossana, 18, 111, 144, 178
reproductive futurism, 43, 57
Richard, Nelly, 17
Ridout, Nicholas, 21–22, 28–29, 45
Rivera, José, 12; *School of the Americas*, 13
Robles, Humberto: *Mujeres de Arena*, 112, 114–16, 118, 120, 137
Rodríguez, Ileana, 9, 18, 111
Rossini, Jon D., 3, 12, 13, 17

Saldaña-Portillo, María Josefina, 13
Saldívar, José David, 21
Saracho, Tanya: *El Nogalar*, 13–14, 20, 21, 97, 139, 162–68, 171, 182, 185, 226n41
Schneider, Rebecca, 21–22, 195, 208n41
Scott, A. O., 147
Segato, Rita Laura, 111
Segura, Andrés, 28, 207m13
seriality, 106–7, 120, 126, 129
Seventh-day Adventism, 168–69
sexual commerce, 117, 131, 164; in Special Period plays, 85, 98–102
Sharif, Abdul Latif, 108
Sicilia, Javier, 191
slavery, legacy of, 9, 47, 122, 198
Slim, Carlos, 160–61, 225n26
Sna Jtz'ibajom, 40, 57–58, 71
Solis, Octavio, 12, 150–62, 175; *Dreamlandia*, 20, 150, 153, 154–62 (**161**), 190, 197; *Lydia*, 160; *Santos y Santos*, 21, 150–54, 161

Solomon, Alisa, 91, 103
Soto, Sandra K., 34
Stoll, David, 220n49
Stuelke, Patricia, 17, 68–69
subaltern studies, 15, 45
Svich, Caridad, 137–38; *Iphigenia Crash Land Falls on the Neon Shell That Was Her Heart*, 11, 121, 123, 138–46, 197, 223n113; *Prodigal Kiss*, 79, 82–83

Taylor, Lib, 17
Teatro Campesino, El (ETC), 25, 27–28, 29, 40, 54, 55–56
teatropoesía, 27
telenovelas, 105–7, 111–12, 126, 129, 199
terrorism, 41–43; state-sponsored, 3, 4, 8, 59
testimonio, 15–17, 30, 51, 107, 134, 137, 139; anti-testimonials, 69, 132–33, 136–37; defined, 113–14; femicide and, 111–21; Garcés and, 69
Theater of the Sphere, 28, 29, 55–56
Third World solidarity, 3, 10, 45
transnationalism, 3, 5, 11, 13, 72, 157, 195; Cazares and, 126–29, 133, 171, 172, 175; Garcés and, 57; Moraga and, 30, 33–34, 40, 41, 52; Orta and, 122
trauma theory, 74
Tropicana, Carmelita: *Leche de Amnesia*, 83–84
Trump, Donald, 166, 199
Tuhiwai Smith, Linda, 30, 50, 54

Valdez, Diana Washington, 110, 134
Valdez, Kinan, 55–56
Valdez, Luis, 27–28, 40, 46–47, 53–56
Valencia, Sayak, 8, 9, 19, 20, 111, 154, 157, 159, 165
Valles García, Marisol, 183–84, 185, 188–91
Vanderwood, Paul, 45
Vasquez, Alexandra, 78
verbatim theater, 17
violence: economic, 3, 6, 8, 20, 107, 111, 122, 131, 154, 195–96; "expressive vs. utilitarian," 18; in seventeenth-century Spain, 158; stage representation of, 18–19, 107, 111, 123, 125, 136–37, 143, 149, 164–65, 185–86; state-sponsored, 16, 110. *See also* capitalismo gore; femicide; narco-violence; necropolitics; neoliberalism; terrorism
Vivancos Pérez, Ricardo F., 29, 207n17

Wang, Meilyn, 185–87, 227n83
War on Drugs (U.S.), 14, 19, 21, 110, 195. *See also* narcoguerra
wetback (term), 57, 211n111

Yarbro-Bejarano, Yvonne, 27, 33, 35
Young, Marion Iris, 106–7

Zapatistas, 15, 22, 26, 29, 40–41, 54, 57, 65, 160, 204n49; Zapatista National Liberation Army (EZLN), 45–46, 56, 65
zombies, 178–79, 186

www.ingramcontent.com/pod-product-compliance
Lightning Source LLC
Chambersburg PA
CBHW032031290426
44110CB00012B/761